NEW RESEARCH ON KNOWLEDGE MANAGEMENT TECHNOLOGY

Edited by **Huei-Tse Hou**

New Research on Knowledge Management Technology
Edited by Huei-Tse Hou

Published by InTech
Janeza Trdine 9, 51000 Rijeka, Croatia

Publishing Process Manager Anja Filipovic

Technical Editor Teodora Smiljanic

Cover Designer InTech Design Team

Additional hard copies can be obtained from orders@intechopen.com

New Research on Knowledge Management Technology, Edited by Huei-Tse Hou
p. cm.
ISBN 978-953-51-0074-4

For EU product safety concerns:
IN TECH d.o.o., Prolaz Marije Krucifikse Kozulić 3, 51000 Rijeka, Croatia,
info@intechopen.com or visit our website at intechopen.com.

Meet the editor

Dr Huei-Tse Hou is an Assistant Professor of Graduate Institute of Applied Science and Technology, National Taiwan University of Science and Technology, Taiwan. He has received the Ta-You Wu Memorial Award (Young Outstanding Researcher Award) (Year 2010) by the National Science Council, Taiwan. His research interest focuses on knowledge management/sharing, e-Learning behavioral pattern analysis, e-Learning system development, and game-based learning systems. Professor Hou has published many academic papers in famous SSCI indexed journals such as *Computers in Human Behavior, Computers & Education, Educational Technology & Society, British Journal of Educational Technology* and *Interactive Learning Environments*.

Contents

Preface

In a highly interactive Internet environment, the research issues in knowledge management vary based on the development of new technology and modes of interaction in the knowledge community. Due to the development of mobile and Web 2.0 technology, knowledge transfer, storage, and retrieval have become much more rapid. The technologies and methods continue to get more and more diverse. At the same time, the types of online communities with high levels of interaction become more and more multi-dimensional. To optimize organizational performance and further promote knowledge innovation and knowledge management in organizations, new and expanded strategies for sharing knowledge within and between knowledge communities are required.

In recent years, there have been more and more new and interesting findings regarding theories, methods, and models in the research field of knowledge management. There are also innovative technologies and tools in knowledge management technology. It is worth noting that the technologies, tools, and models in technology have been applied to more fields (e.g., education and digital learning) as technology and management concepts have continued to develop. These trends speak to the importance of studies of knowledge management, and the studies expand their influence on more multidisciplinary applications. New research issues in knowledge management await researchers. A comprehensive understanding of these novel research issues will assist with the academic development and practical applications in the field of knowledge management.

Therefore, this book aims to introduce readers to the recent research topics in knowledge management, it is titled "New Research on Knowledge Management Technology" and includes 13 chapters. In it new KM technologies and systems are proposed, the applications and potentials of all KM technologies are explored and discussed.

I expect this book to provide relevant information about new research trends in comprehensive and novel knowledge management studies. This information will serve as an important resource for researchers, teachers and students, and will further scholarly work and the development of practices in the knowledge management field.

Prof. Huei-Tse Hou
Graduate Institute of Applied Science and Technology
National Taiwan University of Science and Technology
Taiwan

1

A Knowledge Management System Embedded in the New Semantic Technologies

Vasile Mazilescu
Dunărea de Jos University of Galați
Faculty of Economics and Business Administration
Romania

1. Introduction

There is a large interest in organizational knowledge in the context of transition to knowledge economy, where knowledge is viewed as the main source of sustainable competitive advantage. Although knowledge management (KM) is primarily concerned with how people and organizations use their knowledge assets, one way to do this efficiently is to employ technology to facilitate the KM processes (Alavi, 1999). Consistent with the growing interest in organizational knowledge and KM, many ICT researchers have been promoting a class of information systems, referred to as Knowledge Management Systems (KMSs). The objective of a KMS is to support knowledge capturing, categorizing, storing, searching, distributing and application within organizations. Technical advances in computers' processing and storage capacity, together with linking these computers into networks of distributed nodes, have greatly increased the organizations' capability to deliver goods and services. Along with these capabilities we need quality, accuracy, responsiveness and capacity. Particular topics of interest on KMSs include among others: Organizational knowledge management approaches, Information management challenges, Service Oriented Architecture (SOA), software environments, Semantic web services environments, Information modeling and the representation of semantics, Intelligent software tools and services, Information management systems in practice.
Semantics is the study of meaning. Semantic Technologies (STs) are distributed software technologies that make the meaning more explicit, principally so that it can be understood by computers. New Semantic Technologies (NSTs) will dramatically influence enterprise's architecture and the engineering of new systems and infrastructure capabilities, so that they act as *disruptive technologies* (so innovative that they have the potential to completely change the way we do business) on capturing and sharing next generation knowledge among workers and organizations in the new economy. NSTs are tools that represent meanings, associations, theories, and know-how about the application of things, separately from data and program codes. These systems must be designed as distributed systems, with the ability to combine different knowledge-based techniques (with the purpose of acquiring and processing information and knowledge), based on approximate reasoning methods (Müller, 1996; Lin, 2008). NSTs will better emulate the human decision-making process, also characterized by imprecise and time-varying knowledge (Knight & Passino, 1987; Barachini, 1990; Dubois et al., 1991; Qian, 1992; Nebel & Bäckström, 1994). Time restrictions are not

excessive in common distributed applications. Critical time reasoning problems may occur in case of faulty operations and overloading. The reasoning depth developed for such systems is still poor (Iqbal et al., 2007; Durán &Aguilo, 2008; Marco & Marley, 2009).
The aim of this paper is to present a Knowledge Management System based on Fuzzy Logic (KMSFL), a real-time expert system to meet the challenges of the dynamic environment. The main feature of our integrated shell KMSFL is that it models and integrates the temporal relationships between the dynamic of the evolution of a technological process with some fuzzy inferential methods, using a knowledge model for control, embedded within the expert system's operational knowledge base. As important contributions of this work, we have integrated some elements of control theory, fuzzy and temporal logics and discrete event systems to increase the decision making capacity (Bylander, 1994; Kim & Lee, 2003; Davis, 2006). We also focused particularly on time, in its many facets (real-time, algorithmic complexity and reasoning over time), by using a time meta-equation. The closed-loop of our KMSFL starts from an initial state and allows planning a number of states to achieve a desired final state. At the end of its operation, the control expert system provides the human decider the possible actions, under specific conditions of the problem. All bibliographic sources are important, because each of the mentioned authors has used a series of concepts that we have integrated in KMSFL.

2. Related work

There is a need for incorporating aspects of time and imprecision into real-time KMSs, considering appropriate semantic foundations (Bobrowitz, 1993; Chen & Parng, 1996; Lau et al. 2008). In reality, it is a common practice for organizations to use one or more of the following (technical) systems and concepts to support their KM efforts (Binney, 2001; Wenger, 2001; Mazilescu, 2009b): Knowledge Maps, Taxonomies, Enterprise search engine, e-collaboration tools, Information repositories, Expert Systems, Data Mining / Knowledge Discovery systems, Case-based Reasoning / Question-Answering tools (for Helpdesk and/or Contact Centers), E-Learning and/or Learning Management Systems (LMS), Enterprise Information Portal, Intellectual Capital (IC) measurement tools. Expert systems are examples of relevant knowledge-based methodologies (as Knowledge Capture Systems) that have much to contribute to KMSs, because they manipulate knowledge in order to implement various tasks (Tsui, 2002; Wang & Lin, 2007; Schwartz, 2006; Omar, 2008). KMSs based on Agent Technology try to provide computers the ability to perform various intelligent tasks, for which their human users resort to their own knowledge and to collective intelligence. Currently, KMSs is a highly economically important field due to their ability of approaching new sets of problems, different from those tackled by the classical systems, such as: perception, decision making, planning, diagnosis, natural language comprehension, enterprise KM, learning, web service interfaces, etc. Conventional expert system shells are too slow for real-time environments, and their inference process is boundless. We need a reactive and interruptible system that can assimilate data and asynchronous events, and present the operator with a reasoned opinion in a timely manner. Only speed is not enough (Stankovic & Ramamritham, 1995; Lassaigne & Rougemont, 1996). While practitioners and researchers continue their efforts in designing and building complex intelligent systems, they became conscious of the fact that uncertainty is present not only in human knowledge. Allowing a certain degree of uncertainty in describing complex systems is perhaps the most significant way to simplify them (Zadeh, 1983; Dubois & Prade, 1992;

Luger & Stubblefield, 1993). Different types of uncertainty can be rigorously characterized and investigated in the context of fuzzy sets theory (Zadeh, 1978; Marco & Marley, 2009). Thus, the ability to operate in an uncertain or partially known environment is one of the basic performances of any real-time intelligent system (Passino & Antsaklis, 1989). Real-time calculation is an area of intense research, since the correctness of a system's functioning in a dynamic and distributed environment depends not only on its operating logic, but also on the temporal aspects involved. Such systems include various solutions of systems, subject to various complex time restrictions, with different granularity levels of the time. Temporal knowledge is an essential element for many applications (planning, process control, dynamic situations control). An intelligent system must have reasoning capabilities that take into account a series of events that may occur in the process: interruptions, limitations on processing time, synchronous and asynchronous nature of the new information occurrence. Considering time, we must highlight two complementary aspects: temporal information management and formalization of the temporal reasoning over time and in real-time (Lunardhi & Passino, 1995). Some approaches are based on numerical models and other on symbolic representations of time. Reasoning under real-time restrictions has specific characteristics. Real-time operations often involve a temporal reasoning, but conversely this is not always true. The control involves a close relation between the process and the control system, which must react to the occurring events. The act of intelligent control is interposed between the process and the various physical entities incorporated in the process' superstructure. In this context, the control system has certain Artificial Intelligence (AI) features, if, in the presence of minimal guidance information from a human expert, it can perform complex actions in response to the events coming from outside. In this case, intelligence includes the ability to accept abstract task specifications in a general form of *goals/restrictions* and to produce reasonable actions, which are consistent with the specifications (Mazilescu, 2009a). In any real-time system like KMSFL, there is a fundamental compromise between action and reasoning. We must notice that logically, the human decider is firmly included in the intelligent control system, which works with certain specific knowledge. The inferential system's logical results can address differently the human operator, the different execution elements or the interfaces with other systems and users. Designing and testing the inferential subsystem for KMSFL, require the existence of certain scientific methods for knowledge acquisition, which, unfortunately, is a heterogeneous, difficult and time consuming process. For this reason, the synthesis of the knowledge management model incorporating human experience was iterative, during a considerably long time, being necessary the indirect development of some methods and environments for testing and simulating some crisp and fuzzy control models, permanently adjusting the inferential subsystem's parameters. For the KMSFL synthesis we adapted and aggregated some AI techniques (possibility theory, symbolic logics, expert systems, etc.) with certain models for technological process control (planning, discrete event systems, qualitative analysis, etc.), closer to human decider's natural way of understanding and operating. This objective was achieved starting from the essential predictability feature that the designed KMSFL must have.

In this respect, we effectively used the notion of microscopic predictability (adopting the Rete compiling technique for the fuzzy processing) and of macroscopic predictability (through KMSFL specification, design and implementation, as a discrete event system). We also introduced logical events. We analyzed and extended the knowledge compilation technique, in order to improve the filtering stage, for the case of fuzzy knowledge (Ghallab,

1988). Furthermore, were used the fuzzy rules along with the fuzzy variables and constants, in the form of possibility distributions, as a basic representation mode for elementary fuzzy knowledge. Choosing between probabilities or possibility distributions and fuzzy sets is not easy, since for finite spaces, the probabilities may have a greater flexibility, in terms of representativeness, but an increased computational complexity. For these reasons, for the KMSFL we have chosen as imprecision measures the possibility measure Π and the necessity measure N (Dubois & Prade, 1992). For the fuzzy variables linking, it was necessary to solve the composition of the fuzzy substitutions, which depends on the compatibility of the fuzzy sets involved in the antecedent of the rules. The necessity measure and the GMP scheme are not independent and the choice of the thresholds for the possibility and necessity measures must be consistent with the chosen inference scheme. This choice is particularly important at all imprecision processing levels within the KMSFL for fuzzy filtering, fuzzy unification, fuzzy conflicts solving, and determination of similar states (Mazilescu, 2011).

We conducted a qualitative analysis of KMSFL using the concepts introduced by (Passino & Antsaklis, 1994). For this, we justified the control system design, in terms of its closed-loop performances, using the traditional concepts of Lyapunov stability of the dynamic systems, applied particularly for KMSLF. Integrating the features of the fuzzy rules base compilation, designing an appropriate inference engine corresponding to the time meta-equation and the corresponding logical justifications are the basic elements in designing the KMSFL. A particularly important issue in designing a control expert system is how the operational knowledge can be acquired and loaded in the knowledge base. In this case, we integrated a model of the process, as a part of the knowledge base. KMSFL was designed so that to coordinate the use of process outputs and reference inputs, to decide how should be synthesized the inferential process' results. In relation to the integration of the expert system within the control expert system's structure, its results can be used by the human decider in decision-making, or can be applied directly on the process.

It was necessary to highlight the knowledge representation in accordance with this system's formalism, to present the basic features of the compiled structure of fuzzy knowledge, the KMSFL parameters, and also to define other logical and computational features of the system. KMSFL-specific knowledge is represented in 1st order logic, aiming the knowledge factorization. We described the design of the fuzzy knowledge compiler, which includes two major parts: static discrimination structure (unification tree, fuzzy unification tree) and variable linking network (algorithms for generating the variable linking network for different rule topologies, fuzzy unification and propagation of the parameters during inferential process) and the system's inference engine algorithm. To highlight the KMSFL applicability, is presented an extended case study (both for the crisp and the fuzzy case). The flexible manufacturing system is composed of many subsystems connected so that they can transmit different amounts of material by means of bond wires, directed according to a given structure schema. For the crisp case, we used the same control model also tested with the G2 generator (Mazilescu, 2009b). This case allowed us to synthesize the fuzzy control model, because of the serious limitations underlined in the tests. KMSFL was implemented in C^{++}. Simulation results have demonstrated the developed system's ability to deal properly with the allocation problem. In addition, we tested a series of parametric dependencies for fuzzy inferential process embedded in the KMSFL engine.

The solution of a control intelligent system as a multi-agent system, presented in *Section 3*, has the quality of emphasizing the place of our fuzzy expert system within a distributed control structure, as well as the integration of other heterogeneous agents. *Section 4* defines KMSFL, designed and implemented by the author as a logical system with discrete logical events resulting from the inferential process. In this section we introduced the time meta-equation (in which each term has its variable part properly defined– according to relationship 1) and the specific model for the KMSFL as a control expert system (according to relationship 2). A very important problem is the way in which operational knowledge on the process control can be acquired and loaded into the knowledge base. For this, we built a model of the process, as a part of the knowledge base. The KMSFL was designed to coordinate the use of process outputs and reference input(s) and to choose the inferential process' results that will be synthesized. In relation to expert system's integration into the control structure, KMSFL results can be used by the human decider in decision-making, or can be applied directly on the process. *Section 5* describes the knowledge representation in accordance with this system's formalism, the basic features of the structure of compiled fuzzy knowledge, and KMSFL system parameters. We have developed and implemented a fuzzy knowledge compiler, similar to the classic Rete compiler, which includes two major parts: static discrimination structure (unification tree, unification fuzzy tree) and the variables linking network (algorithms for generating the variables linking network for different topologies of rules, fuzzy unification and spreading of parameters during inferential process). To highlight the applicability of KMSFL, we present in *Section 6* an extended case study relative to a balancing problem for a flexible manufacturing system (both for classical and fuzzy case), formulated as follows: the flexible manufacturing system consists of a set of components (machines, subsystems, etc.) connected so that they can transfer different amounts (parts) of material through bond wires, directed according to a given structure scheme. Such a system can be represented through a graph (M, A), where M={1, ..., N} is the set of identical components in its structure and $A \subset M \times M$. Assume that (M, A) is strongly connected, i.e. for $(\forall)\ i \in M$ there is a path from i to $(\forall)\ j \in M$ and moreover, if $(i, j) \in A$, $i \neq j$). Each component has a quantity of material that can be processed. We assume that any quantity of component i, denoted by $x_i \geq 0$, for $x_i \in N_+^*$ or $\mu_{xi} \in R_+^*$ (for the fuzzy case), can be partially transferred to component j. The control expert system for this problem area must be able to transfer the whole amounts of material (discrete case) or fractions of the quantity x_i (continuous case) from component i to another component j, if there exists $(i, j) \in A$. For the crisp case, we used the same control model also tested with G2 generator. This case allowed us to synthesize the fuzzy control model, due to the serious limitations outlined in its previously conducted crisp tests. Finally, *section 7*, concludes and introduces the future research work in order to synthesize KMSs more integrated into the NSTs.

3. KMSFL in a distributed control structure

KMSFL, as a control agent, is an expert system that integrates imprecise knowledge. The reasoning specific to this agent is performed by the inference engine based on fuzzy logic. This agent's architecture follows the general characteristics of any agent like in (Jennings & Wittig, 1992). However, there are several new elements which we emphasize in fig. 1.

It is noted that planning and coordination module (PC_{io}) comprises three levels: the level of evaluation of the global situation, the meta-planning level and the level of coordination of cooperation. Its main functions are dedicated to monitoring the activity of other agents, choosing the communication protocol, analyzing whether to respond to other agents and detecting global conflicts. The major difference between the monitoring function of PC_{io} and the monitor is that the monitor supervises the activity of its own system based on fuzzy knowledge. The monitor is the only link between the system based on imprecise knowledge and the $ISICMA_{io}$ interface, and implicitly between the system based on imprecise knowledge and the whole multi-agent control system. Its basic role is of remote control of its own system based on fuzzy logic, meaning that the monitor will communicate through messages, because it is not a part of the AI system based on imprecise knowledge. Decisions concerning the control of the intelligent control system based on fuzzy knowledge are made at the level of $Monitor_{io}$, whose main functions are: retrieving information from various sources, granting access to MS_{io}, evaluating the local situation, updating the local information, describing high-level goals, planning the decisions and actions. In order to eliminate the possible conflicts between these functions and the ones of the AI system based on imprecise knowledge, $Monitor_{io}$ invokes the low-level behaviors stored in MS_{io}.

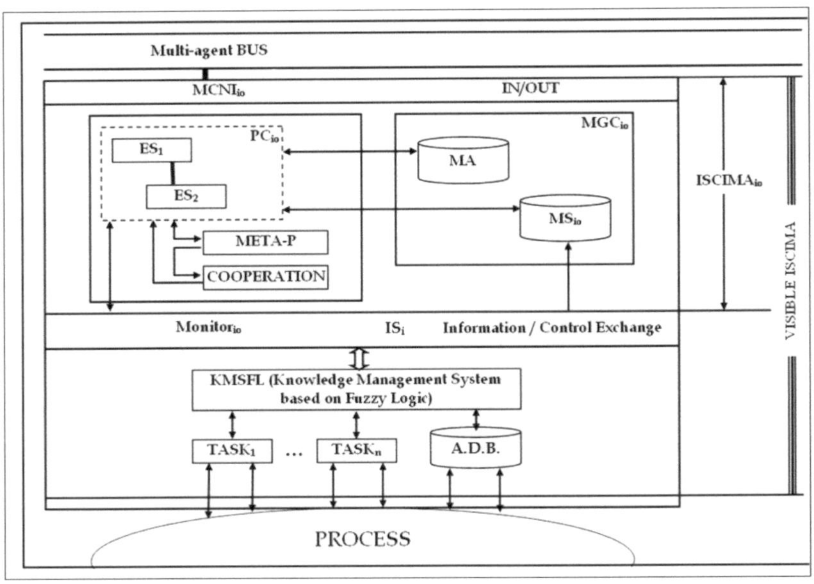

Fig. 1. KMSFL in a multi-agent structure

Fuzzy logic is a generalization of bivalent logic, replacing the discreet nature of the latter with one of continuous nature. While in bivalent logic, in order to demonstrate the validity of formulas, are used methods that use up all the possibilities of evaluation according to the interpretation function, in fuzzy logic this is no longer possible. A special feature of human reasoning is the effective use of natural language, even in the logical reasoning. According to this observation, we may conclude that the mathematical model of how a man thinks during a control process and at a certain level of decision synthesis may be based on fuzzy logic combined with modal temporal attributes (Mazilescu, 2010). Approximate reasoning theory, as a methodology for exploiting imprecise knowledge relative to the control expert system's state (denoted $\mathbf{x}^{CES} \in X^{CES}$ and represented in the form of possibility distributions), allows, by means of logical inferences, to obtain rigorous characterizations of the values of linguistic variables within the structure of state $\mathbf{x}^{CES}$, according to the control goal (Mazilescu, 2009a). The set X^{CES} can be defined as a Cartesian product $X^b \times X^{int} \times X$, where $\mathbf{x}^b = [x_1^b, x_2^b, \ldots x_{k_1}^b]^t \in X^b$. For example, the component x_1^b indicates, through its values, the potential command events for the process, $x_i^b \in U^{(i)}$, i=2, ..., k_1, where $U^{(i)}$ are the universes of discourse attached to linguistic variables $x^{(i)}$ (chosen to characterize the state $\mathbf{x}^{ES} \in X^b \times X^{int}$), X^{int} is the set of internal states of the inference engine and X is the set of states of the process. Thus, we can model KMSFL and the corresponding reasoning as a possibilistic expert system, that allows us to characterize a state $\mathbf{x}^{CES} \in X^{CES}$ based on imprecise information relative to the state $\mathbf{x}^{CES}$, i.e. with a subset $E \subseteq X^{CES}$, for which $\mathbf{x}^{CES} \in E$. We assume that there may be components of state $\mathbf{x}^{CES}$, defined as predicates that have firm truth values. Moreover, in this case is met the condition of membership of truth values to the interval [0,1] and thus we can work only with interval [0,1]. The control expert system manages knowledge specific to a state of the closed-loop system $x^{CES} \in X^{CES}$, characterized at time k by $x_k^{CES} = (x_k, x_k^{ES})$. The class of possibilistic expert systems can encompass also temporal reasoning. In this case, the rules base consists no longer of relationships, but of multi-dimensional possibility distributions to which are attached temporal descriptors, modeled in turn by means of possibility distributions, in order to attach the fuzzy statements to temporal features. Attaching the fuzzy temporal descriptors is specific to AI techniques, while in terms of control, this corresponds to fuzzifying the moments of time in the theory of discrete event systems.

4. Defining KMSFL as a discrete system based on logical events

Temporal aspects are important in areas such as planning, qualitative simulation, cognitive modeling, and natural language semantics. There are two basic approaches to the integration of temporal aspects in terms of AI logical systems: **i)** first-order logic can be directly used to formulate statements that contain symbols for time positions; **ii)** first-order logic can be extended with modal operators. Introducing the temporal aspects aims at designing the means for solving the meta-equation:

$$\text{time} = \text{complexity} \oplus \text{real\_time} \oplus \text{temporal\_reasoning} \quad (1)$$

which was proposed and used for integrating time in an application of AI, dedicated to technological process control. This meta-equation will be particularly applied for the inference engine developed, which is able to exploit knowledge specific to control applications. Operator ⊕ is an aggregation symbolic meta-operator, which can be instantiated in different classes of specific operators. Relation 1 can be viewed as a meta-equation as it contains several variable elements, such as: i) the first term has as variable the time component defined in the algorithms' analysis, and the compiled knowledge structure specific to KMSFL system tries to improve exactly this value; ii) the second term includes the time variable in the form of the length of the control expert system's inferential chain, which depends on how the events occur; iii) the last term was included to highlight the possibility of adding temporal attributes, which was not clearly necessary for KMSFL system, at least not for the case study solved. We define all elements describing KMSFL as a Control Expert System (CES). Defining the model for KMSFL as a closed-loop system is important, if we consider some of its features (Passino & Antsaklis, 1994). At this level, we emphasize a series of features of the control expert system, the elements of qualitative analysis of the control expert system, as well as a crisp version of a simplified example, to demonstrate the theoretical aspects.

Definition The control expert system (CES) is a formal system, defined as:

$$CES = (X^{CES}, E^{CES}, f_e^{CES}, \delta_e^{CES}, g^{CES}, x_o^{CES}, E_v^{CES}) \tag{2}$$

where: $X^{CES}=X\times X^{ES}$ is the set of states x^{CES} of the control expert system
$E^{CES}=E_u\cup E_d^{CES}\cup E_o$, with $E_d^{CES}=E_d\cup E_r^{ES}\cup UI$. Sets E_u, E_d, E_r^{ES} and UI are the input events of the control expert system and E_o the output events of the process;
g^{CES}: $X^{CES}\to\mathcal{P}(E_u\cup E_d^{CES})$-{∅} is the activation function of the CES;
f_e^{CES} : $X^{CES}\to X^{CES}$, $e\in\mathcal{P}(E_u\cup E_d^{CES})$-{∅} is the set of state transition functions;
δ_e^{CES} : $X^{CES}\to E_o$, $e\in\mathcal{P}(E_u\cup E_d^{CES})$-{∅} is the output function; $x_o^{CES}\in X^{CES}$ is the initial state; $E_v^{CES}\subset E^{CES}$, where E^{CES} is the set of all trajectories (finite or not) of events in closed loop, which can be generated by the control expert system, based on g^{CES} and f_e^{CES}, and E_v^{CES} is the set of all trajectories of allowed events in closed loop (a subset of trajectories of events that may result, knowing the trajectories of events of the process and of the expert system, connected together). Thus, E_v and E_v^{CES} are viewed as some restrictions in the structure of E_v^{CES}. Based on the trajectories of allowed events, we can highlight additional restrictions which are possible sequences of events within the closed loop system. The output events of fuzzy expert system are considered, in this case, logical events. These issues are particularly important for the future possibility of a qualitative analysis of the closed-loop system (admissibility, cyclical behavior and stability). Conventional knowledge-based systems can ignore the dynamic behavior of the control expert system caused by user inputs and process outputs. Many expert systems' evaluation is done either through difficult simulations, or by comparing its behavior with the one of human experts. The fuzzy control expert system is like a planner, because it can predict a number of states in the evolution of the process. An expert system (fig. 2) should be designed to remove unwanted behaviors of closed-loop system. Initial state x_o^{CES} is necessary both from theoretical and practical considerations. From the theoretical point of view, it is the beginning of a formal system, in which derivation relations will be the inferential processes, and from the practical point of view, it is necessary to define the initial state of the control expert system in order to reduce possible unwanted combinations of states that could unduly complicate the model. If the initial state of the closed loop system is known, the state transitions can be restricted to the acceptable states of the system. Once specified the initial state $x_o^{CES}=(x_0, x_o^{ES})$ for the state $x_k^{CES}=(x_k, x_k^{ES})$ at time k, we get, based on the definition of activation function $g^{CES}(x_k^{CES})$, the following form:

$$g^{CES}(x_k^{CES})=[g^{ES}(x_k^{ES})\cap E_r^{ES}\cap UI]\cup\delta^{ES}(x_k^{ES})\cap g(x_k)\cap HC]\cup[g(x_k)\cap E_d], \tag{3}$$

where:

i. $g^{ES}(x_k^{ES})\cap E_r^{ES}\cap UI=(\mathcal{P}(E_1^{ES}\cup\mathcal{R})\setminus\{\varnothing\})\cap E_r^{ES}\cap UI$ is the set of input and internal events of the expert system, allowed for the state x_k^{ES};
ii. $\delta^{ES}(x_k^{ES})\cap g(x_k)\cap HC=E_0^{ES}\cap\mathcal{P}(E_u\cup E_d)\cap HC$ is the set of command input events of the process, allowed for the state x_k^{ES};
iii. $g(x_k)\cap E_d=(\mathcal{P}(E_u\cup E_d)\setminus\{\varnothing\})\cap E_d$ is the set of input disturbance events of the process, allowed in the current state x_k of the process.

The input events allowed in the process for the control expert system in closed-loop are the events allowed both by the current state of the process $\mathbf{x}_k$ or by the states x_k^{ES}, and the events caused by input disturbances of the process, allowed in the state $\mathbf{x}_k$. The expert system must control only the activation of the events of type $E_u\cup HC$. It is built in such a way that its transition from a current state in a future state is achieved in response to any output event of the process. Notice that the control expert system's dynamic must be properly defined, even for the particular case in which the expert system also comprises imprecise knowledge, and its reasoning must reflect the temporal characteristics, specific to process (according to relationship 3). Assume that $e_k \subset g^{CES}(x_k^{CES})$ is an allowed event of the control expert system in closed loop, currently in the state $x_k^{CES}=(x_k, x_k^{ES})$. Under these conditions, if the events $e_{\eta_k}^{ES} \in g^{ES}(x_k^{ES}) \cap E_r^{ES} \cap UI$, $e_{uk} \in \delta^{ES}(x_k^{ES}) \cap g(x_k) \cap HC$ and $e_{dk} \in g(x_k) \cap E_d$, then e_k can be defined in various ways. These depend on the type of input command events of the process, or on the type of disturbance events, which may occur simultaneously. There is thus a finite number of ways $i_0 \in N^*$, so that for $(\forall)$ $i \in \{1, ..., i_0\}$, e_k^i can be properly defined. Corresponding to each type of event e_k^i, $i=1,...,i_o$, then:

$$f_{e_k^i}^{CES}(x_k^{CES}) = x_{k+1}^{CES}, \text{ where } x_{k+1}^{CES}=(x_{k+1}, x_{k-1}^{ES}).$$

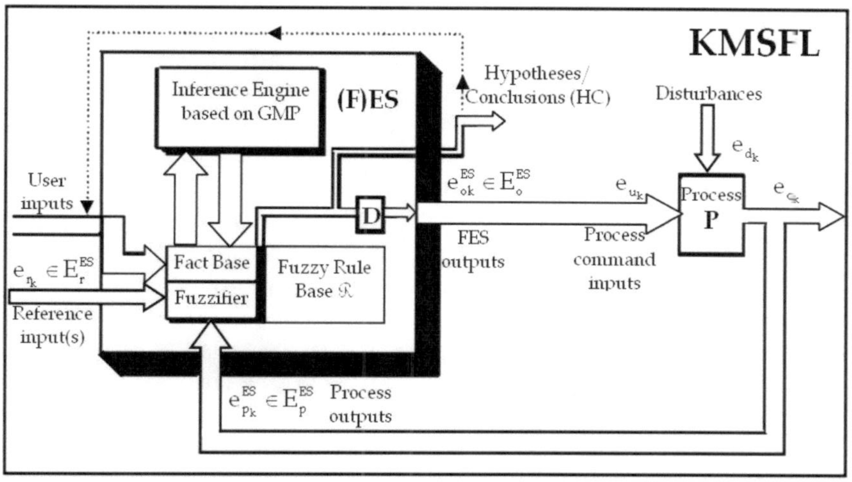

Fig. 2. The basic architecture for KMSFL

5. The characteristics of KMSFL as a fuzzy expert system

Knowledge representation and exploitation within an expert system are rather conflicting characteristics, whereas the increase in knowledge representation power reduces system's efficiency and increases the difficulty of developing it. Many AI problems are difficult to solve from the computational point of view. An observation which may help to reduce this complexity is that often these problems have the following property: inputs can be divided into two parts, of which, a part is relatively constant long time, compared with the second part. In such situations, seems right to make some changes in the constant part, in order to reduce the time of obtaining the solution for the AI problem, if the second part varies, but is known at certain moments of time. Transformations made in advance are called pre-processing or knowledge compilation. Using variables in an expert system allows knowledge factorization. First order predicates language facilitates expressing complex knowledge rigorously, imposing appropriate reasoning techniques. Definition of certain propagation and inference procedures for real-time expert systems, involves the development of powerful reasoning mechanisms, as well as adapting the control algorithms to the state spaces, which are often very large. KMSFL is conceptually based on all the properties summarized above and consists of the compiled fuzzy rules base (control model) and the inference engine. In order to highlight the characteristics of this system, the following elements must be described: i) *The formalism,* specifying the types of knowledge supported by the system. Are presented, in order, the fuzzy knowledge syntax and the basic features of the compiled linguistic models, system's parameters, the elementary fuzzy filtering, the compatibility of possibility distributions for GMP inference scheme; ii) *Compiler properties,* which include the static structural discrimination component of the fuzzy state x^{CES}, the fuzzy unification tree as the basic element of the structure of compiled fuzzy knowledge (aimed at checking the consistency of fuzzy substitutions), the algorithm that generates the variables linking network.

Network's terminal nodes correspond bijectively to the fuzzy rules; iii) *Inference engine algorithm based on fuzzy logic,* which includes techniques for reasoning in the presence of compiled imprecise knowledge.

As a first step in the practical implementation of an expert system, knowledge representation aims to describe the problem domain as a model that includes relational entities and symbols, according to an appropriate formalism. The types of knowledge accepted by KMSFL are: **i)** variables (symbols always preceded by '?', such as ?x, ?y, and which will occur only in rules); **ii)** atomic constants (numbers or strings); **iii)** possibility distributions or fuzzy constants (symbols always preceded by the character '*' and used to represent imprecision); **iv)** logical operators. Possibility distribution can take any form. This complexity can cause a number of difficulties for the application of possibility theory. In practice, when the variable is numeric, it appears that a trapezoidal possibility distribution on continuous referential is well suited. It can be represented through four parameters (g, d, φ, δ). The trapezoidal form of possibility distributions is preserved in most of the inference and calculation operations. All the fuzzy constants used in knowledge representation and modeling, for the synthesis of fuzzy reasoning algorithms, are represented by trapezoidal possibility distributions, such as $g \leq d$, $\varphi, \delta \geq 0$, called T-numbers. Fuzzy constants can occur both in facts and rules, and are always associated to fuzzy sets (T-numbers) through *constfaz* function. Within KMSFL, we can equate the fuzzy set to a fuzzy constant. Undefined fuzzy constants are not allowed.

A fuzzy constant has always a value corresponding to a continuous, trapezoidal and normalized fuzzy set. Using possibility distributions provides an unified framework for representing imprecision and uncertainty. Parameter ζ is used to measure fuzzy sets' uncertainty ($0 \leq \zeta \leq 1$). If a fuzzy set is uncertain, parameter ζ must be defined in *constfaz* function through a list (uncertain ζ). We admit that a completely uncertain fuzzy set ($\zeta=1$) has no effect on system's behavior. In contrast to facts, a motive is a structured list in which variables may occur. This indicates the presence of variables, atomic constants and of fuzzy constants within motive's structure. In addition, the motives may occur in both the conditional part and in rules' conclusion. Uncertainty is allowed in the conditional part and in the consequent of GMP inference scheme, only if a particular linguistic model requires it. In order to increase the knowledge representation capacity, are introduced *predicates* that appear as motives in the left side of the rules. We emphasize the presence, within the knowledge model, of predicates F(a), which are flags that emulate human reasoning sequences, in order to achieve the control expert system's goal. The knowledge representation formalism for KMSFL is:

Antecedent	:: = condition*
Condition	:: = motive | motive motive_index | predicate
motive_index	:: =<atomic constant>
motive	:: = expression in which are allowed the three types of data;
predicate	:: = (predicate_sym predicate_arg predicate_arg)
predicate_arg	:: = predicate | atomic constant | fuzzy constant | variable
predicate_sym	:: = {=*, *<, >*, *Π, *N}
consequent	:: = conclusion*
conclusion	:: = motive | motive motive_index | predicate | procedure

Predicates =*, *< and >* have binary values, while *Π, *N are fuzzy predicates. If fuzzy linguistic models are introduced in a expert system, it becomes more complex due to considering the fuzzy processing at all system's levels, such as: fuzzy filtering, imprecise sets compatibility, fuzzy unification, calculation of the inferred conclusion together with the calculation of spreading for the parameters that manage imprecision, selection of strategies in which are naturally embedded also elements of factual knowledge imprecision. The fuzzy pattern-matching aims to determine the instantiations set of the causes. It is stronger than the classic one due to its capacity of processing the fuzzy knowledge. It is a matter of evaluating the degree of this pattern-matching between a fuzzy cause and a fuzzy fact (the fact filters more or less the cause). In order to put a fact in relation with a cause, we can build up a recursive algorithm, comparing the two associated trees step by step. It follows beyond doubt that the knowledge pattern-matching is the basic operation. Generally speaking, it is a matter of pattern-matching between a model P and a data D, to which we attach μ_P respectively Π_D ($\mu_P(u)$ is the degree of the compatibility between the value u and the meaning of P, while $\Pi_D(u)$ is the degree of possibility that the value u represents the value of the attribute which describes an object modeled through the data D). The degree of compatibility has the membership function $\mu_{P|D}$ defined through the extension principle. Though it translates relevant information related to the degree of the pattern matching between P and D, it is difficult to use $\mu_{P|D}$. We prefer two scalar measures in order to evaluate the compatibility: Π(P,D) and N(P,D). Let us consider the most simple case ((*f, *m→*c),*c'), where *m is the cause of the rule, *m→*c, *f is the fact, each of them being expressed by fuzzy sets. In order to deduce the conclusion *c', it is to be known if the fact is compatible with the rule condition. We can try to calculate GMP for the inferred conclusion *c'. The theory of possibilities provides two measures, which are very useful to evaluate the compatibility of the fuzzy sets:

$$\Pi(*m,*f)=\sup_u \min(\mu_{*m}(u), \mu_{*f}(u)),\ N(*m,*f)=1-\Pi(\neg *m, *f)=\inf_u \max(1-\mu_{*m}(u), \mu_{*f}(u))$$

Generally, it is much complicated to calculate N than Π. A simple calculating method is based on the separation of the complementary of *m. Analyzing the form of ¬*m, we find that this can be divided into two fuzzy sets L_s and L_d. The fuzzy set $L_s=(-\infty,g_m-\varphi_m,-\infty,\varphi_m)$ is always on the left of *m, while $L_d=(d_n+\delta_m,\infty,\delta_m,\infty)$ is always on the right of *m, and $L_s \cap L_d=\varnothing$. It follows that $\neg *m=\max(L_s, L_d)$. We get:

$$N(*m,*f)=1-\Pi(\neg *m,*f)=1-\Pi(\max(L_s,L_d),*f)=1-\max(\Pi(L_s,*f),\Pi(L_d,*f)).$$

Having Π and N, defined and calculated this way, we distinguish several classes of decreasing compatibility. Even if the measures Π and N correctly estimate the degree of compatibility between the fuzzy constants, these measures cannot be used directly to infer the conclusions in the case of an inference engine based on GMP. If the measures Π and N satisfy some thresholds, then the pattern matching is successful. To calculate GMP we need the parameters θ and K, in the following form:

$$\theta=(*m,*f)=\max(\mu_{*f}(g_m-\gamma_m),\mu_{*f}(d_m-\varphi_m)),\ K=(*m,*f)=\min(\mu_{*m}(g_f),\mu_{*m}(d_f))$$

At the end of the fuzzy condition/fact pattern-matching stage for the cause C and the fact F, if the degrees of the pattern matching satisfy the chosen thresholds and if there is a consistent substitution σ, then the pattern matching is successful. The substitution σ is a particular case when the variables in the causes can be associated to some fuzzy constants present in the facts. If the instance σ·C, obtained through the application of the fuzzy substitution σ to the condition C, is not totally equal with F, i.e. the expression F=σ·C is not always true, then σ is fuzzy. We can take into account the problem of finding the proper thresholds for measures Π and N in order to determine the facts that do not filter the causes at all. The choice is not made randomly, as between the two parameters of GMP it must be a tight link. Because of all these remarks and in order to correctly solve the problem, there are the links between Π, N, θ, K.

Fuzzy variables linking. The fuzzy condition/fact pattern matching is the first stage in the running of the inference engine, which takes into account the imprecision. After this stage, it results a lot of instantiations of the causes. Each motive's instantiation will be associated to a fuzzy substitution and to the four parameters Π, N, θ, K. The second stage is represented by the linking of the variables and it aims to determine the consistent instantiations at the level of rules' full conditions.

Fuzzy unification. The purpose of the fuzzy unification is to verify the consistency of the fuzzy substitutions, where the variables can be associated with fuzzy sets. Let's consider a rule (*D *H ?x) (B ?x)→(act(C *E ?x)). In the antecedent of the rule there are two causes C_1= (*D *H ?x) and C_2=(B ?x). We suppose the facts to be specified: F_1=(*d_1 *h_1 *w) and F_2=(B *r). For certain chosen fuzzy sets, the fuzzy constant *d_1 filters *D and *h_1 filters *H. The only result for the pattern-matching between C_2 and the fact F_2 is the fuzzy substitution σ=(* /?x) and the pattern-matching parameters. If all the parameters satisfy the designed thresholds, then the facts unify totally with the causes. After the fuzzy condition/fact pattern-matching, we obtained two fuzzy substitutions: σ={*w/?x} and σ = {*r/?x}, where *w and *r are fuzzy sets. The fuzzy unification contains, on the one hand, the evaluation of the consistency degree of the fuzzy substitutions on a certain norm and, on the other hand, the fuzzy substitutions composition.

Let us consider a rule R with k conditions, under the form COND(R)=(C_1,...,C_k). After the fuzzy condition/fact pattern-matching, if each condition C_i, filters a fact F_i, then there are a fuzzy substitution σ_I, so that $F_i=\sigma_i\cdot C_i$, and the four parameters Π_i, N_i, θ_i, K_i. Let us consider a variable ?v within the rule; assume that it appears n times in the conditional part of the rule. ?v_i is used for the representation of ith of the variable ?v. In this case, all the occurrences of the variable ?v within the global condition of the rule can be represented through the following list: {?v_1, ?v_2,...,?v_n}. Each ?v_i will be certainly associated with a term t_i, which can be an atomic or a fuzzy constant, denoted: {t_1/?v_1, t_2/?v_2,..., t_n/?v_n}. All the various variables present within a rule are independent. Each variable can occur in a rule several times. Each occurrence of the variable is independent of the other occurrences. Nearly all expert systems preserve this hypothesis. The fuzzy unification consists of: **i)** The consistency verification of the element in list {t_1/?v_1, t_2/?v_2,...t_n/?v_n}→{t_p/?v_p}, as against a certain norm; **ii)** The composition of the fuzzy substitutions. In order to eliminate any confusion, $?v_p$ is used to represent the variable ?v after the fuzzy unification. Finally, the fuzzy unification can be represented through the following expression: $\{t_1/?v_1, t_2/?v_2,...t_n/?v_n\}$ $\{t_p/?v_p\}$, where t_p is going to be calculated. Let us consider a simple case. If t_i is a fuzzy set, i.e. t_i=*t(i), (i=1,2), then the symbolic or numerical comparison is no longer sufficient to evaluate the consistency between *t(1) and *t(2). When $?v_1$ and $?v_2$ are independent, the cartesian product *t(1)×*t(2) is defined by:

$$*t(1)\times *t(2)=\{((x_1, x_2), \mu_{*t(1)\times *t(2)}(x_1,x_2)/x_1\in X_1, x_2\in X_2, X_1, X_2\subset R\}, \mu_{*t(1)\times *t(2)}(x_1,x_2) =\min(\mu_{*t(1)}(x_1)_{*t(2)}(x_2))$$

The compatibility between *t(1) and *t(2) can only be clarified through a reasonable explanation of the criterion relative to which compatibility is judged. In the classic situation, the criterion is given by the equality relation. It is quite natural to introduce appropriate criteria for fuzzy unification in both stages: to check the consistency and to make up the fuzzy substitutions. These criteria should be more general; the equality relation can be defined through a binary fuzzy relation R. Defining the fuzzy set *t(1) and the relation R, we obtain $\mu_{R\circ *t(1)}(x_2)$, defined by:

$$\mu_{R\circ *t(1)}(x_2)=\sup_u \min(\mu_R(x_1,x_2),\mu_{*t(1)}(x_1))$$

Since we know both the relation R and the Cartesian product (t(1)×*t(2), we can use measures Π and N to estimate the consistency of fuzzy sets *t(1) and *t(2) relative to R. Thus we have:

$$\Pi(R,*t(1)\times *t(2)) = \sup_{x1,x2}\min(\mu_R(x_1,x_2),\mu_{*t(1)}(x_1),\mu_{*t(2)}(x_2)),$$

$$N(R, *t(1)\times *t(2)) =\inf_{x1,x2}\max(\mu_R(x_1, x_2), 1-\mu_{*t(1)}(x_1),1-\mu_{*t(2)}(x_2))$$

It is interesting to note that the fuzzy binary relation R, can be interpreted in various ways. The equality relation may be regarded as a particular case of relation R. A last important problem is the parameters spreading. At the end of the elementary fuzzy pattern-matching stage, if the pattern-matching degree satisfies the chosen threshold and if there is a consistent substitution σ, then the pattern-matching process is successful. The fuzzy condition–fact pattern-matching process is the first stage, part of the overall cycle of the inference engine, able to take into consideration the imprecision. Each instance of a fuzzy motive is associated with a fuzzy substitution σ and with the parameters Π, N, θ, K. Following all these remarks and in order to correctly solve the problem, there are the links between Π, N, θ, K. As already shown, GMP verifies the following proposition:

Proposition i) $K = 0 \Leftrightarrow \theta = 1$; $K > 0 \Leftrightarrow \theta < 1$; ii) The conclusion *c' inferred through GMP is uncertain: $(\mu_{*c'}=1) \Leftrightarrow \theta = 1$; iii) N (*m, *f) $> 0 \Leftrightarrow \theta <1$.

The second stage in the pattern-matching process, on a global scale of the fuzzy rules, is the fuzzy linking of variables. This conducts the fuzzy unification, whose main purpose is to verify the consistency of fuzzy substitutes, for which we have already presented a series of theoretical results. Using the tests present in the linking nodes, we can build a dynamic tree that allows adding or suppressing facts. Within each test node of this tree, the values of the variables are tested. If two facts go on the same path, then it is possible that the two facts are consistent. We may use this tree in order to avoid combination challenges. This tree is called *linking tree* and it is associated to the linking nodes. It has some difficulties for the

discrimination of the fuzzy sets within its linking nodes, since certain parts (leaves) of the tree may contain multiple fuzzy facts.
That is why the efficiency of this solution decreases, being similar to the use of the unification tree, in order to discriminate the fuzzy motives. The main inefficiency factor is related to the disorder of the fuzzy facts in the tree leaves.
In order to improve this situation, we may use the characteristics of the fuzzy sets in order to sort out the facts. This approach was used to adapt the unification tree for the processing of fuzzy motives. The major difference that appears between the two situations is the fact that the unification tree is a static tree, i.e. the discriminator motives do not change, whereas the linking tree is dynamic, the discriminator facts being updated during the functioning period of the inference engine.
The fuzzy variables linking process consists of the fuzzy unification and the spreading of Π, N, θ, K parameters, evaluated on a global scale of the antecedent of the rule. We will further insist on the parameters spreading process, obtained at the end of the filtering stage, in the consequent of the rules. The Π possibility and N necessity degrees represent the extent to which a rule is satisfied in the current state within the facts base. During the selection stage, the system selects the rule that satisfies best these conditions in order to activate it, and the parameters θ and K serve to applying the GMP inference scheme. In the conclusion part of a rule there may be multiple motives (some may be added, others may be deleted, once the rule has been activated).

6. Case study

For the synthesis of fuzzy knowledge control model for the flexible production system, we considered the loads as fuzzy T-numbers, expressed linguistically as "around" or "approximately", and we introduced intermediate variables in the knowledge model's structure, such as: global balance degree *bd* (for the whole flexible manufacturing system) with the fuzzy values *satisfactory* and *unsatisfactory*, partial balance degrees pbd_i, i = 1, ..., 5 (per groups of subsystems), corresponding to certain situations unresolved in the crisp model, and fuzzy variables d_{56}, d_{42}, d_{13}, d_{21}, d_{43} and d_{35}, whose values can be the fuzzy T-numbers *small, large* or *zero*. The currently used partial balance degrees have as imprecise characteristics the linguistic values *good* and *unsatisfactory* (*unsatisfactory* value, in this case, is similar, in fuzzy number, to the one associated with the linguistic value *unsatisfactory* of the global balance degree). It was also useful to introduce knowledge in the form of imprecise facts of type (X1 X2 X3 X4 ?v_q), (X1 X2 X4 ?v_q), (X3 X4 X5 X6 ?v_q), (X1 X3 X4 X5 X6 ?v_q), (X2 X4 X5 X6 ?v_q), ensuring that the balancing is continuously accomplished, partially and gradually, and a number of *meta-rules* in which these facts are present. They will be activated chained, as (R13, R14) (R13, R15) (R16, R17) (R16, R24) (R18, R19) (R18, R25) (R20, R21) (R22, R23)) and support the synthesis of fuzzy decision. We may notice that, for this control model, we followed the stages for the synthesis of a linguistic model, in terms of knowledge acquisition process, and the knowledge and meta-knowledge are represented according to KMSFL formalism.
Exploiting this model requires calculating the fuzzy unification and the partial conclusion inferred through the GMP scheme, the call of procedures in rules' consequent and of a control module, dynamically updating the priorities of the rules according to the current imprecision of all knowledge involved at some point in the decision synthesis, chaining the fuzzy meta-rules and demonstrating the global asymptotically stable behavior of the closed-

loop system. Intermediate fuzzy variables pbd_1, pbd_2, pbd_3, pbd_4 and pbd_5 are degrees of partial balance between groups of subsystems (1, 2, 3, 4), (1, 2, 4), (3, 4, 5, 6), (1, 3, 4, 5, 6) and (2, 4, 5, 6). These variables were used to eliminate the unbalance situations obtained in the crisp case, these being the control meta-knowledge of the expert in the field. They depend essentially on the structure of flexible manufacturing system and are actually imprecise knowledge used in decision synthesis. For each inference cycle it must calculate all the corresponding fuzzy values and generate the updated facts, thus, the current state of the control system.

The fuzzy control model has the following properties: *i*) variable pbd_1 appears in rules 14 and 15, and its value is recalculated after the pattern-matching between its current fuzzy value and the motive (pbd_1 *b) by applying the GMP inference scheme. The same calculation method is applied to other partial balance degrees; *ii*) for meta-rules 14, 16, 18, 20 and 22 fuzzy unification is applied differently, requiring the calculation of the resulting fuzzy value for the variable $?v_q$ from the consequent; *iii*) variable $?v_q$, together with variables pbd_1, pbd_2, pbd_3, pbd_4 and pbd_5, allow chaining the fuzzy rules while the control model is used by the KMSFL inference engine; iv) within the structure of meta-rules 13-25 are present fuzzy variables d_{56}, d_{35}, d_{13}, d_{21}, d_{43}, d_{42}, representing the fuzzy instant differences between machine loads, referenced by the corresponding indexes, in the appropriate order. The values of these variables are fuzzy numbers tp *ma(2 pbd_j 1 1), j=1 ... 5 and tp *mi(0 1 0 1). Fuzzy value *b is generated similarly. To clarify how the fuzzy model for flexible production system is initialized and exploited, follow the *Algorithm_KMSFL*, in which are also presented some functional aspects of the control expert system.

This algorithm associated with the inference subsystem within the KMSFL was developed in close relation with fuzzy knowledge representation formalism. In addition, we tested the knowledge model using the generator G2 (only for the crisp case) to highlight some of the advantages and limitations of the knowledge management model and of the inference engine. However, fuzzy processing is specific to the expert system developed, this being the major objective of this work.

Algorithm_KMSFL

1. Enter the initial fuzzy loads $\mu_{x_{i0}}$;
2. Calculate the expected average value $\mu_{c_0} = \sum_{i=1}^{6} x_{i_0} /6$, the fuzzy distances $\mu_{d_{i0}} = \mu_{x_{i0}} - \mu_{c_0}$ and the initial balance degree $bd_0 = \max_{i=1,\ldots,6} \{\mu_{d_{i0}}\}$;
3. Generate sets *s (the characteristics of fuzzy sets *s are checked in tests, in relation to the initial loads), *n = tp(3 bd_0 2 2) (d and δ are checked in tests in relation to the initial loads) and the facts (bd *n) and (bd *s);
4. Initialize $x^b=(x^{b1},x^{b2})$ where $x^{b1}=\mathbf{0}$ and $\dim(\mathbf{x}^{b1})=12$, $\mathbf{x}^{b2}$ contains the initial facts attached to all linguistic variables involved in the control model, such as: ((X1 ?x), (X2 ?y), (X3 ?z), (X4 ?v), (X5 ?w), (X6 ?ξ), (X1 X2 X3 X4 $?v_q$), (X1 X2 X4 $?v_q$), (X3 X4 X5 X6 $?v_q$), (X1 X3 X4 X5 X6 $?v_q$), (X2 X4 X5 X6 $?v_q$), (X1 X2 X4 $?v_q$), (X12b 1), (bd *n), (CFS *zero), (pbd_1 *b), (d_{56} *ma), (d_{35} *ma), (pbd_2 *b), (d_{13} *ma), (pbd_3 *b), (d_{21} *ma), (pbd_4 *b), (d_{42} *ma), (pbd_5 *b), (d_{43} *ma), to evaluate the effect of all fuzzy variables that appear in structure of this state component of KMSFL. As initial fact attached to the reason (bd *n), is launched the fact (bd *v_0), where *v_0 is generated as a fuzzy set around the value of bd_0, of the form (*constfaz* *v_0(tp bd_0-1 bd_0+1 2 2)). Is also initialized $\mathbf{x}^{int} = 0$.

5. In the consequent of rules R1-R10, along with the deduction of fact (xib i), corresponding to a procedure call, is attached the calculation of the balance degree bd with its new fuzzy value, i.e. is generated the new fact (bd $*v_k$), $k \geq 1$. Value $*v_k$ can filter or not *n or *s, and properly the fuzzy values of partial balance degrees and the fuzzy distances between the physically interconnected subsystems;
6. If the inference engine stops on a different event than on the one corresponding to the activation and execution of rule 11, then are recalculated the fuzzy differences $\mu_{d_{i_k}} = \mu_{x_{i_k}} - \mu_{c_0}$, along with determining the subsystem (i = 1, ... 6) and the corresponding rule j (j = 1 ,..., 25) to be activated, to satisfy the balancing goal at the current time, by using meta-rules (R13-R25) or by launching the *control module.*

For each inference cycle must calculate all the corresponding fuzzy values, and generate the updated facts and thus the current state of the control system.

Implementation results for KMSFL

Test A. This test aims to prove the functioning of the KMSFL prototype for a first set of knowledge. Fuzzy values involved in testing the control model by using the corresponding inference engine are: (*constfaz* *s(tp 0 1 0 1)), (*constfaz* *n(tp 2 ∞ 1 1)), (*constfaz* *ma(tp 2 ∞ 1 1)), (*constfaz* *mi(tp 0 1 0 1)), (*constfaz* *b(tp 0 1 0 1)), $\varepsilon=1$, $\eta= 0$, $\mu_{x_1} = \mu_{x_2}=\mu_{x_3}$=(199.5 200.5 1 1), $\mu_{x_4}=\mu_{x_5}=\mu_{x_6}$=(-0.5 0.5 1 1), "around x_0"=(x_0-0.5 x_0+0.5 x_0-1.5 x_0+1.5)="x_0", x^{b1}=**0**. We get the following results: the first complete execution of the inference engine implies a number of 118 inferences and the values of subsystems' loads and of the global balance degree are: μ_{x_1}="101.33"=(100.83 101.83 0.5 0.5), μ_{x_2}="102.60"=(101.56 102.56 0.5 0.5), μ_{x_3}="101.33"=(100.83 101.83 0.5 0.5), μ_{x_4}="102.04"=(101.54 102.54 0.5 0.5), μ_{x_5}="100.61"=(100.11 101.11 0.5 0.5), μ_{x_6}="92.627"=(92.127 93.127 0.5 0.5), bd=(6.87 7.87 0.5 0.5). In this case, the balance degree bd="7.3731" is an unsatisfactory value, which means that the balancing problem is not completely solved (fig. 3, fig.4). For inferences 42, 43, 54, 55, 58, 59, 70, 71, 82, 83, 86, 87, 95, 96, 100, 101, 103, 104, 105, 106 are activated meta-rules 16, 17, 13, 14, 13, 15, 16, 17, 13, 14.13, 15, 16, 17, 16, 17, 13, 14, 13, 15 respectively, the rest of the inferences activating the basic rules R1-R10.

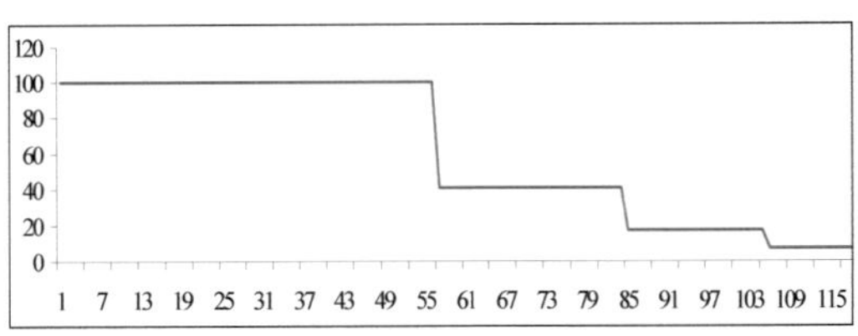

Fig. 3. The evolution of balance degree bd

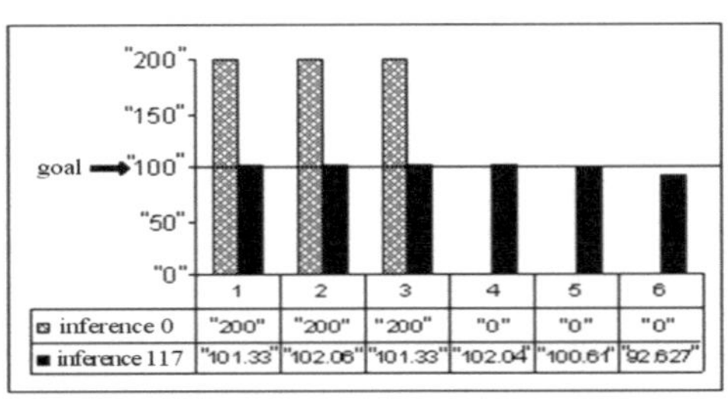

Fig. 4. The loads evolution for test A

After resetting the inference engine with the values previously obtained, we get a total of 18 inferences, whose result is presented in Table 1 (SC=Set of Conflicts, ER=Executed rule):

No.	μ_{x1}	μ_{x2}	μ_{x3}	μ_{x4}	μ_{x5}	μ_{x6}	x_{b1}	x^{b1}	SC_k	ER	Event	bd
0	101.33	102.01	101.33	102.00	100.61	92.627	0	00000000000	7	7	e_{43}	7.3575
1	101.33	102.01	101.67	101.67	100.61	92.627	7	00000010000	4	4	e_{35}	7.3575
2	101.33	102.01	101.14	101.67	101.14	92.627	4	00010010000	8	8	e_{56}	7.3575
3	101.33	102.01	101.14	101.67	96.883	96.883	8	00000011000	4	4	e_{35}	3.1018
4	101.33	102.01	99.011	101.67	99.011	96.883	4	00010010000	2	2	e_{13}	3.1018
5	100.17	102.01	100.17	101.67	99.011	96.883	2	01010010000	3	3	e_{21}	3.1018
6	101.09	101.09	100.17	101.67	99.011	96.883	3	00100010000	13	13		3.1018
7	101.09	101.09	100.17	101.67	99.011	96.883	3	00100010000	13,14	14	[e_{56}]	3.1018
8	101.09	101.09	100.17	101.67	97.947	97.947	8	00000011000	13	13		2.0378
9	101.09	101.09	100.17	101.67	97.947	97.947	8	00000011000	13,15	15	[e_{35}]	2.0378
10	101.09	101.09	99.058	101.67	99.058	97.947	4	00010010000	2	2	e_{13}	2.0378
11	100.07	101.09	100.07	101.67	99.058	97.947	2	01010010000	3	3	e_{21}	2.0378
12	100.58	100.58	100.07	101.67	99.058	97.947	3	00100010000	6	6	e_{42}	2.0378
13	100.58	101.12	100.07	101.12	99.058	97.947	6	00000100000	7	7	e_{43}	2.0378
14	100.58	101.12	100.60	100.60	99.058	97.947	7	00000010000	4	4	e_{35}	2.0378
15	100.58	101.12	99.829	100.60	99.829	97.947	4	00010010000	13	13		2.0378
16	100.58	101.12	99.829	100.60	99.829	97.947	4	00010010000	13,14	14	[e_{56}]	2.0378
17	100.58	101.12	99.829	100.60	98.888	98.888	8	00000011000		0	$e \neq e_{00}$	1.1394

Table 1. Inference process results for test A (case a2)

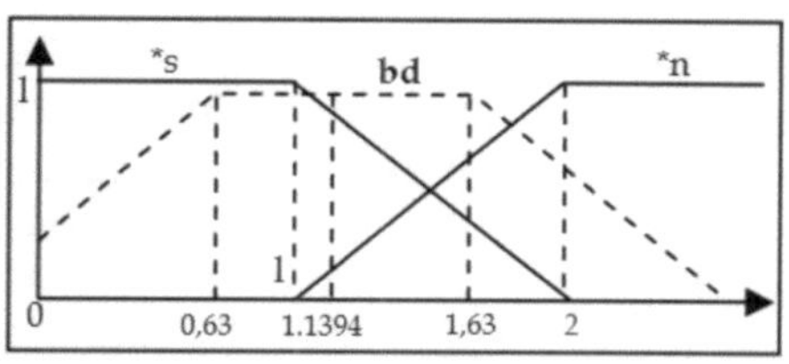

Fig. 5. The fuzzy final balance degree

We notice that, at the end of inference engine execution, in accordance with the reset, the balance degree is bd="1.1394", which corresponds to linguistic value *satisfactory* (fig. 5) because Π(*s, "bd")=1 and N(*s, "bd")=0246>0. The balance degree is satisfactory but the fuzzy differences between the final values of subsystems' loads and the expected average value are not similar (i.e. they are not all around zero). This is proved by the inference engine stop after the execution of meta-rule 14 (after which it cannot infer anything) and not of rule 11, as is conceived the control model. This is due to improper choice of the fuzzy set for the linguistic value *unsatisfactory*.

Test B. The purpose of this test is to highlight that, for other initial subsystems' loads, the control model achieves its intended objective, in terms of balance degree (which must be satisfactory at the end of the execution), and that the final loads are similar to the expected average value, given by $\mu_{\bar{x}}$=(*constfaz* *$\mu_{\bar{x}}$ (tp 32.83 33.83 1 1)), according to the similarity criteria adopted within the KMSFL. In this case μ_{x_1}="200", μ_{x_2}=...=μ_{x_6}="0", x^{b1}=**0**, and the other fuzzy values of the knowledge model are initialized and are similar to those in the test A. After the first execution, the inference engine performs 67 inferences and the values of fuzzy loads are: μ_{x_1} ="33.419", μ_{x_2} ="34.289", μ_{x_3} ="33.419", μ_{x_4} ="34.961", μ_{x_5} ="32.55", μ_{x_6} ="31.361". The last rule activated is meta-rule 13, and the balance degree at this stage is bd="1.9725". It is noted that the balance degree is satisfactory (Π(*s, "0.967") = 1 and N(*s, "0.967")=0.266>0), the fuzzy differences between the final loads and the expected average value are approximately zero, but the loads of the subsystems analyzed in pairs, according to the reasons within antecedent of rule 11, are not all similar to each other, because the execution does not end with rule 11. The observation above is based on the following calculations: for $\mu_{\bar{x}}$ =(32.83 33.83 1 1), μ_{x_1} =(32.919 33.919 1 1), μ_{x_2} =(33.789 34.789 1 1), μ_{x_3} =(32.87 33.87 1 1), μ_{x_4} =(33.69 34.69 1 1), $\mu_{x_5} = \mu_{x_6}$ =(31.865 32.865 1 1) we get respectively the following pairs: $\Pi(\mu_{x_1}, \mu_{\bar{x}})$ = 1, $N(\mu_{x_1}, \mu_{\bar{x}})$=0.455, $\Pi(\mu_{x_2}, \mu_{\bar{x}})$=1, $N(\mu_{x_2}, \mu_{\bar{x}})$=0.02, $\Pi(\mu_{x_3}, \mu_{\bar{x}})$=1, $N(\mu_{x_3}, \mu_{\bar{x}})$ =0.48, $\Pi(\mu_{x_4}, \mu_{\bar{x}})$=1, $N(\mu_{x_4}, \mu_{\bar{x}})$=0.07, $\Pi(\mu_{x_5}, \mu_{\bar{x}})$=1, $N(\mu_{x_5}, \mu_{\bar{x}})$=0.01 that satisfy the condition of similarity between any of the final states of the loads and the expected average value.

Test C. This test emphasizes the *dynamic circularity*. All subsystems are loaded with fuzzy values different from "0", and the characteristics of the associated fuzzy numbers are closer to the case of natural perception, i.e. have been increased the cores and the imprecision areas of fuzzy values, as follows: *s = *b = *mi = (-1 1 2 2), *n =* ma = (3 ∞ 3 3), "around x_0" = (x_0-1 x_0+1 x_0-3 x_0+3), $\varepsilon = 1$, $\eta = 0$, μ_{x_1} = (1222 1224 2 2) = "1223", μ_{x_2} = (309 311 2 2) = "310", μ_{x_3} = (444 446 2 2) = "445", μ_{x_5} = (37 39 2 2) = "38", μ_{x_6} = (741 743 2 2) = "742", $x^{b1} = 0$. We may notice the intensive use of meta-rules in the second part of the execution and the correct ending of the balancing problem, in terms of final state. The expected average fuzzy value is $\mu_{\bar{x}}$ = "610.8(3)". After the first execution of the inference engine of KMSFL, starting from inference 39, the system goes in a cyclical operation (dynamic circularity), since all inferences starting from inference 40 do not change the KMSFL state so that to achieve the intended objective correctly. This is justified by the value of bd = "3.7213", with Π(*n, "3.7213") = 1 and N = (*n, "3.7213") = 0.54426. In this example is not activated the control module from rule 12 consequent, whose purpose is to eliminate the cycles from inference engine operation. To solve this problem, which is not allowed in the operation of an expert system, in the next we will highlight the behavior of inference engine when activating the control module. Solving the above listed deficiencies is founded on resetting the inference engine operation, based on user inputs UI, in order to achieve the goal. Reset is done by positioning the vector $x^{b1} = 0$, the subsystems' loads and the other fuzzy values being equal to the last values previously used.

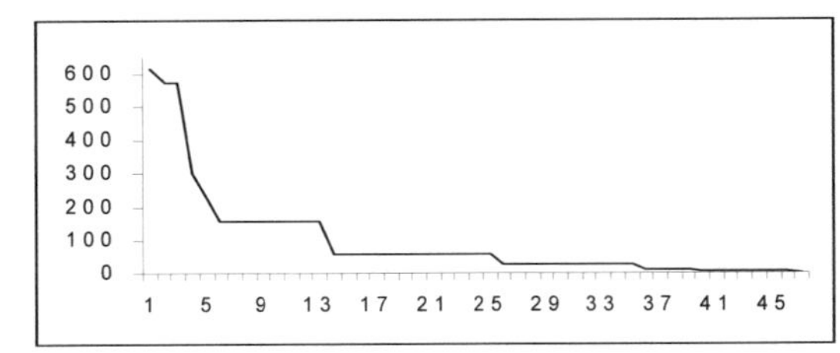

Fig. 6. Balance degree evolution for case C

After the reset, are used the meta-rules from the structure of knowledge management model to achieve the goal state. We get the following final fuzzy values of subsystems' loads: μ_{x_1} = (609.87 611.87 2 2), μ_{x_2} = (611.76 613.76 2 2), μ_{x_3} = (609.34 611.34 2 2), μ_{x_4} = (611.71 613.71 2 2), $\mu_{x_5} = \mu_{x_6}$ = (608.16 610.16 2 2). The final balance degree is satisfactory because Π((-1 1 2 2),

(0.9311 2.9311 2 2)) = 1 and N((-1 1 2 2), (0.9311 2.9311 2 2)) = 0.017225 > 0. The evolution of the balance degree is shown in fig. 6. Final loads above are similar to each other because: $\Pi(\mu_{x_1}, \mu_{x_2}) = 1$, $N(\mu_{x_1}, \mu_{x_2}) = 0.275 > 0$, $\theta(\mu_{x_1}, \mu_{x_2}) = 0.945$, $K(\mu_{x_1}, \mu_{x_2}) = 0.055$, $\Pi(\mu_{x_1}, \mu_{x_3})=1$, $N(\mu_{x_1}, \mu_{x_3}) = 0.367 > 0$, $\theta(\mu_{x_1}, \mu_{x_3}) = 0.265$, $K(\mu_{x_1}, \mu_{x_3}) = 0.75$, $\Pi(\mu_{x_1}, \mu_{x_4}) = 1$, $N(\mu_{x_1}, \mu_{x_4}) = 0.04>0$, $\theta(\mu_{x_1}, \mu_{x_4})= 0.92$, $K(\mu_{x_1}, \mu_{x_4}) = 0.145$, $\Pi(\mu_{x_1}, \mu_{x_5}) = \Pi(\mu_{x_1}, \mu_{x_6}) = 1$, $N(\mu_{x_1}, \mu_{x_5}) = N(\mu_{x_1}, \mu_{x_6}) = 0.725 > 0$, $\theta(\mu_{x_1}, \mu_{x_5}) = \theta(\mu_{x_1}, \mu_{x_6}) = 0.855$, $K(\mu_{x_1}, \mu_{x_5}) = K(\mu_{x_1}, \mu_{x_6}) = 0.145$.
It is noted that all criteria regarding the correct stop off the inference engine are met, thus obtaining the solution, whose value must be calculated through unification according to rule 11 antecedent. Thus, is revealed the inference engine behavior in order to avoid dynamic circularity presented in this example. The KMSFL can effectively predict a number of states that characterize the process, for a finite time horizon, as a result of its own inferences and of its knowledge management model.

7. Conclusions and future work

Designing and testing KMSFL system requires the existence of some scientific methods for knowledge acquisition, which unfortunately is a heterogeneous and time-consuming process. The synthesis of the control model for the case study presented, encompassing human control experience, was iterative, being necessary to indirectly develop some methods and testing and simulating environments for some crisp and fuzzy control models, permanently adjusting the inferential subsystem.
The importance of this paper consists of demonstrating the possibility of employing an expert KMS in problems of process control and planning, using imprecise knowledge. It was necessary to continuously adapt known models (e.g. theory of possibilities, discrete event systems) to synthesize a control structure based on fuzzy knowledge. We also tried to conceptually develop a multi-agent real control structure, which is a solution to meet a series of demands on the complexity of the control process. Such systems, especially those based on communication between agents by sharing memory, bring up features well suited for real-time applications, such as: integration of heterogeneous agents, interaction between activities of acquisition, reasoning and action on the external environment, fusion of data coming from sensors of different nature and operation, flexibility and efficiency in the integration of new data needed for reasoning, by simply writing them in the common memory. Real-time applications require the cooperation of elaborate reasoning processes. The essential point in integrating the cognitive/reactive aspects is the modeling of the relations between the process evolution and certain inferential methods, to allow the closed-loop system to achieve a range of required performances. Temporal aspects are an important dimension of any KMS embedded in NSTs. There is a distinction between real-time reasoning and reasoning over time, the latter being a feature of the knowledge-based systems. For this reason, it was absolutely necessary to explain the significance of time in the design and implementation of KMSFL, emphasizing its implications in the specific case of the developed application.
Following the tests presented and the knowledge representation and exploitation structures within KMSFL, we may outline the following conclusions:

i. the formalism chosen for knowledge representation is strong enough to support the representation of some types of knowledge underlying the synthesis of control decisions. It has the advantage of factorizing the knowledge, which substantially reduced the size of fuzzy rules base. Also, this knowledge representation method is more appropriate to express some types of knowledge similar to those commonly used in the decision synthesis through natural language;

ii. the knowledge fuzzy model for the problem presented was developed incrementally, as was embedded in the model sufficient domain knowledge, resulting from the limitations observed in the crisp case. Is it possible to constantly adapt the fuzzy model through simulations;
iii. the inferential subsystem based on fuzzy logic solves the control situations correctly, both from the computational point of view and in terms of the semantics of the conclusions inferred through the chosen inference scheme;
iv. modeling the process and the expert system as systems with logical events allowed the qualitative analysis of KMSFL;
v. the control module integrated into the inferential subsystem automatically adapts the problem-solving process, being equivalent to closed-loop system input, denoted UI (user input). In this way, through the control meta-rule 12, we can simulate practically the activation of the relation between output Hypotheses/Conclusions and user inputs. This component is not activated in every case (initial loads). This justifies a major feature of the designed control expert system: its ability to correctly solve the problem, under the conditions specified for each case; vi) The case when $c_k \in \mathbf{N}^+$ is not a particular case for $\mu_{ck} \in \mathbf{R}^+$ due to certain restrictions on the events trajectories and to system's lack of flexibility in achieving the balance, thus leading to partial balance. For the discrete case, there is a tolerated unbalance value, denoted ψ and for which $|x_i - x_j| \leq \psi$, which defines the invariant set. For the fuzzy case, is achieved a good balancing solution, regardless of the initial subsystems' loads. In this case the system is broadly asymptotically stable relative to event trajectories.

We also summarize possible further development, which inherently can be obtained starting from KMSFL: identifying stronger planning characteristics, the logical specification of the real-time expert systems so that to describe how the statements change their truth values, depending on time or in order to meet some strong real-time restrictions, knowledge acquisition (as a difficult and insufficiently formalized problem), as well as the correct choice of the inference operators that lead to consistent results with regard to the well-defined knowledge semantics, integrating a control expert system like the one developed (agent) into a multi-agent system structure, identifying real problems in different application areas that can be solved using the expert system developed.

8. Acknowledgments

I would like to acknowledge my heartfelt and sincere gratitude to my family. A special thanks to all my projects partners and various anonymous reviewers for their valuable advice, insight, comments, and suggestions. This research is funded by a private company in cooperation with Dunărea de Jos University of Galati, Romania, under the research Projects 556/2009 and 557/2010. I am extremely thankful for their financial assistance.

9. References

Alavi, M. (1999), Knowledge Management and Knowledge Management Systems: Conceptual Foundations and Research Issues

Barachini, F. (1990), Match-Time Predictability in Real-Time Production Systems, Lecture Notes in Artificial Intelligence, nº 462, Expert Systems in Engineering, Principles and Applications, International Workshop, Viena, Austria, September, 1990, Proceedings, Springer-Verlag, p. 190-203, ISBN 3-540-53104-1

Binney, D. (2001), The knowledge management spectrum - understanding the KM landscape, Journal of Knowledge Management, 5, 1, 33-42

Bobrowitz , O. (1993), La représentation et l'utilisation des connaissances imprécises pour l'aide à la conduite des procédés, Thèse en Automatique et Informatique, Franche-Comté, 1991

Bylander, T. (1994), The computational complexity of propositional STRIPS planning, Artificial Intelligence, nº 69, 1994, p. 165-204

Chen, H.P.; Parng, T.M. (1996), A new approach of multi-stage fuzzy logic inference, Fuzzy Sets and Systems, Vol. 78, nº 1, feb. 26, 1996, p. 51-72

Davis, M. (2006), Semantic Wave 2006, Part-1: Executive Guide to Billion Dollar Markets, A Project10X Special Report

Dubois, D.; Lang, J.; Prade, H. (1991), Fuzzy sets in aproximate reasoning - Part 2: Logical approaches, Fuzzy Sets and Systems, nº 40, 1991, p. 203-244

Dubois, D.; Prade ,H. (1992), Fuzzy rules in knowledge-based systems, An introduction to fuzzy logic applications in intelligent systems (edited by R. Yager, L. A. Zadeh), Kluwer Academic Publishers, p. 45-68

Durán, O.; Aguilo, J. (2008), *Computer-aided machine-tool selection based on a Fuzzy-AHP approach*, Expert Systems with Applications, Volume 34, Issue 3, p. 1787-1794, 2008, www.elsevier.com

Ghallab, M. (1988), Compilation de bases de connaissances, PRC GRECO IA, Actes des Journées Nationales, p. 231-253

Iqbal, A.; He, N., Ullah Dar, N.; Li, L.- *Comparison of fuzzy expert system based strategies of offline and online estimation of flank wear in hard milling process*, Expert Systems with Applications, Volume 33, Issue 1, p. 61-66, 2007, www.elsevier.com

Jennings, N. R. and Wittig, T. (1992) ARCHON: Theory and Practice. In: Distributed Artificial Intelligence: Theory and Praxis. Kluwer Academic Press, pp.179-195

Kim, YG.; Yu, SH.; Lee, J.H. (2003), *Knowledge strategy planning: methodology and case*, Expert Systems with Applications, Volume 24, Issue 3, 1 April 2003, p. 295-307, 2003, www.elsevier.com

Kingston, J. (2001), *High Performance Knowledge Bases: four approaches to knowledge acquisition, representation and reasoning for workaround planning*, Expert Systems with Applications, Volume 21, Issue 4, p. 181-190, 2001, www.elsevier.com

Knight, J.F.; Passino, K.M. (1987), Decidability for temporal logic in control theory, Proceedings of the Twenty-Fifth Allerton Conference on Communication, Control and Computing, University of Illinois at Urbara-Champaign, p. 335-344

Lassaigne, R.; Rougemont, M. (1996), Logique et complexité, Hermes, Paris, 1996

Lau, H.C.W.; Cheng, E.N.M.; Lee, C.K.M.; Ho, G.T.S. (2008), *A fuzzy logic approach to forecast energy consumption change in a manufacturing system*, Expert Systems with Applications, Volume 34, Issue 3, April 2008, p. 1813-1824, 2008, www.elsevier.com

Lin, C.J.; Wu, W.W. (2008), *A causal analytical method for group decision-making under fuzzy environment*, Expert Systems with Applications, Volume 34, Issue 1, p. 205-213, 2008, www.elsevier.com

Luger, G.F.; Stubblefield, W.A. (1993), Artificial Intelligence, Structures and Strategies for Complex Problem Solving, Second Edition, The Benjamin/Cummings Publishing Company, Inc., ISBN 0-8053-4780-1

Lunardhi, A.D.; Passino, K.M. (1995), Verification of qualitative properties of rule-based expert systems, in Applied Artificial Intelligence, p. 587-621

Marco A.C. Pacheco, Marley M.B.R. Vellasco (2009), Intelligent Systems in Oil Field Development under Uncertainty, Studies in Computational Intelligence 183, Springer

Mazilescu, V. (2009a), A Real Time Control System based on a Fuzzy Compiled Knowledge Base, Proceedings of The 13th WSEAS International Conference on COMPUTERS, CSCC Multiconference, Rodos Island, Greece, July 23-25, Conference track: Artificial Intelligence. Computational Intelligence, p. 459-464

Mazilescu, V. (2009b), Knowledge Management & Intelligent Economic Systems, Europlus Publishing House, ISBN 978-973-1950-79-2

Mazilescu, V. (2010) Characterizing an Extended Fuzzy Logic System with Temporal Attributes for Real-Time Expert Systems, The 10th WSEAS International Conference on Systems Theory and Scientific Computation (ISTASC'10), Taipei, TAIWAN, p.159-165

Mazilescu, V. (2011), An Intelligent System for a Resource Allocation Problem based on Fuzzy Reasoning, Computer Technology and Application, David Publishing Company, From Knowledge to Wisdom, ISSN 1934-7332, p. 247-255

Müller, J.P. (1996), The design of intelligent agents: a layered approach, Lecture Notes in Artificial Intelligence (Subseries of Lecture Notes in Computer Science), nº 1177, ISBN 3-540-62003-6

Nebel, B.; Bäckström, C. (1994), On the computational complexity of temporal projection, planning and plan validation, Artificial Intelligence 66, p. 125-160

Omar, L.O. (2008), *Java Fuzzy Kit (JFK): A shell to build fuzzy inference systems according to the generalized principle of extension*, Expert Systems with Applications, Volume 34, Issue 1, p. 796-804, 2008, www.elsevier.com

Passino, K.M.; Antsaklis, P.J. (1989), A system and control theoretic perspective on artificial Intelligence planning systems, Int. Journal of Applied Artificial Intelligence, Vol. 3, p. 1-32

Passino, K.M.; Antsaklis, P.J. (1994), Lyapunov stability of a class of discrete event systems, IEEE Transaction on Automatic Control, Vol. 39, p. 269- 279

Ponnurangam, D.; Uma, G.V. (2005), *Fuzzy complexity assessment model for resource negotiation and allocation in agent-based software testing framework*, Expert Systems with Applications, Volume 29, Issue 1, p. 105-119, 2005, www.elsevier.com

Qian, D. (1992), Representation and use of imprecise temporal knowledge in dynamic systems, Fuzzy Sets and Systems, Vol. 50, nº 1, Aug. 25, p. 59-77

Schwartz, D.G. (2006), Encyclopedia of Knowledge Management, Idea Group Inc., ISBN 1-59140-573-4 (hc)

Stankovic, J.A.; Ramamritham, K. (1995), What is Predictability for Real-Time Systems?, Advances in Real-Time Systems, IEEE Computer Society Press, p.26-33, ISBN 0-8186-3792-7

Tsui, E. (2002), The role of Artificial Intelligence in Knowledge Management, Knowledge-Based Systems, 13, 5, October, 235-239, URL= http://www.aifb.uni-karlsruhe.de/~sst/Research/ Publications/kbs-editorial-note2000.pdf

Wang, K.J.; Lin, Y.S. (2007), *Resource allocation by genetic algorithm with fuzzy inference*, Expert Systems with Applications, Volume 33, Issue 4, November 2007, p. 1025-1035, 2007, www.elsevier.com

Wenger, E. (2001), Supporting communities of practice: a survey of community-oriented technologies, 2001, URL=http://www.ewenger.com/tech/index.htm

Zadeh, L.A. (1978), Fuzzy sets as a basis for a theory of possibility, Fuzzy Sets and Systems, nº1, 1978, p.3-28

Zadeh, L.A. (1983), Knowledge Representation in Fuzzy Logic, in An introduction to fuzzy logic applications in intelligent systems (edited by R. Yager, L. A. Zadeh), Kluwer Academic Publishers, p. 1-26

2

Integration of Knowledge Management in the MIB for the Network Management

Antonio Martín and Carlos León
Dpto. Tecnología Electrónica. University of Sevilla
Spain

1. Introduction

In a heterogeneous and distributed context, the management of telecommunication networks and services is becoming increasingly important in operator and service provider environments. This management cannot be performed without the contribution of intelligent management functions, which ensure the most important management operations of provisioning, assurance and billing. More advanced tools are needed to support this activity. It is necessary to develop new models, which offer more possibilities.
To resolve this difficulty in this chapter we study the integration of advanced artificial intelligence technology into existing network management models. We describe the design and implementation of a management platform using Artificial Intelligent reasoning technique.
This study focuses on an intelligent framework and a language for formalizing knowledge management descriptions and combining them with existing OSI management model. In this chapter we present a methodology to specify intelligent agents, based on management OSI model.
We propose a new paradigm where the intelligent network management is integrated into the conceptual repository of management information. In modern network elements management information is increasingly stored in a distributed manner locally with the network elements into Management Information Base (MIB) databases. These databases contain all relevant configuration data and the dynamic state data (measurements and alarms) in a standardized format. We study a technique which integrates the knowledge base of expert system within the MIB used to manage a network.
A new property named RULE has been added in the MIB, which gathers important aspects of the facts and the knowledge base of the embedded expert system. By integrating the knowledge base in resources specifications, system has the power to provide diagnosis of fault network, which can assist engineering trainees, inspectorate staff and professional. Furthermore this paper outlines the development of an expert system prototype based in our propose GDMO+ standard and describes the most important facets, advantages and drawbacks that were found after prototyping our proposal.
This paper is organized as follows. In the section immediately below, we describe the evolution of network management and the role of network management functions. We will examine the management network, including the concepts, major approaches, and management models. It starts with specific applications and work on expert systems in similar fields. We propose a new Intelligent Integrated Management Model and an extension of

standard called Extended GDMO or simply GDMO+, for the incorporation of the management expert rules. Next will examined the design and development of a prototype. From there, we present the concept the formulation of the system design proposal and also an outline of the various stages in the system development cycle. Next section summarizes the performance of the system and the results of the research. Finally we outline the conclusion and future works.

2. Management network overview

The purpose of network management is the assignment and control of proper network resources, both hardware and software, to address service performance needs and the network's objectives. With the ever-increasing size and complexity of underlying networks and services, it has become impossible to carry out these functions without the support of automated tools (Zuidweg, 2002). As the size of communication networks keeps on growing, with more subscribers, faster connections and competing and cooperating technologies and the divergence of computers, data communications and telecommunications, the management of the resulting networks gets more important and time-critical. Telecommunication and services are in the process of revolutionary yet evolutionary changes due to transformation of the regulatory environment that in turn has given rise to rapid improvements in the underlying application, networking, computing, and transmission technologies.
There are two dominant network management models, which have been used to administration and control the most of existing networks: TMN and SNMP. Both network management systems operate using client/server architecture. SNMP standards are defined in a series of documents, called request for comments or RFCs proposed by the Internet Engineering Task Force (IETF) and Telecommunications Management Network TMN is introduced by the ITU-T (the former CCITT). Of these two TMN is gaining popularity for large complex networks.
In private network environment, SNMP enjoys near-universal support. In the public environment, however, a more heterogeneous mix of de facto telecommunications industry standards has prevailed, with a move toward TMN support. Moreover TMN was the first who started, as part of its Open Systems Interconnection (OSI) program, the development of the architecture for network management. The OSI management environment consists of tools and services need to control and supervise the management networks.

2.1 OSI network management model

The OSI network management model is a starting point for understanding network management. There are three basic components comprising the elements of the management architecture to support a successful implementation of the OSI Network Management Model, figure 1:

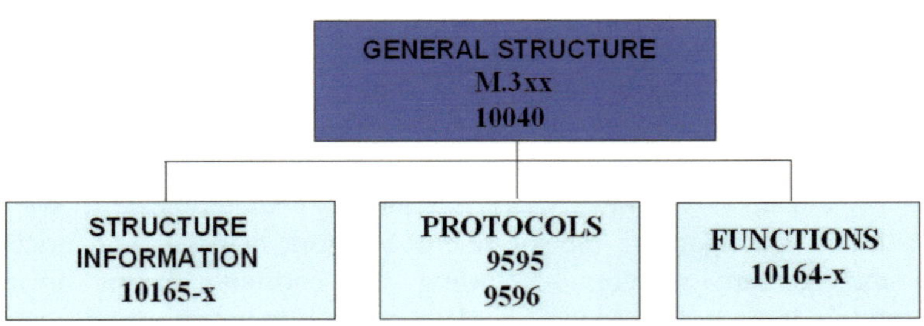

Fig. 1. Overview of OSI Network Management Model.

- An information component involved with five major functional areas: fault, configuration, accounting, performance, and security management in network management which facilitate rapid and consistent progress within each category's individual areas (International Organization for Standardization [ISO], 1993).
- A communication component which focuses upon how the information is exchanged between the managed systems (International Telecommunication Union [ITU-T], 1992).
- A functional component involved with the various activities performed in support of network management (International Telecommunication Union [ITU-T], 1996).

According to the International Organization for Standardization (ISO), the OSI network management model defines a conceptual model for managing all communication entities within a network. This main concept is the managed object, which is an abstract view of a logical o physical resource to be managed in the network (Hebrawi, 1995). Managed objects provide the necessary operations for the administration, monitoring and control of the telecommunications network. These operations are realized through the use the Common Management Information Protocol (CMIP) (International Telecommunication Union [ITU-T], 1997). This is a network management protocol built on the OSI communication model. The related Common Management Information Services (CMIS) (International Organization for Standardization [ISO], 1998) defines services for accessing information about network objects or devices, controlling them, and receiving status reports from them. For a specific management system, the management process involved will take on one of two possible roles, Figure 2:

- A Manager or Manager Role is an element that provides information to users, issues requests to devices in a network, receives responses to the requests and receives notifications. These notifications are unsolicited information from devices in the network concerning the status of the devices.
- Agent or Agent Role is an unit that is part of a device in the network that monitors and maintains status about that device. It can act and respond to requests from a manager and can provide unsolicited information (or notifications) to a manager.

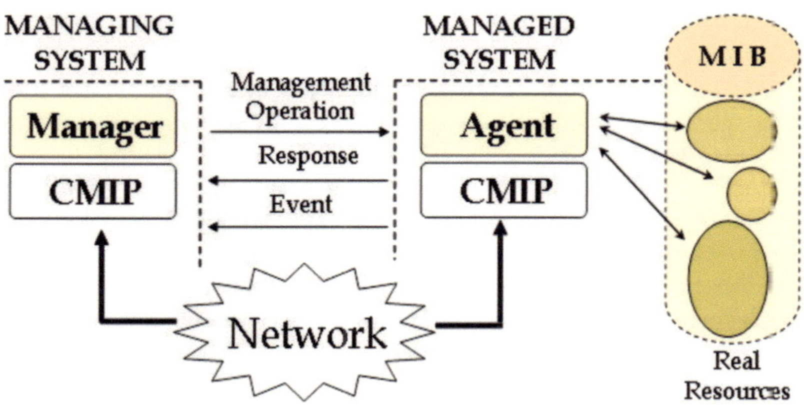

Fig. 2. OSI manager/agent architecture

These managed objects are defined according the ISO Guidelines for Definition of Managed Objects (GDMO). GDMO language uses the object orient programming and defines how network objects and their behaviour are to be specified, including the syntax and semantics.

This standard has been standardized by ITU-T in ITU-T X.722 and is now widely used to specify interfaces between different components of the TMN architecture. GDMO properties values types are described using the abstract syntax notation one (ASN.1) (Morris, 2003). ASN.1 describes an abstract syntax for data types and values.
Nowadays there are different domains of application of the expert systems in topics related with the network management. OSI classifies the systems management activities into five functional areas. We can categorize the expert systems used in network management within these five groups. Some expert system examples are Max & Opti, ANSWER, Trouble Locator, and CRITTER in fault diagnosis area, ESS-ES, ECXpert, and APRI in accounting management area, ACE, XCON, SMCS, and EXSim in configuration management area, TASA, NETTRA, and Scout in performance management area, NIDES, P-BEST, and NIDX in security management area. In this context the expert system that we have built, would be included in the area of work of the fault management (Liao, 2005; Negnevitsky, 2002; Yaguo & Zhengjia, 2009).
After this brief introduction to management elements, we will approach our research in the integration of knowledge management of expert system into MIB in the OSI management model. We are studying the way to integrate the expert knowledge in the management Internet model. Internet management model doesn't use the Object Oriented Programming such as it is used by the OSI model. This is one of the reasons for the Internet model simplicity. The definitions contain objects, specified with ASN.1 macros. In internet model the resources specifications can only be groups of scalar variables and cells tables in spite of not being an Object Oriented Programming model. We can use the tables of the Internet model as classes of the OSI model, where the attributes are the table columns and every file contains an instance of the class. The same as in OSI every object has an OID associated identifier.

3. Management knowledge definition

After describing a number of important aspects which have to be considered when designing a language for behaviour descriptions, this section focuses on the syntax and semantics of the language GDMO which is discussed in this paper. Practical experience with GDMO shows that, from an intelligent point of view, the quality of GDMO specifications is not satisfactory. The managed object specifications are incomplete to define the management knowledge of a specific resource. As consequence a new element is necessary.
To solve the current problem to undertake an intelligent integrated management we offer an original contribution to include expert rules in the specifications of the network features. To answer these questions, it will be necessary to make changes on the template of the GDMO standard. To formalize the main proposal of the paper, we analyze necessary requirements area to undertake the related aspects with the knowledge integration in the managed objects. We present an extension of the standard GDMO, to accommodate the intelligent management requirements, figure 3.
GDMO is organized into templates, which are standard formats used in the definition of a particular aspect of the object. A complete object definition is a combination of interrelated templates. There are nine of these templates: class of managed objects, package, attribute, group of attributes, action, notification, parameter, connection of name and behaviour (Morris, 2003), figure 4.

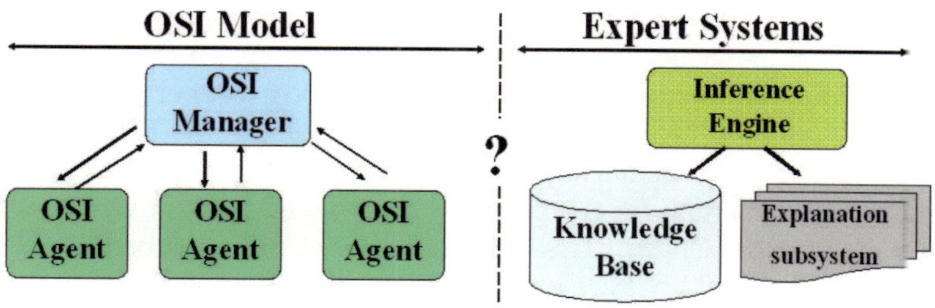

Fig. 3. Independence of Objects and Expert Management

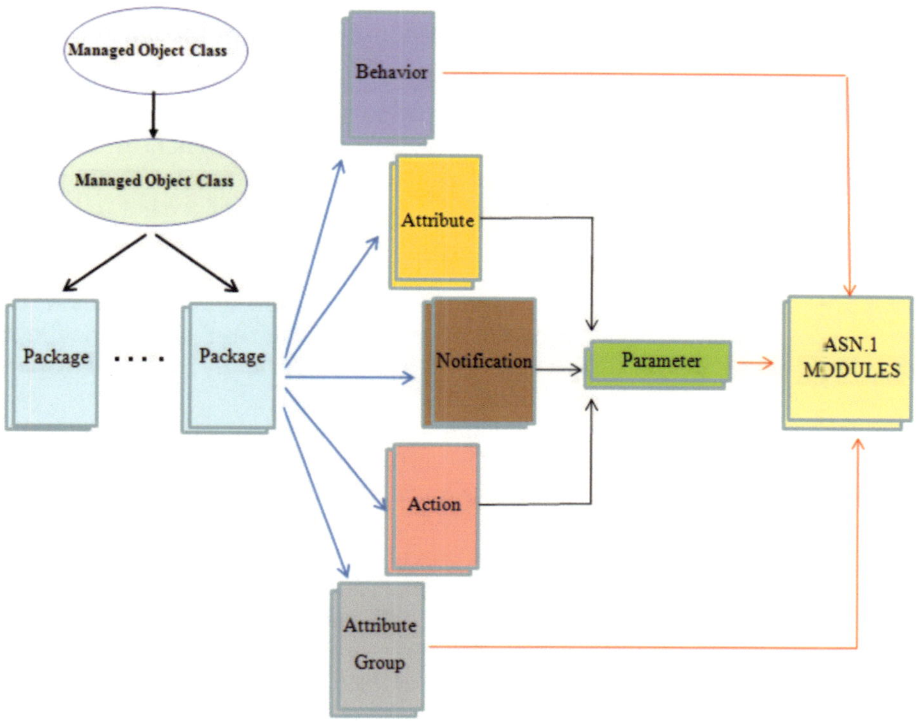

Fig. 4. Independence of Objects and Expert Management

The elements that at the moment form the GDMO standard do not make a reference to the knowledge base of an expert system. Until now the managed objects are not able to use the knowledge that the base of knowledge provides which collects the management operations and control of a management domain. We observe the need to define new structures for those cases in which it is necessary to express the knowledge. To solve this problem we suggest a refinement of the package template. We propose to extend the Guidelines for Definition of Managed Objects with the following goals: facilitate the normalization and integration of the knowledge base of expert system into resources specifications.

These goals will allow to developers specify the storage location and the update method of intelligent managed and provide a way to specify complex managed. Thus the description of certain aspects of managed object knowledge, e.g. the definition of expert rules, can be supported. We proposed adding a new property in GDMO standard named "rule". This attribute will define all the aspect about the management knowledge in a specific managed object class. The set of managed object classes and instances under the control of an agent is knows as it's a MIB, an abstraction of network resources properties and states for the purpose or management. The MIB, which is specified using the Structure Management Information (SMI) defines the actual objects to be managed (Clemm, 2006).

Two relationships are essential for the inclusion of knowledge in the component definition of the network: Managed Object Class and Package. GDMO includes the basic template MANAGED OBJECT CLASS, which is always implemented and GDMO also defines an optional template named PACKAGE, which defines a combination of properties for later inclusion in a managed object class template.

4. Management information and knowledge management structure

Management information models are abstractions of the network resources. They define the structures and contents of management information that the management functions act upon. A management information model provides a common characterization of the network resources, enables multiple management functions to interact with each other, and supports different management functions (Huang, 2008). Management information is exchanged among management systems where management functions are implemented (Goleniewski & Jarrett), 2006).

Attaining interoperability of network management systems and a common view of managed resources in a managed network environment requires that information models comply with standard models. The management functions currently exchange management information by means of techniques defined in ITU-T X.700.

These recommendations incorporate the important object-oriented and manager/agent paradigms for information modelling. The object-oriented approach for information exchange allows for grouping of data and the executable operations to be fully encapsulated into an object and object properties to be extended through "inheritance." The data can be manipulated only via the access operations provided in the object. The guidelines for the definition of managed objects, ITU-T Recommendation X.722 allow for a common data structure for managed objects in the managed and managing systems. Managed objects include their names, attributes, operations that can be performed on attributes, notifications that objects can emit, and behaviour descriptions of the objects.

The definition of a managed object class is made uniformly in the standard template, eliminating the confusion that may result when different persons define objects of different forms. This template is used to define the different kinds of objects that exist in the system. Classes describe what information and services they provide each manage object and GDMO defines format for this information (Kuo et al., 2005). This way we ensure that the classes and the management expert rules defined in system A can be easily interpreted in system B. Managed object class structure is show here:

```
<class-label> MANAGED OBJECT CLASS
    [DERIVED FROM <class-label> [,<class-label>]*;]
    [CHARACTERIZED BY <package-label> [,<package-label]*;]
    [CONDITIONAL PACKAGES                                        (1)
        <package-label> PRESENT IF condition;
        ,<package-label>] PRESENT IF condition]*;]
REGISTERED AS object-identifier;
```

DERIVED FROM clause specifies the superclass or superclasses from which this managed object is derived (inherited). This plays a very important role, when determining the relations of inheritance which makes it possible to reutilize specific characteristics in other classes of managed objects. In addition, a great advantage is the reusability of the object classes and therefore of the expert rules which are defined. By using this clause, any attribute, operation, notification, and behaviour exposed by managed objects, as well as inheritance and containment relationships among managed objects and managed object classes, can be defined, figure 5.

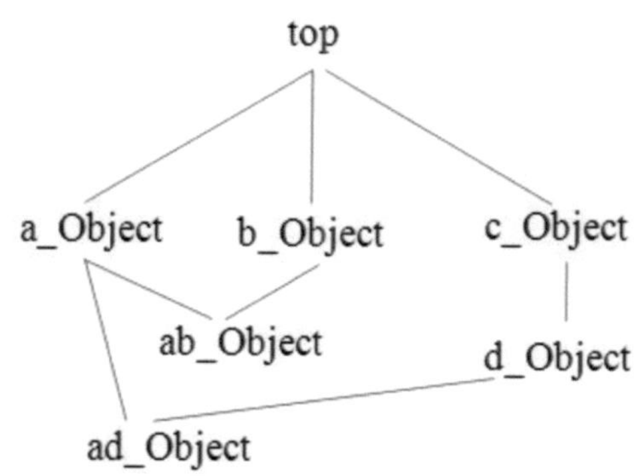

Fig. 5. Inheritance between classes

Packages included in the object class definition are identified by the CHARACTERIZED BY and CONDITIONAL PACKAGES clauses. The CHARACTERIZED BY clause identifies the package or packages that are always present when the managed object is included in the system. The CONDITIONAL PACKAGES clause is used to identify those packages that may or may not be included each time the managed object of this class is instantiated. Finally, the REGISTERED AS clause identifies the location of the managed object class on the OSI registration tree (Stallings, 2000).

4.1 Package template

The PACKAGE template is used to specify the characteristics that represent a consistent set of specifications about a network resource. One purpose of the package is to provide a set of re-useable definitions that can be used in several managed object class specifications. All the properties that we define in the package will be included later in the Managed Object Class Template, where the package is incorporated. A same package can be referenced by more than one class of managed objects. For each managed objects class, the following information is defined:

1. Attributes: are the types of data supported by the class (managed object).
2. Operations: are the actions supported by the class.
3. The behaviour of the managed object.
4. Notifications: are the types of unsolicited information a managed object can send to a manager.

The current template package in GDMO standard is adapted and we add a new feature. In addition to the properties indicated above, we suggest the incorporation of a new property called RULES and its associated template called "RULE", which contains all the specifications of the knowledge base for the expert system, figure 6.

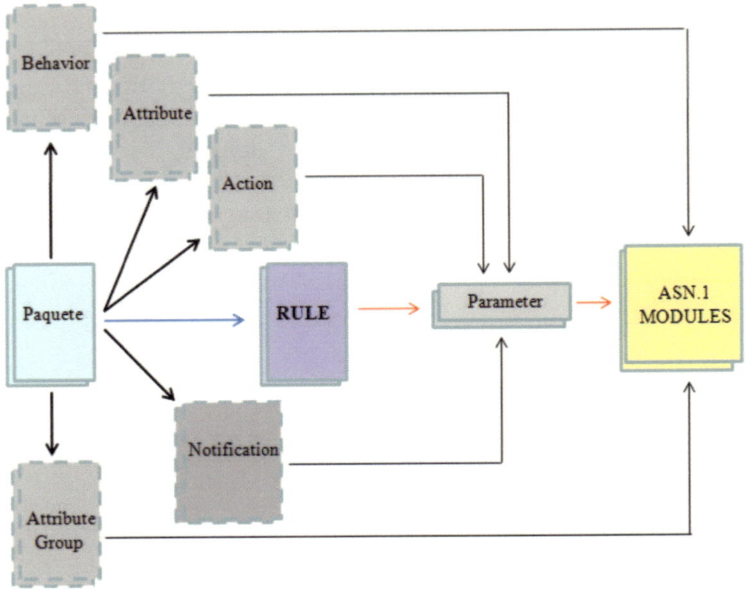

Fig. 6. New rule template.

Next definition shows the elements of a package template, in which it is possible to observe the new property RULES.

<package-label> PACKAGE
[BEHAVIOUR <behaviour-label> [,<behaviour-label>]*;]
[ATTRIBUTES <attribute-label> propertylist [,<parameter-label>]*
,<attribute-label> propertylist [,<parameter-label>]*]*;]
[ACTIONS <action-label> [<parameter-label>]*
[<action-label> [<parameter-label>]*]* ; (2)
[NOTIFICATIONS <notification-label> [<parameter-label>]*
[<notification-label> [<parameter-label>]*]* ;]
[RULES <rule-label> [,<rule-label>]*;]
REGISTERED AS object-identifier;

The property RULES allows a treatment similar to the other properties, including the possibility of inheritance of rules between classes. Like the rest of the other properties defined in a package, the property RULES needs a corresponding associated template.

4.2 Expert rule template

There are a number of different knowledge representation techniques for structuring knowledge in an expert system. The three most widely used techniques are expert rules, semantic nets and frames (Brachman & Levesque, 2004). For this study we use expert rules. We represented the knowledge in production rules or simply rules. Rules are expressed as IF-THEN statements which are relatively simple, very powerful as well as very natural to represent expert knowledge. A major feature of a rule-based system is its modularity and modifiability which allow for incremental improvement and fine tuning of the system with virtually no degradation of performance.

In our study case the template RULE permits the normalized definition of the specifications of the expert rule to which it is related. This template allows a particular managed object class to have properties that provide a normalized knowledge of a management dominion. The structure of the RULE template is shown here:

```
<rule-label> RULE
        [PRIORITY      <priority> ;]
        [BEHAVIOUR <behaviour-label> [,<behaviour-label>]*;]
        [IF occurred-event-pattern [,occurred-event-pattern]*]          (3)
        [THEN     sentence [, sentence]* ;]
REGISTERED AS object-identifier;
```

The first element in a template definition is headed. It consists of two sections:

- <rule-label>: This is the name of the management expert rule. Rule definitions must have a unique characterizing name.
- RULE: A key word indicates the type of template, in our case a definition template and the specifications for the management expert rule.

After the head, the following elements compose a normalized definition of an expert rule.

- BEHAVIOUR: This construct is used to extend the semantics of previously defined templates. It describes the behaviour of the rule. This element is common to the others templates of the GDMO standard.
- PRIORITY: This represents the priority of the rule, that is, the order in which competing rules will be executed.
- IF: It contains all the events that must be true to activate a rule. Those events must be defined in the Notification template. The occurrence of these events is necessary for the activation of the rule and the execution of their associated actions. We can add a logical condition that will be applied on the events occurred or their parameters.
- THEN: This gives details of the operations performed when the rule is executed. Those operations must be previously defined in the Action template. These are actions and diagnoses that the management platform makes as an answer to network events occurred.
- REGISTERED AS is an object-identifier: A clause identifies the location of the expert rule on the OSI registration tree. The identifier is compulsory.

5. Fault management application using GDMO+ specifications

In order to evaluate the fault management capabilities of the integrate management solution proposed we have simulated an application that monitors an environment to collect fault event data (Baker et al., 2008). As said before we have considered a private network. We suppose this network as being heterogeneous and hierarchical. The intelligent sensor nodes only disseminate data when the network is being monitored and an error occurs in a resource (Premchand et al., 2008), figure 7.

The use of integrate knowledge in agents can help the system administrator in using the maximum capabilities of the intelligent network management platform without having to use other specification language to customize the application (Akinyokun & Imianvan, 2006).

Our system has the following components: an inference engine, a knowledge base, and a user interface, figure 8.

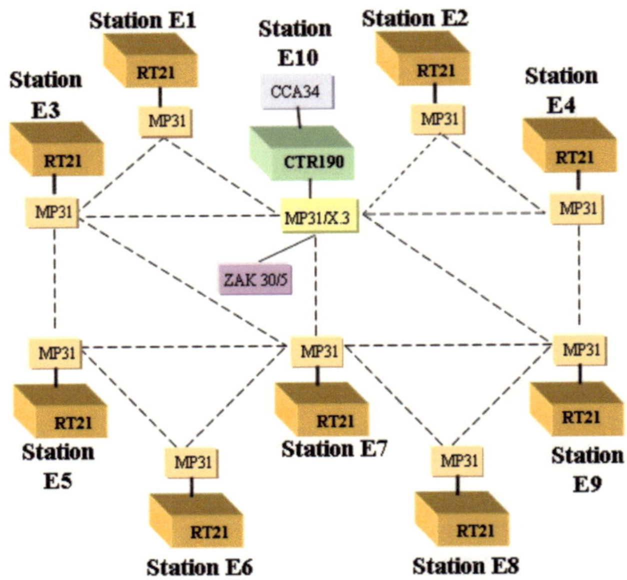

Fig. 7. Power Company Network

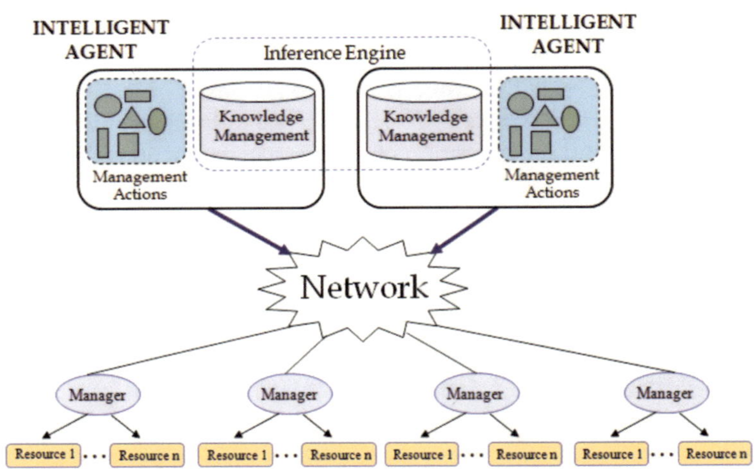

Fig. 8. Architecture System

- The inference engine: This is the processing unit that solves any given problems by making logical inferences on the given facts and rules stored in the knowledge base. It defines the managed objects and the expert rules belonging to the Expert System that manages this network (Waiman et al., 2005). Our system is implemented in Brightware's ART*Enterprise, an expert system shell. ART*Enterprise is a set of programming paradigms and tools that are focused on the development of efficient, flexible, and commercially deployable knowledge-based systems. Expert system shells simplify developer interactions by eliminating the developer's concern with operating system requirements. Its use can therefore reduce the design and implementation time of a program considerably. By using an existing general purpose tool we were able to build a standard and extensible platform with proven performance and quality. The experience with our prototype is that ART Enterprise is a useful tool for developing expert systems.

- The knowledge base: The core of the system, this is a collection of facts and if-then production rules that represent stored knowledge about the problem domain (Power & Bahri, 2005). The knowledge base of our system is a collection of expert rules and facts expressed in the ARTScript programming language ART*Enterprise. The knowledge base contains both static and dynamic information and knowledge about different network resources and common failures. The resultant expert system has about 600 rules and it has been employed Workstation to program the expert system. This initial knowledge has been acquired from the experts in the management domain. The knowledge base of our system can be extended by adding new higher level rules and facts.
- The user interface controls the inference engine and manages system input and output. It is a set of I/O handling routines for managing the system. This includes tools for browsing the inheritance architecture classes generated by both GDMO and ASN.1 compilers. Moreover our system includes facilities to browse the GDMO classes using a Web browser such as Explorer o Mozilla (Hui et al., 2005).

6. Control centre

Detection mechanisms are implemented real-time in our prototype and have been embedded with the network elements, network protocols and devices. System operations, uses a supervision system called CSS (Communication Supervisory System) (Lei et al., 2009). This system can monitor, in real time, the network's main parameters, making use of the information supplied by a Supervisory Control and Data Acquisition (SCADA), formed by a Control Center (placed on the main CSE building), and Remote Terminal Units (RTUs) installed into different stations. The use of a SCADA system is due to the management limitations of network communication equipment. Fault identification involves testing the hypothetical faulty components. Repair is achieved by taking intelligent corrective actions.
The CSS allows the operator to acquire information, alarms or digital and analogical parameters of measure, registered on each RTU (Doukas et al, 2007). Starting from the supplied information, the operator is able to undertake actions through the CSS in order to solve the failures that could appear or to send a technician to repair the stations equipment.
The management system in normal operation generates different notifications and alarms. An alarm is an event generated asynchronously whenever the value of some quality indicator crosses a predefined threshold (either positively or negatively) (Maggiora et al., 2000). Those alarms are caused when an incident occurs. These events are accompanied by parameters that show different aspects of the events (León et al., 1999).

```
...
(31/01 1100.200 stat1 7_TX_C2 stat2 Alarm)                      1
(31/01 1103.106 stat1 7_TX_C2 stat2 Alarm_Disappears)           2
(31/01 1122.168 stat1 CTR190/7_RX stat2 Alarm)                  3
(31/01 1134.169 Mux3 EXT_FONIA MAD Alarm_Disappears)            4
(31/01 1134.122 stat4 CCA34C_C1C2 stat3 LOCAL_CHANEL_2)         5
(01/02 1034.135 Transc_1 SPU1_BER_1 BER Alarm)                  6
(01/02 1034.146 Transc_1 SPU1_BER_1 BER Alarm_Disappears)       7
...
```

Each alarm contains information about circumstances that caused the incident. The working memory is where all knowledge is contained each item of knowledge is called a Fact. In a previous relation, taking as an example the third fact, the following information is obtained:

- Date alarm: 31/01.
- Time: 1122.168.
- Alarm kind: CTR190/7_RX. (This case means "Reception error")
- Implied equipments:
  - Origin: stat1, "station1".
  - Destiny: stat2, "station2".

These events or notifications used, they are previously defined using the corresponding notification template and are including in the same class of managed objects in which the expert rule acts. When a connection error occurs the device returns the following error messages.

F1 (31/01 1100.200 stat4 7_TX_C2 stat2 ALARM)
F2 (31/01 1103.168 stat4 7_TX_C2 stat2 ALARM)

These alarms indicate problems that require corrective actions. The management system analyzes and checks the rules that match these conditions. If the antecedent of some rule is satisfied, this rule is ready to fire and is placed in system the agenda. When a rule is ready to fire it means that since the antecedent is satisfied, the consequent can be executed. The executed management expert rule in this case is transmissionError. The results generated by the management system are show following:

```
FIRE 1: transmissionError f-2
  Severity 4
  Diagnostic: It damages in the modulate transmission between station4 and station2.
  Recommendation "Revision transceiver
  1 rules fired.
  Run time is 0.074 seconds, 27.0270 Rules/Sec.
```

7. Final prototype verification

The purpose is to achieve a functionally correct prototype. Validation constitutes an inherent part of the knowledge based expert system development and is intrinsically linked to the development cycle. Validation is essential to the decision-making success of the system and to its continued use. An expert system not validated sufficiently may make poor decisions. Validation certainly gives confidence in the system which affects the value of the prototype.

Validation concerns have the following objectives:

- to ascertain what the system knows, does not know, or knows incorrectly.
- to ascertain the level of decision expertise of the system.
- to determine whether the system is adequately theory based.
- to analyze the reliability of system.

To verify the system we feed it with an alarms arbitrary amount. As described our system has been validated with respect to the following aspects: system validation using test cases, validation by case studies, validation against human experts, validation against tough case and validation on site, etc. The result of this proof are including in Table 1.

Alarms Initial Number	Number After Filtration	Filtered Alarms	Fired Rules	Proceeding time	Rules/Sec.	Indications to the Operator
100	1	99	51	0,118 Sec.	432,2034	1
200	10	95	102	0,412 Sec.	247,5728	6
300	31	89,6	155	1,250 Sec.	124,0000	20
400	31	92,25	201	1,438 Sec.	139,7775	16
500	32	93,6	254	2,975 Sec.	85,3782	19
600	38	93,66	293	5,249 Sec.	55,8202	16
700	44	93,71	346	17,982 Sec.	19,2415	18
800	55	93,125	394	26,938 Sec.	14,6262	23

Table 1. Prototype Testing Results

From these result we can establish the fallowing conclusions:

- Filtration process effectiveness is very high: almost 90% of the whole. This has the advantage of a decreasing percentage in the amount of indications presented to the operator.
- The speed of the system improves diminishing the number of alarms on which the rest of rules act.

The expert system, with over 600 operation rules, has produced excellent results which, after extensive field-testing, proved to be capable of filtering 90% of produced alarms with a precision of 95% in locating them, Figure 9.

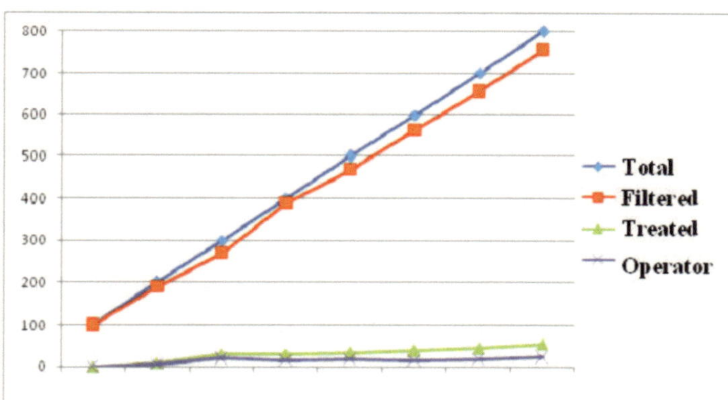

Fig. 9. Filtration Process Effectiveness

As noted above, the system performs satisfactorily with about a 95% rate of success in real cases. The confidence values provided were also found to be in reasonable relative order. It is also noted that the performance of the system depends considerably in the facts happened. The more information is input, the better the chance of diagnosing the likely causes of the problems in the network.

8. Conclusion

Current networks are very complex and demand ever-increasing levels of quality, making their management a very important aspect to take into account. The traditional model of network administration has certain deficiencies that we have tried to overcome by using a model of intelligent integrated management. To improve the techniques of expert management in a communications network, we propose the possibility of integrating and normalising the expert rules of management within the actual definition of the managed objects. Intelligent managed objects characteristics are autonomy, reactivity, pro-activeness, mobility and learning.

In this chapter we showed possibilities to apply and integrated the artificial intelligence techniques in network management and supervision, using OSI. We showed possibilities to apply and integrated the artificial intelligence techniques in network management and supervision, using ISO network management standard.

Unfortunately, the knowledge management is defined in using different intelligent techniques. This results in knowledge specifications which are often ambiguous, increasing the possibility of different implementations not being interoperable. To achieve consistent, clear, concise, and unambiguous specifications, a formal methodology has to be utilized. This paper introduces a framework for the inclusion of formal knowledge descriptions into GDMO specifications. An object-oriented logic programming language is presented, which can be used in conjunction with the framework to specify the management knowledge of managed objects.

We have supplied an original contribution to include expert rules in the specifications of the network elements; for this purpose we have proposed a new standard called Extension of GDMO standard or simply GDMO+. Through the integration of the knowledge within the new extension of the GDMO standard, we can simultaneously define the management information and knowledge. Thus, the management platform is more easily integrated and allows a better adaptation for the network management. Moreover we have built a prototype and experiments have been carried out in order to test the efficiency of our proposal. This demonstrated that GDMO+ is capable of specifying the knowledge of a reasonably sized information model. A large amount of the management knowledge could be described in a surprisingly short and easy to understand manner.

It is suggested that future work should aim to further development of this prototype system by adding more modules based on the framework provided by the system so that more in-depth knowledge and specialized subjects may be captured; in particular the following are of great interest: Development of a design module, possibly a large system, for identifying specific areas like accounting management, configuration management, performance management and security management. Moreover use of external programs and graphics interface to enhance the functions of the system will be desirable. Finally study the possibility of using another method of knowledge representation and reasoning different to the rules: Semantic nets, neuronal nets, frameworks, etc.

9. References

Akinyokun, O.C., Imianvan, A.A. (2006). Mobile agent system for computer network management Proceedings from the International Conference on Advances in Engineering and Technology, Pages 796-808

Baker, D.; Nodine, M.; Chadha, R.; Chiang, C.J. (2008). "Computing diagnostic explanations of network faults from monitoring data," Proc. of IEEE Military Communication Conference, CA, USA, pp. 1-7.

Brachman, R.J., & Levesque, H. J. (2004). Representation and reasoning. San Francisco, CA: Elsevier/Morgan Kaufmann.

Clemm, A. Network Management Fundamentals. Cisco Press, 2006.

Doukas, H., Patlitzianas, K. D., Iatropoulos, K., Psarras, J. (2007). Intelligent building energy management system using rule sets. Building and Environment, Volume 42, Issue 10, Pages 3562-3569.

Goleniewski L. & Jarrett, K.W. (2006). Telecommunications Essentials, Second Edition: The Complete Global Source. Addison Wesley Professional.

Hebrawi, N. (1995). GDMO, Object modelling and definition for network management. Technology appraisals.

Hui, S. C., Fong, A. C. M., Jha. G. (2001). A web-based intelligent fault diagnosis system for customer service support. Original Research Article. Engineering Applications of Artificial Intelligence, Volume 14, Issue 4, Pages 537-548.

Huang, C.W. (2008). Introduction to Communication Systems of Network Management, Chinese Taipei Components Certification Board, Taipei, Taiwan.

ISO/IEC and ITU-T. (1998), Information Processing Systems - Open Systems Interconnection - Systems Management Overview. Standard 10040-2, Recommendation X.701.

ISO/IEC DIS 10165-4 / ITU-T. (1993). Recommendation X.722, Information Technology - Open Systems Interconnection - Structure of Management Information - Part 4: Guidelines for the Definition of Managed Objects (GDMO), International Organization for Standardization and International Electrotechnical Committee.

ITU-T. (1992). Recommendation X.700, Management Framework for Open Systems Interconnection (OSI). CCITT Applications.

ITU-T. (1996). Recommendation M.3400, TMN Management Functions. Study Group IV.

ITU-T Rec. X.711. (1997). Common Management Information Protocol (CMIP) Specification.

Kuo, S.Y.; Liao, F.P. and Chen, K.L. (2005). NetworkManagement: Concepts and Practice, A Hands-On Approach, GoTop Book Corporation, Taipei, Taiwan.

Lei, Y., He, Z., & Zi, Y. (2009). Application of an intelligent classification method to mechanical fault diagnosis, Expert Systems with Applications, Volume 36, Issue 6, August 2009, Pages 9941-9948.

León, C., Mejias, M., Luque, J., & Gonzalo, F. (1999). Expert System for the Integrated Management of a Power Utility's Communication System. IEEE Trans on Power Delivery, Vol. 14, No. 4, 1208-1212.

Liao, S. (2005). Expert system methodologies and applications - a decade review from 1995 to 2004. Expert Systems with Applications, Volume 28, Issue 1, Pages 93-103.

Maggiora, P. L. Della., .E, Christopher E., Pavone, R.L., Phelps, K. J., Thompson, J.M. (2000). Performance and Fault Management. Cisco Press

Morris, Stephen B. (2003). Network Management, MIBs and MPLS: Principles, Design and Implementation by Publisher: Addison Wesley.

Negnevitsky, Michael. (2002). Artificial intelligence: a guide to intelligent systems. New York:Addison Wesley.

Power, Y., Bahri., P. A. (2005). Integration techniques in intelligent operational management: a review Knowledge-Based Systems, Volume 18, Issues 2-3, Pages 89-97

Premchand Boyapati, Krishna Shenai, Bradford R. Lilly. (2008). "Sensors and Sensor Network". U.S. 1-50400 (D2008-48, 49, 50, 51 and 52).

Stallings, W. (2000). SNMP, SNMPv2, and CMIP: the practical guide to network. Publication Reading, Mass. Addison-Wesley.

Waiman, C., Leung, L. C., & Tam, P. C. F. (2005). An intelligent decision support system for service network planning. Decision Support Systems, Volume 39, Issue 3, Pages 415-428.

Yaguo, L., Zhengjia H., Yanyang Z. (2009). Application of an intelligent classification method to mechanical fault diagnosis. Expert Systems with Applications, Volume 36, Issue 6, Pages 9941-9948

Zuidweg, J. (2002). Next generation intelligent networks. Boston: Artech House.

Management of Knowledge Acquisition from Human Sources in Innovation Transfer

Antoni Zwiefka and Malgorzata Nycz
Lower Silesian Voivodeship Marshal Office, Health Policy Department, Wroclaw
Wroclaw University of Economics, Faculty of Management
Finances and Business Informatics
Department of Artificial Intelligence Systems, Wroclaw
Poland

1. Introduction

The term 'Knowledge Management' (KM) appeared several years ago and at first it was applied only to information systems. It was obvious soon that its meaning was broader and connected with business processes reengineering and management of quality. Knowledge management concentrates on recognition of all intellectual assets within an organization as well as on managing them. The main purpose of KM was obvious: better achievement of business goals.
In knowledge based economy the role and importance of information and knowledge is still growing. Knowledge is becoming one of the most valuable assets in any organizations. Fast progress at the field of scientific research - especially in medicine, new information and communication technologies, etc. enforce not only the necessity of innovation transfers but also the necessity of developing and creating knowledge.
Knowledge management can be seen as a result of evolutionary human development. In the last quarter of the 20th century this development was observed in continuously growing application of information and knowledge in societies and in organizations. Today information and knowledge are crucial and especially valuable due to the rapid developed and continuous progress in every sector of our life. Fast exchange of medical knowledge, new medicals, creation and propagation of new knowledge etc. are possible due to the achievements of 'informational revolution'.
For our further investigation we have taken into account medicine as a domain/discipline. Why medicine? For some quite obvious facts: our health is of great importance not only to us (people) but also for our countries. And on the other hand, medical clinics have a high intellectual potential for product innovation, process and service development. There are many reasons why this potential of innovation is not sufficiently transferred to the results, such as product development by companies and better health care. The barriers concern, among others, different interests. Clinics are mainly focused on the efficient management and welfare of patients. Whereas the objective of the industrial units is all about economy and economic importance. Today big business companies and corporations dominate as suppliers of ready innovative products. So far, the changes initiated by the employees of clinics and small and medium-sized enterprises (SMEs) have no chance to transfer knowledge and ideas. But this is the flexibility of SMEs in developing lab types, prototypes

and small business solutions , that can help to improve the daily work of clinics and, in particular, its quality[1].
The chapter consists of six parts. After a brief introduction to the subject, there are basic definitions. The following definitions are characterized: knowledge management, information society, knowledge based economy, knowledge based organization, knowledge and its classifications, intellectual capital, sources of knowledge, gaining knowledge from different sources (knowledge discovery from databases and knowledge acquisition from human sources). Part three has been devoted to modeling of knowledge management. Then we describe the acquisition of knowledge treated as a process. In this part we present a model of knowledge management system in which we distinguish: input, processing and output. Within the processing module we distinguish discovery of evident knowledge from databases and acquisition of tacit (human) knowledge. In the next part we focus on knowledge acquisition and present some techniques of obtaining the knowledge (topic maps, skill maps, knowledge maps, contact books, knowledge sources maps, knowledge matrix, competency matrix). Part five presents ontology impact on knowledge management. Consequently, it has effects on the performances and validity of the KM system. Short summary ends the paper.

2. Basic definitions

Knowledge management can be seen as a result of evolutionary human development. In the last quarter of the 20th century this development was observed in still growing application of information and knowledge in societies and in organizations. In the 80th of XX century, the group work systems appeared. The next steps towards knowledge management were document management as well as information management systems. Diffusion of Internet in a global scale can be treated as a mile step in KM because new forms appeared in the shape of corporate portals. At the end of the last century we could observe a new type of systems: knowledge management systems. This evolution can be presented as in fig 1.
Today information and knowledge are crucial and especially valuable due to the fact that the progress in all sectors of our life is still growing. Our society is becoming more and more information society. Sometimes we can say we live in the information and knowledge era and our economy is based on knowledge.
The role and importance of innovation and creativity in the information society is becoming more and more important. The main features of the information society are as follows:

- Domination of services in economy,
- Domination of specialists and scientists,
- Importance of theoretical knowledge as a source of innovations,
- Tendency to social control of technical development,
- Permanent life learning,
- Creation of 'intellectual technologies' that are treated as a basis of social and political Decision making process.

[1] The authors participate in the IntraMED-C2C project. This project began to develop and provide the tools for increasing the access of small and medium-sized enterprises (on a European scale) to the innovation potential in clinics. This will open up new markets for their products. Workshops may be a good tool for initiating SMEs' access to clinics. Within the project, in accordance with the needs of the regions, there are arranged such pilot workshops.

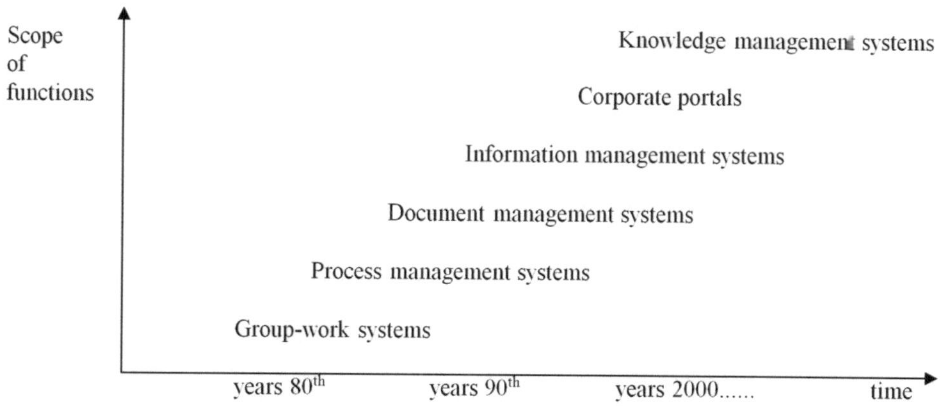

Source: based on (Wierzbicki, 2004)

Fig. 1. Evolution of information systems: from group-work systems to knowledge management systems

Knowledge based organization is a system basing on a permanent process of gaining knowledge from any possible sources and using it. It possesses, inbuilt into its organization structure, learning, knowledge creating and innovative processes. There is a permanent process of knowledge exchange and conversion between external structure, internal one and individual competences of workers (Sveiby, 2003).

The intensive development of information and communication technologies increases the number of accessible information and enables its fast processing. In modern management it is neither structure, rules nor the newest methods and instruments, but well educated, creative, innovative, intelligent people and teams created by them, that decide about success of the organization.

If a modern organization wants to be competitive on a global as well as local market, it should meet two general conditions. It has to possess the appropriate knowledge and be able, to know how to use this knowledge.

New economy can be called knowledge based economy, new economy, digital economy or network economy and be applied to all sectors of economy, also to the medical one. Knowledge based economy is based on six following pillars:

1. innovation system,
2. education system,
3. communication and information system,
4. business and institutional surrounding,
5. knowledge management in organization,
6. regional aspects

which are shown in fig. 2. All these elements influence each other.

When we realize that our health is one of the most important features not only for a given person but also should be seen in a larger scale, we understand how important the medical knowledge management is for a given country, region, etc. Fast exchange of medical knowledge, new medicals, creation and propagation of new knowledge, etc. is possible due to the achievements of 'informational revolution'.

There are many definitions of knowledge that can be found in literature. Knowledge can be seen either in a narrower or broader meaning. According to an encyclopedia definition knowledge in its narrower meaning is understood as the whole credible information about the reality with the ability to use it. In its broader meaning knowledge is a set of information, believes, etc. that are of practical or recognizable value (Encyklopedia Powszechna, 2005). Knowledge can be described as all information and skills used by people to solve their problems which cover practical and theoretical elements as well as hints and rules how to proceed. Knowledge can be treated as the implementation of information in practice. It also can be seen as early collected and cumulated information. From the information systems point of view, knowledge consists of facts and reasoning rules. And another definition of knowledge says that data are transformed into information, then into knowledge by adding context, experience and interpretation. Knowledge is a skill to realize concrete tasks basing on information (Probst & Raub & Romhardt, 2002). Dependencies among data, information, knowledge and wisdom are shown in fig. 3.

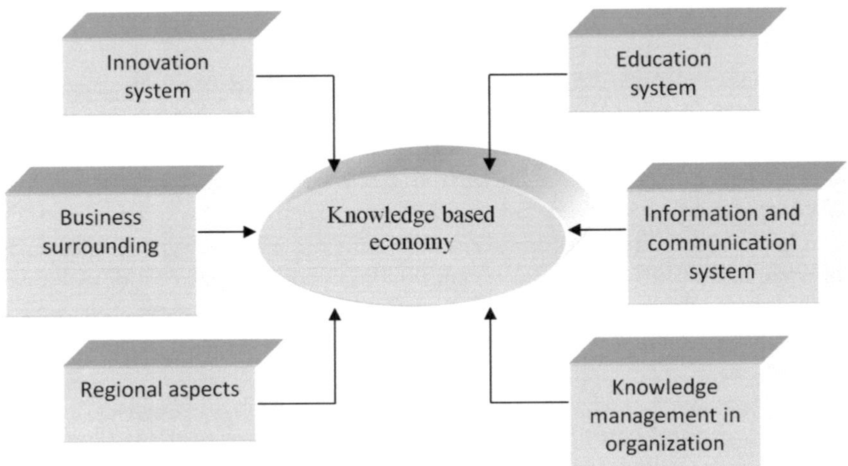

Source: (Nycz, 2007)

Fig. 2. Basic pillars of knowledge based economy

Classifications of knowledge can be different, depending on the criterion which has been taken into account. Knowledge can be *a priori* or *a posteriori* one. Knowledge can be divided into *science* that is general knowledge and *techniques* used in achieving economical effects. We can also distinguish knowledge which is conscious and unconscious (tacit) one (Nonaka & Takeuchi, 2000). Tacit knowledge is our knowledge, experience or context, in which we see information. Knowledge can be classified into *procedural, declarative* or *mixed* one. Knowledge can be also seen as *domain knowledge* (e.g. medical, technical, financial, managerial etc.) or *meta-knowledge* (knowledge about knowledge). Knowledge can also be static, dynamic, causal, full or not full, sure or unsure, primordial or secondary, secret or open, managerial or technological.

Knowledge is connected with innovations; knowledge and innovations – with creativity of people. Knowledge as any other asset in organization has to be managed.

In knowledge based economy we treat intellectual capital as a strategic asset. It is a sum of knowledge of people in the organization and it decides about the value of the organization, the value that is different from the financial one. Intellectual capital consists of patents, workers skills, technologies, information about clients and suppliers and experience (Stewart, 1997) and it can be presented as in fig. 4.

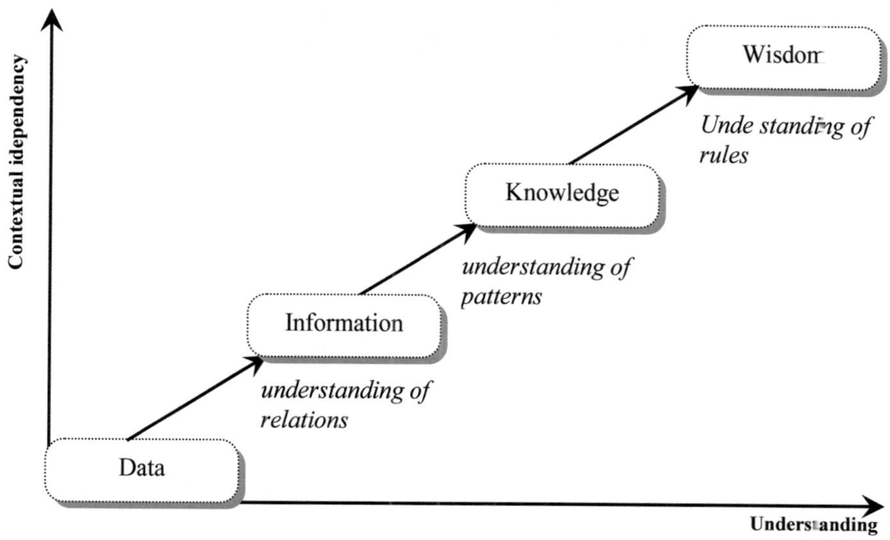

Source: (Chauvel & Despres, 2002)

Fig. 3. From data to wisdom

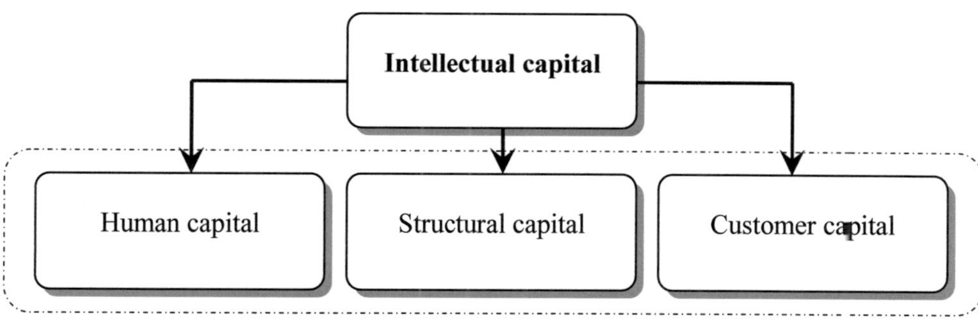

Source: (Stewart, 1997)

Fig. 4. Forms of intellectual capital

Knowledge management covers such areas as information management, management of conscious knowledge (that has been previously codified in structural and non-structural databases and data warehouses - knowledge about processes), management of non-conscious knowledge (that workers possess in their brains), and management of intellectual capital (that means management of production processes basing on intellectual assets of the organization) (Caldwell & Harris, 2002).

When talking about knowledge management we should think also about such aspects as law conditions which are applied in a particular country, norms, standards, disposals, law regulations within organization as well as those coming from the outside, cultural and technological regulations. Considering these aspects, it is useful to define some layers of medical knowledge management. They can be distinguished as following: (1) law regulations, (2) knowledge assets of the organization and particular workers, (3) scientific researches carried out with cooperation with medical universities – they can be treated as processes enhancing general as well as specialized knowledge, (4) general information standards that are obligatory in a country, (5) universal systems of economic object identification, (6) infrastructure information systems in medical sector.

As we have already said, knowledge, as any other asset in organization, should be managed. There are many descriptions and definitions of KM in literature. For the purpose of this book we propose the following definition:

Knowledge Management is such an approach that covers identification, collecting (storing), development, enlargement, co-usage of both material and non-material information assets in organization. Our further investigations will be based on this definition.

Sources of medical knowledge can be different. They are grouped according to different criteria. When we consider how 'modern' they are, we can distinguish traditional sources (written on paper like books, articles in medical journals, scientific reports, etc.) in the shape of traditional documents (e.g. patents, certifications), and electronic sources, like traditional databases and data files, audio and video documents, hypertexts, multi-media databases, data warehouses, knowledge bases, located inside the organization as well as outside, which are accessible via Internet or other nets. These sources are depicted to the conscious knowledge which is structuralized and accessible to those who need it (in fact it is only theoretically, because not all the knowledge especially this very new, innovative one is open to everybody).

But what about the tacit knowledge? Its importance is still growing and this is the obvious truth we all know. But how to manage it? How to convince people to share their knowledge, experience, results of their experiments, etc.? We will try to answer these questions below.

3. Modeling of knowledge management

In the process of gathering information, documents, professional experiences and know-how at a corporate level, a big issue is modeling of *knowledge management. It is used t*o understand easily and clearly how knowledge may be dealt with, **transforming tacit knowledge into more explicit forms**. The Nonaka's and Takeuchi's KM model, as one of the most famous among the existing models, focuses on a knowledge spiral that explains the transformation of tacit knowledge into explicit knowledge and then back again as the basis for individual, group, and organizational innovation and learning" (Dalkir, 2011).

The concept of knowledge socialization must be understood in the conversion of tacit knowledge into the explicit knowledge by sharing the hidden (internal) knowledge during the implementation of joint activities by members of the organization. External expression is (in turn) understood as a process of translation of tacit knowledge into the explicit one by expressing it in a generally accessible, acceptable and digestible form. Combination model, is treated as the expression of explicit knowledge in another form or its conversion into a new form. In addition, it is treated as a combination of communication, distribution and systematics of explicit knowledge. The fourth and final element in the model is a learning process - the conversion of the explicit knowledge into the tacit one.

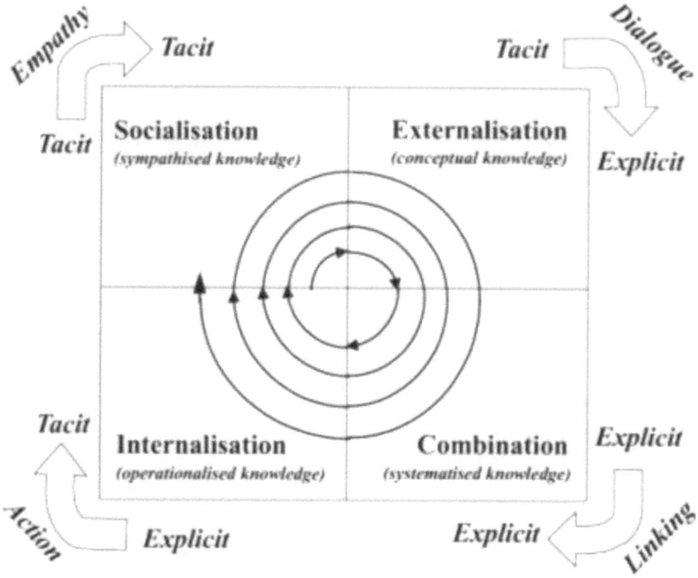

Source: www.emeraldinsight.com

Fig. 5. Nonaka's and Takeuchi's knowledge management model

The key to this model is the interaction between forms of knowledge and levels of the organization. The spiral resulting from the conversion of the explicit knowledge into the hidden one on each level, is the basis for the creation and playback of knowledge in the organization. Knowledge of the Japanese model is individual, group, organizational and inter-organizational. The spiral of knowledge creation in organizations can be activated by fulfilling the following demands:

- Spiral is driven by the intentions, aspirations and objectives of the organization – it must be present and makes the workers until they become their targets,
- It must provide employees with autonomy because it is a catalyst for the emergence of new ideas and positive motivation,
- Organization should be characterized by the creative chaos and instability. It can be used to violate workers' routines and interaction with the rapidly changing environment. It also allows more reliable and faster respond in the event of a crisis.
- In the organization, there should be some redundant information - going beyond the needs of operational activity, and the organization should be as internally differentiated as its surrounding.

Members of the organization more easily adapt to their environment when they differ from each other.

The Ba concept (model) by I.Nonaka and L.Konno can be seen as the enhancement of the Nonaka's and Takeuchi's model. It can be understood as a space where there is a dynamic exchange of knowledge and there are knowledge-conversion processes listed above. Within this model four spaces have been characterized:

- "original space - space to share emotions, experiences and mental models,
- interaction space - space to convert tacit knowledge into the explicit one, the key here are dialogues and metaphors,

- cyberspace - virtual space of interaction – it is a combination of new and the existing explicit knowledge in the organization, and
- exercise spaces - supports internalization, learning" (Nonaka & Takeuchi, 2000).

The authors of the concept of Ba believe that the creation of knowledge in the organization runs perfectly in the following five phases:

- "dissemination of tacit knowledge (…),
- search of ideas - in the course of brainstorming, the concept of dialogue is created, which eventually takes the form of public - this phase corresponds to the externalization,
- confirmation of ideas - because according to Nonaka knowledge is the confirmation of convictions, therefore the ideas created in the previous phase should be verified - that will be beneficial to the organization,
- building pattern - in production it corresponds to the creation of a prototype. In this phase, the concept takes a material form,
    - leveling of knowledge - both in the inside as well as inter-organizational. A concepts arising in one cycle become the beginning of another process at a higher level" (Nonaka & Takeuchi, 2000).

4. Knowledge acquisition as a process

According to the technological approach to knowledge management, the system of KM can be seen as any other information system. It consists of three modules: input, processing and output and among them we distinguish feedbacks (see fig. 6.)

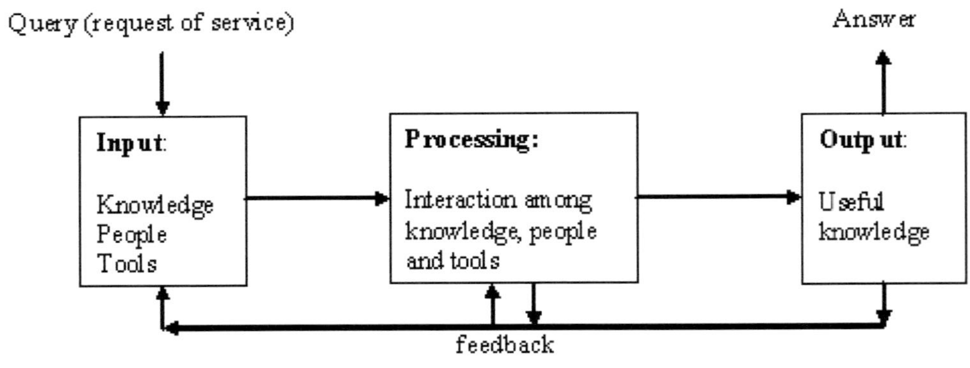

Source: (Nycz, 2007)

Fig. 6. Model of knowledge management system

Input module enables introducing the query to the system that can be in the shape of a request to realize the knowledge service, e.g. finding necessary knowledge. Each request of service has to be identified and authorized. Each request is monitored till its end. Through the input module, new knowledge and any updating are introduced to the system.

The processing module realizes interactions among knowledge assets, information tools and people who need knowledge, people who are responsible for system administration tasks and people who possess necessary, required knowledge. Within the processing module, the process of knowledge management is realized. It consists of some sub-processes such as:

knowledge localization, knowledge collecting and storing, acquisition of knowledge, knowledge sharing and its broadcasting, usage of knowledge and its development. The processing module can use one or more knowledge sources. It can also use data mininig techniques to find/generate required knowledge from accessible databases. But it can also find knowledge from personal sources (tacit knowledge). It can deliver information about where and who possesses the required knowledge and how to achieve him/her. In the frame of this module, the appropriate infrastructure of services has to be done, through which knowledge sources are accessible.
Before the obtained knowledge is to be delivered to the user, it has to be verified and assessed and visualized in the form required by the user.
Now let's concentrate on the processing module. Interactions among sub-processes can be presented as shown in fig. 7.

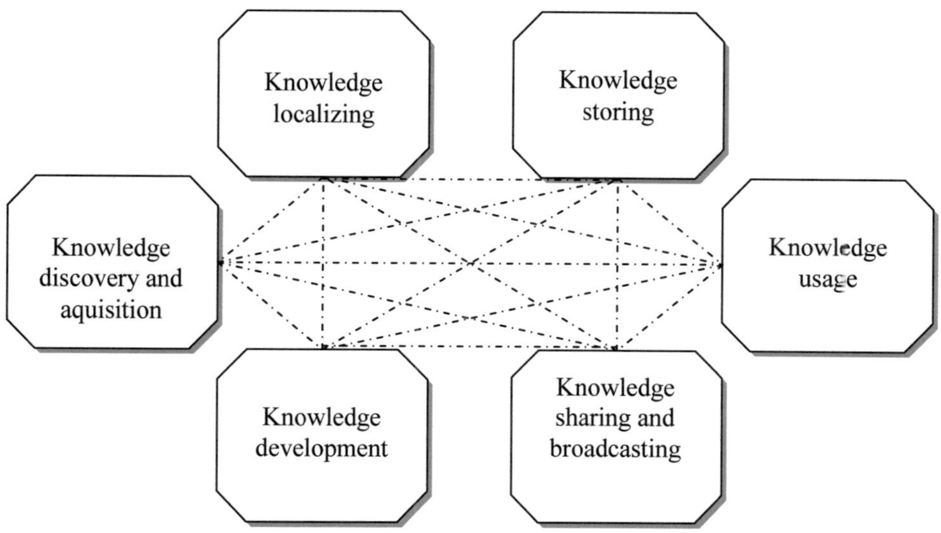

Source: (Probst & Raub & Romhardt, 2002)

Fig. 7. Interaction between sub-processes of knowledge management

Knowledge management process is realized all the time. It can be in one of two states: active, when the request of service appeared, or stand by, when waiting for the request.
Gaining of knowledge means obtaining knowledge from the sources where it is. These are: 1) sources connected with human factor; in this case we talk about *knowledge acquisition* or sources in a raditional shape (paper sources) as well as in 2) a digital form (e.g. databases) from which we *discover* the required *knowledge*. If we want to use information techniques to obtain knowledge from paper sources, first they have to be converted into a digital form. There are many different techniques of knowledge acquisition from human sources and we will present them below.

5. Techniques of knowledge acquisition

Knowledge acquisition relates to human sources. In a modern organization workers contact each other in many ways: e.g. personally, using fax, email. It is important to know where, at whom, in which documents, data files, law regulations we should seek necessary knowledge. Knowledge acquisition can be realized by topic maps, skill maps, contact books, knowledge maps, knowledge matrix, competency matrix (Supply_Chain Council, Supply-Chain Operations Reference-model Overview Version 5.0, 2003).

Topic maps are the ISO standard (ISO/IEC 13250). The basic elements in a topic map are: subject, associations and occurrences (fig. 8.)

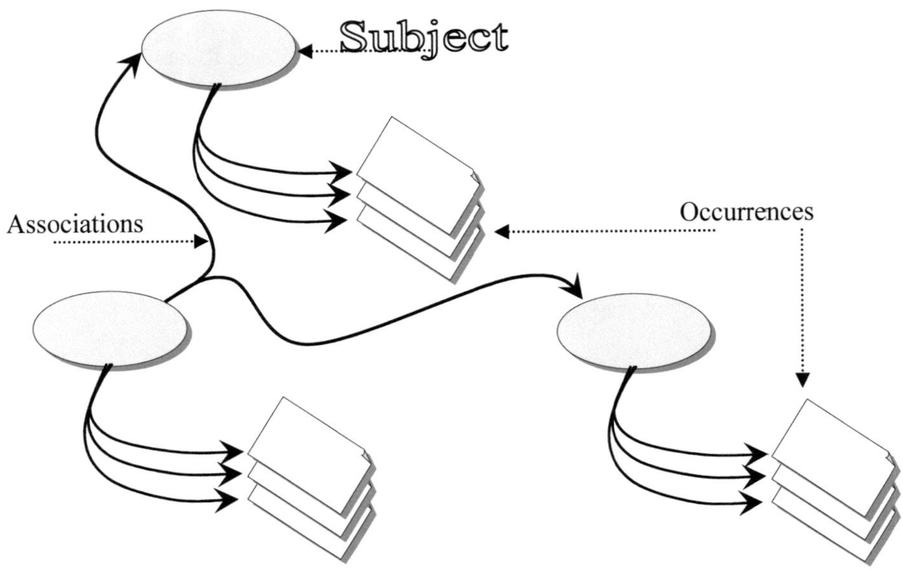

Source: ibidem

Fig. 8. Topic map structure

Subject is a basic element in a topic map and it can be a person, document or any other thing. It can be an abstract idea or a real one.

Occurrence is an assignment between the subject and the information source, e.g. a document on a given subject, video or/and audio sequences, archives collecting documents on a given subject.

Associations among subjects can be understood as a binding element showing relations between subjects of different types. There are two subjects in any association and each subject may realize different function, e.g. association of 'is father' type can have the subject of 'human being' type and one of them is 'father' and the other - 'child'.

Topic maps are the advanced solution of structuralization, gathering and knowledge representation problem. But, they deliver limited set of instruments especially when we want to use them to present our workers knowledge or to assure them the possibility to use more advanced mechanisms of database searching, e.g. navigation mechanisms. To implement such functions, it is necessary to enlarge the technology of topic maps by creating new structures that are needed to store information about the workers, their knowledge and skills.

Skill map has been created by adding new, the third layer to a topic map. There are new created objects (e.g. skills, associations between them) as well as associations with their occurrences (subjects) in this layer (fig. 9.).

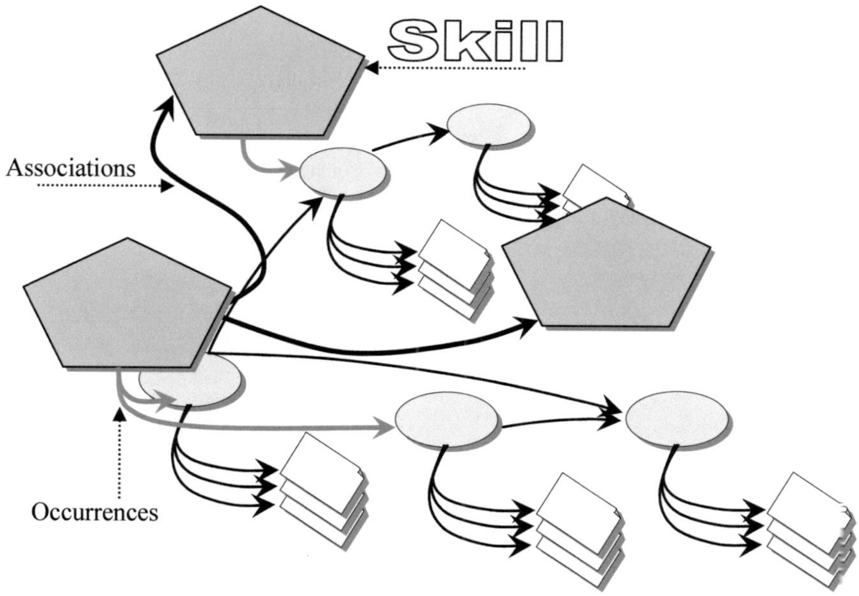

Source: ibidem

Fig. 9. Exemplary skill map

Contact books are a very simple way to localize knowledge sources. Such a book contains information about our employees or experts within our organization. Contacts can be categorized due to e.g. competences, departments, potential problems, etc. Those workers who need specialized knowledge from experts should have access to contact books. The advantage of contact books is obvious: saving time when looking for the desired knowledge.
Knowledge maps called also knowledge sources maps are especially useful when we want to find location of required knowledge assets. They present graphically dependencies among intellectual actives, their sources of origin and applications. Knowledge maps have been created to answer the requests coming from users to systematize assets connected with human capital (still growing) as well as associations of tasks with the appropriate intellectual assets in the organization.
Taking structure as a criterion we can distinguish several types of knowledge maps, e.g. topographical knowledge maps, information assets maps, geographical information maps, knowledge sources maps. Exemplary map of knowledge sources is shown in fig. 10.
Knowledge matrix can be very useful in presentation of intellectual assets. It can be seen as another way of knowledge assets presentation that is collected in the organization. Knowledge matrix consists of carefully selected categories. For example, it may be the pairs of appropriate matched types of knowledge (explicit and tacit, internal and external).
Competency matrix is used when we want to define how particular knowledge areas influence the management of organization. The matrix possesses two dimensions. It consists of four parts (fig. 11.).
They are created when crossing two-dimensional space of knowledge assets with two axis: vertical that represents e.g. competitiveness of organization assets, and horizontal one representing the degree of knowledge usage in organization. All assets can be assigned to one of four matrix areas. Each area represents the strategy of usage of 'its' knowledge source.

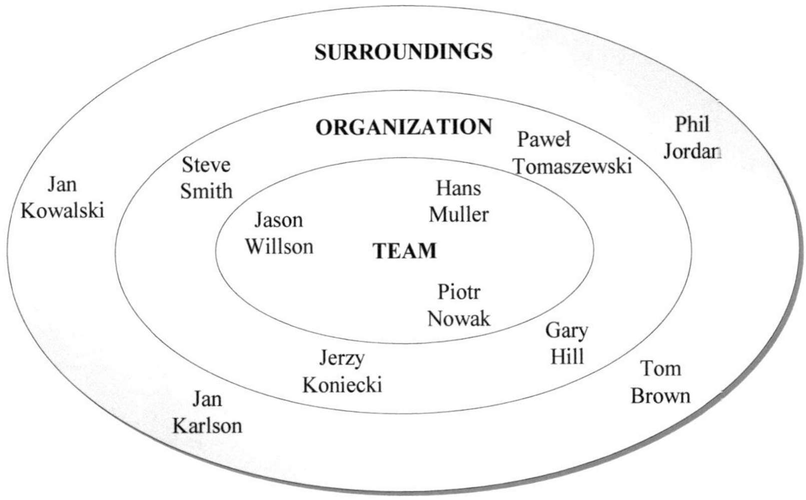

Source: (Probst & Raub & Romhardt, 2002)

Fig. 10. Knowledge sources map

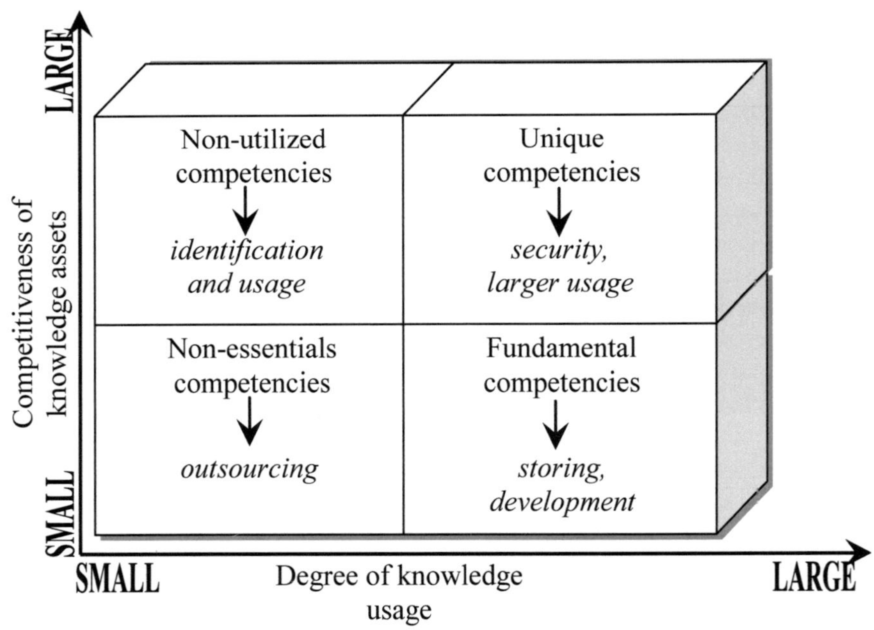

Source: ibidem

Fig. 11. Competency matrix

6. Ontology impact on knowledge management

Taking into account the definition of knowledge management and its elements (see the previous sections of this chapter), now we have to consider how knowledge is to be collected (and then processed) within the information system. One general condition has to be fulfilled: knowledge must be written in knowledge base using such formalism of its representation that can be understood by both people and computer. Ontology is one of such mechanisms and seems to be especially useful when we talk about tacit knowledge. There are some expectations put towards ontology[2]. These expectations can be described in the following way:

- to make easier the communication between people and organizations by common understanding of ideas, reduction of any possible misunderstandings, synonymous definitions of ideas and integration of many points of view,
- to make possible the representation and usage of knowledge in any part of information system,
- to assure the cooperation of many components, modules and systems by sharing and mapping of knowledge,
- to use the system dictionaries by delivering coherent and rich user interfaces, reduction of system creation time, multilingualism maintenance, many ways of visualization, etc.,
- to modify the systems during their activity by introducing the parameterization of functionalities within ontology as well as by the usage of generative user interface.

6.1 Ontology definitions

There are some definitions of ontology known from the literature[3]. For example J.A.Hendler says that "an ontology is a formal definition of a body of knowledge"[4]. Another definition explains ontology as a theory of a particular domain or sphere of knowledge, describing the kinds of entity involved in it and the relationships that can hold among different entities"[5]. One more definition says "An ontology defines the terms used to describe and represent an area of knowledge. Ontologies are used by people, databases, knowledge-bases and applications that need to share domain information (a domain is just a specific subject area or area of knowledge, like medicine, tool manufacturing, real estate, automobile repair, financial management, etc.)[6].

In our further investigations we would like to concentrate on the definition proposed by J.F.Sowa who says that "the subject of *ontology* is the study of the *categories* of things that exist or may exist in some domain. The product of such a study, called *an ontology*, is a catalog of the types of things that are assumed to exist in a domain of interest *D* from the perspective of a person who uses a language *L* for the purpose of talking about *D*. The types in the ontology represent the *predicates, word senses,* or *concept and relation types* of the language *L* when used to discuss topics in the domain *D*"[7].

---

[2] http: //www.rodan.pl/web/guest/oferta/platforma_officeobjects/officeobjectsontology_manager, 8.07.2011

[3] See e.g. http://www.aaai.org/AITopics/pmwiki/pmwiki.php/AITopics/Ontologies, 9.07.2011

[4] ibidem

[5] D.S.Weld (ed.): The role of Intelligent Systems in the National Information Infrastructure, The American Association for Artificial Intelligence, 1995, http://www.aaai.org/AITopics/pmwiki/pmwiki.php/AITopics/Ontologies, 9.07.2011

[6] J.Heflin (ed.): OWL Web Ontology Language Use Cases and requirements, 2004, http://www.aaai.org/AITopics/pmwiki/pmwiki.php/AITopics/Ontologies 9.07.2011

[7] http://www.jfsowa.com/ontology, 9.07.2011

6.2 System of medical ontologies as an exemplary ontology

The treatment of patients is the main goal in medicine. When a doctor has made (after examination) a diagnosis, the next step is to select the best form of treatment. Parallel to this, is a pathway of solving the patient's problems. Both are typical ways to get experience. There is a hypothesis that the proposed system of nodes feature different ontologies of expertise. These domains of influence have to be taken into account because of the diversity of knowledge involved in health-care.

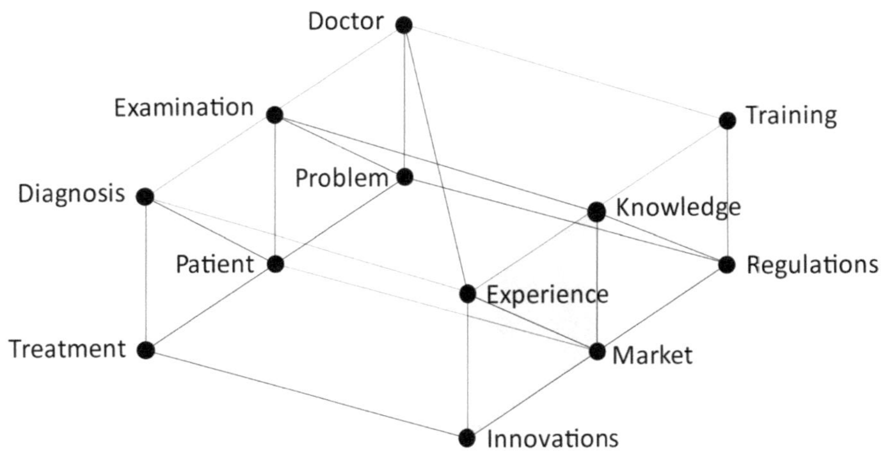

Source: own elaboration

Fig. 12. Relations in the process of medical innovations

Evolution of medical practice (treatment) involves interactions both within and among the foregoing aspects. Thereby, in Fig. 12 nodes correspond to the subcomponents of aspects of the patient-practitioner correlation. The system includes the provision of patient services. This process is supported by training and regulations having influence on the knowledge used for examination. There are two kinds of knowledge in the medical sector. Tacit knowledge is generated e.g. within experience. The emergence of relations in the presented system reflects both the application of knowledge into specific activities as well as the exchange of information across the relations.

Differently from linear or flat models of medical innovation, the undirectionality of pathways within this scheme does not confine the potential of innovation (grey area) only to scientific breakthroughs but at calls for appreciation of multiple sources across all domains. It is worth mentioning that the importance of variety in the system of innovation draws attention to the central role of institutions. Scientific progress requires such clearly defined system of understanding to describe the space in which ontological solutions are searched.

7. Conclusions

In knowledge based economy the role and importance of information and knowledge is still growing. Knowledge is becoming one of the most valuable assets in any organizations. Rapid progress in the field of scientific research – especially in medicine, new information and communication technologies, etc. enforce not only the necessity of innovation transfers but also the need of development and creation of knowledge. Knowledge discovery from the existing databases have been known for +- 30 years, but the acquisition of tacit knowledge is much younger. Human capital consists of creativity, an innovative way of reasoning, experience and knowledge of people and – as any other assets in the organization – should be managed. This chapter covers some problems of tacit knowledge management. We have chosen medicine as an exemplary discipline where transfer of knowledge is of special importance.

In the medical sector innovation transfer will open up new markets for SMEs' products. This may be a good possibility for clinics to become a part of that. Clinics have a high potential for product innovation, process and service development. There are many reasons why this potential of innovation is not sufficiently transferred to the results, such as product development by companies and better health care. The barriers concern, among others, different interests. Clinics are mainly focused on the efficient management and welfare of patients. Access of small and medium-sized enterprises (on a European scale) to the innovation potential in clinics can improve their economy. Whereas the objective of the industrial units is all about economy and economic importance. Today big business companies and corporations dominate as suppliers of ready innovative products. So far, the changes initiated by the employees of clinics and small and medium-sized enterprises (SMEs) have no chance to transfer knowledge and ideas. But this is the flexibility of SMEs in developing lab types, prototypes and small business solutions , that can help to improve the daily work of clinics and in particular its quality.

When we consider knowledge management in context of the innovation transfer, we should remember about new possibilities of processing that is cloud computing. It is – according to the National Institute of Standards and Technology – "a model for enabling convenient, on-demand network access to a shared pool of configurable computing resources (e.g. networks, servers, storage, applications and services) that can be rapidly provisioned and released with minimal management effort or services provider interaction". There have been distinguished three sorts of services in cloud computing: infrastructure as a service, platform as a service and software as a service. Knowledge management within cloud computing seems to be the field for further investigations.

8. Acknowledgement

The presented studies were conducted in frame of InTraMed-C2C Project (2CE096P1 - CENTRAL EUROPE Programme 2007 – 2013) in cooperation with Wroclaw University of Economics. The co-operation is much indeed appreciated.

9. References

Caldwell F., Harris K. (2002). *Cykl popularności metod zarządzania wiedzą w roku 2002, [in:] Knowledge Management. Zarządzanie wiedzą w organizacji*, ComputerWorld Custom Publishing, May 2002 (in Polish)

Chauvel D., Despres C. (2002). *Intellectual Roots of Knowledge Management*, KMSS 2002, Sophia Antipolis, September 2-6, 2002

Dalkir K. (2011). *Knowledge management theory and practice.* Second Edition. Boston, MA: MIT Press, 2011

Davenport T., Prusak L. (1998). *Working Knowledge*, Harvard Business School Press, Boston 1998

Encyklopedia Powszechna, PWN, Warszawa 2002, http://encyklopedia.pwn.pl/, 22.01.2005 (in Polish)

Nonaka I., Takeuchi H. (2000). *Kreowanie wiedzy w organizacji*, Polska Fundacja Promocji Kadr, Warszawa 2000 (in Polish)

Nycz M. (2007). *Pozyskiwanie wiedzy menedżerskiej. Podejście technologiczne*, Wyd. AE im. O.Langego we Wrocławiu, Wrocław 2007 (in Polish)

Probst G., Raub S., Romhardt K. (2002). *Zarządzanie wiedzą w organizacji*, Oficyna Ekonomiczna, Kraków 2002 (in Polish)

Stewart T.A. (1997). *Intellectual Capital*. The New Wealth of Organisations, New York 1997

Wierzbicki M. (2004). *Czy e-learning, zarządzanie wiedzą, jakością i procesami to oddzielne wyspy*, MacroSoft S.A., 2004 (in Polish)

Supply_Chain Council, Supply-Chain Operations Reference-model Overview Version 5.0, http://supply-chain.org/slides/SCOR5.0OverviewBooklet.pdf, 4.03.2003

Sveiby E. (2003). *A Knowledge-Based Theory of the Firm to Guide Strategy Formulation*, http://www.sveiby.com.au, 15.11.2003

4

A Roadmap for Requirements Elicitation of Knowledge Management Systems: A Delphi Study

Sanath Sukumaran[1], Hemalatha Ramalingam[1], Lorna Uden[2], Akmal Rahim[1] and Kanchana Chandran[3]
[1]*Taylor's University*
[2]*Staffordshire University*
[3]*Freelance*
[1,3]*Malaysia*
[2]*UK*

1. Introduction

The discipline of Knowledge Management (KM) has been around for quite some time. However, it has yet to find a successful formula of assimilation to benefit organizations today. Organisations are not able to leverage on its past successes, experiences and lessons learnt without an effective mode to capture tacit requirements. Knowledge Management bridges this gap.

An organization's continued maturity is assessed not only for its financial strength but from its ability to leverage and build upon mainly its tacit and at times explicit nature of its intellectual capital whilst enabling co-creation of values (Lee & Choi, 2003). To manage both tacit and explicit knowledge in an organisation, it is imperative that a Knowledge Management System (KMS) be deployed.

2. Problem statement

KMS requires a synergetic effort from an array of disciplines and perspectives armed with the correct technological tools to be the driving force towards a knowledge-sharing environment. Any KMS ought to look into the needs and demands of its people including cultural and organizational norms should it live up to its expectations and survive the test of time.

Software engineering as a body of knowledge does not encapsulate people, cultural and organizational facets in a holistic sense within its software development processes. Herein lies the gap.

3. Research question

To explore how knowledge can be elicited to suit the needs of its stakeholder taking into account cultural and organizational norms.

4. Research objectives

- To review weaknesses of present KMS in achieving its intended goal.
- To ascertain how KMS differ from conventional systems to warrant a different approach.
- To propose a roadmap for requirements elicitation for Knowledge Management Systems using Activity Theory

5. Literature review

5.1 Overview

KM emerged as a scientific discipline in the early 1990s. It was initially supported solely by practitioners, when Scandia hired Leif Edvinsson of Sweden as the world's first Chief Knowledge Officer (CKO). Hubert Saint-Onge started investigating various sides of KM long before that.

The idea of a KMS is to enable employees to have ready access to the organization's documented base of facts, sources of information, and solutions. For example, an engineer could know the metallurgical composition of an alloy that reduces sound in gear systems. Sharing this information organization wide can lead to more effective engine design and it could also lead to ideas for new or improved equipment. (Langton & Robbins, 2006).

5.2 Knowledge management systems

It has been suggested that the term "KMS project" should never be used as if it pertained to the same category as an IT or IM project (Terra & Gordon, 2002). KMS projects should take a holistic or organic view of the enterprise and should encompass different initiatives in many areas: certainly in IM, but also in HR, organizational design, internal communications and so forth. KM is more closely associated with the "act of managing" than IM.

In this sense, KM is never-ending. It is defined by the identification of people's expertise and the interplay of people with people (tacit knowledge-sharing) and people with information systems (two-way road of knowledge capture, reuse and recreation). Given that they are highly dependent on people's previous knowledge, motivation and willingness to create, act, share and or codify their own individual knowledge, KM processes are far more complex than IM projects. However, KMS is increasingly dependent on the support of a solid IT infrastructure.

5.3 Activity theory

Initial large-scale software development efforts were chaotic, often resulting in an explosion of costs and development times which were much larger than originally predicted. The outcome was typically quite different from the original objective of the activity. Many times the object was simply not produced and the effort was abandoned after the investment of considerable resources, (Barthelmess & Anderson, n.d).

As a result, practitioners turned their attention to the development process itself. A new term, software engineering, was coined to represent this endeavour. Software engineering strives to further define techniques, processes, methodologies, and languages to ease the development of large software systems, (Barthelmess & Anderson, n.d).

Software engineering approaches the problem of collective development from a production-oriented viewpoint. While this view allows a certain amount of anticipatory reflection, e.g., the ability for subjects to predict important aspects of development prior to initiation and to assess results after completion (Floyd,1992), it blinds software engineers to the communicative aspects of a collaborative software development activity; (Barthelmess & Anderson, n.d).

Activity Theory (AT) is a philosophical and cross-disciplinary framework for studying different forms of human practices as development processes, with both individual and social levels interlinked at the same time, (Nardi, 1996).

AT is a development theory that seeks and explains qualitative changes in human practices over time (Uden, n.d). KMS also involves in qualitative changes in human practices, therefore AT is required in the development of KMS. AT helps to maintain adequately the relationship between the individual and social levels (Uden, n.d). KM Systems also incorporates relationship between the managerial personnel and its co-worker to the benefit of the organization (Nardi, 1996). This further emphasizes how AT can play an important role in the development of KM Systems.

AT helps to maintain adequately the relationship between the individual and social levels (Uden, n.d). KM Systems also incorporates relation between the managerial personnel and its co-worker to the benefit of the organization (Stahl, 2006), this emphasizes AT definitely plays an important role in the development of KM Systems.

5.4 The connection between knowledge management system and software engineering

KMS is developed in order to convince the need for improving productivity and the potential of employees and the company as a whole. The existing knowledge infrastructure is evaluated so that it can convey the idea that the present ways of doing things are not just sidelined in preference for a new system. KMS is a commercial system, generally IT based, mainly for managing knowledge and experience in organizations supporting creation, capture, storage and dissemination of information (Benbye, 2008).

In essence, KM is a method that simplifies the process of sharing, distributing, creating, capturing and understanding of a company's knowledge (Davenport & Prusak, 1998). KM starts with a problem and ends with a solution.

Software Engineering (SE) concerns methods and techniques to develop large software systems. The engineering metaphor is used to emphasize a systematic approach to develop systems that satisfy organizational requirements and constraints. Since SE is a typical knowledge-intensive discipline that evolves very fast and involves a large number of people, different phases and different activities (Rus & Lindvall, 2002), it is one of the disciplines that can benefits most from KM (Edwards, 2003). Does this mean that KMS follows SE principles?

It can be derived that both practices (KM & SE) start with a problem. For an example, one of the challenges in KM is to change organizational culture, whereby it involves changing the people attitudes and behaviours to ensure that they contribute to the sharing of knowledge to the organization. However to use SE to develop a large software system in the industry, the processes also follow a number of defined steps which are accepted as best practice by the software engineers. The early phase for SE starts with information or requirements gathering while KMS requires knowledge capture in order to kick-start the development phases. Both the software engineers and the knowledge developer need to specify the suitable tools for designing their intended systems. From this discussion, both practices have the same concept, which is problem solving but the approach and the domain may possibly be different. KM involves organizational, human and technical issues, with the advice that the technical should be treated as least important of the three and the most important part of the KMS is to capture experience which is the knowledge itself (Davenport & Prusak, 1998).

We should see KMS and SE principles differently even though both these practices have the same goal which is to develop a system that help solve problems but the end product of both will not be the same. We use SE principles to develop a conventional system to solve day to day problems such as library system, content management system, point of sales software and other software that are related to our daily use.

The real purpose of the software that has been developed is achieved by looking inside the software as to what does the software or the system contain? Based on simple logic, we can say that the library system contains information about books, names, authors, locations and the ISBN codes and this is what distinguishes a library system from other systems. What then makes a system that is based on SE principles different from KMS?

SE principles may not be sufficient for KMS because to some extent KMS is completely different from a SE system. Both are software, but what goes inside the software might be different as stated earlier. What goes inside the SE system consists of information such as account numbers, stock quantities and others, which are explicit as opposed to KMS, which consist of tacit knowledge which is completely different from information.

Knowledge is distinguished from information by the addition of 'truths, beliefs, perspectives and concepts, judgments and expectations, methodologies and know-how'. Based on opinions, the way we capture information is different than knowledge because knowledge is tacit and from tacit, one can capture experience.

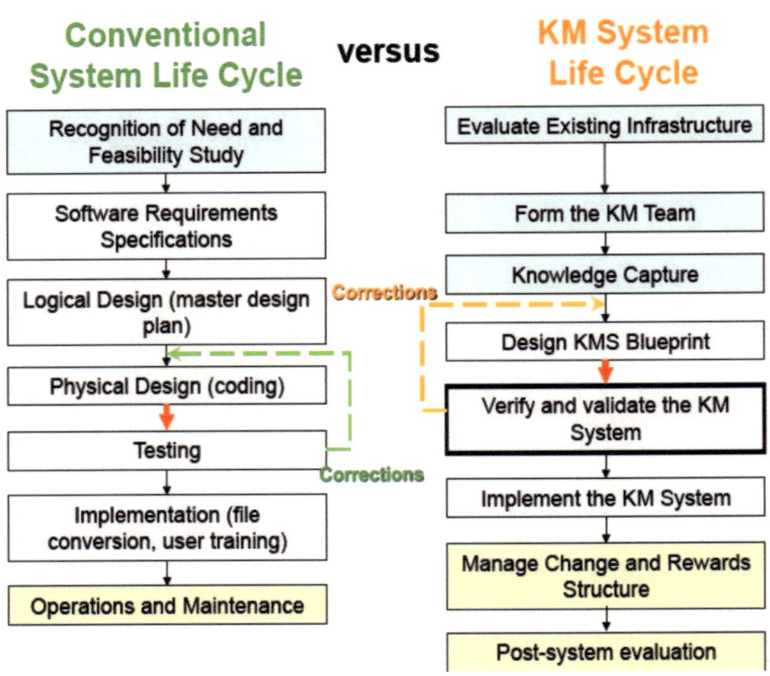

Fig. 1. Adapted from Sornlertlamvanich, V. (Sornlertlamvanich, n.d)

From the table below, we can see how KM systems differ from conventional systems to warrant a different approach:

KM System	Conventional System
Knowledge developer gathers knowledge from people with the given knowledge and the developer depends on them for the solution	Systems analyst gathers data and information from the users and the users depend on analysts for the solution
Knowledge developer deals with the domain expert	Conventional system developer deals with the user
Experts know the solution and problem	Users know the problem, not solution
Result oriented, incremental, interactive	Process driven, sequential
Testing phase at the beginning	Testing phase at the end

Fig. 2. Adapted from Sornlertlamvanich, V. (Sornlertlamvanich, n.d)

KM team must capture the knowledge requirements for the system to be built so that the end product will be meaningful to the organization and its users. Conventional systems development is primarily sequential, whereas KMS is incremental and interactive. In the case of a conventional system, testing is usually done towards the end of the cycle (after the system has been built), whereas in KMS, the evolving system is verified and validated from the beginning of the cycle. Systems development and systems management is much more extensive for conventional information systems than it is for KMS. The conventional systems life cycle is usually process-driven and documentation-oriented whereas KMS is result-oriented (Sornlertlamvanich, n.d).

5.5 The weakness of present KMS in achieving its intended goal

KMS can be a very complex system which comprises of expensive hardware solutions and complex indexed database. When KMS is completed, the developers of the system need to ensure that KMS is able to store tacit knowledge so that their effort proves to be successful. KMS has a reputation for costing a lot to set up, running into difficulties when trying to get everyone to contribute and ending up with a great deal of information that is inconsistent and irrelevant for most of its users (Straker, 2009).

Organizations tend to focus more on the technology used in the development of KMS rather than the requirements or extraction of tacit knowledge to be stored in the KMS. Organizations think that investment in expensive technology can provide them with a good KMS. KM involves organizational, human and technical issues, with the advice that the technical should be treated as least important of the three (Davenport & Prusak, 1998). Complex IT infrastructures for KMS prove to be costly because the effort need to maintain, update and develop is huge. Instead of focusing too much on the technical view, the developer should focus more on the human part where the KM team should play their role by dealing with the domain experts, experts that know the solution, problem and also can contribute how to make sure the data inside the KMS is tacit knowledge. Knowledge capturing is crucial in developing KMS because before implementing or designing the system, the knowledge has to properly assign to the intended user for future usage.

Failing to capture tacit knowledge will result in the KMS just being a normal database system containing data that is not meaningful for the organization. Tacit knowledge is the result of the human brain processing, analyzing and filtering information to reach conclusions. Information is not knowledge. Yet many organizations fail to understand the difference and are disappointed when a huge investment in technology does not deliver the expected results (Hurley, 2010). Organizations need tacit knowledge because it can drive the organization forward and increase the efficiency on how the organization can operate and be more competitive. In an organization, workers come and go and some of them might have ten to fifteen years of working experience. Their invaluable experience in handling certain practices is important for the organization to expand its potential and knowledge capabilities.

Building a system for KM is thoroughly different from building a system for conventional purpose. As discussed earlier, abandoning social, cultural and organizational issues may interrupt the development process of a good KMS. The character of learning and sharing needs to be cultivated in the foundation of any given organization. Workforces that are willing to learn and share their ideas and experiences in an organization can enable the KMS to perform better. When a knowledge management initiative is seen as the exclusive mandate of the technological department it can become an exercise in information and document storage and retrieval. Successful knowledge management is about fostering an environment in which knowledge is shared and questions asked and answered across the internal barriers of departments and teams.

Most organizations are still structured along hierarchical lines that are not conducive to interdepartmental collaboration or cooperation and yet this collaboration is essential to knowledge management. Finding and managing the flow of knowledge in an organization requires a very different approach to managing information. Creating an organizational culture where knowledge sharing is the norm is the most important and most difficult part of implementing knowledge management within a business. As with all organizational change, technology can and does play an important and integral part but it cannot alone be the driver (Hurley, 2010).

KMS approach without input from all stakeholders can interrupt KMS intended goal. Current knowledge management technologies cannot yet handle uncertainties with inadequate information. They cannot deliver the right information to the right person at the right time because companies cannot predict what the right information to distribute is and who the right people to distribute it to are (Lang, 2001). Stakeholders need to anticipate the prospect of building the KMS and also to identify the experts needed to collaborate with the developers of KMS. Besides, inadequate knowledge or data in the KMS may perhaps be one of the weaknesses of the current KMS available. The quality of information can also be a turn-off. If the first item the user opens is unexpectedly scrappy, then the user will not look further (Straker, 2009). The user's experience is important when navigating the KMS in order to look for specific knowledge. If the experience is not worth a visit due to the poor quality of data stored, then the user might not consider using the system again.

Other than the quality of the data in KMS, a complex user interface and a complex operation can also be an obstacle for the user to use the KMS. When the users only want a simple system and do not have the time to learn how to use it fully then such systems are liable to fall into disuse (Straker, 2009).

Another strong reason why KMS fails in achieving its intended goal is because people are unwilling to cooperate during requirement elicitation for KMS. Apart from that, when the KMS is completed, there is no valuable knowledge input to the KMS itself. People are reluctant to share their invaluable experience and knowledge that they have acquired over the years to their organization. They may feel they are 'giving away the shop', deskilling their job and reducing their employability or potential to earn higher wages. Experts, in particular, live and die on what they know. Where knowledge is power, to give freely what you know to others can seem like professional suicide. It may also be work that is rewarded relatively poorly and can lead to people following up and asking you for further information (Straker, 2009).

5.6 Research gaps

KM approaches should include methods to overcome impediments to knowledge transfer. Implementing effective methods to counteract impediments in this way may not always be possible (Szulanski, 1996). For example, it may be too much to expect that contributors describe a knowledge artifact, including the factors that associate the strategy with the original context, and how the strategy should change when applied to different contexts.
KM approaches may fail when they attempt to create a monolithic organization memory. Organizations that have tried to develop a massive organization memory as a whole have failed (Ackerman, M. S. and Halverson, C. A. (2000)). Among other reasons, such organizations are distributed and may have conflicting goals.
Such organizations may fail when they do not incorporate with humans, processes, and technology (Ackerman & Halverson, 2000). This is justified by the limitations and importance of each of these components. Humans alone are slow and have limited capacities. Processes are the main component in delivering organizational goals. Thus, any approach that is not associated with processes will tend to fail or be perceived as failures.

6. Research method

Most KMS are so diverse, spanning across industries. In order to obtain necessary data to answer the research question, it is imperative that the research method employed is flexible enough to cater the needs of a variety of situations and to a wide range of complex problems, for which there is often no other suitable means of analysis. The Delphi technique is a systematic method of collecting opinions from a group of experts through a series of questionnaires. The iterative approach espoused in Delphi allows KM experts to reconsider their judgements in the light of feedback from peers. The anonymity of the approach enables experts to express their opinions freely, without institutional loyalties or peer group pressures getting in the way.
The aforementioned iterative approach also gives KM experts more time to think through their ideas before committing themselves to them, leading to a better quality of response. Since AT emphasises on human activity as the basic unit of analysis, the research is able to uses human activities (supervision of projects) to analyse responses garnered from Delphi.

7. Scenario

The Five-Year Strategic Plan of University X has made teaching and learning a major priority. Under the said target plan, technology is identified as one of the drivers that will shape the future direction of the University's learning experience. Hence, the gradual adoption of e-Learning tools and strategies is currently being investigated. On that note, the critical success factor and challenges for the implementation of e-Learning at the University is the willingness and ability of existing faculty members to adopt technology into their teaching and learning activities. The key thrust is to ensure that lecturers, as front liners, are the ones driving and advocating technology.

Ensuring sustainable buy-in from the academic staff can only be possible when strong structural and technical support is in place. In doing so, tacit knowledge from experts is to be obtained to better comprehend the intended requirements of the tools that would be acquired. To guarantee success in implementation, there must be significant reliance on sound planning and on the provision of appropriate developmental interventions. This would include obtaining tacit knowledge as an input capture into the KMS system from selected experts of best practices, opinions and solutions via the Delphi method.

The process of Delphi mindfully uses the Activity Theory notion in obtaining human related information allowing social-organization processes to be accounted. With this in mind the KMS system would visibly include all needs and demands of the experts including cultural and organizational norm in living up to its expectations and survive the test of time hence productively achieving and solving the software engineering practices of today.

The initial groundwork of the Delphi process taken on for this research study obtained relevant requirements from knowledge experts based on their respective specialization areas. Only five identifiable experts in the cluster of major specialization areas of Information Technology were consulted into providing these relevant feedbacks. These five areas broadly covers the relevant domains in Computing. The major specialization areas include algorithms and network security, multimedia, object oriented programming and game development, databases and software development concepts and strategies.

Upon identifying the experts, the first round of the Delphi process addressed relevant questions directed to the selected experts taking into consideration both the human expert opinions in the subject domain areas together with the social and organizational requirements of the system. They were directed in such a way that the opinions incorporated issue that affected the outside boundary of the organization - the external environment. By driving these questions, the research pilot study enabled the experts to provide opinions that not only drives or shares their current best practices utilized but envisages the possible needs of what makes an outstanding learning Institution.

Further to this, the second round of the Delphi process initiated a set of questions via a questionnaire to the same selected sets of experts. The objective of this stage of the Delphi process is to obtain a consolidated wholesome viewpoint of all experts concerned regarding feasible requirements of the blended learning tools and strategies. A system perspective view on their feedback, opinions and knowledge better enables the complete requirements acquisition process. By doing so, the team is able to obtain a collective consensus in achieving the purpose of the intended change.

8. The findings

8.1 Delphi process step 1 – Outcome

1. Requirements and effective elicitation results on the blended learning tools.
2. Identifiable assistance that would be required in adopting blended learning.

Expert 1-Algorithms and Computer Security

1.	The learning tools should be able to simulate animations via multimedia or games. It should have the features or options to simulate or modelling via a request from expert (lecturer). Choice of simulation should be based on the topic at hand and the guidance

of the lecturer. The simulation options should have common characters available, hence having the option of choosing the match of which characters are to be adopted or used for the topic or scenario at hand. Simulation via game infuses students to think logically and analytically hence drawing the results via a step-by- step momentum governing a build-up of interest on the topic at hand. A video capture of the lecture with the ability of conversion to audio form provides a thinking flow in the students mind hence mind provoking to empower and challenge the questioning technique. These applications can be converted to any choice of language hence making it multi-lingual. It supports and garners a cultural openness in assisting students from all walks of life. In addition to this there is a feature of an SMS option linking the lecturer to the student enabling the sharing of instant up-to date information.

2. The need for relevant training from prospective vendors enabling the maximization of the learning tool at hand is required. A testing period performed on a trial basis on the relevant tools should be incorporated to better understand, enable gradual adoption and gauge the capabilities of the software. In the case of minimal support, the success of the software could be jeopardized. It is only feasible through teamwork for a better understanding of the stakeholders of the software.

Expert 2- Multimedia

1. Taking into consideration that this specialization area covers more of the tool manipulation in multiple media format, the provision for recording of visual screen movement enabling the capture of the instructors input entry would be substantial in the display of the software's capabilities. Alongside this would be the creation of a central repository for all visual capture in support of the teaching materials. Again, the provision to support these visual content via narration to a multi-lingual audio content well establishes an open community support culture for international students. The strength of a two-way communication through a discussion forum would enable students to highlight concerns or ideas in the area of module coverage – hence exploring many horizons of skills, capabilities and doubts. Possible inclusion of various on-line games highlighting usage of various media format could also be added as a repository in understanding the "real-life" production conceptualization in a practical way.
2. To consider various vendors who could propose some viable tools that could be adopted into teaching Multimedia using blended strategies in particular the best practices that have been successful in leading institutions that have incorporated blended strategies in their teaching and learning. For that, essential training is required for the adoption of any of the tools that are viable. A considerable time for planning would be required in the rollout of the tools to best enable positive adoption amongst all stakeholders. Facilitators should be equipped with financial support in acquiring some state-of-the art technological tool to better support the upgrade of the technological adoption in the institution.

Expert 3 - object oriented programming and game development

1. One blended tool that could be incorporated should enable programming to be visually guided (screen view) as video captured files which could be made

available publicly via YouTube. This would be possible with screen capture software highlighting the visual movement of the input device hence enabling the students to revisit lectures. The capture of the lecture (visual input screen movement) could be utilized as a revision through examples given or perhaps be used as an alternative mode of teaching. Simulation depicting object oriented programming principles would also be viable to better understand the topic at hand. We could also use gaming software's which would strengthen the knowledge of students via a self -guided realization. Another feature that could be added in the imperative technology of making communication effective both ways is to enable the blended learning tool available via mobile applications. The objective here is mobility of being able to gain access to the expert (lecturer) anytime and anywhere. Students and lecturers at the University are respectively logged on the system. This could be featured as a Universities "Facebook" application. Another interesting requirement is acquiring tools that enable group collaboration that logs problems and shares solutions with individuals and or groups thus enabling feedback from lecturers to be appropriately provided. The additional feature of the blended tool to enable on-line video conferencing with students and potential speakers and clients could also carve a niche in overcoming the communication and requirement gap.

2. There is a need for vendors support on the software's adopted. Training is essential on the best technical video capture (awareness of all possible tools and methods of video or audio capture) in adopting the right blended learning strategy. Quality of tool is essential. It is equally important to ensure that the content of the video is appropriately suitable for the nature of the study or practice in accordance with the current Gen Y. It also provides support to experts looking for the best simulators available in teaching object oriented programming at a higher level other than ALICE. There is a visible need for up to date technological gadgets and tools with the objective of keeping up with the current trends hence making it appealing to try out new techniques and styles of blended learning. Recognition and reward should be given to individual experts in taking the initiative to appropriately apply blended learning into their classroom. This serves as an internal and external motivational factor to many.

Expert 4 – Databases

1. There should visibly be simulation of the programming of SQL through a recorded session thus enabling students to conceptualize the practical sessions through a simulation learning system, serving as a recap or perhaps a revision of the topic at hand. The need to establish an online forum to ensure that the students are able to interact with lecturers who serve as a support mechanism to students and lecturers enabling better understanding of topics and ideas discussed. Example: freeforum.org. There should also be access to video files depicting real life industry case studies to be viewed by the students for practical experience and analysis. Students need to be provided with real-time data which could be used to train the students on database development for high end industries.
2. There is visible need for trainings from the suppliers or vendors on the usage of the specific product. Lecturers should be able to gain access to up-to-date resource

materials through the University's library. Financial support into the investment on technological gadgets such as Ipad could develop a new culture towards the ecosystem of the University.

Expert 5 - Software development concepts and strategies.

1. The tools should enable facilitated collaboration with industry stakeholders thus providing an avenue for direct interaction of problem and solutions. How can this be done? Via a forum that could automatically send out "invites" to industry experts. This would be a specialized tool that caters to the requirements of round trip engineering (software). The tools should contain a database, self- available samples of past models or solutions with feedback and comments attached to each, hence becoming a repository of knowledge base. Inside the repository would be viable and non-viable solutions.
2. The need for collaboration with vendors is crucial in building the intended applications best suiting the user at hand. Clientele assistance is needed in identifying committed clients who are willing (via a Memorandum of Understanding) to be pro-actively involved in injecting real-life industry inputs. There is a need for assistance in identifying real-life projects to be used for assignments. The repository has to be current and updated with solutions for future reference and commercialization purposes (if required).

9. The interview process

The goal of this questionnaire process at the end is to reach a consensus of opinion among the group of experts. The uniqueness of Delphi lies in its reliability, given the variableness of human opinion, and in its ability to be administered remotely without direct participant interaction. Hence, this process gathers a reconfirmation of the experts' knowledge and opinions on forming the basis of a collective organizational goal that is to be achieved. The individual experts will be given a brief explanation of the selection options, criteria settings which will then guide them to provide their opinions.
Questions:

1. What would you want in a tool to assist you in incorporating Blended Learning in or outside classrooms?
2. The effectiveness of the tools based on subject domain?
3. What assistance would you as an expert require in adopting Blended learning?

Expert 1

Q1.

- Simulation Capabilities – simulates the concepts with most familiar characters (ex: game)
- Mobile application capability – information on ad-hoc situations
- Multi-lingual – enabling international students to convert materials to their choice of language
- Audio or Video conversions – various media options in the learning process

Q2.

- Provides options of teaching process and styles

• Increase support to students – building closer ties • Enables self-study • Availability – mobility • Creates an environment of competitiveness (students) Q3. • Vendor Support • Training
Expert 2 Q1. • Simulation capabilities – make it interesting • Mobile application capability – fast accessibility to lecturers • Multi-lingual – to assist international students as a supporting application • Visual screen capture – to be stored in repository for reference • Real-time data capture • User friendly Q2 • Enables self-study • Available – mobility • Improves logical thinking process – via games or simulations • Builds interest – current technology trends being practiced – keeping up with IT savvy skills of students Q3 • Management support • Training • Technology devices – current trends – Ipad
Expert 3 Q1 • Simulation capabilities – able to help simulate programming topics • Mobile application capability – making communication effective • Visual screen capture – to capture screen of programming process • Forum – all stakeholders – industry based online forum where we assist industry personnel's in given advice and solutions • Games simulation capabilities – enabling better understanding of programming principles Q2 • Provides options of teaching process – different from traditional method of teaching using technology as an aided tool • Increases student support – building closer ties – anywhere, anytime concept • Enables self-study – encourages independent study of student • Available – mobility – accessing the materials becomes easily accessible • Engaging in industrial relation or ties – real experience gained on real work scenarios • Improves logical thinking process via games or simulations – logic approaches simplified.

Q3 • Vendor support – to suggest simulation activity • Training – to be able to guide other team members • Technology devices – current trends – latest gadgets to achieve intended target • Gradual adoption trial and error – time required to change and familiarize • Recognition – efforts should be recognized and rewarded
Expert 4 Q1 • Simulation capabilities – database simulation properties • Audio-Video or Video-Audio conversion – conference system • Forum for all stakeholders – improves interaction with industry specialist • Central repository – case stories problems and solutions • Real time data capture – keeping abreast with updated data content for ease of manipulation • User-friendly Q2 • Provides options of teaching process – recorded sessions for repeated preview • Enables self-study • Engaging in industrial relations or ties • Improves logical thinking process – via games or simulations – able to develop analytical thinking process • Builds interest – current technology trends being practices Q3 • Vendor support – technological infrastructure must be available and strong in terms of support mechanism • Management support • Training • "Exploration time" • Technological devices – current trends - Ipads
Expert 5 Q1 • Forum for all stakeholders – live input from stakeholders • Central repository – case stories problems and solutions – historical information can be archived and decisions made in the past can be documented Q2 • Provides options of teaching process – students are looking towards creativity • Increase support to students – building closer ties – additional ways to engage with students • Enables self-study – students can learn and explore at their own pace • Available – mobility – students can proactively network anytime anywhere • Builds interest – current technology trends being practiced – students can assimilate better given the fact that they are largely familiar with the current technological tools and trends Q3 • Vendor support – additional requirements can be filled in • Management support – in terms of supporting resources • "Exploration" time – before it gains maturity

10. Analysis of findings and conclusion

The success of any KMS lies in the effective input of knowledge from all stakeholders concerned. Knowledge, which transforms itself as requirements into the KMS system, has to evidently involve proactive input from experts. These experts are those who understand the organization's processes and culture better and thus able to provide valuable and imperative input. Hence, one way of analysing this human activity occurrence serving as tacit knowledge into the KMS system is by using the Activity Theory. Since AT focuses on the interaction of human activity and consciousness within its relevant environmental context, the eventual KMS developed around these fundamentals would have an achievable and sustainable success rate of enabling employees to seamlessly access the organization's documented facts, best practices and solutions.

The Delphi technique utilized in this research study involved firstly gathering opinions and knowledge from selected experts concerned. The process went through a second round that led to a re-confirmation of opinions and knowledge serving as a building block for the solutions at hand. The research concluded from the Delphi process documented above evidently shows common opinions and knowledge that were gathered from the experts. It is apparent that all experts are in agreement for a blended learning initiative with the support and involvement from all stakeholders concerned.

By using both activity theory and Delphi technique, deep analysis can be performed within the activities of the experts and from these activities, tacit and explicit knowledge can be observed and analyzed. During the interview process, especially during the second round of interviews, when the questions were asked to the panel of experts, some of the experts realized that there existed divergent approaches exist in supervision style. Not only was the knowledge engineer able to garner further insights, the exercise also proved by an eye-opener for experts themselves which would have inadvertently increased their body of knowledge.

As espoused in this research, software engineering practice generally does not amalgamate people, cultural and organizations factors when gathering requirements. Since it is imperative that KM Systems consider the aforementioned factors, AT coupled with Delphi technique was applied in this research. This approach is not only holistic but also more dynamic with thorough investigations built in to the roadmap involving people, cultural, and organization dimension. The investigations details how using AT, a knowledge engineer is able to harvest tacit knowledge allowing every situation and scenes to evolve gives them different meaning and context. In conclusion, this research espouses a combination of KM practices, AT and Delphi technique in an integrated roadmap to provide a solid foundation for requirements elicitation in developing KM system.

11. Research outcome and limitations

The proposed research will shed new insights on the roadmap required to implement an effective KMS that will survive the test of time. The roadmap will ensure that KMS maps the interest of its stakeholders alike since it encapsulates their interest from the onset. The roadmap embodies an interesting fusion of people, cultural and organizational aspects required of a successful KMS.

However, it must be noted that even when the aforementioned system is in place, it still does not eliminate the perennial challenge of most knowledge management systems in place today which is the aspect of contribution. If contributions are not forthcoming, then even the most illustrious KMS will not serve its intended purpose. The proposed KMS roadmap does not illustrate a detailed outline of the development processes required to implement a KMS but rather elicitation of requirements required as building blocks to build a KMS.

12. References

Abecker, A., Decker, S. and Maurer, F. (2000) 'Organizational Memory and Knowledge Management', Guest editorial, Information Systems Frontiers, vol. 2, no. 3-4, pp. 251-252.

Ackerman, M. S. and Halverson, C. A. (2000) 'Reexamining Organizational Memory', Communications of the ACM, vol. 43, no. 1, pp. 59-64.

Benbye, H (2008). Knowledge Management Systems Implementation: Lessons from the Valley. Oxford, Chandos Publishing.

Davenport, T.H. and Prusak, L. (1998), Working Knowledge: How Organizations Manage what they Know, Harvard Business School Press, Boston, MA.

Floyd, C.: 1992, 'Software Development as Reality Construction'. In: C. Floyd, H. Zullighoven, R. Budde, and R. Keil-Slawik (eds.): Software Development and Reality Construction. Springer-Verlag, Chapt. 3.2.

Hurley.L (2010) Reasons knowledge management information systems fail (n.d.).

I. Rus, and M. Lindvall, "Knowledge management in software engineering," IEEE Software, vol. 19(3), 2002, pp. 26-38.

J. S. Edwards, "Managing software engineers and their knowledge," in Managing Software Engineering Knowledge, A. Aurum, R. Jeffery, C. Wohlin, and M. Handzic, Eds., Berlin: Springer-Verlag, 2003, pp. 5-27.

Lang, J. C. (2001). Managerial concerns in knowledge management. *Journal of Knowledge Management*, *5*(1), 43-59. doi:10.1108 or 13673270110384392

Langton, N & Robbins, S. (2006). Organizational Behaviour (Fourth Canadian Edition). Toronto, Ontario: Pearson Prentice Hall.

Lee, H. and Choi, B., Knowledge Management Enablers, Processes, and Organizational Performance: An Integrative View and Empirical Examination, Journal of Management Information Systems, Volume 20, Number 1, 2003, pp. 179 – 228.

Nardi, B., Ed. Context and Consciousness: Activity Theory and Human-Computer Interaction.Cambridge, MA, MIT Press, 1996.

P. Barthelmess and K.M. Anderson University of Colorado at Boulder A View of Software Development Environments Based on Activity Theory

Sornlertlamvanich, V. (n.d.). 2: Knowledge Management Systems Life Cycle. Knowledge Management.

Stahl, G. (2006), Group cognition: Computer Support for Building Collaborative Knowledge, MIT Press, Cambridge, MA.

Straker, D. (2009). How Knowledge Management Systems Fail and Succeed. *syque.com*. Syque.

Szulanski, G. (1996) 'Exploring Internal Stickiness: Impediments to the Transfer of Best Practice within Firms', Strategic Management Journal, vol. 17, Special Issue Winter, pp. 27-44.

Terra, J.C. & Gordon, C. (2002) Realizing the promise of corporate portals: Leveraging knowledge for business success, Boston: Butterworth Heinemann

Uden, Lorna Department of Computing, Engineering and Technology, Staffordshire University, Beaconside, Stafford, ST18 0AD, UK E-mail: l.uden@staffs.ac.uk
Activity theory for designing mobile learning

5

Fuzzy-Monte Carlo Simulation for Cost Benefit Analysis of Knowledge Management System Investment

Ferdinand Murni Hamundu[1],
Ahmad Suhaimi Baharudin[2] and Rahmat Budiarto[3]
[1,2]*School of Computer Sciences-Universiti Sains Malaysia,*[3]*InterNetWorks Research Group College of Arts and Sciences-Universiti Utara Malaysia*

1. Introduction

Nowadays, knowledge management system is not doubtful as an important tool in an enterprise business process by reason of the effective knowledge management system can give a competitive advantage. Knowledge management system (KMS) is an information technology (IT) based system, which is developed to support and enhance the processes of knowledge creation, storage or retrieval, transfer, and application (Alavi & Leidner., 2001;Tseng, 2008). There are some benefits that can be achieved by implementing KMS such as increased employee productivity, better quality of a finished product, production and labor cost saving (M.-Y. Chen et. al, 2009; Wickhorst, 2002). Many managers know these benefits, but they are still vacillating to decide for investing KMS in their structure. This vacillation comes from consideration of budget and uncertainties or risk of economic constrained. In addition, the managers do not know how to analyze cost and benefit of KMS investment correctly. Without being able to make the analysis, managers cannot determine whether investing a KMS is worthwhile or a waste for the enterprise. Therefore, the cost-benefit analysis of KMS investment is necessary in order to evaluate its attractiveness.
The traditional cost-benefit analysis that always used in KMS and other enterprise information system (EIS) investment evaluation such as net present value (NPV), internal rate of return (IRR), and payback period (PB) seek to adopt a monetary unit as a basis of analysis, in which all non-monetary parameters are given monetary values (TBC, 1998; Tang and Beynon, 2005). However, it is observed in (Phillips-Wren et al., 2004) that most benefits associated with EIS like KMS are mostly intangible, which makes the use of traditional quantitative financial models heavily biased towards tangible costs and benefits. In an attempt to bridging the intangible towards tangible in the benefits related decision-making process, some enterprises analyze based on subjective judgement. This approach constantly in linguistic term contains ambiguity data that has a number of weaknesses (Uzoka, 2009) such as: inaccurate representation of the uncertainty lack of historical data, inability to understand completely and reproduce the results, poor explanation of a decision process and associated reasoning, a possibility of missing out important problem details for the evaluation, high probability of different experts producing different results without the

ability to decide which one is correct, difficulty in exploiting past evaluations, and the risk of producing meaningless or highly faulty results.

In this paper, a fuzzy rule based system is proposed to bridging the tangibles and intangible benefits of KMS investment. The fuzzy component addresses the vagueness associated with human judgement, especially of intangible parameters. Furthermore, a Monte-Carlo simulation method is used to consider the uncertainty of economic in calculating an expected net present value (NPV). The Monte Carlo simulation is a method that appropriate for estimating the impact of KMS critical factors to the financial result by randomizing value from each of the uncertain variables and calculating the objective or target value of an investment model.

This paper starts with an introduction about problem of KMS investment decision in section 1, and then followed by discussion about cost and benefit of KMS investment, related works in cost-benefit analysis of KMS investment, and including the Fuzzy-Monte Carlo simulation as the proposed approach for this paper in section 2. Section 3 provides a framework for cost benefit analysis of KMS investment. The real life problem that the authors dealt with and intangible benefit analysis due to this problem are introduced in Sections 4 and 5, respectively. Section 6 provides a mathematical model of cost-benefit impact to KMS investment. In Section 7, the results of the Monte-Carlo simulation are analyzed and discussed. Finally, Section 8 presents the conclusions and outlines for further research.

2. Literature review

As managers became aware that the power of knowledge is the most valuable strategic resource, knowledge management (KM) became widely recognized as essential for the success or failure of enterprises. Consequently, over the past 20 years, KM has progressed from an emergent concept to an important factor in sustainable competitive advantage of business (Wagner et al., 2011). According to one estimate, 81% of the leading organizations in Europe and the U.S. are utilizing some form of KM (Grossman, 2006). Knowledge is based on data and information. Data represents the raw facts without meaning; information symbolized to what is obtained when data is organized in a meaningful context, while knowledge is characterized as the meaningfully organized accumulation of information (Zack, 1999). Nonaka (1994) points out that there are two different types of knowledge in an organization: explicit and tacit knowledge. Explicit knowledge is formal and systemic, while tacit knowledge is highly personal and difficult to formalize. These two types of knowledge are both essential to the organization and must be captured and shared for others to benefit. Thus, knowledge in the organization should be managed properly and carefully.

The KMS refers to the set of processes or practice to develop the ability of an employee in creating, acquiring, capturing, storing, maintaining and disseminating the enterprise's knowledge (Hamundu & Budiarto, 2010). Many companies are building KMS to manage their organizational learning and business "know-how". For instance, a software engineer is able to know immediately the algorithm of a security system in prior software development. Sharing this information organization widely can lead to more effective security design, and it could also lead to ideas for new or improved software. Indeed, the ability to perform all functions of KMS depends on the information technology (IT) role. Facing a tremendous amount of data on a daily basis, enterprises only use IT to integrate each division of various tools, such as intranet, data warehouse, electronic whiteboard, artificial intelligence and expert systems so that the jumbled business data is well-organized and more integrated (Khandelwal, 2003). During the development of KMS, attention should be paid to various issues and challenges related to using IT to support KM (Jungpil & Mani, 2000). This issue is considered by the managers to evaluate whether the KMS investment is feasible or not. Thus, the accurately calculating the cost and the benefit of KMS investment are necessary.

2.1 Costs

The first step of cost-benefit analysis for a KMS investment is to determine the costs. On the surface, this may seem deceptively simple, but there are costs involved in a knowledge management investment that may not be readily obvious to the manager. In fact, investment cost of EIS likes KMS is a common factor influencing the purchaser to choose the EIS (Davis & Williams, 1994). Obviously, the project will incur the cost of whatever EIS to be used. This can range from free, to nearly free, to several thousand dollars for an EIS. In addition, any technical infrastructure for the EIS that is needed will also have to be counted in the costs.

Investment costs of KMS include, but are not limited to the costs of software, hardware, incentive programs, implementing and maintaining. Technically, these costs can be grouped under two major criteria, namely, capital expenditures and operating expenditures (Ngai & Chan, 2005). Capital expenditures are the non-recurring costs involved in setting up the KMS such as product costs (the basic cost of the KM tool), license costs (the cost of the KM tools in terms of number of users) and training costs. Operating expenditures are the recurring costs involved in operating the KMS, which include maintenance costs and software subscription costs (the annual, pre-paid cost of upgrading the product to a major software release when it is launched).

2.1.1 Software

The standard software such as e-mail, web servers, corporate intranets, newsgroups, shared file systems, or centralized databases in an enterprise is commonly already existed. Hence, there is no software cost even only transfer knowledge such as the exchange of e-mail, the use of instant messaging tools, or the use of internet search engines. However, if the enterprise wishes to establish a level of knowledge integration and wishes to manage, encourage, and shepherd the transfer of knowledge, these tools are probably inadequate for the task.

In this case, the enterprise will want to invest in a commercially available product designed specifically for the tasks that the company wishes to be able to accomplish with the KMS. Costs for this may be quite high, but this KMS will be more likely to be utilized by the users, even if more user friendly than competing products.

2.1.2 Hardware

Along with the cost of software, the enterprise must also consider the costs of the infrastructure or hardware that will be needed to support the KMS. The application that is chosen may need its own application server on which to run or it may co-locate with existing applications on a server that the company already owns. If the system is placed on a server with applications already running, the company will have to consider the cost of any performance degradations that the other applications may occurrence. A server will need rack space in the server room, a universal power supply, and a network connection. Any upgrades to the enterprises network for handling an increased traffic attributable to the KMS should be considered.

Even if the company chooses to use the current systems and equipment, this equipment will be experiencing heavier loads than in the past, and this should be considered. If e-mail is chosen as a required tool, the mail server should be able to handle the increased traffic. The database server is needed to handle increased loads if it is to host a KM database. If the internet is required as part of a KMS, then the enterprise should be ensured that there is enough bandwidth available to handle all incoming and outgoing traffic and purchase more if needed.

2.1.3 Incentive programs

Another cost that should be considered, which is easily overlooked especially in the planning stages of a KMS investment, is the cost of programs that will be instituted to encourage employees to use the new system. A KMS is only useful when it is being used heavily, and the use of the system must likewise be encouraged by management. This means that the investment cost of a KMS must include the costs of awards and rewards that will be distributed to employees to encourage adoption and participation. In addition to the material costs involved, this program will also need an employee or group of employees to administer the program, determining the criteria for receiving an award, and determining the employees who are to be rewarded for their levels of participation. Managers will need to make their employees aware of the rewards program and encourage their charges to participate.

2.1.4 Implementing and maintaining cost

The implementing and maintaining cost of a KMS comes in many forms and all forms must be considered when calculating total costs. One implementing cost that should be considered is the cost for employing a member of the IT staff to install the KM hardware and software on all needed servers and client machines. In addition, the IT staff will need to configure the application to meet the needs of the business. This will require input from members of the business units that will be participating in the project, and their labor must be considered in the costs.

Once the system has been installed and is running, it will need to be maintained. A properly configured KMS will likely require little if any daily maintenance, but a member of the IT staff will need to contribute at least a few hours a month to backups, system administration, and the occasional restart. Knowledge will need to be input into the system in order for it to be useful, and in most cases this will require a substantial investment of labor capital from those possessing the knowledge to add this information to the system. The costs for the addition of knowledge will be heavy early on, but will steady out in the future, and will be based on the use of the system. In order for employees to be able to use the system, they will need to be trained on its use and the goals of the project. This training will take them away from other productive tasks and should be considered as one of the costs of the KMS investment. Once the employees have been trained, the time they spend using the system should also be considered as a labor cost attributable to the KMS investment.

2.2 Benefits

Once the costs have been calculated, the benefits of KMS investment either tangible or intangible must also be figured. One intangible benefit that will be gained after utilizing the

KMS is an increased quality of a finished product. Quality, which is delivered by KMS accounts for 20% of benefits (Anderson, 2002). An employee who uses the KMS might be able to obtain knowledge that will reduce the amount of defective finished products or will increase the effectiveness and quality or innovation of the products (Plessis, 2007). Another intangible benefit that will be recognized from the KMS is an increase in employee productivity. Productivity and speed, which is delivered by KMS account for 55% of benefits (Anderson, 2002). Employees, who use the KMS will be able to think creatively, innovatively, and also work faster, because they will find information on the KM environment that allows them to avoid repeating the work of others, such as a snippet of computer code (Chen & Huang, 2009).

The higher-quality product means potential to increase product sale or to decrease customers' dissatisfaction (Berry & Waldfogel, 2010). Consequently, it will improve the company's revenues and profit. Furthermore, an employee productivity and speed are strong related to delivery time of a finished product, while one factor that causes increase order of the finished product is an improved delivery time to customer (Ustundag et al., 2010). In addition, cost saving is also a benefit that can be realized through utilization of KMS. The practices of learning new knowledge, and sharing what is known by individuals, would enhance organizational capabilities and firm performance in terms of cost saving (Law & Ngai, 2008). Cost saving represents approximately one-quarter of benefits from KM investment (Anderson, 2002). The KMS can save in a labor costs and material costs, but the true benefit of cost saving through a KMS is realized when employees discover and share methods for reducing costs on final products.

2.3 Related works in cost-benefit analysis of KMS investment

Benefits might be difficult to measure, because many of the benefits are intangible, and cost savings delivered by KMS investment with an amount of USD*xxx* in the balance sheet will not be immediately illustrated. In addition, it is almost impossible to find metrics that will produce a one-to-one correlation between KM and financial impact (Vestal, 2002). The measurement of intangible benefits such as increased customer satisfaction and increased productivity of an employee, or cost savings is the key to evaluate the attractiveness of KMS investment. Furthermore, an evaluation of financially risk of KMS investment is needed by using objectives and parameters such as revenue, other benefits, capital and operating costs. A suitable investment model needs to be developed in order to estimate the financial outcome of the project and ascertain whether it meets any predetermined financial criteria as to what constitutes an attractive project (Ustundag et al., 2010).

Traditional cost-benefit analysis used in evaluating the value of EIS investment likes KMS relies on cash flow measures. Cost-benefit analysis include: payback period, rate of return on investment (ROI), net present value (NPV), profitability index, and internal rate of return (IRR) (TBC, 1998; Tang and Beynon, 2005). They assume that all costs and benefits are known, and it can be illustrated in a common metric–money. However, these assumptions are rarely met in the real life (K.C. Laudon and J.P. Laudon, 2005). They observed that most of the traditional cost-benefit analysis methods miss out a great deal of strategic considerations in an attempt to quantify and discount monetary units of intangibles. Therefore, this paper introduces an approach that can handle the problem that had defined earlier such as;(1) how to bridging the tangible and intangible benefits for cost-benefit analysis of KMS investment, (2) how to assess and manage the key factors as a reason the KMS success or failure, which is in uncertainty matters.

Over the years, Artificial Intelligence (AI) techniques such as Artificial Neural Network (ANN), Genetic Algorithm (GA), and Fuzzy Logic (FL) have been studied and employed in such kinds of investment decision making. Fuzzy Logic (Zadeh, 1965) has been widely used because of its obvious advantages of effectively dealing with linguistic expressions and capturing experts' knowledge on a specific problem. One of the key advantages of intelligent systems or such as fuzzy logic, is the modelling of unstructured variables and an attempt to utilize linguistic values in the evaluation process (Harmon and King, 1985). Fuzziness is inherent in many problems of knowledge representation, and the other is that high level managers or complex decision processes often deal with generalized concepts and linguistic expressions, which are generally fuzzy in nature. Modelling of imprecise and qualitative knowledge, as well as the transmission and handling of uncertainty at various stages are possible through the use of fuzzy sets. Fuzzy logic is capable of supporting to a reasonable extent, human type reasoning in a natural form. Examples of intelligent and soft computing techniques utilized in cost-benefit analysis of EIS can be found in (Uzoka, 2009). The framework of Uzoka (2009) is oriented for providing a cost-benefit analysis in EIS investment evaluation. However, cost-benefit analysis still need to provide an approach that not only includes the tangible and intangible benefits, but also provides the relationship among them and how they affect the investment output. All these benefits impact should be incorporated into an economic model with the purpose of informing the decision-maker about the amount of loss, cost saving, or revenue increase with an intention to inform the manager whether investing a KMS is worthwhile or a waste for the enterprise.

Therefore, this paper primarily concerns with providing such a framework for the cost-benefit analysis of KMS investment, which is utilized for assessment of the customer sales increase. Fuzzy rule based systems have been the most popular and easiest way to capture and represent fuzzy, vague, imprecise and uncertain domain knowledge. The fuzzy rule based systems (FRBS) uses fuzzy IF-THEN rules to determine a mapping from fuzzy sets in the input universe of discourse to fuzzy sets in the output universe of discourse based on fuzzy logic principles. In recent years, many researchers use the concept of a pure fuzzy logic system where the fuzzy rule base consists of a collection of fuzzy IF-THEN rules for many objectives such as flow time prediction in semi conductor manufacturing system (Chang et al., 2006), and Ustundag et al. (2010) who use FRBS for determining the revenue increase due to the quality of supply chain of companies after RFID implementation. Furthermore, the Monte Carlo simulation is implemented to calculate the expected net present value (NPV) for evaluating the attractiveness of KMS investment. Investment appraisal based on Monte-Carlo simulation of net present value (NPV) is a suitable methodology for KMS investment by which the uncertainty encompassing the main variables projected in a forecasting model is processed in order to estimate the impact of risk on the projected results. It is a technique in which a mathematical model is subjected to a number of simulation runs, usually with the aid of a computer. During this process, successive scenarios are built up using input values for the investment key uncertain variables which are selected at random from multi-value probability distributions. The simulation is controlled so that the random selection of values from the specified probability distributions does not violate the existence of known or suspected relationships among the investment variables.

The motivation of this paper is the lack of studies in the literature about how the expected revenue increase of KMS investment is determined by using NPV calculations. Therefore, the fuzzy rule-based system is used to calculate the expected revenue increase, and the Monte-Carlo simulation method is applied to determine the expected NPV of KMS investment at different certainty levels.

3. Cost benefit analysis of KMS investment

Referring to the limitations of existing cost-benefit analysis as discussed in Section 2, a new mechanism that can solve the problem must be established. This paper proposes framework that able to bridging intangible and tangible benefit for cost-benefit analysis as shown in Figure 1. The framework consists of four main process and one sub process namely benefit identification, knowledge acquisition, determine the probability distribution, modelling of risk impact to economic model, and performing simulation for risk analysis.

The proposed framework starts with to identify the benefit of KMS investment (See Figure 1, Benefit Identification process). Once the benefit identification has been done, the knowledge acquisition for handling the intangible benefits by using fuzzy rule-based system (FRBS) is conducted (See Figure 1, Knowledge Acquisition process). Furthermore, the output of knowledge acquisition process and tangible benefit are determined their probability distribution based on the characteristic of data (See Figure 1, Determine the Probability Distribution for Each Benefit). Once a FRBS has been set up, the probability distributions of those intangible and tangible benefits are linked to an economic model (See Figure 1, Modelling of Cost Benefit Impact to KMS Investment). Finally, perform the simulation for forecasting the certainty level of expected NPV (See Figure 1 Performing Simulation).

In order to illustrate how the proposed framework works, a cost benefit analysis of KMS investment for a software house company ABC is given in the following section.

4. A software house company ABC

An ABC company of software house has three branches in different cities, which meets the demand based on job order. The company plans to integrate KMS in their information and communication technology infrastructure. The management board of the company requests a cost-benefit analysis for the KMS investment. In the cost-benefit analysis, costs is categorized in capital expenditures and operating expenditures. On the contrary, the cost saving, increasing the quality of products, and employee productivity and speed are considered as benefits of the KMS investment. The cost savings contribute to increase the profits, while increasing orders due to the customer satisfaction is defined in expressions of productivity-speed time and quality of product impact. The benefits is identified and discussed in Section 2.2.

The revenue element of ABC Company consists of total of orders with the yearly amount before KMS adoption is 200 units with standard deviation 18% and the price per unit of USD5000. The investment costs of KMS are structured by capital expenditure (C_{Xn}) and operating expenditure (C_{Yn}) as USD200000 and USD20000 per year respectively, while the cost unit for the target of cost savings consists of average of annual direct labor cost per unit product (20 labor) of USD100, annual purchase material cost per unit product of USD800, annual method for final product per unit of USD500.

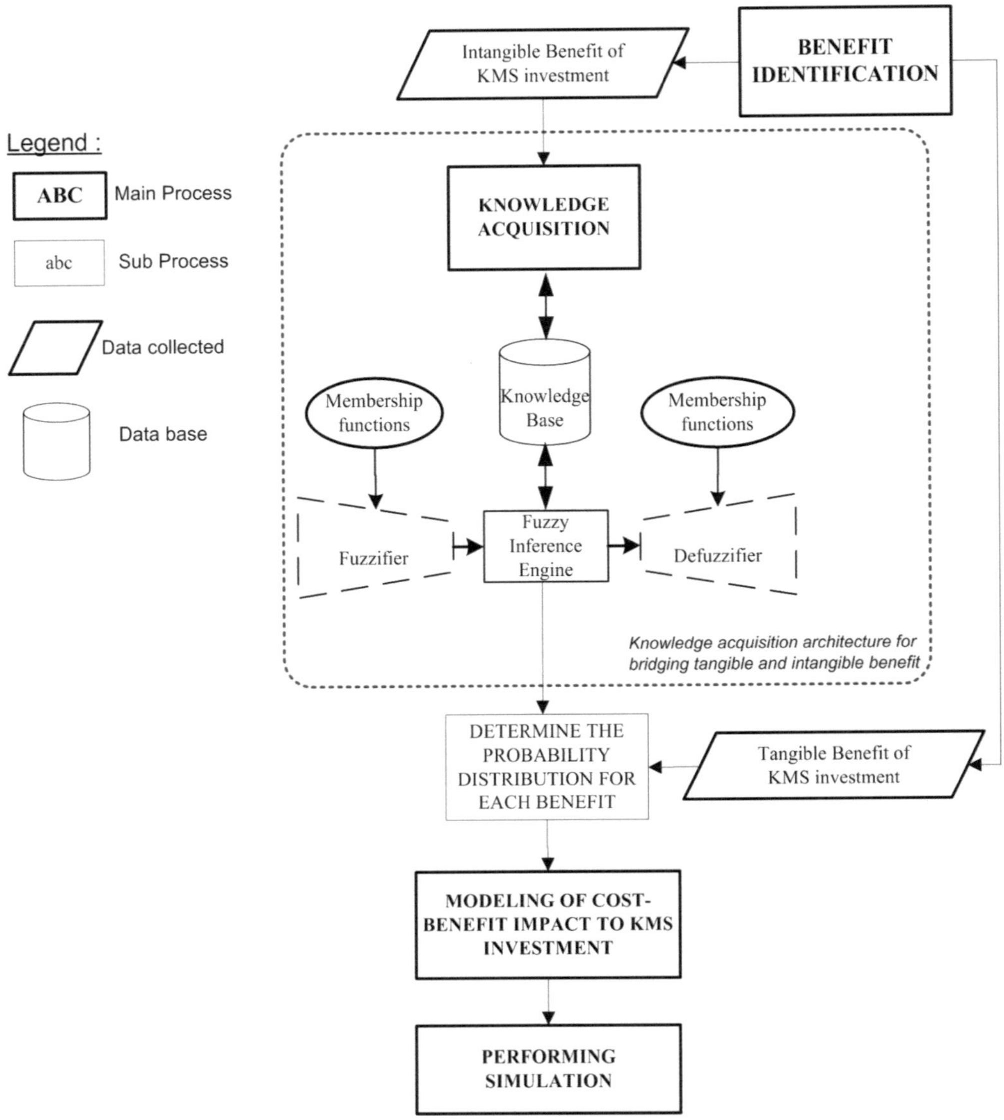

Fig. 1. Framework for Cost-Benefit Analysis of KMS Investment

Due to the fact that to illustrate the increase customer orders as an impact of intangible benefits in a balance sheet is difficult, a fuzzy rule-based system is developed. Consequently, net present value (NPV) as the feasibility indicator of the investment is computed using Monte-Carlo simulation.

5. Knowledge acquisition

Regarding the impact of intangible benefits of KMS investment to a revenue model, which is represented by increased customer orders, this paper involves expert's opinion to handle the increased by producing a fuzzy rule-based system (FRBS). This system is a systematic reasoning methodology that can capture the contextual judgment of experts by using fuzzy set theory.

This paper employs Mamdani model due to its advantages in representation of expert knowledge and in linguistic interpretation of dependencies. Hence, the increase in orders is calculated in a Mamdani-type. The composition of Mamdani-type fuzzy logic rule bases is in the following form (Tosun et al., 2010).

$$\text{If } x_1 \text{ is } A_1,\ x_2 \text{ is } A_2 \ldots \text{ And } x_n \text{ is } A_n \text{ then } y \text{ is } B$$

where A and B are linguistic variables defined by fuzzy sets of the universe of discourse x and y respectively. The output of the fuzzy rule based model whose rule base is constructed using Mamdani-type fuzzy logic rules is shown in Equation (1) (Jang and Gulley, 1997).

$$Z_{MOM} = \frac{\int_{z'} z dz}{\int_{z'} dz} \tag{1}$$

where Z_{MOM} is the defuzzified output, z' is the maximizing z at which the membership function reaches its maximum. In this paper, both triangular and trapezoidal fuzzy numbers are used to consider the fuzziness of the decision elements. The rules established for the increase rate in orders is structured such as follows:

Rule 1: IF delivery time is Short AND quality of product is High THEN Increase Rate in Orders is High.

Rule 2: IF delivery Time is Short AND quality of product is Medium THEN Increase Rate in Orders is Medium.

Rule 3: IF delivery Time is Normal AND quality of product is High THEN Increase Rate in Orders is Medium.

Rule 4: IF delivery Time is Normal AND quality of product is Medium THEN Increase Rate in Orders is Medium.

Rule 5: IF delivery Time is Long AND quality of product is Low THEN Increase Rate in Orders is Low.

All rules defined by the experts, and then calculated in Matlab Fuzzy Toolbox. The max–min method is used for the aggregation mechanism whereas the mean of maximum method is used for the defuzzification process of fuzzy outputs. Furthermore, the membership functions of delivery time that represent of productivity and speed of employee, quality of product and increase rate in orders are defined by the experts and given in Figure 2, Figure 3, and Figure 4, respectively.

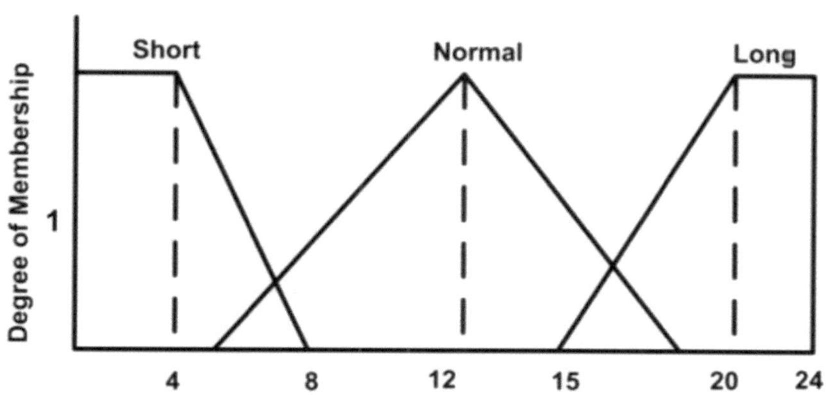

Fig. 2. The MFS of delivery time

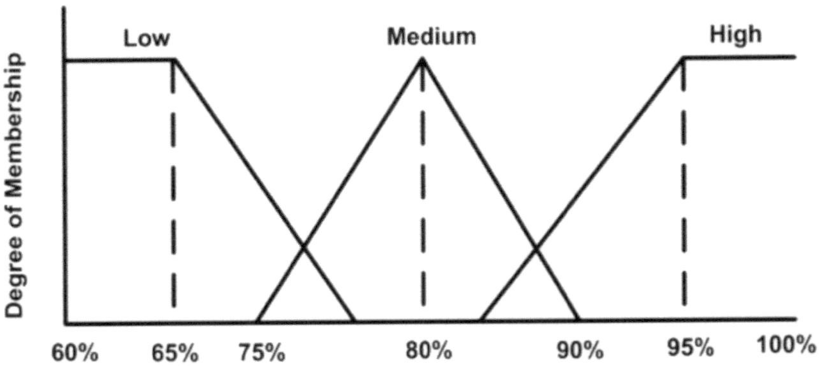

Fig. 3. The MFS of quality of product

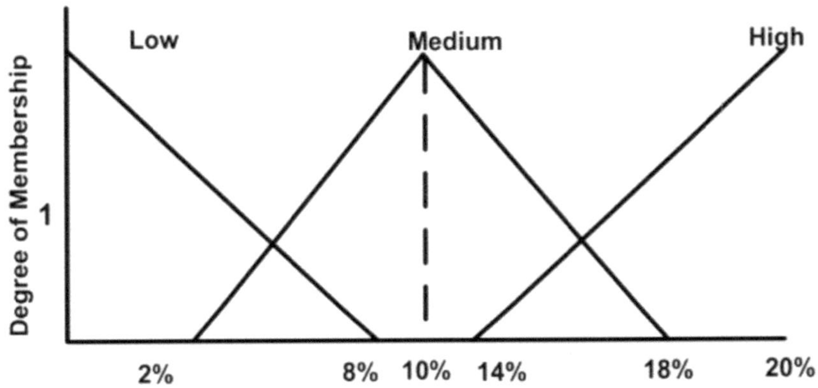

Fig. 4. The MFS of increase rate in orders

By implementing the input data into the system, the probability distribution of expected increase rate in orders is generated as shown in Table 1. In addition, the experts' also predict the expected cost savings rate (r) which is delivered by KMS investment with probabilities of 10%, 30% and 60% as shown in Table 2.

Probability (%)	Delivery Time (h)	Quality (%)	Increase Rate in Orders (%)
0	48	65	3.3
30	30	80	10
60	20	95	18.5

Table 1. The expected increase in sales

Probability (%)	Cost saving rates (%)		
	Labor Cost	Material Cost	Cost on Final Products
10	2	6	15
30	3	8	20
60	5	10	25

Table 2. The expected cost saving rates

6. Model of cost-benefit Impact to KMS investment

In the KMS cost-benefit analysis of KMS investment, the costs calculation is structured by capital expenditures (C_{Xn}) and operating expenditures (C_{Yn}). On the other hand, the benefits of KMS (B) that calculated in Eq. (2) are derived from revenue increase (RI) and costs saving such as annual purchase material cost saving (CS_m), cost saving on final product (CS_i), and labor cost saving (CS_l). Indeed, the variables of total benefit are calculated considering the increase rate in orders (s) which has been estimated by fuzzy rule based system as shown in Table 1. The increased orders (S') is calculated by Eq. (3).

$$B = (CSm + CSi + CSl) + RI \tag{2}$$

$$S' = S(\mu,\sigma)\ x\ (1+s) \tag{3}$$

where $S(\mu,\sigma)$ is the yearly orders with a mean μ and standard deviation σ. The cost savings are computed considering the increased orders (S'), cost unit (c), cost saving rates (r) as shown in Table 2. The cost saving is calculated by Eqs. (4)-(6).

$$CS_m = S' + c_{material} + r_{material} \tag{4}$$

$$CSi = S' + c_{final\ product} + r_{final\ product} \tag{5}$$

$$CSl = S' + c_{labor} + r_{labor} \tag{6}$$

The revenue increase is calculated considering yearly total orders (S), the increase rate in orders (s) and profit for each unit (p) in Eq. (7). Finally, the NPV of the total KMS investment is determined for n years in Eq. (8) where i indexed as discount rate.

$$RI = S(\mu,\sigma)\ x\ s\ x\ p \tag{7}$$

$$NPV = -(C_{X1} + .. + C_{Xn}) + \sum_{n=1}^{t} \frac{[B - (C_{Y1} + .. + C_{Yn})]}{(1+i)^n} \tag{8}$$

In relation to investment analysis, the Monte Carlo simulation is the appropriate method for estimating the impact of KMS costs and benefits to the investment result by randomizing value from each of the uncertain variables and calculating the objective or target value of the investment model (Hacura et al., 2001). This method uses random numbers from probability distributions of increase rate in orders and cost saving rates to compute the probability distribution of NPV, which meant not only produce one value of NPV.

7. Simulation, results, and discussion

The simulation to calculate the NPV of KMS investment is carried out using software Crystal Ball Version 7.2.1. In addition, the simulations are run 500 times to minimize the possible errors arising from the random variables. A simulation generates the probability distribution for the total revenue increase, the total cost saving, and the total benefit which is the sum of total revenue increase and total cost saving as shown in Fig. 5, 6, and 7 respectively. Furthermore, the distribution of NPV in 3 years horizon is shown in Fig. 8 with the probability of a discount rate (i) of mean of 8% and standard deviation of logarithmic value of 0.22. The cost savings of material, labor and method on a final product are

computed considering the increased orders, unit costs and cost saving rates using Eqs. (3)–(6). For calculating the total revenue increase, the estimated demand increase of the company is multiplied with the profit for each unit as in Equation (7). The total yearly benefit is calculated by Eq. (1), while the NPV by Eq. (8).
According to the results of the simulation, the cost saving varies between USD35,675 and USD64,772 while the revenue increase varies between USD38,128 and USD296,894. The simulation result for total benefit varies between USD75,307 and USD360,368. The distribution of the NPV of KMS investment has the mean value of USD355,492 and the standard deviation USD254,519, which varies between USD -48,705 and USD731,091.

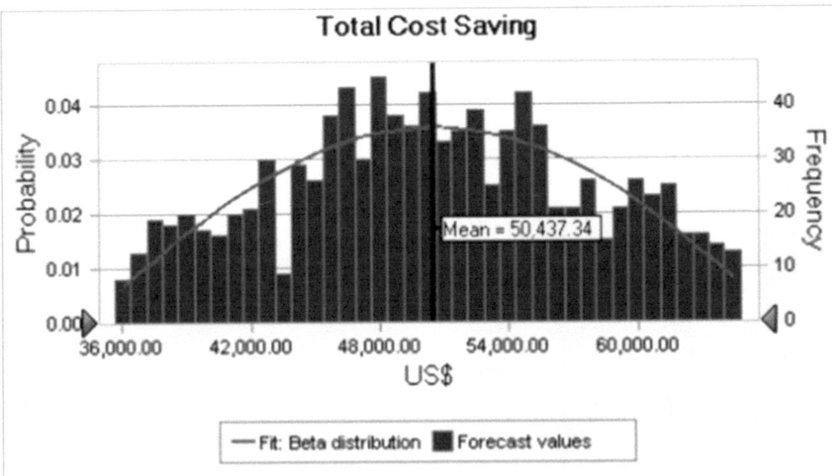

Fig. 5. The simulation results for the total cost saving

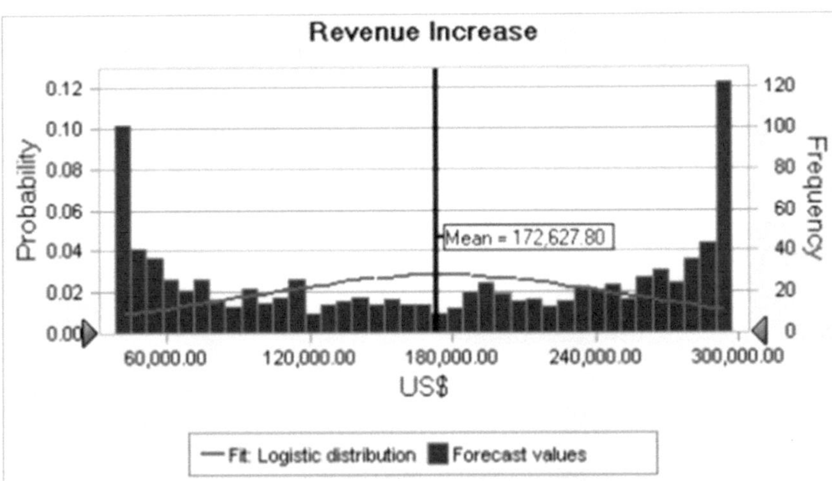

Fig. 6. The simulation results for the total revenue increase

The NPV, which is defined as the difference between a present value of cash inflow and cash outflow by considering a discount rate is important for managers to know whether the attractiveness of an investment is good or bad. If NPV is positive, then the investment decision is acceptable. Otherwise, the investment should be rejected.

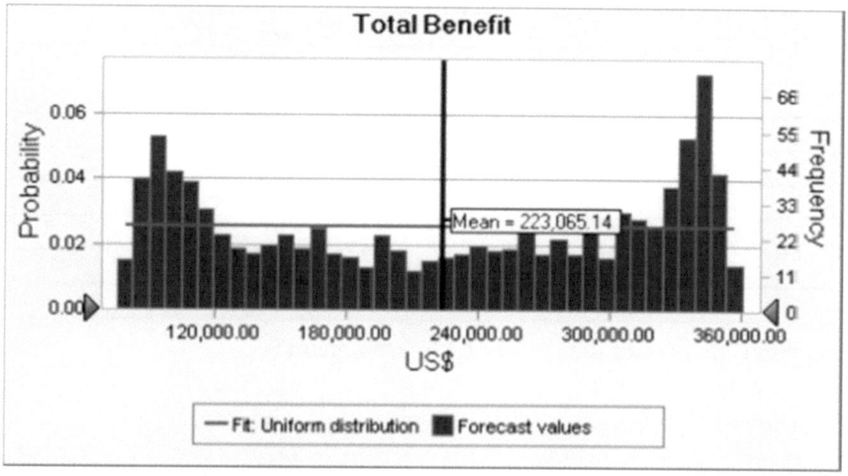

Fig. 7. The simulation results for the total benefit

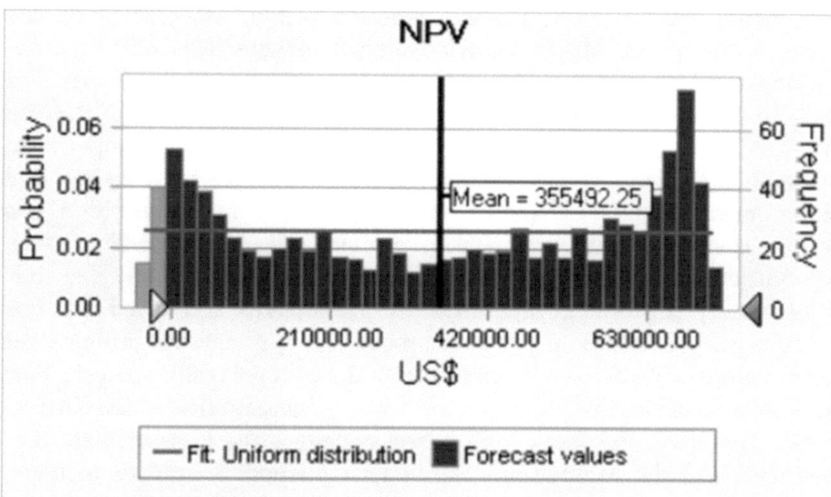

Fig. 8. The simulation results for the NPV of KMS investment

As shown in Table 3, the KMS investment for three years horizon is more than 90% certainty that the NPVs will be positive. Therefore, the managers of the software house company ABC should decide to invest in KMS. However, there is small probability (<10%) that the KMS investment will be a loss with an amount of less than -USD48,705. This may be due to the uncertainty or risk of economic constrained, which can be represented by probability distribution of the discount rate. As a summary, although the managers should invest the KMS, they should also consider the small probability of loss by ensuring the effective performance of the KMS. In order to ensure that KMS performance is effective, the managers should assure both IT infrastructure support as well as the employee participants for the KMS adoption.

Probability (%)	Net present value of KMS investment (USD)
0%	(48,705)
10%	7,401
20%	57,059
30%	151,300
40%	251,613
50%	377,746
60%	473,571
70%	573,595
80%	642,519
90%	681,202
100%	731,092

Table 3. Percentile analysis of the NPV of KMS investment

8. Conclusion

Knowledge management system (KMS) is developed to support and enhance the processes of knowledge creation, storage or retrieval, transfer, and application. There are some benefits that can be achieved by implementing KMS such as increased employee productivity, better quality of a finished product, production and labor cost saving. However, many enterprises fail in knowledge management activities, because they are unwilling to invest time and money in developing the knowledge when they do not know how to measure the benefits. For managers, it is very important to accurately measure the benefits of a KMS investment in the planning phase. Using the most proper attractiveness evaluation methods, the managers can take the accurate decisions on KMS investment.

In this study, attractiveness evaluation of a KMS investment within a company is investigated by cost-benefit analysis. The investment cost of the KMS is categorized in capital expenditures and operating expenditures. On the contrary, the cost saving, increasing the quality of products, and employee productivity and speed are considered as the benefits. The purpose of this paper is to propose an approach for bridging the tangible and intangible values of KMS investment into a model of cost-benefit analysis. Furthermore, an integrated model considering the expected revenue increase due to the KMS investment is determined. Therefore, the fuzzy rule based system is used to calculate the expected revenue increase, and the Monte-Carlo simulation method is applied to determine the expected NPV of KMS investment at different certainty levels. In the future study, the proposed model will be improved by considering risk and opportunity factors in KMS investment evaluation. In decision-making, there are criteria that are opposite in direction to other criteria, such as criteria in benefits (B) versus those in costs (C), and criteria in opportunities (O) versus those in risks (R). Thus, the BOCR should be involved into a quantitative financial model to assist the managers in KMS investment decision.

9. References

Alavi, M., & Leidner., D. E. (2001). Review: Knowledge management and knowledge management:Conceptual foundations and research issues. *MIS Quartely, 25*(1), 107-136.

Anderson, M. (2002, November). Measuring intangible value: The ROI of knowledge management. ASTD Links, 1(5). Retrieved July 7, 2003, from ASTD Links Web site: http://www1.astd.org/news_letter/November/Links/anderson.htm

Berry, S., & Waldfogel, J. (2010). Product Quality and Market Size. *The Journal of Industrial Economics, 58*(1), 1-31.

Chang, P.-C., Liu, C.-H., & Wang, Y.-W. (2006). A hybrid model by clustering and evolving fuzzy rules for sales decision supports in printed circuit board industry. *Decision Support Systems*, 42, 1254-1269.

Chen, C.-J., & Huang, J.-W. (2009). Strategic human resource practices and innovation performance -- The mediating role of knowledge management capacity. *Journal of Business Research, 62*(1), 104-114.

Chen, M.-Y., Huang, M.-J., & Cheng, Y.-C. (2009). Measuring knowledge management performance using a competitive perspective: An empirical study. *Expert Systems with Applications*, 36(4), 8449-8459.

Grossman, M. (2006), "An Overview of Knowledge Management Assessment Approaches", *The Journal of American Academy of Business*, 8(2): 242-247.

Hacura, A., Jadamus-Hacura, M., & Kocot, A. (2001). Risk analysis in investment appraisal based on the Monte Carlo simulation technique. *The European Physical Journal B - Condensed Matter and Complex Systems*, 20, 551-553.

Hamundu, F. M., & Budiarto, R. (2010, 24-26 March 2010). *A Fuzzy Inference System Approach for Knowledge Management Tools Evaluation. International Conference on Computer Modelling and Simulation, 2010* uksim, pp.305-310, 2010 12th.

Jungpil, H., & Mani, R. S. (2000). A framework of knowledge management systems: issues and challenges for theory and practice. *Paper presented at the Proceedings of the twenty first international conference on information systems.*

Khandelwal, V. K., & Gottschalk, P. (2003). Information technology support for interorganizational knowledge transfer: An empirical study of law firms in Norway and Australia. *Information Resources Management Journal, 16*(1), 14-23.

Law, C. C. H., & Ngai, E. W. T. (2008). An empirical study of the effects of knowledge sharing and learning behaviors on firm performance. *Expert Systems with Applications, 34*(4), 2342-2349.

Martin, K. (2002). Show me the money: Measuring the return on knowledge management. Retrieved July 7, 2003, from http://www.llrx.com/features/kmroi.htm

Ngai, E. W. T., & Chan, E. W. C. (2005). Evaluation of knowledge management tools using AHP. *Expert Systems with Applications, 29*(4), 889-899.

Nonaka, I. (1991). The knowledge creating company. Harvard Business Review, 69(6), 96–104.

Phillips-Wren G.E., Hahn E.D. and Forgionne G.A. (2004); A Multiple Criteria Framework for Evaluation of Decision Support Systems. Omega, 32:323-332

Plessis, M. d. (2007). The role of knowledge management in innovation. *Journal of Knowledge Management, 11*(4), 20-29.

Tang Y. and Beynon M. J.(2005);Application and development of Fuzzy Analytical Hierarchy Process within a capital Investment Study. *Journal of Economics and Management*, 1(2):207-230.

TBC[Treasury Board of Canada] (1998); Benefit cost analysis guide. Downloaded on February 2007 from http://www.tbssct.gc.ca/fin/sigs/revolving_funds/bcag/bca2_e.asp

Tosun, M., Dincer, K., & Baskaya, S. (2010). Rule-based Mamdani-type fuzzy modelling of thermal performance of multi-layer precast concrete panels used in residential buildings in Turkey. *Expert Systems with Applications, 38*(5), 5553-5560.

Tseng, S.-M. (2008). The effects of information technology on knowledge management systems. *Expert Systems with Applications, 35*(1-2), 150-160.

Ustundag, A., Kilınç, M. S., & Cevikcan, E. (2010). Fuzzy rule-based system for the economic analysis of RFID investments. *Expert Systems with Applications, 37*(7), 5300-5306.

Uzoka, F. (2009). Fuzzy-Expert system for cost Benefit Analysis of Enterprise information systems, A Frame work. I*nternational Journal on Computers Science and Engineering,* 1(3):254–262

Wagner, H. T., Dum, T., Scha, x, fferling, A., & Schulz, M. (2011, 4-7 Jan. 2011). The Effect of Knowledge Management Systems on Absorptive Capacity: The Case of a German Law Firm. *Paper presented at Hawaii International Conference on the System Sciences (HICSS), 2011 44th*

Vestal, W. (2002). Measuring knowledge management. Retrieved July 7, 2003, from Knowledge Management Advantage Web site: http://www.kmadvantage.com/docs/km_articles/Measuring_km.pdf

Zack, M. (1999). Managing codified knowledge. Sloan Management Review, 40(4), 45–58.

Zadeh, L. A. (1965). Fuzzy Sets. *Information and Control, 8*, 338-353.

6

The Semantic Web-Based Collaborative Knowledge Management

Lemen Chao[1,2], Yong Zhang[2] and Chunxiao Xing[2]
[1]*Beijing Institute of Petrol-Chemical Technology, Beijing*
[2]*Research Institute of Information Technology, Tsinghua University, Beijing*
P. R. China

1. Introduction

The current knowledge processing models can be classified into two categories—Man's Knowledge Processing Model and Machine's Knowledge Processing Model—according to literature reviews of knowledge processing studies in knowledge management and Artificial Intelligence. Man's Knowledge Processing Model is based on knowledge management theory, especially the Second Generation Knowledge Management (SGKM), and focuses on processing tacit knowledge by human brains. Machine's Knowledge Processing Model is based on Artificial Intelligence or First Generation Knowledge Management (FGKM), and engages in processing explicit knowledge by computers. Furthermore, there are two challenges faced by current research of knowledge processing. One of these challenges is how to break through bottlenecks in the two knowledge processing model by lowering the cost of knowledge sharing and innovation and adopting machine-readable knowledge reorientation technology; the other one is how to make full use the complementary advantages of human and computer through combining the two models [1].

In this chapter, we carry out in-depth study of knowledge life cycle on the semantic web and propose the model for collaborative knowledge processing and its implementation framework. The remainder of this paper is organized as follows. In Section 2, we review the development of semantic web technologies and discuss machine readability of semantic web knowledge representation. In the next part, section 3, we describe the knowledge life cycle on the semantic web. Then, section 4 proposes a model for collaborative knowledge management on the semantic web and section 5 discusses how to implement the model. Section 6 provides a case study by analyzing the FOAF project. In the conclusion (section 7) some topics that should be further studied are proposed.

2. Related work

The term "Semantic Web" was coined by Tim Berners-Lee in 1998 and defined as not a separate Web but an extension of the current one, in which information is given well-defined meaning, better enabling computers and people to work in cooperation [2]. The layer cake framework of the semantic web implicates that the development of Semantic Web technologies proceeds in steps and each step building a layer on the top of another. It mainly includes seven different layers, namely Unicode and namespace, XML, RDF(S), ontology, logic, proof and trust. Two principles, those are downward compatibility and upward partial understanding, were usually recommended to build adjacent layers [3].

There has been noticeable improvement in the studies of semantic web technologies over the past ten years. Some of them, especially the technologies at lower levels of the layered cake, such as XML, RDF(S), OWL and SPARQL, have been standardized by W3C knowledge representation, knowledge searching, knowledge mining, semantic web services, semantic grid, application integration and social network analysis are becoming research hotspots in knowledge processing. Project10X examined over more than 270 companies providing semantic products and services and published a semantic web wave report[4].The ReadWriteWeb picked out top ten semantic web products of 2009[5], including Google Search Options , Rich Snippets, Open Calais 4.0,BBC's Semantic Music Project, Freebase, and Data.gov.

It is one of revolutionary innovations in the semantic web that human-centric knowledge representation, which has been widely used in traditional web, is substituted for machine-centric knowledge representation. Therefore, knowledge on the semantic web is machine-readable. Machine readability of semantic web knowledge representation is implemented by:

2.1 Knowledge atom

The semantic web makes it possible to process knowledge by a smallest atomic unit of it. There are two knowledge representation technologies are commonly used on the semantic web, one is XML-based RDF(S) and the other is OWL Language. However, the core ideas behind them are similar: describing a knowledge atom as an object-attribute-vale triple and converting non atomic knowledge representation units into knowledge atoms by Reification Mechanism. Take a knowledge atom that represents 20100808's name is Zhang as example, its XML based RDF syntax knowledge representation is the following:

```
<?xml version="1.0" encoding="UTF-8"?>
<rdf:RDF xmlns:owl=http://www.w3.org/2002/07/owl#
xmlns:rdf="http://www.w3.org/1999/02/22-rdf-syntax-ns#"
xmlns:rdfs="http://www.w3.org/2000/01/rdf-schema#"
xmlns:my="http://www.chaolemen.com/ University#" >
<rdf:Description rdf:about="20100808">
   <my:name>Zhang</my:name>
</rdf:Description>
</rdf:RDF>
```

2.2 Machine readability of knowledge atom

The meaning of knowledge atom is declared in domain ontology which is written by XML-based RDF schema or OWL language. Therefore, the semantic web allocates a unique specific meaning to each of knowledge atoms in a semantic web document and can avoid the two well-known semantic problems: homonymy and polysemy. Take knowledge atom 20100808 as example, the meaning that 20100808 represents a student could be described as follows:

```
<?xml version="1.0" encoding="UTF-8"?>
<rdf:RDF xmlns:owl="http://www.w3.org/2002/07/owl#"
xmlns:rdf="http://www.w3.org/1999/02/22-rdf-syntax-ns#"
xmlns:rdfs="http://www.w3.org/2000/01/rdf-schema#"
 xmlns:my="http://www.chaolemen.com/University#" >
<rdf:Description rdf:about="20100808">
   <rdf:type rdf:resource= "&my;Stuedent"/>
   <my:name>Zhang</my:name>
</rdf:Description>
 </rdf:RDF>
```

2.3 Machine readability of relation between knowledge atoms

The machine readability of knowledge atom is a necessary condition for that of web knowledge and not the sufficient condition of it. There is another necessary condition which is machine readability of relations between knowledge atoms. Semantic web makes it possible to represent the knowledge relations in machine readable syntax. For example, a knowledge atom 20101881 is the teacher of another knowledge atom 20100808, the machine readable relation between them can be shown as follows in XML-based RDF(S) syntax.

```
<?xml version="1.0" encoding="UTF-8"?>
<rdf:RDF xmlns:owl="http://www.w3.org/2002/07/owl#"
 xmlns:rdf="http://www.w3.org/1999/02/22-rdf-syntax-ns#"
 xmlns:rdfs="http://www.w3.org/2000/01/rdf-schema#"
   xmlns:my="http://www.chaolemen.com/University#" >
<rdf:Description rdf:about="20101881">
   <rdf:type rdf:resource= "&my;Teacher"/>
   <my:name>Wang</my:name>
   <my:isSupervisorOf rdf:resource="20100808"/>
</rdf:Description>
 </rdf:RDF>
```

3. Knowledge Life Cycle on the semantic web

Knowledge Life Cycle (KLC) is one of the most important concepts in New Generation Knowledge Management (NGKM). The NGKM for the first time allows for the production of new knowledge in knowledge management, while the First Generation Knowledge Management concerns itself mainly with the distribution, sharing and use of existing knowledge. Existing knowledge can be categorized into knowledge in human brain and knowledge stored on the Web. In this paper, the topic is just limited to the existing knowledge, namely knowledge stored on the Web.

The production of new knowledge form existing knowledge mainly relies on the technologies of Artificial Intelligence (AI) to date. However, the AI hasn't made much progress with knowledge production yet.

Semantic Web is not a separate Web but an extension of the current one, in which information is given well-defined meaning, better enabling computers and people to work in cooperation[6]. Semantic web having well structured data provides a new solution for producing new knowledge based on existing knowledge.

3.1 KLC in next generation knowledge management

KLC shown as Figure 1 was developed by members at the Knowledge Management Consortium International (KMCI), especially by Joseph M. Firestone and Mark W. McElroy[7]. In that Figure, the life cycle of knowledge is a continuum regime of knowledge process and it can be divided into three fundamental phases: knowledge production, knowledge validation and knowledge integration.

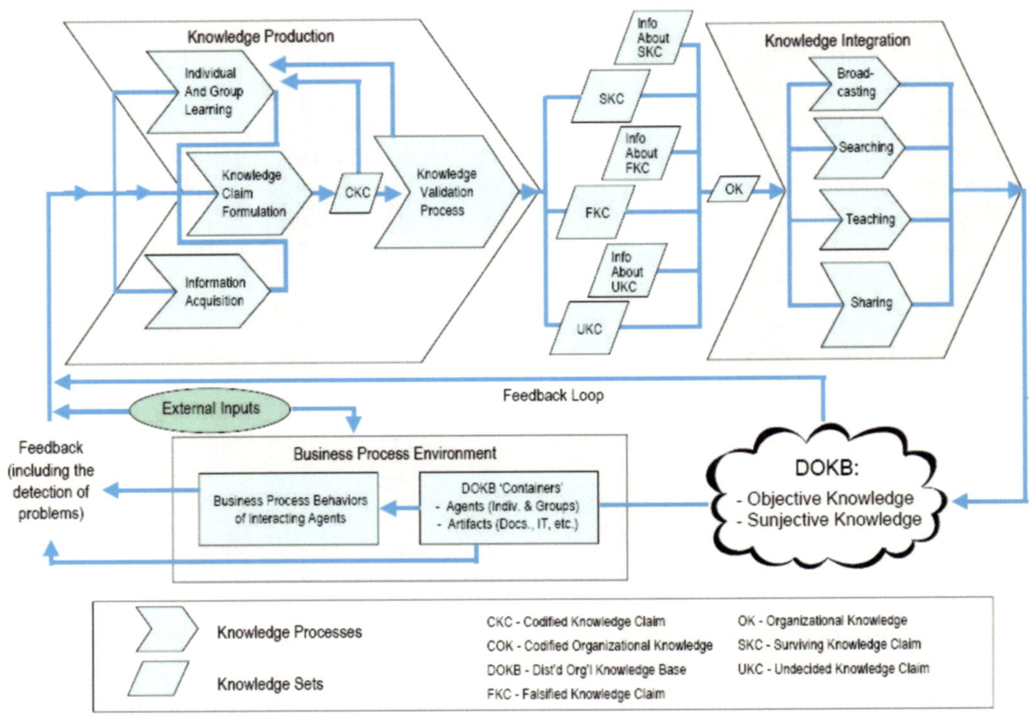

Fig. 1. KLC in NGKM (Source: Mark W. McElroy, The new knowledge management: Complexity, learning, and sustainable innovation, KMCI Press, USA, 2002.)

The theoretical foundation of KLC is Complex Adaptive System Theory (CAS theory). This theory views a system as a fluidly changing collection of distributed interacting components that react to both their environments and to one another. Therefore, CAS theory makes KLC possible to study organizational knowledge management from a new perspective, in which the complexity of managing knowledge comes from not only the external environment, but also the internal adaptive components.

The most significant contribution of KLC to knowledge management is for the first time arguing that the knowledge process is one kind of natural process of living systems. The first generation knowledge management theory places too much emphasis on supply side of knowledge process (such as the sharing and use of existing knowledge), while neglecting the importance of demand side knowledge process (including the production, validation and integration of knowledge).The introduction of KLC changes the conventional ways of thinking on knowledge management into a more effective way – Next Generation Knowledge Management (NGKM).

3.2 KLC on the semantic web

Semantic Web makes it possible for AI to manage the knowledge on the web effectively. Semantic Web is an evolving extension of the World Wide Web in which the semantics of information and services on the web is defined, making it possible for the web to understand and satisfy the requests of people and machines to use the web content [2]. Therefore, this new technology will definitely introduce a new research domain into current knowledge management theory.

Contrary to knowledge in human organizations, the knowledge on semantic web is created, processed, stored, and transferred by machine agents, not directly by human brain. Semantic knowledge management turns much attention to sharing and reusing the knowledge while organizational knowledge management places more emphasis on the continuous production of new knowledge through enhancing the conditions in which innovation and creativity naturally occur and organizational learning happen. In other words, Knowledge management on semantic web belongs to supply side knowledge management while organizational knowledge management belongs to demand side knowledge management. Currently, KLC is limited to life cycle of knowledge in human organizations, not considering the knowledge management on semantic web.

The different stages in semantic KLC are representation, interconnection, reasoning, retrieving, validation and integration (Figure 2).

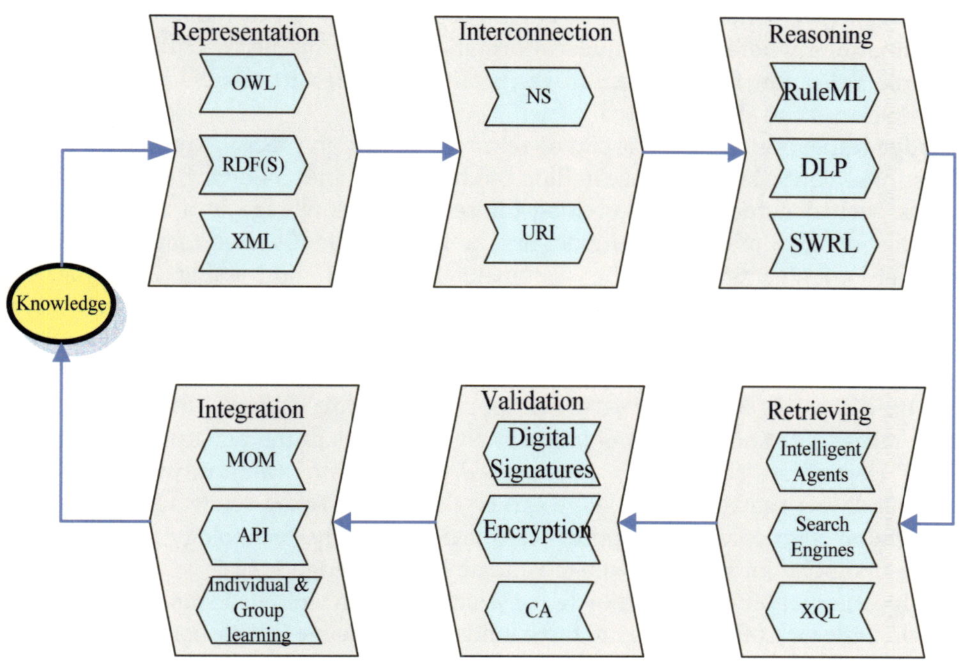

Fig. 2. KLC on the Semantic Web

(1)Knowledge representation: The main purpose of knowledge representing is changed on semantic web. Traditionally, web content is formatted for human readers rather than computer applications. As a result, the machines hardly find, organize, integrate or validate knowledge on the traditional web without man's intervention. We have been tended to believe that Artificial Intelligence is the only way to manage the web data by machines or applications. AI hasn't been, however, made much progress with data management yet and therefore many scholars of knowledge management have to grant a higher value on human-centric knowledge management instead of machine- centric knowledge management. Semantic web, for the first time, make it easier for machines to manage web knowledge because data are represented to be machine readable. The main semantic technologies to represent data semantically are Unicode, XML (Extensive markup language), RDF/RDFs (Resources Description Framework / Resources Description Framework Schema), and OWL (Web Ontology Language) [8].

(2)Knowledge interconnection: Another main purpose of semantic web is to build a web between data. Today's web is not a web of data, but a web of computers or applications. Knowledge on the current web doesn't connect with or be related to each other. Uniform(URI) and Namespace (NS) are most common used technologies to build connection between semantic knowledge.

(3)Knowledge reasoning: Semantic web's strength lies in its ability to knowledge reasoning. It is very difficult for today's web to reason knowledge because of lacking metadata and rules. Semantic web makes knowledge reasoning possible by adding semantic metadata and a rule system to semantic data. By adding new rule system to the semantic web, new knowledge can be inferred and existing knowledge can be validated. Rule system may be Monotonic or Nonmonotonic. Monotonic rule system, which is a special care of predicate logic, can be combined with semantic web by Semantic Web Rules Language (SWRL) or Description Logic Programs (DLP). No monotonic rules are useful in situations where the available information is incomplete [9]. Through RuleML, Nonmontonic rules can be represented easily and priorities to resolve some conflicts between these rules can also be added.

(4)Knowledge retrieving: Knowledge can be retrieved with high precision on semantic web. The process of semantic knowledge searching can be divided into following steps: searching for semantic web document and searching for semantic knowledge in a web document found. Intelligent agent and search engines are the most frequently used tools to search for semantic web documents. After the document is located, addressing and querying languages, such as XQL, XQuery, X-Path, RQL and SPARQL, can be used to further search for semantic web parts.

(5)Knowledge validation: As knowledge on semantic web may be redundant, out-of-date, incorrect, or distorted, it is necessary for semantic web to validate the result set of knowledge retrieving. Knowledge validation in NGKM refers to the process by which new "knowledge claims" are subjected to peer review and a test of value in practice [10]. The process of validating semantic knowledge can be carried out based on its authenticity and integrity. Digital signatures, encryption, certificate authority technology are the most prevalent technologies for semantic web to validate its knowledge.

(6)Knowledge integration: Diverse knowledge which has been validated sometimes needs to be integrated with each other. There are three kinds of knowledge integration technologies:

- Technologies to integrate knowledge with each other, such as Message-oriented Middleware (MOM), Message Broker or Adapters.

- Application programming interface (API) to integrate knowledge with applications, such as ADO.NET, ODBC, and JDBC.
- Technologies to integrate knowledge with business process including Individual and Group Learning.

Though knowledge management on semantic web is only in the initial phase, it looks quite promising. That knowledge life cycle on semantic has three features: 1) the life cycles of knowledge on semantic web is a continuums regime of knowledge process, 2) six distinct stages in semantic knowledge management are representation, interconnection, reasoning, retrieving , validation and integration, and 3) semantic knowledge management requires different methodologies or technologies for different stages.[11]

4. Modelling collabrative knowledge management on the semantic web

4.1 Web2.0 and its implications

The concept of "Web 2.0" began with a conference brainstorming session between O'Reilly and MediaLive International [12]. Web 2.0 is not a new technology, but a new shift in the application model of the World Wide Web. Design principles behind web 2.0 include: The web as platform, harnessing collective intelligence, data is the next Intel inside, end of the software release cycle, lightweight programming models, software above the level of a single device and rich user experience [13].There are some typical applications of web 2.0 such as Blog,RSS,Wiki,Tag,SNS,P2P which has been widely used on existing web. The reasons why web2.0 has been successfully accepted are as follows: users create value, networks multiply effects, people build connections, companies capitalize competences, new recombines with old, and businesses incorporate strategies [14].

	Principles	*Lessons*
1	*The web as platform*	*Leveraging customer-self service and algorithmic data management to reach out to the long tail and not just the head.*
2	*harnessing collective intelligence*	*Network effects from user contributions are the key to market dominance in the Web 2.0 era.*
3	*data is the next Intel inside*	*Database management is a core competency of Web 2.0 companies*
4	*end of the software release cycle*	*Operations must become a core competency and users must be treated as co-developers*
5	*lightweight programming models*	*Support lightweight programming models that allow for loosely coupled systems ; Think syndication, not coordination ; Design for "hackability" and remixability*
6	*software above the level of a single device*	*The PC is no longer the only access device for internet applications, and applications that are limited to a single device are less valuable than those that are connected*
7	*rich user experience*	*Companies that succeed will create applications that learn from their users, using architecture of participation to build a commanding advantage not just in the software interface, but in the richness of the shared data.*

Table 1. Design principles behind web 2.0

In contrast to web1.0, web2.0 extends the coverage of knowledge management to the long tail of organizational knowledge chain so that it can nurture knowledge ecosystems for contemporary organizations. Some of the key implications of web2.0 on knowledge processing are as following:

(1)Mass-Collaborative Knowledge Processing: It can be easily inferred from some principles behind web2.0 such as harnessing wisdom of crowds, lightweight programming models, software above the level of a single device and rich user experience, that knowledge processing activities on web 2.0 environments are mass-collaborative. All volunteers who located on long tail of organizational knowledge chains would be encouraged to participate in organizational knowledge intervention and can save the cost of knowledge sharing and innovation in organizations.

(2)Self- Organized Knowledge Processing: Web2.0 applications allow users to cooperate with each other rather than controlled by other. Wiki, for example, allows anyone not only to contribute his or her own knowledge but also to edit the knowledge provided by others Therefore, a self-organized knowledge processing platform forms on web2.0 and facilitates ongoing knowledge sharing and innovation activities in organizational knowledge ecosystems.

(3)Meta-synthestive Knowledge Processing: The three main elements of knowledge processing system -content, machine and man- can be integrated seamlessly in web2.0 environments. The increasing popularity of Internet technology highlights limitations of human brain in the speed, accuracy, strength, storage capacity, storage time and standardization of knowledge processing. As a result, computer is becoming an alternative tool of knowledge processing. The abilities of human brain and computers in knowledge processing are complementary with each other so that man-machine collaborative knowledge processing will be one of the basic models for computing knowledge on the web.

4.2 Integrating semantic web with web2.0

Table 1 conducts a comparison between the semantic web and web2.0 from a knowledge processing perspective. There is a growing awareness that integrating semantic web with web2.0 is reasonable and practical [15] .Web3.0, which is the third wave to hit the web in future, should be an integration of semantic web into web2.0 [16]. The semantic web and web2.0 are complementary with each other [17], for example the semantic web can be used for linking and reusing data across Web 2.0 communities [18].

		Web 2.0	The Semantic Web
Similarities	*Platform*	*Internet, especially world wide web*	
	Purpose	*To Improve the efficiency of Knowledge Processing*	
Differences	*Level*	*Applications*	*Data*
	Unit	*Micro contents*	*Knowledge atom*
	focus	*Man*	*Machine*

Table 2. A comparation between the semantic web and web2.0

According to the seven basic principles of Web2.0 and main outcomes of organizational knowledge management, we can propose a novel collaborative knowledge management model by the holistic systems approach. The model has three different layers: knowledge chain management, knowledge base management and knowledge ecosystem management, as shown in Figure 3. These three levels correspond to the three different objectives of organization knowledge management respectively: accumulating or creating organizational knowledge, mining or utilizing organizational knowledge and building a knowledge ecosystem for the organization. The theoretical foundation of knowledge chain management is Web2.0 based organizational knowledge management. Knowledge chain management plays a role of knowledge provider for organizational knowledge base. The management of knowledge base in turn could promote the further development of the knowledge chain management. Knowledge base management is a prerequisite for building a knowledge ecosystem and a well developed knowledge ecosystem can provide a better environment for construction of knowledge base. Organizational knowledge management should cultivate its knowledge chain, knowledge base and knowledge ecosystem at the same time.

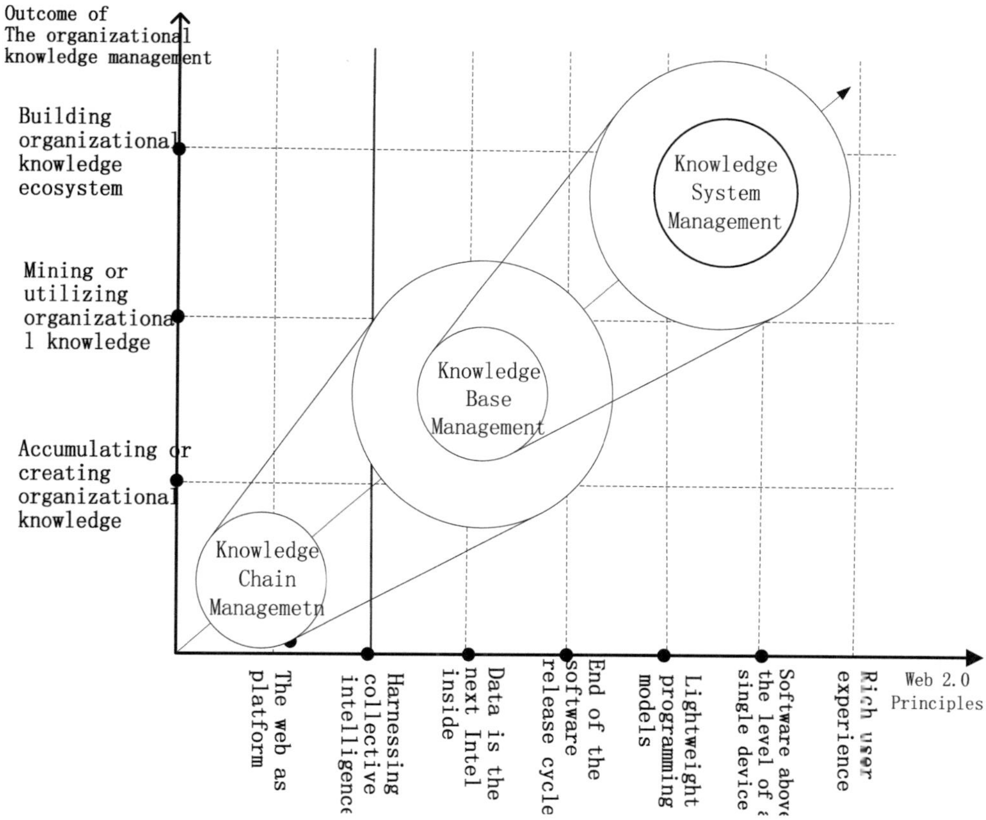

Fig. 3. A Model for Collaborative Knowledge Management on the Semantic Web

5. Implementing collaborative knowledge management on the semantic web

Figure 4 introduces a new framework that integrates semantic web with web2.0 to make full use the mutually complementary natures of them. The framework consists of following five layers in top-down direction: user layer, application layer, computing layer, knowledge layer and networking layer. The building activities of the five different layers should also follow the two basic principles of semantic web layered cake -downward compatibility and upward partial understanding- has been discussed in previous section.

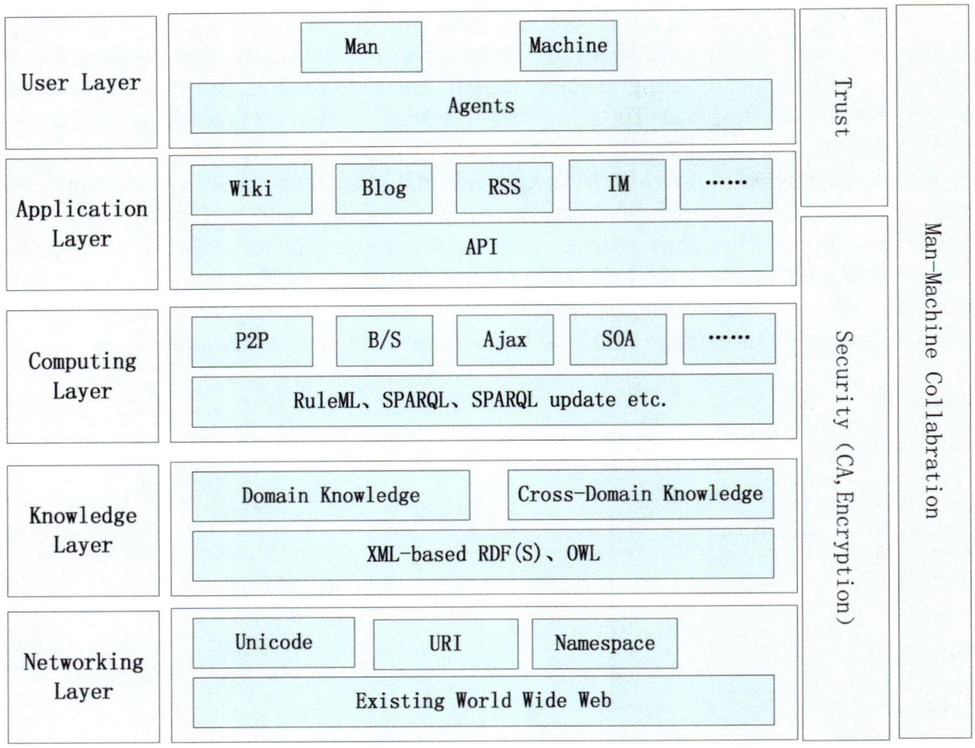

Fig. 4. Knowledge Processing Framework for Integrationg Semantic Web with Web2.0

5.1 Networking layer

The new framework is built on the top of traditional World Wide Web technologies and provides the knowledge layer with the services of data interconnecting and transferring. Some current web technologies, including Unicode, URI and namespaces, form part of the basic structure of this layer.

5.2 Knowledge layer

The knowledge layer is located between the networking layer and computing layer and provides the upper layer with machine readable knowledge representation services. This layer involves two kinds of knowledge: domain knowledge and non-domain knowledge. The latter can be described, retrieved, inferred and validated by the former. Unlike domain knowledge, non-domain knowledge can be maintained by collaborative efforts of domain experts and grass root users. XML-based RDF and OWL language is two most prevailing technologies in the knowledge layer.

5.3 Computing layer

The computing layer bridges the gap between the computing layer and the application layer and be responsible for knowledge retrieving, inferring, extracting and mining of the whole framework. Therefore, its knowledge processing technology depends on the two other layers. Some semantic web knowledge processing technologies, including RuleML,SPARQL and SPARQL-update , are used for knowledge computing in the computing layer because of its lower layer and some web2.0 technologies, such as P2P,B/S,Ajax and SOA , are also used to keep align with its upper layer.

5.4 Application layer

The application layer is the upper layer of the computing layer and provides the user layer with web2.0 application environments, such as Wiki, Blog, RSS and IM. The layer combines web2.0 with semantic web so that improves the effects of knowledge processing by man-machine collaboration. At the same time, the technologies of Application Programming Interface are usually required in this layer for keeping its independence with computing layer.

5.5 User layer

At the top of the framework, we can find user layer including agents, men and machines. Men and machines can use web2.0 application of application layer by intelligent agents. Men, machines and agents at the long tail of organizational knowledge chain are encourage to take part in knowledge processing activities in order to build organizational knowledge ecosystems which support mass-collaborative, self-organized, and Meta-synthesized Knowledge Processing.

5.6 Trust and security

Shown as figure 1, it is evident that trust and security are common challenge for all the layers and can't be ignored by any of the layers. Therefore, a holistic security and trust solution is required in the framework. In general, the trust of two top layers- user layer and application layer - could be implemented by interaction between agents, at the same time, the security of the other three layers should use information security technologies, including encryption or certificate authentication.

5.7 Man-machine collaboration

Man-machine collaborative knowledge processing is one of most protruding features in the framework which inherits from web2.0. It should be put on top of the list to maximize the complementary advantages of man and machine when developing or selecting methods and technologies for each layer.

6. Case study

In this section, we're going to make an in-depth study of applications built on the top of FOAF project and to provide insights into the semantic web based collaborative knowledge management.

The Friend of a Friend (FOAF) is a project about creating a web of machine-readable homepages describing people, the links between them and the things they create and do[19]. The project accumulates various kinds of data, such as text, photo and records, from real practices and defines relations between different data source by social relations[20][21][22].Knowledge life cycle of a typical FOAF application is as follows:

(1) Knowledge representation. Users of these applications can publish their personnel information in FOAF language , an XML-based RDF knowledge representation language introduced by the FOAF project. The language employs classes FOAF:Agent,

FOAF:Document, FOAF:Group, FOAF:Image, FOAF:OnlineAccount, FOAF:Orgnization, FOAF:Person, FOAF:PersonalProfileDocument, FOAF:Project to represent an agent, document, group, image, account, organization, person, personal profile information or project respectively. Currently, although some tools are developed to capture FOAF information automatically from the web, the reliability of those tools is not enough to be completed the task by computers itself. The machine's knowledge presentation is in need of man's intervention. As a result, knowledge representation in FOAF project should be conducted by the collaboration of men and machines.

(2) Knowledge interconnection: The FOAF language defines tags FOAF:knows, FOAF:made, FOAF:maker, FOAF:fundBy, FOAF:member, FOAF:member, FOAF:currentProjects, FOAF:pastProjects, FOAF:SchoolHomepag to represent relationships between friends, resource and its makers, resource and its funders, organization and its members ,a project and its relevant projects, persons and schools. Therefore, applications on the top of FOAF can build a machine readable web of knowledge elements.

(3) Knowledge reasoning: Applications built on the top of FOAF can conduct social network analysis and compute the size or density of a collaborative network, degree of or distances between actors, length of a collaborative walk, diameter and radius of a collaborative network, reachability between enablers, and centrality of an agent.

(4) Knowledge retrieving: Queries of knowledge retrieving in these applications can be written in the SPARQL language, a query language for RDF recommended by W3C.As SPARQL has a good support for expressing queries across diverse data sources, applications built on the FOAF can provide cross domain data sharing and on-demand knowledge services.

(5) Knowledge validation: FOAF applications can validate the results sets of retrieving activities by integration the semantic web with web2.0. The knowledge represented by semantic web technologies has good support for machine readability and be convenient to validate automatically. However, machines are not always competent at automatic knowledge validation and in need of human intervention. Pro-Ams (Profession Amateurs) from the long tails of web2.0 applications have good domain knowledge and can be used to make up for deficiencies in knowledge validation by computers.

(6) Knowledge integration: the Knowledge validation could be followed by integration of knowledge from different sources. A semantic web-based collaborative knowledge processing system built on FOAF project has a good capability for integrating personal information with tacit knowledge, explicit knowledge or application by integration the semantic web technologies with web2.0 principles.

While FOAF is a simple application of the Semantic Web, it has been widely used in social network analysis[23], search engine[24], e-commerce partner query [25].The success of FOAF application not only stress the necessity for studying human-machine collaborative knowledge management, but also highlights the importance of human intervention in knowledge processing by computers.

7. Conclusions

The increasing popularity of Internet technology highlights limitations of human brain in the speed, accuracy, strength, storage capacity, storage time and standardization of knowledge processing. As a result, computer is becoming an alternative tool of knowledge processing. However, the human-oriented knowledge representation, which is a common feature of traditional knowledge representation technologies, makes the machines'

knowledge processing activities complex. The Semantic Web provides a new platform for Man-Machine cooperative knowledge processing because of its computer-readable knowledge representation technologies. Therefore, Man-Machine cooperative knowledge processing is becoming one of the hot research topics in knowledge management.
This chapter discussed new features of the Semantic Web-based knowledge processing, designed a model to combine the Semantic Web with Web2.0 for knowledge processing and proposed a unified framework of organizational knowledge ecosystems and knowledge processing software systems, after in-depth studies on the Semantic Web, Web 2.0 and Knowledge Ecology. Research methods such as literature review, case study, system study, and knowledge engineering methodologies are used to conduct the research.

8. Acknowledgments

This research was supported by Natural Science Foundation of China (No. 71103020), Key Laboratory of Data Engineering and Knowledge Engineering (Renmin University of China), Ministry of Education (No. KF2011001), Funding Project for Academic Human Resources Development in Institutions of Higher Learning Under the Jurisdiction of Beijing Municipality(No. PHR201108368), and National Basic Research Program of China (973 Program, No.2011CB302302).

9. References

[1] Chao Lemen. The New Knowledge Processing:Integrating Semantic Web with Web 2.0[C].2010 International Conference on Computer Application and System Modeling.

[2] Tim Berners-Lee, James Hendler, Ora Lassila.The Semantic Web[J].Scientific American, 2001(5):34-43.

[3] Grigoris Antoniou, Frank van Harmelen. A Semantic Web Primer (Second Edition) [M]. The MIT Press, 2008:17-18.

[4] Project10X. Semantic Wave 2008 Report: Industry Roadmap to Web 3.0 and Multibillion Dollar Market Opportunities[R/OL]. (2008-9) [2011-3-19]. http://www.project10x.com/.

[5] Richard MacManus. Top 10 Semantic Web Products of 2009[OL]. (2009-12-20) [2009-12-19]. http://www.readwriteweb.com/archives/top_10_semantic_web_products_of_2009.php

[6] T.Berners-Lee, J. Hendler and O. Lassila. "The Semantic Web", Scientific American, Scientific American, Inc., 2001(5), pp. 34-43

[7] Mark W. McElroy, The new knowledge management: Complexity, learning, and sustainable innovation[M], KMCI Press, USA, 2002.

[8] Thomas B. Passin, Explorer's Guide To The Semantic Web, Manning Publications Co., USA, 2004.

[9] G. Antoniou, F. Van Harmelen, a Semantic Primer, The MIT Press, London, England, 2008.

[10] Mark W. McElroy, Second Generation KM a White Paper[J], EMERGENCE, Lawrence Erlbaum Associates, Inc., 2002(3), pp. 90–100

[11] Chao Lemen,An Xiaomi,Ye Liuqi,Knowledge Life Cycle on Semantic Web,Proceedings of 2009 International Forum on Information Technology and Applications[C],IEEE Computer Society,2009.

[12] Tim O'Reilly. What Is Web 2.0,Design Patterns and Business Models for the Next Generation of Software.(2005-9-30)[2011-07-11]. http://oreilly.com/web2/archive/what-is-web-20.html.

[13] Colin White. The Impact of Web 2.0[J].DM Review, 2007(8):14.

[14] Amy Shuen.Web 2.0: A Strategy Guide[M].O'Reilly Media, Inc.2008:1-266.

[15] James Hendler, Jennifer Golbeck. Metcalfe's law, Web 2.0, and the Semantic Web [J]: Journal of Web Semantics, 2008(6):14-20.

[16] Ora Lassila, James Hendler.Embracing Web 3.0 [J].IEEE Internet Computing,2007(3):90-93.

[17] Anupriya Ankolekar, Markus Krotzsch, Thanh Tran, Denny Vrandecic. The two cultures: Mashing up Web 2.0 and the Semantic Web [J].Journal of Web Semantics, 2008(6):70-75

[18] U. Bojars, J.G. Breslin, A. Finn, S. Decker. Using the Semantic Web for linking and reusing data across Web 2.0 communities [J].Journal of Web Semantics, 2008(6): 21-28

[19] foaf-project.org. About FOAF [OL][2011-09-01]. http://www.foaf-project.org/about/

[20] Dan Brickley and Libby Miller. FOAF Vocabulary Specification 0.91 Namespace Document 2 November 2007 - OpenID Edition [EB/OL]. http://xmlns.com/foaf/spec/,2007.

[21] Edd Dumbill, XML Watch: Finding friends with XML and RDF[EB/OL] (2002-6-1) [2009-4-5]. http://www.ibm.com/developerworks/xml/library/x-foaf.html]

[22] The Friend of a Friend Project.RDFWeb: Friend of a Friend (FOAF)[OL].[2011-10-20]. http://rdfweb.org/foaf/

[23] Guillaume Erétéo, Michel Buffa, Fabien Gandon, Patrick Grohan, Mylène Leitzelman, Peter Sander.A State of the Art on Social Network Analysis and its Applications on a Semantic Web[C].In: Proc. SDoW2008 Social Data on the Web, Workshop held with the 7th International Semantic Web Conference Karlsruhe, Germany: (October 2008)

[24] Google.Social Graph API[OL].[2011-9-20]. http://code.google.com/intl/EN/apis/socialgraph/

[25] WANG Xu-ping,NI Zi-jian,HU Xiang-pei. A method of searching e-commerce partner based on FOAF and RDQL [J]. Journal of Harbin Institute of Technology, 2008(4):661-665.

7

Digestion of Knowledge in a KM System to Reveal Implicit Knowledge

Jaime Moreno-Llorena and Xavier Alamán Roldán
Universidad Autónoma de Madrid
Spain

1. Introduction

The motivation of this work is the problem of information overload in the ICT-based systems. We think network knowledge management systems have the most important characteristics of systems with this problem, but they are more scalable and controllable than others, so they might be used as a research experimental model.

Our assumption is that there are several hidden aspects in the systems with information overload, which can be used to try to solve this problem. On the one hand, taking advantage of the excess energy of the active elements that are involved in the systems, such as users, services or applications and other entities related to them. One the other hand, using the properties of both the elements and the activities related to the systems affected by the problem, such as network, active entities, information and knowledge involved, or processes and interactions of these elements and activities.

In applying this assumption to proposed simplified experimental model of knowledge management systems, we try to discover ways to reduce information overload in these systems, which could be applied in broader areas such as the Web.

Our approach is based on a knowledge management system called KnowCat (KC) (Alamán & Cobos, 1999; Cobos, 2003; Cobos & Pifarré, 2008), which is a groupware system that facilitates the management of a knowledge repository by means of user community interaction through the Web. KC achieves a selection of the best documents without supervision by anyone, using information about users' activity and users' opinion about knowledge. KC knowledge repository is formed by documents and topics structured as a knowledge tree. Each KC instance is a KC Node and has a subject, a user community and a knowledge repository. Crystallization is the KC's process of knowledge selection by its quality using information about users' activity and their opinion about the knowledge items. For more information, please see the chapter about KC in this book.

In order to support the assumption, a prototype has been developed on KnowCat, which is called Semantic KnowCat (SKC) (Moreno-Llorena, 2008; Moreno-Llorena & Alamán, 2005) incorporating ideas and techniques from different research areas that converge on the Semantic Web (Berners-Lee, 2000): Knowledge Management, Human Computer Interaction, Collaborative Work, and Data and Information Mining (Baeza & Ribeiro, 1999).

This article shows how some of the techniques and ideas mentioned are integrated to implement an Analysis Module (AM) of SKC on a KC system. This module is in charge of processing explicit knowledge of the system in order to develop another latent and return it to the system in a way that it can be used. For this reason, the module uses texts associated with the knowledge, the way the latter is structured and the way its components interact. As a result, the knowledge developed provides new access opportunities and interaction with the system and knowledge.

The knowledge tree of a KC node represents the common and shared understanding of the corresponding community on the domain dealt by the node. This tree may be considered a representation of an ontology underlying the domain (Gruber, 1993). Assignment of documents to topics in the knowledge tree involves semantic annotation of these documents within an ontology scope. This is the AM view of the knowledge tree node where it works. It is in this context, that one should be interested in the automatic annotation of documents - automatic assignment of documents to topics- (Kiryakov et al., 2004) or in mapping between ontologies -trees- with different nodes (Noy & Musen, 2002).

In AM text mining techniques that allow poorly structured textual data processing through the use of vectorial models are being used (Baeza & Ribeiro, 1999; Chang et al., 2001). These techniques are currently very popular, especially for their use in automatic indexing of the Web contents. In addition, AM uses analysis language processing (Carreras et al., 2004) appropriate for natural language processing. Application of these techniques in the field data recovery is not widely used because the computing effort of its use does not justify the benefits it provides in most common cases, where some of the texts compared are small and the repository to be dealt with is big -as it happens when using conventional search engines on the Web-. However, it seems that the situation may be different when comparing larger texts on moderate- sized repositories, which is the case we are concerned with and why we thought it would be a good idea to use this technique (Brants, 2004). There are other alternatives to this approach (Baeza & Ribeiro, 1999) that the prototype could be included in the future to contrast the results.

The ultimate aim of the module is to convert the result obtained into something useful to interact with the system and its contents. For this reason, it is essential to resolve problems related to the information filtering to be shown, typical of recommendation systems (Adomavicius & Tuzhilin, 2005), and with data visualization (Geroimenko & Chen, 2002).

To check the viability of the proposed approach several experiments have been performed with four KC nodes in learning activities carried out in the Universidad Autónoma de Madrid (Spain). The experimental results have shown evidences about how to take advantage of latent knowledge to enrich knowledge base and to facilitate the management task fulfilled by the system, the interaction among its entities and users' access to the contents that have been processed, among other interesting applications (Moreno-Llorena, 2008; Moreno-Llorena & Alamán, 2005; Moreno-Llorena et al., 2009a, 2009b). The enrichment of the proposed content seems to provide a very powerful support for automatic exchange of knowledge among knowledge management systems opening a way to the development of the latter on the semantic Web field (Berners-Lee, 2000).

2. SKC analysis module

The knowledge process that the Analysis Module (AM) produces for the Semantic KnowCat (SKC) (Moreno-Llorena, 2008; Moreno-Llorena & Alamán, 2005; Moreno-Llorena et al., 2009a, 2009b) system may be considered a digestion because its intention is to extract something new and assimilating by the system from the existing knowledge.

The AM works on the system knowledge base, depositing the result of its activity in the same repository, in a way in which both the system and users may use the module's contributions in a transparent way. The AM considers that the knowledge is formed by items. These items may be documents, topics, knowledge trees, nodes, users, etc.

With the new knowledge the system may improve the management it carries out in different ways, for instance, providing different views of the repository and new access services; simplifying users' classification of knowledge items in the system; or informing users about implicit relation between items, given the context of interaction.

Each knowledge item that is considered by the AM must have a description text associated, which may be assigned either manually or automatically; for the second option the module itself may deal with it on some occasions. The descriptive texts that are associated with the documents that SKC currently manages are the documents themselves, given that they contain textual information. In the case of the topics -that is a collection of documents-, are given by the descriptive texts of documents classified within themselves or of the subtopics they contain; although initially model texts that don´t necessarily have to be part of the system knowledge repository, may be used. Nodes are the same way in that they may be considered the root topics of a knowledge tree constituted by the topics and the documents included within it. Regarding users, several description texts may be associated with them, considering the documents or topics that, for instance, they provide or use frequently.

The AM carries out two fundamental tasks: on the one hand, it develops knowledge that is latent in the system; and on the other hand it incorporates it within the system itself in an explicit way in order to allow its exploitation. Implicit knowledge is found in relations that are established among the different knowledge items, for instance within the contents included or within interactions that ones and others establish. Explicit knowledge is incorporated into the system in its clear new state, describing the existing knowledge items, or in the form of new knowledge items that are added to the repository.

The link through the contents is established, in this approach, obtaining vectorial descriptors of the weight of the terms from text documents associated with the items. With these descriptors items may be compared, the distance that separates them may be determined and groups among them may be formed.

Associations based on the interaction between knowledge items are determined by analyzing how items relate among themselves. Like this, the way in which topics group documents and other topics in the knowledge tree of nodes may be considered, and how users provide documents to the system.

The knowledge incorporated into the system, as a result of the analysis, provides new repository exploitation opportunities. On one hand, the enriched knowledge items may be shown from new perspectives thanks to the new attributes. On the other hand, the items incorporated into the system by the knowledge assimilated by the latter, allow offering users different views of the repository and new services.

2.1 Linking by content

In our approach we have considered, initially, four types of knowledge items: nodes that are system instances in charge of the knowledge management about an area with the help of a user community; topics structured in the form of a knowledge tree that develop the different aspects of the main node topic; users that constitute the community that participates in the node; and documents that describe the different topics and are provided by the users, searched by them and which are the object of their consideration.

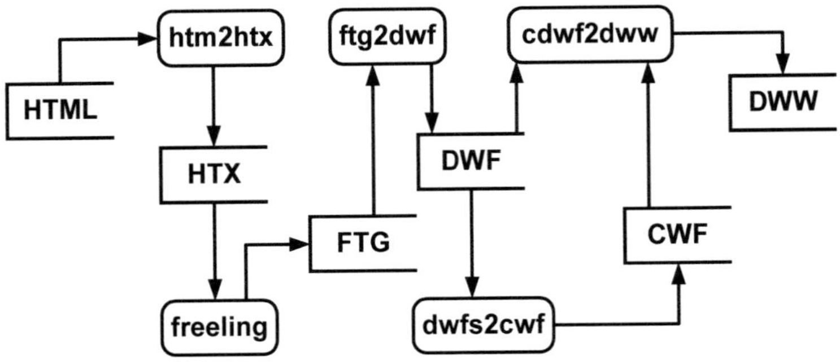

Fig. 1. Process obtaining weight of words vectors for knowledge items from HTML

It is possible to associate a text document with all the knowledge items that are considered in the system that describes them. These contributions may have several backgrounds. First, text associations to knowledge items may come from the nature of these items; for instance the documents used in experiments are textual type. Secondly, these associations may stem from the explicit relations of knowledge items with other items that already have associated texts. This occurs with topics that organize the documents, users that provide documents to the system or the node that contains both. Thirdly, text associations descriptive to the items may be inferred from more dynamic relations, like the one that is established between users and the documents that are more frequently visited by them or the ones they give their opinion about, or like the ones that are shown between documents referenced among them. Lastly, it is always possible to associate texts descriptive to the items that affect some aspects of utility, such as users' curriculums, their topics of interest, key words associated with documents or descriptions of topics. This case is completely general and may be applied to non textual documents, such as images, sound, etc.

Once a descriptive text has been associated with one of the items considered, it is necessary to put it in a way that it can be used as a comparison instrument. This is achieved by converting the text into a descriptor that shall be connected to the aspect it is referring to. For instance, if the text associated with a user describes the topics of interest for the latter, the corresponding descriptor shall refer to the users' preferences; but if the text describes the documents it itself has elaborated, the corresponding descriptor shall refer to its creative job. Like this, items shall be able to have as many descriptors as aspects of them are taken into account.

```
<html>
 <head>
    <meta http-equiv="Content-Type" content="text/html; charset=iso-8859-1">
    <title>Arquitectura de Linux</title>
 </head>
 <body text="#330033" bgcolor="#CCCCCC" link="#3366FF" vlink="#000099" alink="#FF0000">
    <center><table COLS=2 WIDTH="73%" ><tr><td>
            <h1><font color="#CC0000">Arquitectura de </font></h1>
            <center><h1><font color="#CC0000">  Linux</font></h1></center></td>
        <td><img SRC="img4.jpg" height=114 width=102></td></tr>
     </table></center>
    <hr WIDTH="100%" color="#FFFFFF">
    <h2>Introducci&oacute;n</h2>
            Por arquitectura de Linux, y
    de cualquier otro sistema operativo en general, podemos entender que es
    la relaci&oacute;n estructurada que tienen los distintos componentes del
    sistema entre ellos, para cumplir su funci&oacute;n: proporcionar al usuario
    una <b>maquina virtual</b> sobre la cual trabajar.
...
```

Fig. 2. HTML file example

In our approach descriptors are weights of words vectors that may be used to determine similarities with other vectors of the same kind and thus relate the corresponding knowledge items (Baeza & Ribeiro, 1999; Chang et al., 2001). The process for obtaining these vectors starts from the texts associated with the items. As texts may be in different formats, they need to be treated in order to obtain their contents "naked" in the form of a flat text. In our approach text files in PDF and HTML (see Fig. 2) format have been considered, although both are transformed into flat text files before starting the process.

```
Arquitectura de Linux
Introducción Por arquitectura de Linux, y de cualquier otro sistema operativo en general,
podemos entender que es la relación estructurada que tienen los distintos componentes del
sistema entre ellos, para cumplir su función: proporcionar al usuario una maquina virtual
sobre la cual trabajar.
...
```

Fig. 3. HTX file example

After the text format has been eliminated- creating flat text files HTX (see Fig. 3)- the lemmas to which the terms refer to must be identified (obviating the grammatical forms in which they are shown) and to determine the grammatical categories to which they belong. With that, references are unified to concepts, the number of different words considered is reduced and the terms with no utility are identified.

In our approach we have used FreeLing language analysis tool (Carreras et al., 2004) that facilitates obtaining all the necessary information to achieve the previous objectives. FreeLing allows to analyse a text to identify the grammatical categories to which the words that form them belong to and to determine the lemmas to which these words correspond in a reference dictionary. When FreeLing cannot find an appropriate lemma to some word, it considers it a new lemma. With all this, the tool may establish the most probable morphologic interpretation of each word that integrates the text that shall be useful to determine a semantic approach of the latter. As a result of the analysis, FreeLing provides tagged version of the text (FTG files), indicating for each appearance of a word its original form together with the lemma and the corresponding morphologic interpretation that are considered more feasible. The Fig. 4 left shows a FTG file example, where for each row, the first string is the word original form, the second is the corresponding lemma, and the third is the encoding of the grammatical category.

```
...
y y CC
de de SPS00
cualquier cualquiera DI0CS0
otro otro DI0MS0
sistema sistema NCMS000
operativo operativo AQ0MS0
en en SPS00
general general AQ0CS0
podemos poder VMIP1P0
entender entender VMN0000
que que PR0CN000
es ser VSIP3S0
la el DA0FS0
relación relación NCFS000
estructurada estructurar VMP00SF
que que CS
tienen tener VMIP3P0
los el DA0MP0
distintos distinto DI0MP0
...
```

```
...
3   2 0.66 ejecutar VMG0000,VMN0000
4   2 0.66 first NCMS000
5   2 0.66 proceso NCMS000,NCMP000
6   1 0.33 Básicamente RG
7   1 0.33 Evidentemente RG
8   1 0.33 Paralelamente RG
9   1 0.33 TM_ms:200 Zu
10  1 0.33 abierto AQ0MSP
11  1 0.33 abrir VMN0000
12  1 0.33 abstraer VMN0000
13  1 0.33 acceder VMP00PM
14  1 0.33 acceso NCMS000
15  1 0.33 acelerar VMN0000
16  1 0.33 además RG
17  1 0.33 administración NP00000
18  1 0.33 administrador NCMS000
19  1 0.33 administrar VMIP3S0
20  1 0.33 affs NCMP000
...
```

Fig. 4. FTG (left) and DWF (right) file examples

The text that has been tagged using FreeLing is processed according to its grammatical categories, in order to completely eliminate entry words that are not considered relevant for the comparison of texts, such as determiners, conjunctions or prepositions. Tags and the original form of other entries are also eliminated. In this way the original text shall remain a sequence of lemmas that already exist in the reference dictionary or that have been minted from outstanding terms that do not appear in it. In this sequence entries for different forms of the same word in the original text appear as a repetition of the same lemmas. Each lemma included in this sequence may be ascribed to a semantic interest in order to contribute to the creation of a descriptor that is the objective of the process.

By counting the appearances of each term in the sequence of lemmas, it is possible to establish the frequency of each of them. In this way, word frequency files are generated for each text associated with a knowledge item (DWF files). DWF files include only one entry for each lemma that contains the corresponding identifier and its frequency, normalised with regard to the maximum appearances of other words taken into account in the document. The Fig. 4 right shows a DWF file example, where each row corresponds to a lemma and the columns are: identifier, appearances number, frequency normalised, lemma and grammatical categories.

Following a similar process to the one described -but working on a collection of representative texts for the general use of the language being used- a reference file is generated with the frequency of words in this collection (CWF file) that represents the frequency of words in the common use of the language (Baeza & Ribeiro, 1999). The document collection is processed as if it were the text associated with a knowledge item. So that the words found and their frequency is representative for the general use of the language, the collection must be broad enough and cover general themes. In our approach the 748 articles included in El País newspaper annuals from four different years that deal with the most outstanding events that took place during that period in the main field of information such as society, culture, sports and so on, have been used.

CWF files are similar to DWF; they include one entry for each lemma, with the identifier in question and its frequency coefficient for the inverse document. This frequency is logarithm to the base ten of the quotient of the total documents in collection N, between number nk of documents where the term appears (see For.1). This coefficient is an indicator frequency of the use of the term in the general use of the language that represents the collection and indicates the rareness of the latter. The Fig. 5 left shows a CWF file example, where each row corresponds to a lemma and the columns are: identifier, appearances number, inverse frequency normalised on document collection, inverse document frequency and lemma.

$$p_{k,i} = f_{k,i} \times fdi_k = f_{k,i} \times \log \frac{N}{n_k} \tag{1}$$

Considering the word frequency files of each knowledge item (DWF), and using the Word frequency file in the reference collection (CWF), a weight for each term is established in the text associated with the item. The weight of a word in a text represents the relevance of the term in it. A term is more characteristic of a text the more frequent it is in the corresponding text and the less frequent it is in the general use of the language in which it is written. Specifically, the weight $p_{k,i}$ of a term k in a document i is the result of the normalised frequency $f_{k,i}$ of the word k in text i, by the term frequency inverse document in the collection used as reference fdi_k (see For.1).

```
...
30 298 2.510 0.400 mayor
31 290 2.579 0.412 deber
32 283 2.643 0.422 mundo
33 278 2.691 0.430 poner
34 277 2.700 0.431 alguno
35 277 2.700 0.431 tres
36 270 2.770 0.443 político
37 268 2.791 0.446 público
38 266 2.812 0.449 Gobierno
39 263 2.844 0.454 económico
40 260 2.877 0.459 decir
41 260 2.877 0.459 día
42 259 2.888 0.461 general
43 253 2.957 0.471 menos
44 252 2.968 0.473 gran
45 251 2.980 0.474 caso
46 249 3.004 0.478 cada
47 248 3.016 0.479 medio
48 246 3.041 0.483 grande
...
```

```
...
1   1 0.333 5.000 1.667 Básicamente
2   1 0.333 2.397 0.799 Evidentemente
3   1 0.333 1.971 0.657 Paralelamente
4   1 0.333 5.000 1.667 TM_ms:200
5   1 0.333 5.000 1.667 abierto
6   1 0.333 0.546 0.182 abrir
7   1 0.333 5.000 1.667 abstraer
8   1 0.333 1.306 0.435 acceder
9   1 0.333 1.175 0.392 acceso
10  1 0.333 1.261 0.420 acelerar
11  1 0.333 0.554 0.185 además
12  1 0.333 1.427 0.476 administración
13  1 0.333 2.175 0.725 administrador
14  1 0.333 2.096 0.699 administrar
15  1 0.333 5.000 1.667 affs
16  1 0.333 5.000 1.667 aleatorio
17  1 0.333 0.806 0.269 algo
18  1 0.333 5.000 1.667 algoritmo
19  1 0.333 0.431 0.144 alguno
...
```

Fig. 5. CWF (left) and DWW (right) file examples.

The vector formed by the terms that appear in the text associated with a knowledge item and their respective weights, constitutes the resulting descriptor to the process, which is kept in the form of a file (DWW files). The Fig. 5 right shows a DWW file example, where each row corresponds to a lemma and the columns are: numeric identifier, appearances number, absolute and normalized frequency on document, inverse document frequency, word weight and lemma.

DWW shall be used to compare the items among one another, calculating the level of similarity among the weight of words vectors they represent. The similarity between two vectors is the measurement of the distance between them. In this approach we have considered the distance between vectors is estimated according to the cosine of the angle they form.

$$sim(v_i, v_j) = \frac{\vec{v}_i \bullet \vec{v}_j}{|\vec{v}_i| \times |\vec{v}_j|} = \frac{\sum_{k=1}^{t} p_{k,i} \times p_{k,j}}{\sqrt{\sum_{k=1}^{t} p_{k,i}^2} \times \sqrt{\sum_{k=1}^{t} p_{k,j}^2}} \tag{2}$$

Therefore, the similarity between two vectors v_i and v_j is the scalar product of the two vectors, broken up by the product of the respective modules. The scalar product of these vectors is calculated by the sum of the components of the product p_k in each of its t dimensions. A module vector is calculated by the sum of the squares of the components of a vector (see For.2).

```
...
          c0   c1   c2   c3   c4   c5   c6   c7   c8   c9   c10  c11  c12  c13  c14  c15
          T102 T103 T104 T105 T106 T107 T109 T110 T111 T112 T53  T54  T55  T56  T57  T58
f0   D100 0.08 0.07 0.04 0.06 0.00 0.16 0.03 0.05 0.01 0.04 0.06 0.04 0.05 0.04 0.02 0.12
f1   D101 0.05 0.05 0.01 0.03 0.00 0.00 0.03 0.01 0.02 0.03 0.04 0.01 0.03 0.03 0.02 0.04
f2   D102 0.07 0.09 0.13 0.13 0.00 0.00 0.10 0.03 0.06 0.11 0.12 0.13 0.16 0.11 0.12 0.21
f3   D105 0.12 0.09 0.05 0.17 0.00 0.00 0.13 0.05 0.12 0.11 0.14 0.05 0.22 0.50 0.20 0.15
f4   D109 0.08 0.13 0.14 0.14 0.00 0.00 0.12 0.08 0.09 0.11 0.12 0.14 0.18 0.13 0.10 0.17
f5   D111 0.12 0.12 0.16 0.17 0.00 0.00 0.11 0.05 0.08 0.11 0.14 0.16 0.22 0.17 0.15 0.19
f6   D113 0.00 0.02 0.00 0.00 0.00 0.85 0.00 0.01 0.00 0.00 0.03 0.00 0.00 0.03 0.01 0.00
f7   D114 0.14 0.19 0.07 0.11 0.00 0.01 0.13 0.09 0.10 0.11 0.14 0.07 0.12 0.12 0.08 0.14
f8   D115 0.02 0.02 0.00 0.03 0.00 0.00 0.00 0.00 0.00 0.00 0.02 0.00 0.00 0.02 0.00 0.03
f9   D116 0.14 0.19 0.07 0.11 0.00 0.00 0.12 0.08 0.11 0.11 0.13 0.07 0.14 0.09 0.08 0.16
f10  D123 0.15 0.21 0.15 0.11 0.00 0.00 0.13 0.08 0.10 0.12 0.11 0.15 0.13 0.13 0.09 0.15
...
```

Fig. 6. CDF file example.

The level of similarity between two vectors is a coefficient between zero and one. The closer the value is to the unit, the more similar vectors are, and the closer to zero, the less similar they shall be. The relation of similarity established between knowledge items is described with this coefficient. In our approach the knowledge items that exceed a specific threshold of similarity coefficient of the relation between both are considered to be related. Unfortunately, this threshold may not be established neither in a fixed way nor in a general way for all cases, given that depending on circumstances such as theme nodes or the nature of the documents taken into account, the election of its value may vary greatly.
The similarity between two set of DWW is summarized in a CDF file. The Fig. 6 shows a CDF file example, where rows f_i and columns c_i represent DWW files (respectively of documents and topics in this case) and he numbers the similarity sim(f_i,c_i) between them. In Fig.6, for instance, sim(f6,c5) (similarity between the document D113 and the topic T107) is 0.85, that is much higher than sim(f6,c10) (similarity between the document D113 and the topic T53), that is 0.03.

2.2 Linking by interaction

This kind of linking between knowledge items is established by analysing how these are related to each other. In our approach we have considered the way in which the documents and the topics within the knowledge tree are organised, and how users relate to the documents they provide to the system. The analysis follows a process that goes through three stages.
Firstly, the AM establishes the knowledge items included in the tree that need to be treated. The first time that a process is carried out in a node, all the tree knowledge items must be processed, but in consecutive processes only the items that have changed need to be treated or the ones linked to these. In our approach, for instance, changes in documents affect the topics of the branch of the knowledge tree where they are located, the node and the items related to ones and others in some way, but do not affect all the elements in the repository. In this selective process of the items it seems to be essential in systems with large knowledge bases or with an intense activity.
Secondly, the AM identifies the users responsible for the valid knowledge items in the knowledge tree. In this approach only the links between users and the valid documents that they have provided to the system are considered. The text associated with each user, according to the documents they provide, is the link to all the descriptive texts. Other kind of links similar to these could be treated in a similar way.
Lastly, the AM recovers the textual components that constitute the texts associated with the knowledge items through the Web. In our approach, we have started from text documents that are linked to them in a consubstantial way, in order to establish the texts associated with other items according to the relationship (above-mentioned) taken into account among them. We have used GNU Wget program (GNU Wget, 2011) in our approach to recover files that contain textual information corresponding to the different knowledge items and to integrate them -where there are more than one- to form the descriptive texts associated. These texts are usually the link to several files; for instance the text associated with a topic shall be made up of texts associated with each document and subtopic included.

2.3 Knowledge enrichment and its exploitation

As mentioned before, in our approach the knowledge developed, as a result of the analysis process, is incorporated into the system in an explicit way; either as descriptors that describe the pre-existing knowledge items or in the form of new knowledge items.

The descriptors added to the knowledge items provide new data to show hidden aspects of the elements they describe. For instance, the interest a particular item arouses may be suitable to make it stand out among the other items or to put all in order. In addition, the most characteristic terms that an item includes may result in an interesting reference to search information related to it in other information repositories.

In our approach, the knowledge specified by the analysis process is incorporated into the system in the form of a new knowledge element category that represents the relation among items of all kinds previously considered (documents, topics, users and nodes). The links incorporated this way in the repository provide the base to offer users new multidimensional views of the knowledge and new services to facilitate its exploitation. In particular, to demonstrate this proposal we have implemented an interactive view of the graph of a relation among knowledge items in the system (see Fig. 7 left), as well as a context sensitive recommendation service that provides reference items -of different kinds- related to the item the user is working with in each moment (see Fig. 7 right).

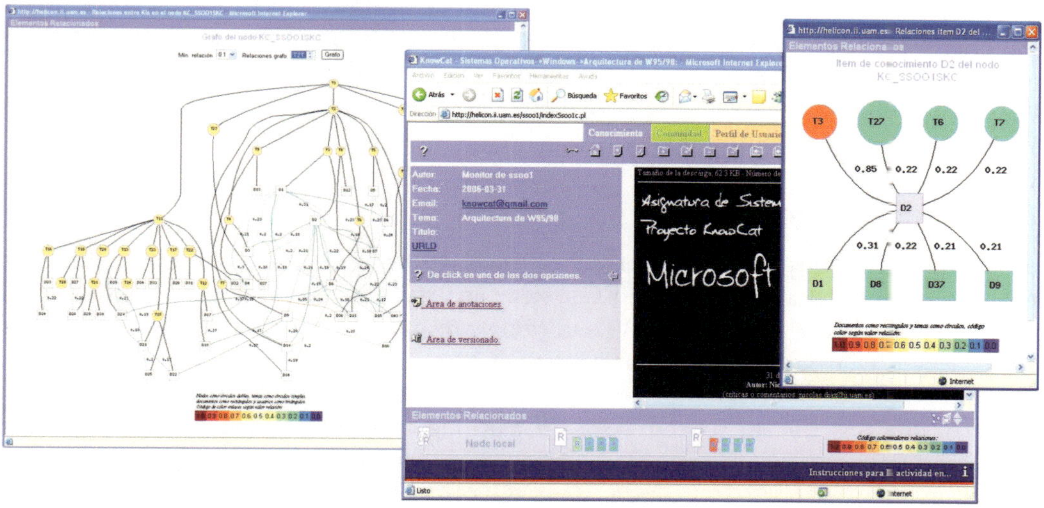

Fig. 7. Interactive view of the knowledge as graph related items (left window) and a context sensitive recommendation (inferior center window and right window).

The view in the form of a graph integrates the static relations established in the system with other dynamics that progress through time. Among the first we can find hierarchical links that join the topics of the knowledge tree or authorship links that connect users to the documents they provide to the knowledge base. Among the dynamic relations the derivation of the item's character present in the repository in each moment and the ones due to the interactions established among them as a result of the system activity may be mentioned. An example of this kind of view can be seen in the illustration above (see Fig. 7 left), where the topics are represented by orange circles, the documents by clear squares, the static relations by black lines and the dynamic relations between the items taken into

account are represented in the form of colour lines according to the level of similarity among the corresponding item vectors, included as a tag.
On the other hand, the recommendation service illustrates how to profit from the new knowledge to facilitate the use of the system and to make interaction with it more dynamic and attractive. In the illustration above (see Fig. 7 right) we can see an example of the window system showing a document and incorporating a recommendation panel on the bottom part, where representative icons of different kinds of knowledge items appear in warmer colours representing the high level of similarity among the vectors associated with the corresponding items. In addition, we can see in the window on top a representation in the form of a graph of the most important relationship that the document we are working with has with other items in the system. In this graph, as in the example of the view, the topics are represented by circles and the documents by parallelograms. However, in this case the colours of the figures represent the coefficient of similarity of the relations that link with the central knowledge item. Other services would be possible applying a similar approach, such as an assistant to locate documents in the most appropriate topic within the knowledge tree, or one to find experts in some topic or other users interested in the same subjects.
Both the view in the form of a graph and the recommendation service implemented allow navigation by mode knowledge different to the one the system allowed before making use of latent knowledge of the system. In both cases, the graphs have been generated by Graphviz (Gansner & North, 2000).

3. Experiments performed

To check the viability of these approaches, we have developed a prototype of the three elements shown that are part of the SKC system: analysis module (AM), graph visualizer for relation among knowledge items (KV) and context recommendation service (RS). They have all been incorporated into a KnowCat system (KC).
The prototype has allowed to perform several experiments with KC nodes, having been prepared for this during several years in teaching activities carried out in la Escuela Politécnica Superior de la Universidad Autónoma de Madrid. In particular, four KC nodes have been used: one node Operating Systems (OOSS); two Formal Languages and Automata Theory (FLAT); and one more Computer systems (CS).
The node Operating Systems is the result of the development of a list of topics on this subject carried out by the students during four consecutive years and which consists of a two level depth knowledge tree with over 20 topics and 350 documents.
The nodes FLAT organise different documents into two knowledge trees provided by the students during the academic year. Both nodes deal with the same subject, but in each of them the documents and the structure of the list of topics are different. Both trees have two levels, one node with 6 topics and 24 documents and the other with 12 topics and 50 documents.
Lastly, in node CS a topic about the corresponding knowledge area has been developed, hence the students from one subject have provided over 180 documents concerning around 40 different topics structured within a knowledge tree during an academic year.
The experiments carried out have been addressed to check the viability of automatic grouping of knowledge items using weight of words vectors assigned by the proposed

procedures. For this, three groups of experiments described in the following paragraphs have been performed.

3.1 Automatic grouping and classification experiments of knowledge items

In order to prove automatic grouping and classification of knowledge items three experiments have been carried out.

The first one starts from node KC on OOSS, where the two most successful documents for each item have been used to establish the weight of words vectors (WWV) for each one of them. Next, the levels of similarity between the WWV for the remaining documents and the WWV for the topics previously mentioned have been established. With these data a graph (see Fig. 8) has been obtained, where each row of points corresponds to one topic and each column to a document. The levels of similarity between documents and topics have been represented by colour points, the higher the value of coefficient, the lighter the colours. The documents have been organised into topics which students had initially classified manually.

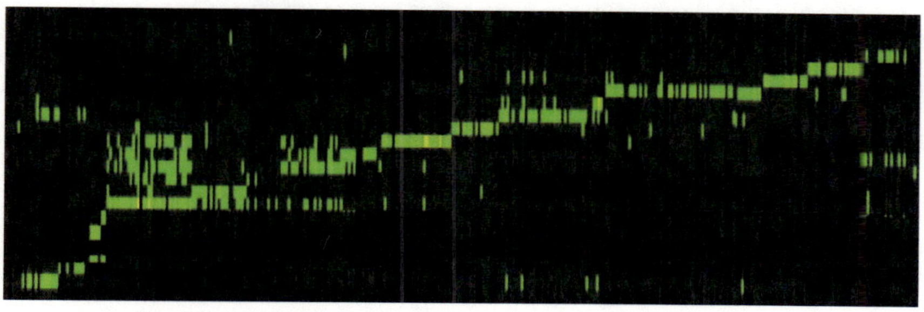

Fig. 8. Automatic classification of documents (rows) by topics (columns) in node KC on OOSS

As a result of the first experiment, in the graph we can see how the highest similarity values -lighter points- are aligned mainly in the rows that correspond to the topics in which they were classified manually. This indicates that automatic classification matches with manual classification in most cases. By analysing the anomalies a posteriori it can be seen that they correspond to ambiguous topics in which heterogeneous documents had been classified.

The second experiment compares the WWV of the documents of the original node OOSS between them. In the graph (see Fig. 9 left) each row of points -vertical and horizontal- correspond to a document and these appear organised into the topics in which they were classified manually. Like in the previous case, the levels of similarity among elements have been represented by colour points, the higher the value of coefficient, the lighter the colours.

As can be seen in the graph corresponding to this second experiment, the highest degrees of similarity are grouped into blocks around the diagonal. Under the conditions shown, this indicates that most documents are more similar to each other when they deal with the same subjects. However, in this case it is interesting to see how the light points outside the groups of the diagonal appear in bands that show how relationships among documents of similar topics are established. In the third experiment performed, the results are similar to the previous one where compared, in the same conditions, the WWV of the documents of a KC node on CS, as can be seen in the corresponding graph (see Fig. 9 right). In this case, as the number of topics is higher and the number of documents per topic is lower, groupings appear like smaller light blocks.

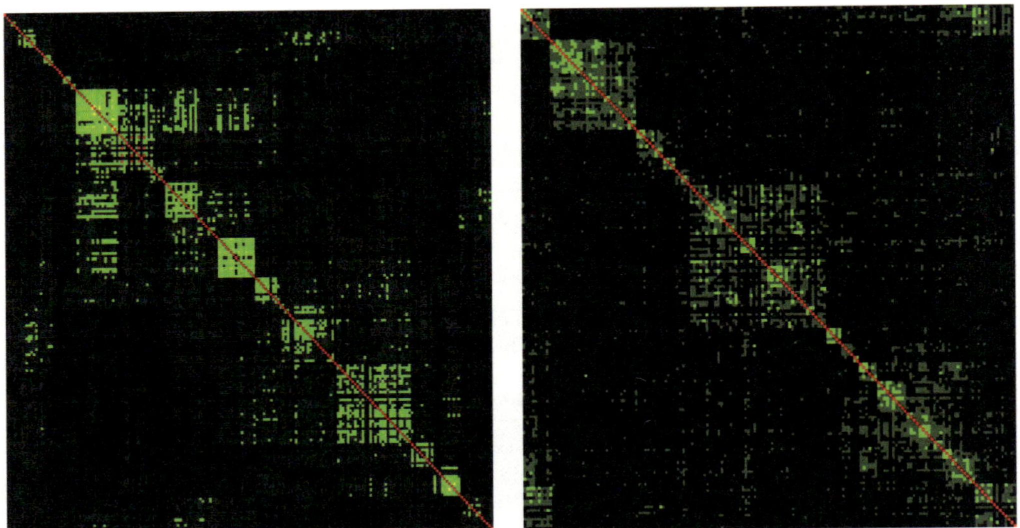

(a) OOSS KC node documents similarity (b) CS KC node documents similarity

Fig. 9. Automatic grouping of documents by topics of knowledge area

3.2 Mapping experiments among knowledge trees

In order to prove mapping among the knowledge trees that represent the ontologies which are taken into account in each node of the system, two experiments have been carried out.

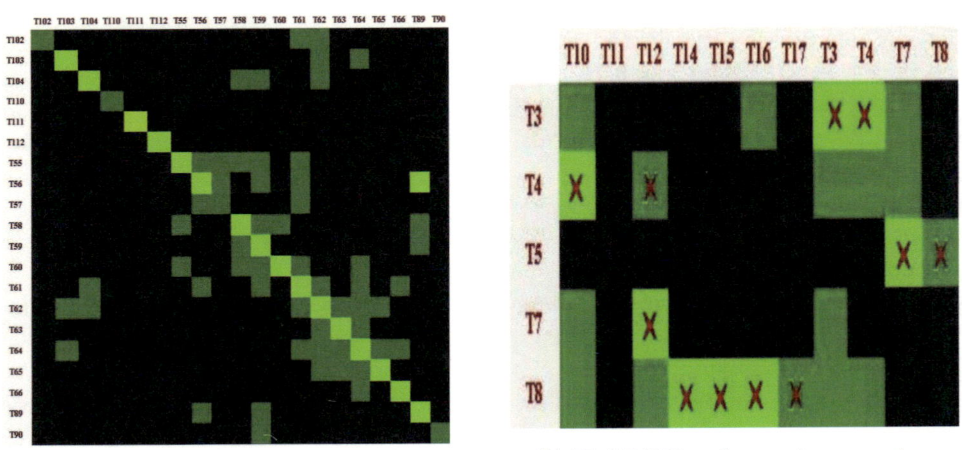

(a) OOSS KC nodes topics mapping (b) FLAT KC nodes topics mapping

Fig. 10. Mapping between topics of KnowCat nodes

In the first experiment of this series, again, we start up with KC node on OOSS, although in this case two new nodes have been created from it with knowledge trees equal to the original. The documents of the initial node have been divided up into the recently created ones, so that every couple of new homologous topics has a similar number of different documents, but relevantly similar. Later the WWV of the topics of the new nodes have been calculated and have been compared with each other. A graph (see Fig. 10 left) has been produced with the values of similarity obtained, where the lines of colour blocks correspond to the topics of one node and the columns to the other. The topics have been organised into both dimensions in order that the homologous topics are in the same position in the corresponding entries of the table. Like in previous graphs, the highest values of similarity are represented by the lighter colours.

As can be seen in the image of this first experiment, the highest grades of similarity -blocks of light colour- are over the diagonal in almost every case. With the proposed approach, this means that it is possible to identify the branches of the knowledge trees that contain documents dealing with the same topics.

For the second experiment two KC nodes on FLAT that have different trees to organise the knowledge have been used. Again the WWV of the topics have been calculated from the documents included within them and the grades of similarity have been calculated from the topics of different nodes comparing their corresponding vectors. The result is shown in a graph (see Fig. 10 right) where the topics of one node are in the axis of abscissa and the other in the organised axis. As on other occasions, the grade levels of similarity are shown in colour blocks, where again, the higher the value of coefficient, the lighter the colours. In this case, the pair of topics that are considered linked to each other through their contents by means of a manual analysis by an expert on the subject have been marked with a cross.

As a result of this second experiment, it can be seen that most of the associations made by an expert fit in over light colour blocks and that every light block is found in topic pairs associated by the expert. Therefore, it is possible to identify the proposed procedure and the topics that deal with related issues in different knowledge trees automatically.

3.3 Automatic association experiment among knowledge nodes

Starting from the documents included in five KC nodes, the one belonging to CS used in the first group of experiments, the two OOSS prepared for the previous group and the two FLAT used in the same group, a WWV has been established for each of them. In every case, the documents included in the nodes are different. By comparing these WWV a graph (see Fig. 11) has been obtained, in which each line of blocks, vertical and horizontal,

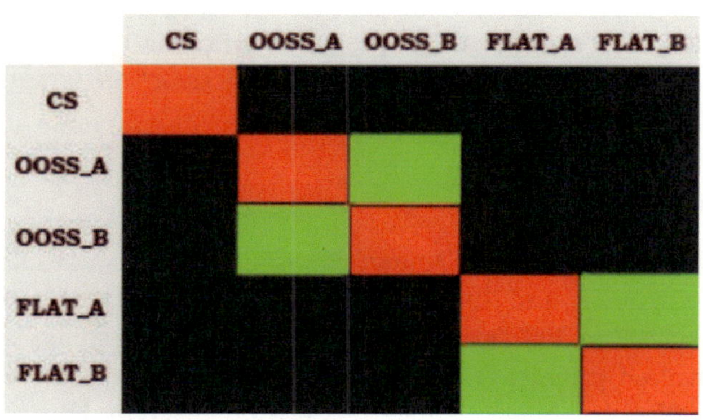

Fig. 11. Grouping of KC nodes per topics

corresponds to a node. Like in previous diagrams, the lighter colours represent a greater similarity.
In the graph we can see that the level of similarity among the WWV of the nodes that deal with the same topics are high compared with the ones obtained where comparing the node vectors on different topics. This means -using this technique- that it is possible to identify nodes that deal with similar contents and to distinguish them from others on different subjects.

4. Conclusions and future projects

Semantic KnowCat (SKC) is a prototype developed on KnowCat to investigate solutions to information overload in ICT-based systems, using knowledge management systems as a model. SKC uses for this purpose some hidden aspects of such systems, as the residual energy of their activity, and properties of both the elements and the activities involved.
The process of the digestion of knowledge proposed seems to be able to specify latent knowledge in a knowledge management field, which may be useful to facilitate the management task fulfilled by the system, the interaction among its entities and users' access to the contents that have been processed, among other interesting applications (Moreno-Llorena, 2008; Moreno-Llorena & Alamán, 2005; Moreno-Llorena et al., 2009a, 2009b). The enrichment of the proposed content seems to provide a very powerful support for automatic exchange of knowledge among knowledge management systems opening a way to the development of the latter on the semantic Web field (Berners-Lee, 2000).
However, the threshold found in the levels of similarity to consider the similar knowledge items is low and higher values are unlikely to appear. In almost every case taken into account most of the items having similarity over 0.3 are related to each other for their contents and the ones that aren't have minor levels, although some objectively related do not reach that value. In some cases the threshold is even lower, between 0.2 and 0.3. It would be highly desirable that the level of similarity would mark more clearly the space between items with different contents and would clarify the similarity between those that have similar contents.
With all this, it is considered highly interesting to continue advancing in an open line of work, paying special attention to specification and contrast of the level of similarity, and searching integration of content analysis proposed with the one for interaction of users (Moreno-Llorena et al., 2009a) and with automatic interaction among nodes (Moreno-Llorena et al., 2009b).

5. Acknowledgements

The system KnowCat and Semantic KnowCat prototype were partially financed by the Spanish Ministry of Science and Technology, project codes TIN2004-03/40 and TSI2005-08225-C07-06. From 2003 to 2007, the system KnowCat was exploited within the frame of four teaching innovation projects (TIP) financed by Universidad Autónoma de Madrid. In the scope of these TIPs, the undergraduate fellow student Javier Hidalgo has collaborated especially on the work shown here. The current research has been partially financed by

Spanish National Plan of R+D, project code TIN2008-02081/TIN, and by the CAM (Autonomous Community of Madrid), project code S2009/TIC-1650.

6. References

Adomavicius, G. & Tuzhilin, A. (2005). *Toward the next generation of recommender systems: a survey of the state-of-the-art and possible extensions,* In : IEEE Transactions on Knowledge and Data Engineering No. 17, pp. 734-749, 2005

Alamán, X. & Cobos, R. (1999). *KnowCat: a Web Application for Knowledge Organization,* LNCS 1727. Eds. Chen, P.P. et al. Springer, 348-359. 1999.

Baeza, R., Ribeiro, B. (1999). *Modern Information Retrieval.* Addison Wesley, 1999.

Berners-Lee, T. (2000). *Semantic Web - XML2000.* Available from http://www.w3.org/2000/Talks/1206-xml2k-tbl

Brants T. (2004). *Natural Language Processing in Information Retrieval.* In proceedings of CLIN 2004 Antwerp, Belgium, 1–13. 2004.

Carreras, X., Chao, I., Padró L. & Padró M. (2004). *FreeLing: An Open-Source Suite of Language Analyzers.* In proceedings of LREC 2004 Lisbon, Portugal. 2004.

Chang, G., Healey, M., McHugh, J., Wang, J. (2001). *Mining the World Wide Web: An introduction search approach.* Kluwer, 2001.

Cobos, R. (2003). *Mechanisms for the Crystallisation of Knowledge, a proposal using a collaborative system.* Doctoral dissertation. Universidad Autónoma de Madrid.

Cobos, R., Pifarré, M., (2008). *Collaborative knowledge construction in the web supported by the KnowCat system.* Computers & Education, Vol.50, No. 3, (April 2009). pp. 962-978, ISSN 0360-1315.

Gansner, E., North, S. (2000). *An open graph visualization system and its applications to software engineering.* Software – Practice and Experience, 30:1203–1233, 2000.

Geroimenko, V., Chen, C. (2002). *Visualizing the Semantic Web.* Springer, 2002.

Gruber, T. R. (1993). A *Translation Approach to Portable Ontology Specifications.* Knowledge Acquisition, 5(2), pp. 199-220, 1993.

Kiryakov, A., Popov, B., Terziev, I., Manov, and D., Ognyanoff, D. (2004). *Semantic Annotation, Indexing, and Retrieval.* Journal of Web Sematics 2, Issue 1. Elsevier 49-79, 2004.

Moreno-Llorena, J. (2008). *Collaborative Knowledge Management By Means Semantic Information.* Doctoral dissertation. Universidad Autónoma de Madrid.

Moreno-Llorena, J., Alamán, X. (2005). *A Proposal of Design for a Collaborative Knowledge Management System by means of Semantic Information.* In: Navarro-Prieto, R. et al., HCI related papers of Interacción 2004, Springer, Dordrecht, The Netherlands,. 307-319, 2005.

Moreno-Llorena, J., Alamán, X., Cobos, R. (2009a). *Modeling of User Interest Based on Its Interaction with a Collaborative Knowledge Management System.* Lecture Notes in Computer Science (ISSN: 0302-9743, impreso y 1611-3349, en línea; ISBN: 978-3-642-02579-2), 330-339, Springer Berlin / Heidelberg. 2009.

Moreno-Llorena, J., Alamán, X., Cobos, R.(2009b). *Establishment and Maintenance of a Knowledge Network by Means of Agents and Implicit Data* . Data Mining and Multi-agent Integration (ISBN: 978-1-4419-0523-9, impreso y 978-1-4419-0522-2, en línea),155-166, Springer US. 2009.

Noy, N. F., Musen, M. A. (2002). Evaluating *Ontology-Mapping Tools: Requeriments and Experience.* In EKAW02 Workshop (WS1) Sep 2002.

GNU Wget (2011). Available from http://www.gnu.org/software/wget

8

A Knowledge Management Framework as Knowledge Bases Development Support to Professional Risk Assessment in SMEs

Sebastian Marius Rosu[1] and George Dragoi[2]
[1]*Special Telecommunications Service & PREMINV Research Centre, Bucharest*
[2]*PREMINV Research Centre, Bucharest & FILS, University POLITEHNICA of Bucharest*
Romania

1. Introduction

The market situation of the European countries is the following: 99% of companies in the EU are small and medium sized enterprises (SMEs) - companies with a maximum of 250 employees and a maximal turnover of € 50 million. In the European Union (Europe have 23 million SMEs and 41 000 large companies) SMEs employ more than 65% of all employees. During past years, SMEs have created 80 % of the new jobs in the EU (IP/08/1003, Brussels, 25th June 2008). SMEs meet the multiple economic, technical and social functions, such as:

- Generate the greater part of GDP in each country, usually between 55% - 95%;
- Provide jobs for majority of employment;
- Produce a large percentage of the applicable technical innovations in the economy;
- Have the highest market dynamism in the economy, a situation evidenced by the evolution of their number, the volume of turnover and size of employment, higher sensitivity to large companies;
- Produce products and services at lower costs than large companies, the main factor causing this difference are lower costs;
- Show high flexibility and adaptability to market requirements and changes favored by smaller size, faster decision-making process, specifically the entrepreneur and his direct involvement in ongoing activities;
- Are the seeds for future large firms, particularly in new areas of the economy, etc.

The SMEs research development activities, products development, new technologies implementation (see figure 1) presupposes knowledge and assumption of multiple risks. As a result of a new product development paradigm, there is a greater need for software tools to risk estimation.

The risk evaluation sustains SMEs in the uncertainties elimination in the development strategy and management policies (see figure 2).

Estimation, evaluation and control of the occupational risk represent prerequisites for grounding and for a continual support of the decision that has been previously taken on occupational safety in a working system (Vasilescu et al., 2008; Tint et al., 2009).

However, in the last time, a lot of research in the field of knowledge management is dedicated to large companies or international concerns and the small and medium-sized enterprises were forgotten. This is the main reason why in this paper analyze the SMEs knowledge and knowledge management, the risk management process and the professional risk assessment as essential part of SMEs business, the knowledge bases built and use to assess the risk at the SMEs level.

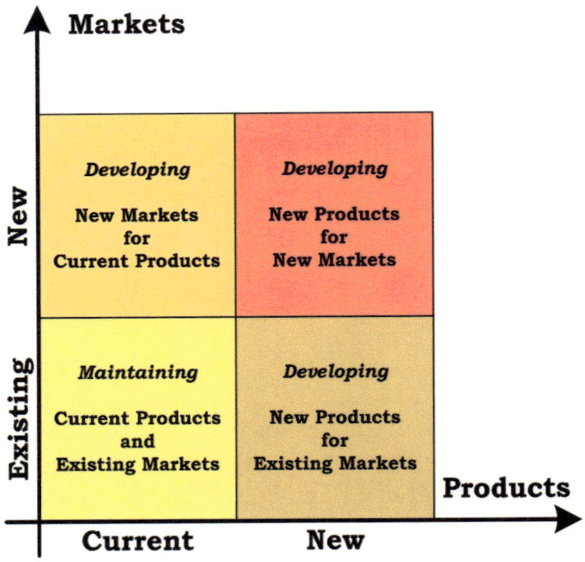

Fig. 1. The SMEs market strategy matrix

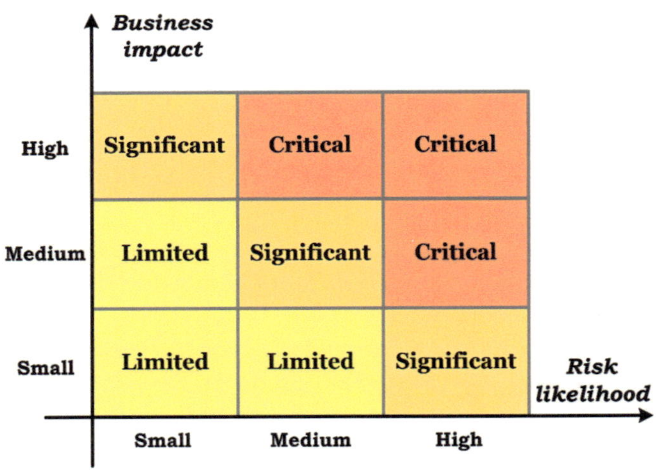

Fig. 2. The SMEs risk assessment matrix

The SMEs product development process has become an intensive process of knowledge application and it consists of a process of transformation of information. The knowledge creation is the major resource of organizational innovation and it, therefore, plays a more crucial role in developing a sustained competitive advantage for organizations, especially in a dynamic environment (Huang, 2009). The business advantage in having knowledge application, lies in the ability to analyze large amounts of data from any business model, determine the personalized preferences of all potentially customers, than rich them with relevant information, wherever they may be (Dragoi et al., 2010). Nowadays, enterprises tend to differentiate themselves from what they know (intellectual capital) and from how they use knowledge. The interest for knowledge within enterprises begins with identification that the value of market of several enterprises is much larger than the value of their own physical patrimony (equipments, facilities etc.) (Rosu et al., 2010b).

2. The SMEs knowledge

Knowledge is power and knowledge has value, but knowledge value is still a challenging topic that has not been completely clarified, whether it be in engineering science or philosophy, economics, etc. (Xu and Bernard, 2011). Over the past 15 years, knowledge management (KM) has progressed from an emergent concept to an increasingly common function in business organizations (Zach et al., 2009). Understanding knowledge management within SMEs is fundamental to economic advancement, particularly if priorities and practices transferred from large organizations are sub-optimal or counter-productive (Sparrow, 2011). Knowledge exists in the mind of people and circulates within organizations (Nonaka and Takeuchi, 1995). For all companies KM and innovation plays an important role (Porter, 2001). Many of KM initiatives are implemented in large companies but in the last years there is a shift towards small and medium-sized enterprises (Fink and Ploder, 2006). Lately, there is increasing realization of need and significance of KM for sustainable competitiveness for SMEs (Pillania, 2008). According to some studies SMEs need a simple framework to organize their key knowledge processes: knowledge identification, knowledge acquisition, knowledge distribution and knowledge preservation (Fink & Ploder, 2007; Ploder & Fink, 2007). The *key knowledge processes* (KKPs) for SMEs (Rosu et al., 2009b) identified (presented in figure 3) are:

- *Knowledge identification* - this process consist in identifying a collection of data, information, text, technical documentation, laws, standards, questionnaires, etc.., thus covering all the basics in a certain area.
- *Knowledge acquisition* - represents the transfer of knowledge from a source of knowledge (e.g. experts, documents, procedures) at a warehouse of knowledge (e.g. organizational memory, intranet, documentation, etc.).
- *Knowledge evaluation* - referring to the interpretation of the acquired knowledge using the techniques, methods and measuring instruments developed in accordance with the objectives and type of assessment, depending on the content and intended purpose, the purpose of issuing value judgments that underlie a particular decision.
- *Knowledge structured* - involves knowledge organization and classification in order to rapid retrieve and complete.
- *Knowledge combination* - should be viewed as a combination (union, alignment) to separate knowledge in order to increase their value.
- *Knowledge shared* - is the process by which knowledge is exchanged (distributed) within the organization.
- *Knowledge utilization* – means the use of scientific and technical knowledge to decision makers and by other members of the organizations in professional practices.
- *Knowledge preservation* – is a process of storage (preservation) of knowledge over time safely to be accessed in the future.

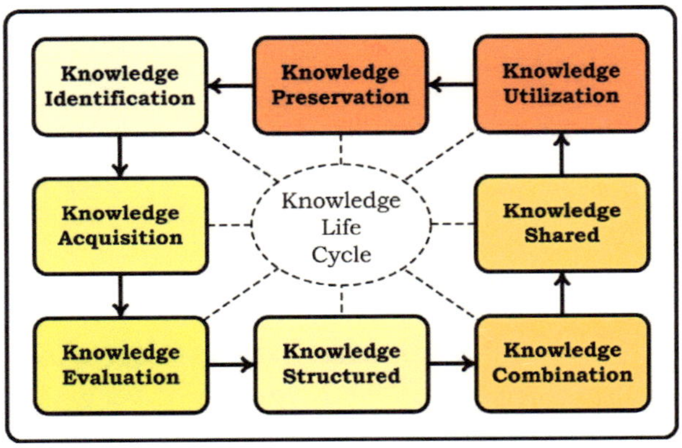

Fig. 3. The *key knowledge processes* (KKPs) for SMEs

Knowledge discovery is widely acknowledged as an interactive and iterative multi-step process ranging from the development of business understanding, data understanding, data preparation, modeling, evaluation and ultimately deployment (consolidation) of discovered knowledge (Sharma and Osei-Bryson, 2010). For SMEs it's necessary that the advantages of KM are clear and the implementation is easy otherwise they will continue to focus on their traditional way of working (Nunes et al., 2006). There are four different roles of knowledge in SMEs business (Fink, 2000; Heinrich & Lehner, 2005):

- *Knowledge as support*: there is a low current strategic position of knowledge and in future too.
- *Knowledge as manufactory*: knowledge plays now an important role but the importance will decrease in future.
- *Knowledge as breakthrough*: in future knowledge will play a very important role for the business still it does not.
- *Knowledge as weapon*: knowledge is important and the importance will increase in future.

Generally, in some SMEs activity sectors, the knowledge generate capacity exceeds the human records and process capacity, which lead to a super sized knowledge offer. In this way can be generated an inefficacy at the organizational and personal level.

Figure 4 shows the relationship among knowledge production, knowledge assimilated and the knowledge uses effect. This figure reflects the three essential trends that characterize the new knowledge society and can influence some SMEs activities (Rosu et al., 2009b):

- Knowledge offer increase;
- Knowledge assimilated increase, but in a much slow rhythm;
- Maintaining an almost constant level for knowledge used.

Short, medium and long term knowledge in handling industrial purposes research will focus on three main directions:

- *Knowledge capitalization;*
- *Knowledge formalization;*
- *Knowledge use.*

The main studies are identified two important distinctions of types of knowledge that has been used (Dragoi et al., 2007; Rosu et al., 2009a, 2009b; Rosu et al., 2010b):

- *The explicit knowledge* - which can be expressed in words and numbers; they can easily be communicated and distributed in the form of data, scientific formulas, codified procedures or universal principles.

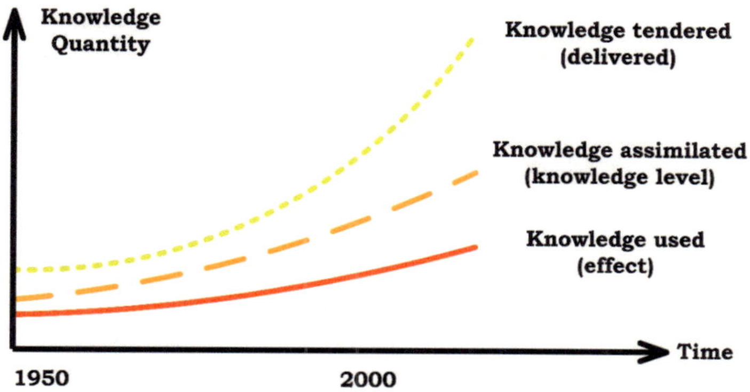

Fig. 4. *Knowledge flow* vs. *knowledge used* in SMEs (Rosu et al., 2009b)

- *The tacit knowledge* - that are very personal and difficult to formalized, dependent on experience and individual characteristics.
- *The implicit knowledge* - stored in the entities that depend on the practical context - products, technologies, processes, etc.; the value of knowledge is manifested in physical goods and services, the intellectual products (patents and licenses), processes (structural capital) and people (intellectual capital).

Enterprises are getting more knowledge intensive, and the integration of various types of knowledge becomes a challenge (Huang, 2008). Success of an enterprise is increasingly dependent on its capability to create an environment in order to improve productivity of knowledge work (Maier et al., 2009). At the enterprise level the knowledge could be found to individual, group or external resources. Professional qualifications, personal experiences, capacity to transform information's in knowledge constitute the individual resources. Patent acts, models, concepts, enterprise culture and management form the group resources. Individual and group resources totality represents the enterprise internal resources. Relations set of external resources with client, suppliers and partners, product and services credibility, offering quality. Tacit or explicit knowledge transfer between these resources

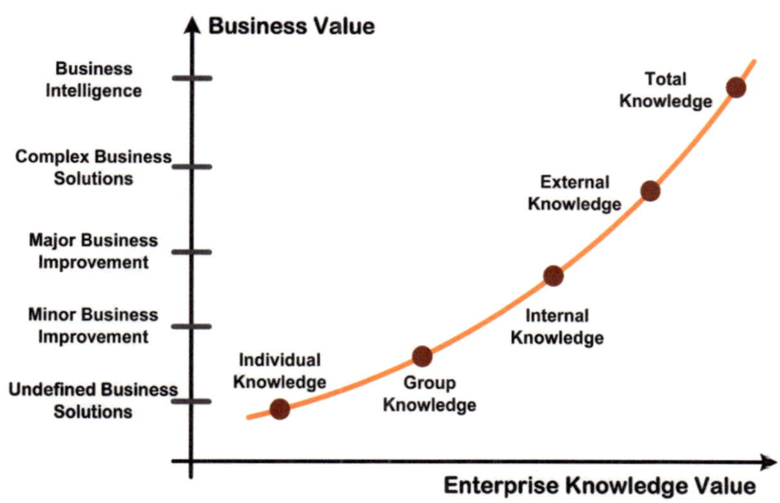

Fig. 5. *Business value* vs. *knowledge value* in SMEs (Rosu et al., 2010b)

and knowledge conversion from a resource to other determines value creation (Rosu et al, 2009a, 2009b). Knowledge from internal and external sources may be categorized into functional or general domain knowledge, organizational knowledge, and problem-specific knowledge (Bolloju et al., 2002). Figure 5 shows how business value is added when the volume and quality of knowledge from the company grows.

The knowledge of employees of an organization is an important asset and such knowledge should be garnered for the ultimate good of the company (Hussain et al., 2010). At the enterprise level knowledge that employees have or should have are varied (see in figure 6 the *key knowledge employees* - KKEs) and can be classified as follows:

- *General Knowledge* - refers to knowledge's that are so popular that would be known by everyone or nearly everyone. The term "general knowledge" is used in everyday conversation (e.g. how good is your general knowledge level?). Another term that could equally well define this type of knowledge might be *Common Knowledge*. Because these skills are widely known would be to restrict general/common knowledge relatively few things taking into account the diversity and geographical distribution of the enterprises. General knowledge doesn't mean special, specialized or specific knowledge. The general/common knowledge is usually limited within certain boundaries (e.g. the general knowledge in a Romanian enterprise are different from general knowledge in a Brazilian company). Commonly, companies require employees with a good level of general knowledge since their recruitment.
- *Commonsense Knowledge* - is a collection of facts and information that an employee is expected to know, which means different people know different things. Common sense refers on the one hand to knowledge and, on the other hand, to solve problems using reasoning skills. Commonsense refers to the everyday knowledge such as to know that every day at work, morning, read the e-mail. Enterprise commonsense knowledge refers to things that an employee has to know just to be able to integrate and work within an enterprise. Employees of different companies may have different commonsense knowledge.
- *Organization Knowledge* - the organization knowledge (*Enterprise Knowledge*) means capitalizing (using information and communications technologies) knowledge employees (knowledge is made jointly). The aim is to build the best alternative use of resources that the enterprise has according to objectives and which, due to internal and external organization developments will be adjusted dynamically. At the enterprise level, employees involved in all activities must be a team and to combine the knowledge and skills for their work to become efficiently.
- *Acquired knowledge* - are the result of a complex process of collection (by the enterprise employees) information and knowledge necessary to develop and improve the activity (in the area in which they work) and problem-solving process. The result of the knowledge acquisition by employees consists of a lot of information and knowledge unordered. This knowledge and information will be selected, analyzed and interpreted by employees during the learning process.
- *Learned Knowledge* - in the enterprise, learning is a process of documentation, experimentation, analysis and interpretation, a process of sharing the knowledge generated by employees in the past. Learning is a process of permanent change, transformation and updating of knowledge resulting in improved ways of thinking and action of employees. An enterprise is more successful if its employees learn quicker, implement and commercialize knowledge faster than the employees of competitors.

The learning knowledge process should receive special attention and organizational structure and culture of the enterprise should stimulate this process in order to improve production by obtaining relevant results in all activities.

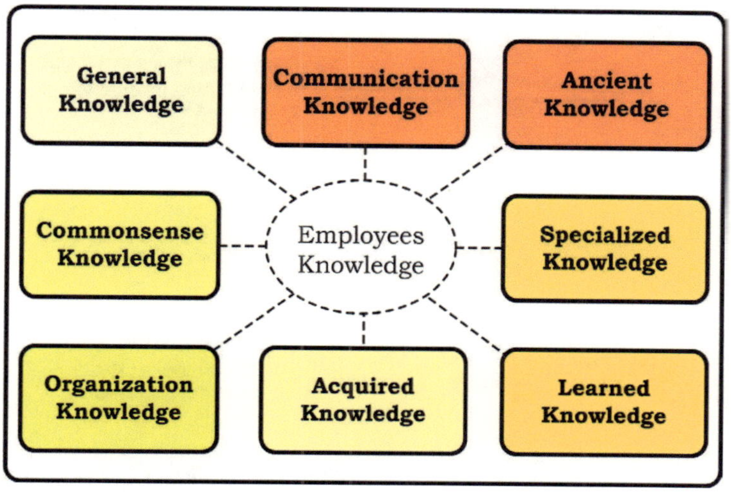

Fig. 6. The *key knowledge employees* (KKEs) in SMEs

- *Specialized Knowledge* - specialized employees knowledge refer to the detailed understanding of enterprise products and services and national and international markets for these products and services, as well as advanced knowledge about enterprise processes and procedures.
- *Ancient Knowledge* - knowledge that is possessed only older employees or employees who have retired. There are cases in which this knowledge has disappeared (and must be recreated) because the documentation doesn't exist or hasn't been adapted by experts or employees haven't shared before they retire. In these cases, enterprises may use the older or retired employees as consultants (for them to outsource their old or lost knowledge).
- *Communication Knowledge* - knowledge about how can be shared knowledge from one employee to another employee or group of employees in the enterprise collaboration and cooperation processes.

In SMEs knowledge can be capitalized (see figure 7) through (Rosu et al., 2009a):

- *Gathering data, information and knowledge from customers, providers and partners:* collecting all data, information, knowledge from clients into a knowledge base; using the info on customers for product and services development and modernization purposes; tight connections with customers through the Internet - maybe opening a forum for discussions; a thorough recording of the staff's contacts with the customers, of customers' wants for anticipations in the future.
- *Creating new incomes by exploiting the existing knowledge:* keeping all patents, licenses, market and necessity research, technical and economic research in a database accessible to the personnel; in case of changing profile within the company into a similar one: keeping all methods and expertise acquired during the former one; selling knowledge/expertise to other companies by means of license, patent, consultancy, etc.

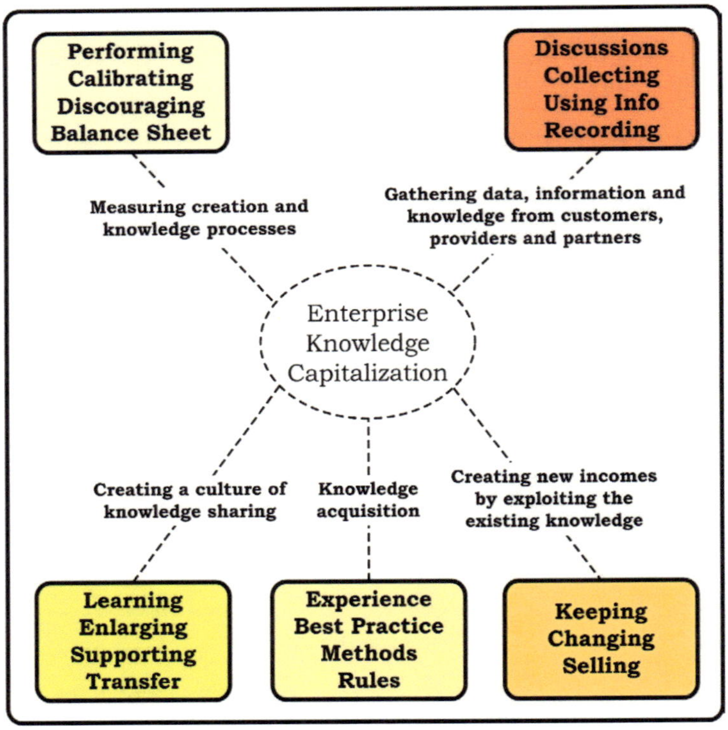

Fig. 7. The key knowledge capitalization processes (KCPs) in SMEs

- *Creating a culture of knowledge sharing:* encouraging learning and improvement; supporting those failing their attempts; upholding a competitive environment and rewarding personal initiative; creating a culture of knowledge sharing from the top of the organization to all its lower levels; enlarging people's knowledge area beyond their field of expertise; setting goals to employees; creating environment for knowledge transfer - such as teamwork, meant especially for knowledge and info transfer from experts to newly employ.
- *Knowledge acquisition:* keeping all experience gained in every (previous) activity in a knowledge or database; creating a knowledge database comprising the best practice, methods, rules and facilitating communication through e-mail, videoconference, Internet forum, etc.; rewarding employees having good results in the acquisition and accumulation process; equal male and female employment, as well as of foreigners; diversity and multicultural representation lead to creativity.
- *Measuring creation and knowledge processes:* performing a knowledge quality audit; calibrating customers, providers and partners according to the value of their contribution to the knowledge process; annual balance-sheet including profit and loss in HR terms and a balance of HR investments; discouraging the use of financial indices in management and mainly in knowledge management.

3. The SMEs knowledge management

Knowledge management (KM) is the process that is organization and coordination of knowledge from the knowledge of the organization. KM is the set of processes that seeks to change the organization's present pattern of knowledge processing to enhance both it and its outcomes (Firestone and McElroy, 2005). Knowledge processes supported by knowledge infrastructures improve individual and team creativity and facilitate innovation (Janev and Vranes, 2005). The processing-driven paradigm of KM has its focus on best practices, training and learning programs, cultural change, collaboration, and virtual organizations (Malhotra, 2005).

The KM processes involves (see in figure 8 the *key knowledge management processes* - KKMPs) (Rosu et al., 2010b):

- *Knowledge clustering* – the kinds of knowledge from the sources of the organization, the processes up to formation of internal memory.
- *Knowledge storage* – this aims to store knowledge in the knowledge infrastructure of the organization, in terms of efficiency.
- *Knowledge classified* – for evaluating and granting priorities that reflect the quality of knowledge and the adequacy requirements processes.
- *Knowledge selection* – this allows the user to use certain criteria for identifying the most appropriate knowledge.
- *Knowledge dissemination* – that knowledge stored in various forms (tacit, explicit or implicit) are accessed by all members of the organization and even stakeholders - customers, suppliers, etc.

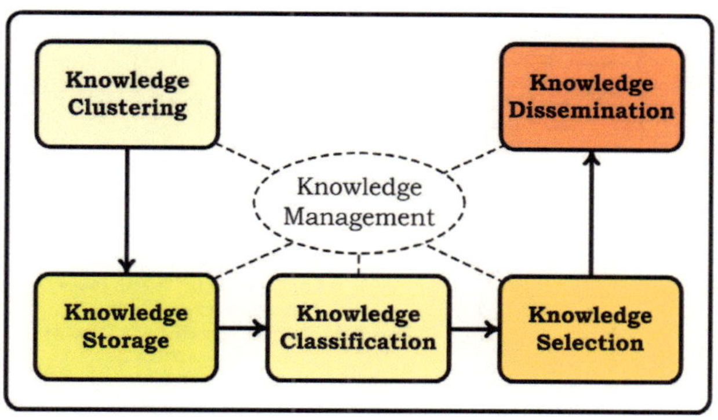

Fig. 8. The key knowledge management processes (KKMPs) in SMEs

Successful SMEs are those who can leverage their knowledge in an effective and efficient manner, so as to make up for deficiencies in traditional resources, like land, labor, and capital (Desouza and Awazu, 2006).The knowledge of the enterprise contains the sharing knowledge of each individual (Dragoi et al., 2007; 2010). For increase the knowledge in SMEs for an efficient management of the intellectual capital and to improve the business value, we proposes a KM scenario in eleven steps: obtains and uses, learn and contribute, evaluates, sustain, support, exchange, combination, transfer,preservation, recovery and discharge (see figure 9), (Rosu et al., 2008, 2009a, 2009b):

1. *The step obtains and use* is well known within organizations. People always seek information and use them later to solve their problems, to take decisions or to create new products. Therefore, new technologies (e.g. Intranet/Internet/Extranet) allow that the large amount of information that flows within organizations can be correctly managed.
2. *The step learn and contribute* are relatively new for organizations. For example, it has been difficult to convince employees to contribute to the organization's knowledge

base. New technologies have helped companies easily organize, send and transfer certain types of information. However, the employee has seen this facility as a threat for his/hers own job security. The most difficult task is to convince individuals that their contribution will give return to their organization as well as to themselves.

3. *The step evaluates* indicate that the organization should define its own necessary knowledge for its mission and classify its own currently intellectual capital. In other words, the knowledge manager does more than organize the content in system on-line; he/she should understand and foresee the community's needs.
4. *The step sustain or maintain* should assure that the future intellectual capital would maintain the organization viable and competitive. Organizations tend to build their own intellectual capital through their relationships with customers, employees, suppliers etc. The knowledge manager should also be responsible for the maintenance of the organizations knowledge base.

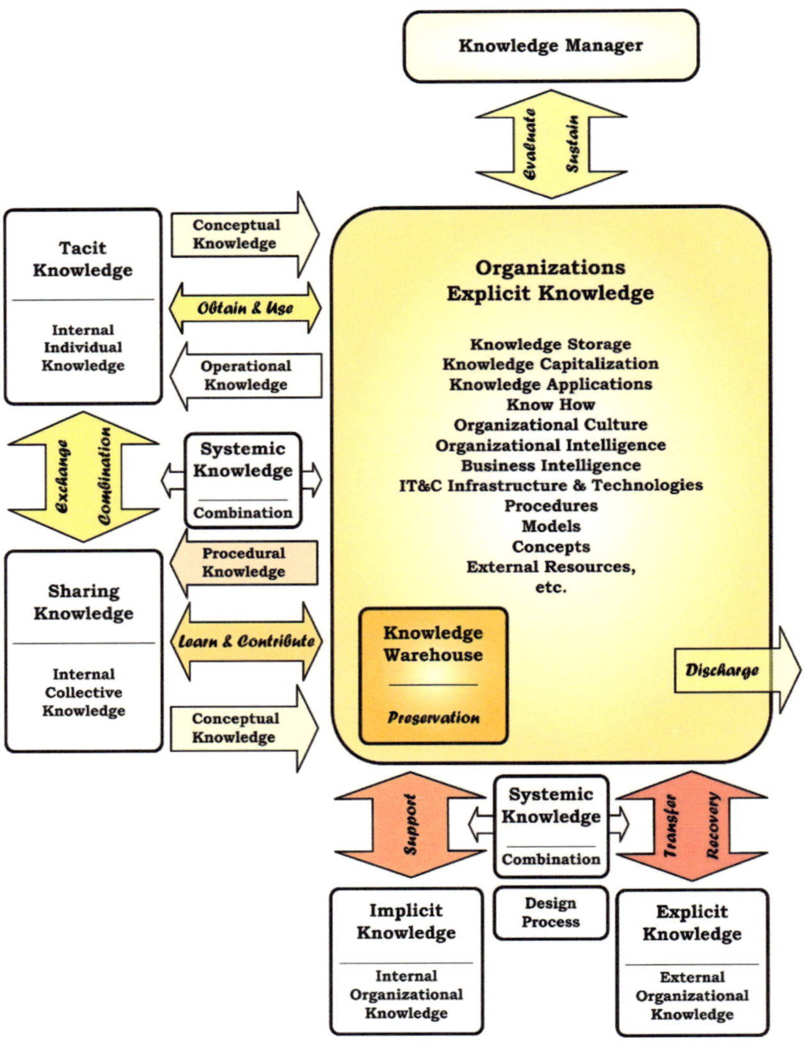

Fig. 9. A *knowledge management scenario* in SMEs as knowledge bases development support

5. *The step support* can be used for the continuous improvement of the product design process.
6. *The step exchange* represents an intelligence and creativity combination of organization employees to find better solutions to their problem. Knowledge exchange involves interaction between decision makers and researchers or project development teams and results in mutual learning through the process of planning, disseminating, and applying existing or new research in decision-making.
7. *The step combination* can be making by means of the Industrial Informatics Systems or Knowledge Work Systems.
8. *The step transfer* realized by teaching process, e-learning and simulations. At the organization level the knowledge could be found to individual or group (collective) resources.
9. *The step preservation* used for knowledge storing in a warehouse. In this repository, knowledge components, structured and classified, are deposited for further use.
10. *The step recovery* utilized when the organization must re-create knowledge that disappears because documentation isn't adequate or experts don't pass along knowledge before they leave.
11. *The step discharge* excludes any useless knowledge from the organizations knowledge base. However, some knowledge can be more valuable if transferred outside the organization.

4. Professional risk assessment as part of risk management process in SMEs

Risk management is the process (see figure 10) of identifying riskand its sources (Gavrilescu, 2009), assessing risk, and taking steps to reduce risk to an acceptable level (Rosu et al., 2010a). Commonly, the risk management process (RMP) includes three phases: *risk identification, risk analyses & risk feedback*. Risk management process is an important component of a successful project development process (see in figure 11 the project management process). Risk is associated with knowledge resources and infers that problems would be caused due to the loss or inadequacy of knowledge (McBriar et al., 2003).

In the enterprise, we can distinguish some basic project components (steps) in the development of a project: start of project study, start project planning, start project execution, basic project design ready, project introduction, project monitoring and controlling, release project product, project product acceptance, close project and retrospective investigation of project. The individual parties involved in a project adopt different terminology for describing risks, use different methods and tehniques for dealing with risk analysis and management, producing different and conflicting results (Tah and Carr, 2001). The complex relationship between an employee's knowledge, attitude, and behavior was not sufficiently explored (Khachkalyan et al., 2006). Enterprise project development presupposes knowledge and assumption of multiple risks. In a project, risks are those conditions or events whose occurrence is not certain, but whether they occur may adversely affect the project. The RMP should not be treated primarily as a technical function carried out by the IT experts who operate and manage the IT system, but as an essential management function of the organization.

In EU countries there is an experience and good practice both in classifying, identifying, and evaluating risks and in eliminating and reducing those (Botezatu et al., 2008). Among others we can mention that at SMEs level, a lot of attention is paid to: air quality (ventilation systems), pressure equipments, elevators, lifting equipments and accessories, noise, construction sites, shipyards, illumination, electricity, individual protection equipments, explosives, extraction of fat using flammable substances, fires, fixed refrigeration systems, heat systems, machinery, flammable liquids or liquefied gases, chemical hazard, depots, air cooling towers, etc. (Yule et al., 2007).

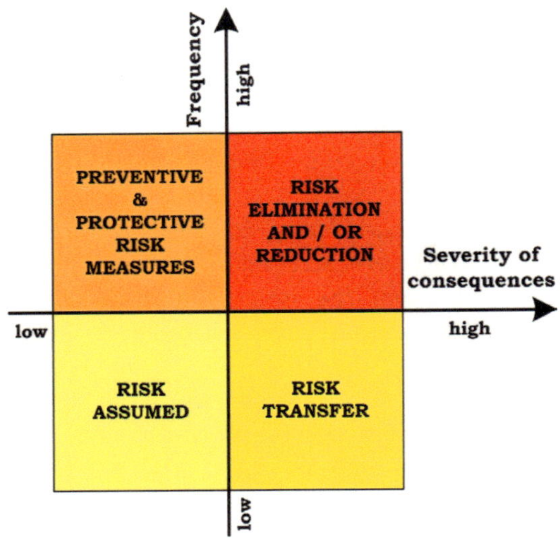

Fig. 10. The SMEs *risk matrix*

Risk identification consist of hazard identification. A hazard is anything that has the potential to cause harm. A hazard is identified as a situation with a potential for causing harm to human safety, the environment, property or business, regardless of how likely or unlikely such an occurence might be (Gasparotti, 2010). Hazards can affect people, property, processes; they can cause accidents and ill-heath, loss of output, damage to machinery, etc. workplace accidents and professional illnesses mustn't be perceived only as fatality, as it is more lucrative to consider them as a malfunction of the processes taking places in SMEs (Botezatu et al., 2008). Occupational risk refers to the likelihood and the severity of an injury or an illness occurring as a result of exposure to a hazard. The main aim of occupational risk assessment is to protect workers health and safety. Risk assessment helps to minimize the possibility of the workers or the environment being harmed due to work-related activities. It also helps to keep your business competitive and effective. Professional risk can be assessed in seven steps, as presented in figure 12 (Rosu et al., 2010a).

But, why is Professional safety and health an essential part of good SMEs business? Professional safety and health (EASHW, 2007b):

- Helps demonstrate that a business is socially responsible;
- Protects and enhances brand image and brand value;
- Helps maximize the productivity of workers;
- Enhances employees' commitment to the business;
- Builds a more competent, healthier workforce;
- Reduces business costs and disruption;
- Enables enterprises to meet customers' OSH expectations;
- Encourages the workforce to stay longer in active life.

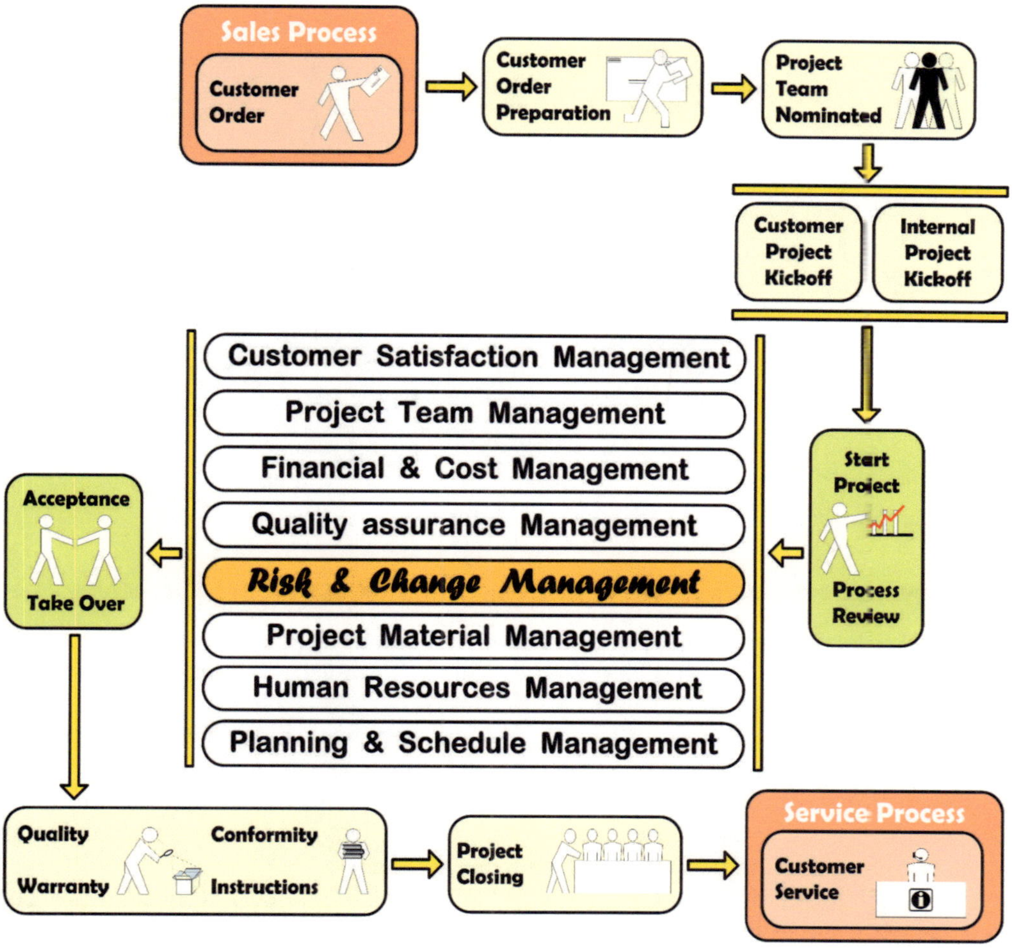

Fig. 11. The *risk management process* (RMP) as part of project management process (PMP)

Under health and safety laws, all employers must carry out regular risk assessment (EASHW, 2007a). To assess professional risk at the workplace we need to know:

- Where the workplace and/or the jobs performed are located and who works there: pay particular attention to those for whom occupational hazard may be more severe than usual, such as pregnant women, young workers or workers with disabilities; remember also about part-time workers, subcontractors and visitors, and employees who work off-site (including drivers, those visiting clients' or customers' homes, etc.);
- What work equipment, materials, and processes are used;
- What tasks are performed;
- What the potential consequences of existing hazards are;
- What protective measures are used;
- What accidents, occupational diseases and other occurrences of ill health have been reported;
- What legal and other requirements are related to the workplace, etc.

Fig. 12. The professional risk assessment (PRA) steps

5. A knowledge based system to professional risk assessment in SMEs

A knowledge-based system (KBS) is the one that captures the expertise of individuals within a particular field and incorporates it and makes it available within a computerized application (Lovett, 2000).

The KBSs help enterprise to diagnose processes in real time, schedule operation, troubleshoots equipment, maintain machinery and design service and production facilities. With the implementation of a KBS in the industrial environments, companies are finding that the real-world problems are best solved by an integrated strategy involving the management of personnel, software and hardware systems.

At PREMINV Research Center, University "POLITEHNICA" of Bucharest, have been implemented some of the KBS modules for risk assessment in various professional fields, system able to provide at the SMEs level the original KM framework (proposed in figure 9) implementation. A first KBS module is focused on professional risk assessment for an *Auto Service Company*.

To identify hazards at the workplace was prepared a General Hazard Checklist (see Table 1). This list can be extended according to specific facilities. Note that, correct identification of hazards involves active involvement of all employees in the process of gathering information.

For each YES answer in the general list is given 0 points and for each answer NO is given 1 point. Depending on the total score obtained and taking into account the probability and severity of consequences risk arising from hazards are evaluated – it may be small, medium or high.

Using expert systems generator VP-Expert (was used the expert system generator - VP-Expert version 2.1, by Brian Sawyer, Educational Version, distributed by Paperback Software International) and based on General Hazard Checklist was built the knowledge base *AUTOSER.KBS* (see figure 13).

The knowledge base rules are following: rules for awarding points variables, rules for calculation of the partial scores and total score and rules for assessment of probability and severity of consequences, and risk arising from hazards in accordance with the total score obtained. To achieve the KBS professional assessment of risk was used the method of representation of knowledge production rules.

No.	Hazard	Yes	No
	Does the hazard exist at the workplace?		
1	Do workers have suitable capabilities and skills to perform their work?		
2	Are flat surfaces (floor, inspection pit, etc.) regularly cleaned?		
3	Are flat surfaces (floor, inspection pit in service station, etc.) paint resistant from substances that are used (e. g., oil, diesel, petrol)?		
4	Is the inspection pit safely covered after work?		
5	Is the inspection pit suitably marked or surrounded with handrails to prevent people from falling down?		
6	Is the inspection pit suitably marked or surrounded with handrails to prevent people from falling down?		
7	Are there marked (e.g. on the floor) ways for cars to enter the service station?		
8	Are employees told not to step on brake tester cylinders?		
9	Are employees told not to step under raised vehicles?		
10	Is the temperature in the service station suitable for work in during both winter and summer?		
11	Are there defined safety rules for assembly work (e. g. bodywork, engine)?		
12	Are there defined safety rules for work with petrol tanks (e. g. repairing)?		
13	Are there instruction to avoid fire in the room in which batteries are stored?		
14	Are there measures implemented to avoid explosion when batteries are charged?		
15	Are there measures in place to protect electrical equipment from water?		
...	… … … … …		
	Answer sum:		

Table 1. The Hazard Checklist

In the *AUTOSER.KBS* knowledge base (KB) there are *if-then* structure rules (excluding the rules for inference engine operations), such as:

```
RULE 0-0
IF      surfaces<>?    AND   clean<>?        AND   surfpaint<>?    AND
        oil<>?         AND   inspit<>?       AND   shoes<>?        AND
        lighting<>?    AND   ventilation<>?
THEN    FIND   rp1     FIND  rp2     FIND   rp3
        FIND   rp4     FIND  rp5     FIND   rp6
        FIND   rp7     FIND  rp8
        r1=(rp1+rp2+rp3+rp4+rp5+rp6+rp7+rp8);
... ... ... ... ...

RULE 6-1
IF      risk>18  AND
        risk<=20
THEN    prob=PROBABLE
        conseq=MODERATELY_HARMFUL
        riskprof=SMALL
CLS
DISPLAY"
EXPLANATIONS ++++++++++++++++++++++++++++++++++++++++++++++++++++
Probable = may materialize only a few times during the occupational career of an employee.
Moderately harmful = accidents and illnesses not causing prolonged distress (such as small
nicks, eye irritations, headaches, etc.).
Small Risk = acceptable.
Conclusion = it is necessary to ensure that it will remain at the same level.
++++++++++++++++++++++++++++++++++++++++++++++++++++++++++++++++";
... ... ... ... ...
RULE 14-0
        IF      inspit=YES
        THEN    rp5=0;
RULE 14-1
        IF      inspit=NO
        THEN    rp5=1;
RULE 15-0
        IF      shoes=YES
        THEN    rp6=0;
RULE 15-1
        IF      shoes=NO
        THEN    rp6=1;
```

After querying the knowledge base will be displayed to evaluate the outcome of risk assessment conclusion and explanations on the likelihood and severity of injury in terms of consequences (see figure 13).

We considered the risk level depending on probability and severity of consequences as follows: *small risk*, *medium risk* and *high risk* and high risk are unacceptable and small and medium risks are acceptable (see figure 14).

In general, if the risk is assessed as unacceptable (height) reduction actions must be taken immediately. If risk is assessed as acceptable (average) is recommended plan of action to reduce or necessary to ensure that it will remain at the same level (in case of risk assessed as small).

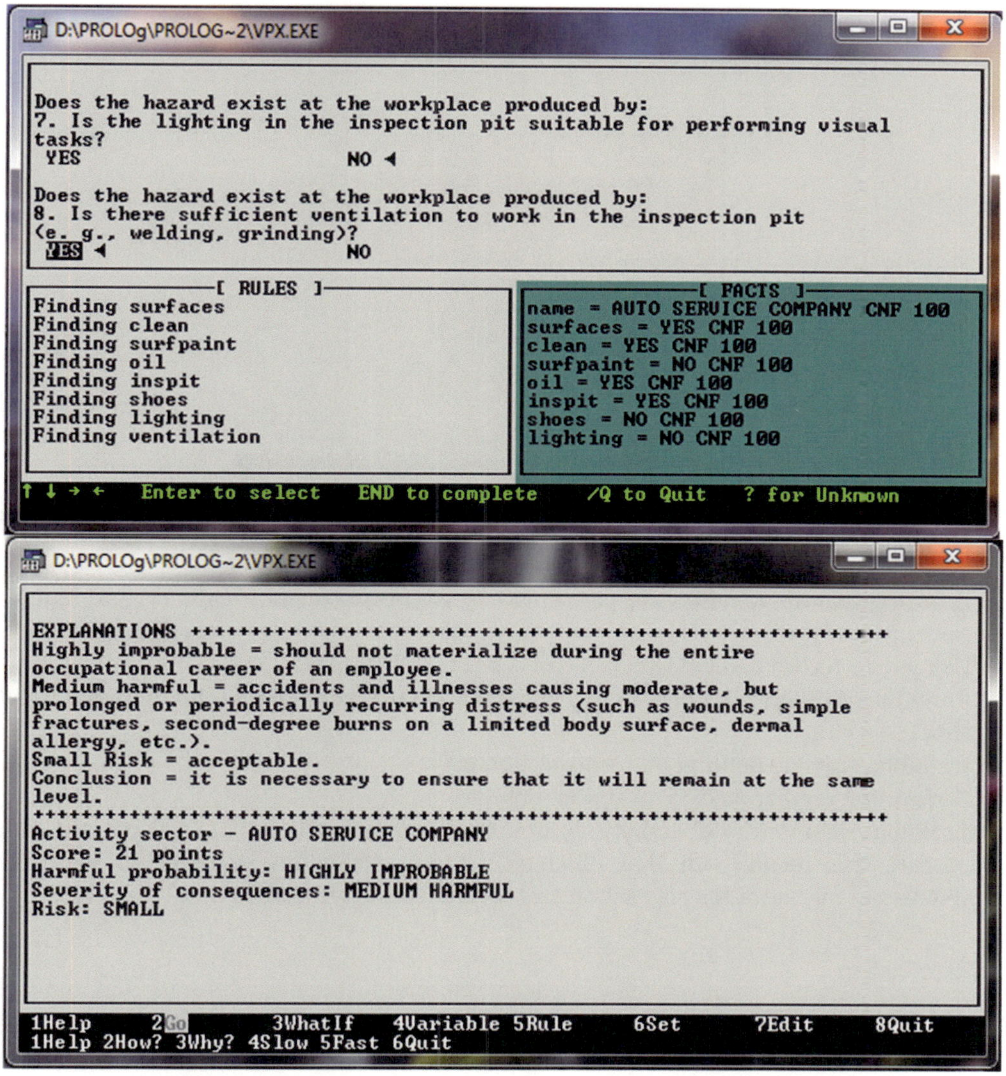

Fig. 13. The *AUTOSER.KBS* knowledge base interrogation and show results

Measures of prevention and protection to be implemented in the organization are to eliminate or reduce to a minimum the danger by organizational measures, or use of collective protection equipment suitable for individual protection. To reduce the risk it is necesary to take preventive measures (EASHW, 2007a), such as:

- Cleaning thoroughly after grinding, painting, etc.
- Wearing protective non-slipping shoes.
- Covering the steps into the inspection pit with non-slipping material.
- Never stepping under raised vehicles.
- Never stepping into a closed inspection pit in a service station.

- Never stepping on brake tester cylinders.
- Keeping inspection pits in service station covered after work.

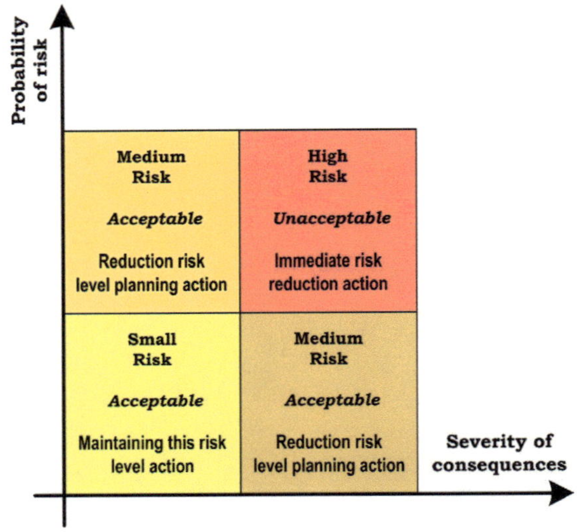

Fig. 14. The risk evaluation based on *probability* and *severity of consequence*

- Ensuring that all activities are performed by well-trained staff; respecting all required safety procedures.
- Using only recommended safe tools for work with batteries.
- Providing workers with necessary personal protective equipment (gloves, masks, safety shoes).
- Installing suitable lighting in the inspection pit.
- Performing regular medical examinations, etc.

It indicated a reassessment of activity sector after the implementation of these measures and to compare this result with that obtained at first evaluation in order to verify the effectiveness of measures for prevention and protection implemented.

6. Conclusion

This paper describes the SMEs knowledge and knowledge management key processes, the professional risk assessment as part of SMEs risk management process and presents a method to build knowledge based system to assess the profesional risks, starting from a SMEs knowledge management framework. Every business decision involves an element of risk (Lam, 2003). General idea that shows the importance of this system of occupational risks assessment consists in the fact that nothing can be achieved without a motivated/interested staff. The new methods, technologies, tools, techniques can be implemented only with the people and for people. It is particularly important that any technique or method to be presented by such a way as to appear in the eyes of the staff as a useful tool, and not as a tool for monitoring employee activity or suppressing it. In the European countries more then 95% of the companies are small and medium-sized enterprises (SMEs) and majority of the European Union employees work in these companies. In Romania just few SMEs develop proper risk measure and cover mechanisms. Regarding our companies the RMP in the majority of annual report of Top 15 BSE (Bucharest Stock Exchange) Romanian listed companies 60 % are in an incipient stage of implementation, only 40 % of this Top 15 companies have already defined their objectives regarding risk management or already have an integrated system of risk management (Blidisel et al., 2008). According to legislation in safety and health, all employers should periodically assess the occupational risks. The main goal of the occupational risk assessment is to protect workers, helping to maintain competitiveness and enterprise productivity.

This work realized at the UPB - PREMINV Research Centre, in University "Politehnica" of Bucharest, is focusing on a university - small and medium-sized enterprise partnership. The validation of this methodology by a case study in the PROGPROC project (CNMP 11014/2007 - between 2007-2010) is to create a support system for resources planning and programming activities according to manufacturing processes management in virtual organizations. The future work in this area includes building other knowledge bases to evaluate eventually other SMEs activities who involve risks.

7. References

Blidisel, R.; Popa, A. & Farcane, N. (2008). Disclosure Level of Risk Management Information: the Case of Romanian Companies. In: *Annals of DAAAM for 2008 & Proceedings of the 19th International DAAAM Symposium*, B. Katalinic (Ed.), 115-116, DAAAM International, ISBN 978-3-901509-68-1, Vienna, Austria

Bolloju, N.; Khalifa, M. & Turban, E. (2002). Integrating knowledge management into enterprise environments for the next generation decision support. *Decision Support Systems*, Vol. 33, No. 2, pp. 163-176, ISSN 0167-9236

Botezatu, C.; Botezatu, C.P. & Carutasu, G. (2008). Conformity Issues for Health and Safety at Work - Part of Integrated Management Systems. In: *Annals of DAAAM for 2008 & Proceedings of the 19th International DAAAM Symposium*, B. Katalinic (Ed.), 151-152, DAAAM International, ISBN 978-3-901509-68-1, Vienna, Austria

Dragoi, G.; Cotet, C.; Rosu, L. & Rosu, S.M. (2007). Internet/Intranet/Extranet-Based Systems in the CESICED Platform for Virtual Product Development Environment. In: *Advances in Integrated Design and Manufacturing in Mechanical Engineering II*, Tichkiewitch, S., Tollenaere, M. & Ray, P. (Eds.), 293-307, Springer, ISBN 978-1-4020-6760-0 (HB), ISBN 978-1-4020-6761-7 (e-book), Dordrecht, Netherlands

Dragoi, G.; Draghici, A.; Rosu, S.M.; Radovici, A. & Cotet, C.E. (2010). Professional Risk Assessment Using Virtual Enterprise Network Support for Knowledge Bases Development. In: *Enterprise Information Systems, Communications in Computer and Information Science*, Vol. 110, No. 3, J.E. Quintela Varajao et al. (Eds.), 168-177, Springer-Verlag Berlin Heidelberg, ISSN 978-972-669-929-6, Germany

Desouza, K.C. & Awazu, Y. (2006). Knowledge management at SMEs: five peculiarities. *Journal of Knowledge Management*, Vol. 10, No. 1, pp. 32-43, ISSN 1367-3270

EASHW (2007a). *Risk Assessment Essentials*, printed in Nurnberg, Germany

EASHW (2007b). *The Business Benefits of Good Occupational Safety and Health*, Fact sheet 77, printed in Belgium

Fink, K. (2000). *Know-how Management*, Oldenbourg Verlag, Munchen/Wien

Fink, K. & Ploder, C. (2006). The Impact of Knowledge Process Modelling on Small and Medium-sized Enterprises. In: *Proceedings of the I-KNOW'06, J.UCS.*, Tochtermann, K. & Maurer, H. (Eds.), 47-51, Graz, Austria

Fink, K. & Ploder, C. (2007). Knowledge Process Modelling in SME and Cost-efficient Software Support - Theoretical Framework and Empirical Studies. In: *Managing Worldwide Operations and Communications with Information Technology*, Khosrow-Pour, M. (Ed.), 479-484, IGI Publishing, ISBN 978-1-59904-929-8, Hershey, USA

Firestone, J. & McElroy, M. (2005). Doing Knowledge Management. *The Learning Organization*, Vol. 12, No. 2, pp. 189-212, ISSN 0969-6474

Gasparotti, C. (2010). Risk assessment of marine oil spills. *Environmental Engineering and Management Journal*, Vol. 9, No. 4, pp. 527-534, ISSN 1582-9596

Gavrilescu, M. (2009). Behaviour of persistent pollutants and risks associated with their presence in the environment-integrated studies. *Environmental Engineering and Management Journal*, Vol. 8, No. 6, pp. 1517-1531, ISSN 1582-9596

Heinrich, L. & Lehner, F. (2005). *Informationsmanagement*. Oldenbourg Verlag, ISBN 3-486-57772-7, Munchen/Wien

Huang, J.J. (2009). The evolutionary perspective of knowledge creation – A mathematical representation. *Knowledge Based Systems*, Vol. 22, No. 6, pp. 430-438, ISSN 0950-7051

Huang, N. & Diao, S. (2008). Ontology-based enterprise knowledge integration. *Robotics and Computer-Integrated Manufacturing*, Vol. 24, No. 4, pp. 562-571, ISSN 0736-5845

Hussain, I.; Si, S. & Ahmed, A. (2010). Knowledge Management for SMEs in Developing Countries. *Journal of Knowledge Management Practice*, Vol. 11, No. 2, ISSN 1705-9232

Janev, V. & Vranes, S. (2005). The role of knowledge management solutions in enterprise business processes. *Journal of Universal Computer Science*, Vol. 11, No. 4, pp. 526-545, ISSN 0948-695x

Khachkalyan, T.; Petrosyan, V. & Soghikian, K. (2006). Association between Health Risk Knowledge and Risk Behavior among Medical Students and Residents in Yerevan. *Californian Journal of Health Promotion*, Vol. 4, No. 2, pp. 197-206, ISSN 1545-8725

Lam, J. 2003. *Enterprise risk management: from incentives to controls*. John Wiley & Sons, Inc., ISBN 0-471-43000-5, Hoboken, New Jersey

Lovett, P.J.; Ingram, A. & Bancroft, C.N. (2000). Knowledge –based engineering for SMEs – a methodology. *Journal of Materials Proccessing Technology*, Vol. 107, pp. 384-389, ISSN 0924-0136

Nonaka, I. & Takeuchi, H. (1995). *The Knowledge-Creating Company: How Japanese Create the Dynamics of Innovation*. Oxford University Press, ISBN 0-19-509269-4, New York

Nunes, M.; Annansingh, F.; Eaglestone, B. & Wakefield, R. (2006). Knowledge Management Issues in Knowledge-Intensive SMEs. *Journal of Documentation*, Vol. 62, No. 1, pp. 101-119, ISSN 0022-0418

Maier, R.; Hadrich, Th. & Peinl, R. (2009). *Enterprise Knowledge Infrastructures*. Springer-Verlag Berlin Heidelberg, ISBN 3-540-23915-4, Germany

Malhotra, Y. (2005). Integrating knowledge management technologies in organizational business processes: getting real time enterprises to deliver real business performance. *Journal of Knowledge Management*, Vol. 9, pp. 7-28, ISSN 1367-3270

McBriar, I.; Smith, C.; Bain, G.; Unsworth, P.; Magraw, S. & Gordon L.J. (2003). Risk, gap and strength: key concepts in knowledge management. *Knowledge-Based Systems*, Vol. 16, No. 1, pp. 29–36, ISSN 0950-7051

Pillania, R.K. (2008). Information technology strategy for knowledge management in Indian automotive components SMEs. *Knowledge and Process Management*, Vol. 15, No. 3, pp. 203-210, ISSN 1099-1441

Ploder, C. & Fink, K. (2007). An Orchestration Model for Knowledge Management Tools in SMEs. In: *Proceedings of the I-KNOW'07, J.UCS*, Tochtermann, K. & Maurer, H. (Eds.), 176-184, Graz, Austria

Porter, M. (2001). Strategy and Internet. *Harvard Business Review*, Vol. 79, No. 3, pp. 62-78, ISSN 0017-8012

Rosu, S.M. (2008). *Research on the implementation of Knowledge Management System for an Industrial Holding*. Ph.D. Diss., Faculty of Automatic Control and Computers, "Politehnica" University of Bucharest

Rosu, S.M.; Dragoi, G.; Cotet, C.E. & Rosu, L. (2010a). Professional Risk Assessment Using Knowledge Bases in Small and Medium Enterprises. *Environmental Engineering and Management Journal*, Vol. 9, No. 4, pp. 489-493, ISSN 1582-9596

Rosu, S.M.; Dragoi, G. & Guran, M. (2009a). Knowledge Management Solutions for Products Development in the Enterprise Business Intelligence. *U.P.B. Scientific Bulletin, Series D*, Vol. 71, No. 4, pp. 97-112, ISSN 1454-2358

Rosu, S.M.; Dragoi, G. & Guran, M. (2009b). A Knowledge Management Scenario to Support Knowledge Applications Development in Small and Medium Enterprises. *Advances in Electrical and Computer Engineering*, Vol. 9, No. 1, pp. 8-15, ISSN 1582-7445

Rosu, S.M.; Dragoi, G.; Guran, M. & Dragomirescu, C. (2010b). The SMEs Knowledge Management. Professional Risk Assessment Using a KBS. In: *DAAAM International Scientific Book 2010*, Chapter 62, B. Katalinic (Ed.), 709-724, DAAAM International, ISSN 1726-9687, ISBN 978-3-901509-74-2, Vienna, Austria,

Sharma, S. & Osei-Bryson, K.M. (2010). Toward an integrated knowledge discovery and data mining process model. *The Knowledge Engineering Review*, Vol. 25, No. 1, pp. 49-67, ISSN 0269-8889

Sparrow, J. (2011). Knowledge Management in Small and Medium Sized Enterprises. In: *Encyclopedia of Knowledge Management*, Second Edition, 671-681, IGI Global Press

Tah, J.H.M. & Carr, V. (2001). Towards a framework for project risk knowledge management in the construction supply chain. *Advances in Engineering Software*, Vol. 32, pp. 835-846, ISSN 0965-9978

Tint, P.; Jarvis, M.; Reinhold, K. & Paas, O. (2009). Risk assessment and measurement of hazards in estonian enterprises. *Environmental Engineering and Management Journal*, Vol. 8, pp. 1165-1170, ISSN 1582-9596

Vasilescu, G.D.; Plesea, V. & Baciu, C. (2008). Establishing the Acceptable Risk Level in Occupational Accidents and Diseases Based on a Formal Analysis. *Environmental Engineering and Management Journal*, Vol. 7, No. 6, pp. 785-789, ISSN 1582-9596

Xu, Y. & Bernard, A. (2011). Quantifying the value of knowledge within the context of product development. *Knowledge-Based Systems*, Vol. 24, No. 1, pp. 166-175, ISSN 0950-7051

Yule, S.; Flin, R. & Murdy, A. (2007). The Role of Management and Safety Climate in Preventing Risk-Taking at Work. *International Journal of Risk Assessment and Management*, Vol. 7, No. 2, pp. 137-151, ISSN 1466-8297

Zach, M.; McKeen, J. & Singh, S. (2009). Knowledge management and organizational performance: an exploratory analysis. *Journal of Knowledge Management*, Vol. 13, No. 6, pp. 392-409, ISSN 1367-3270

Agent Based Personal Knowledge Management System Supported by Mobile Technology Cross-Platform Solution

Kaspars Osis[1] and Janis Grundspenkis[2]
[1]Faculty of Engineering, Vidzeme University of Applied Sciences, Valmiera
[2]Institute of Applied Computer Systems, Riga Technical University, Riga
Latvia

1. Introduction

A historic transition from the industrial age to the information age has happened during several previous decades. The industrial age can be characterized by following: standardized information routines, usage of fixed procedures, and creation of material goods and consumption of them. In opposite the information age is focusing on creation and consumption of information, usage of ad-hoc approaches and non-standardized information for decision making. During this time of transition the Web has developed very rapidly along with information explosion. That has led to a notion of information overload. In organizations workspace environment and equipment is turning to be more sophisticated. Also learning environment is becoming more information and technology dense. As a result work is becoming increasingly complex (Wiig, 2004) requiring additional knowledge and skills to handle it. In turn that leads to recognition that knowledge has become a very important asset both for individuals and for organizations. Thus knowledge more increasingly has been seen as an active area of research. Notions of knowledge work and accordingly of knowledge worker have strengthen their positions out of transition from information to knowledge.

Much of attention is focused towards researching different knowledge related areas. Knowledge management (KM) is one of such areas. It was first defined by Wiig in 1986 (Wiig, 1997). As per (Tiwana, 2002) KM has three basic processes: knowledge acquisition, sharing, and utilization. Knowledge is divided in two broad categories: tacit (i.e. tacit knowing) and explicit (i.e. explicit knowing) (Polanyi, 1966). There are also several other ways of classifying knowledge based on particular perspective of research (Maier, 2004). Majority of research is connected with knowledge that we do know and with knowledge we know that we do not know. However per (Frappaolo, 2004) there still remains knowledge which we do not know that we know and knowledge which we do not know that we do not know. Thus we propose a new concept of knowledge substance to encompass all knowledge elements (KE) as a basis for further research.

New technological solutions such as mobile technology and accordingly different types of mobile devices have appeared in addition of transition to the information age and development of the Web and the Internet. These devices have greatly influenced individuals' habits and their ways of consuming, sharing and storing information. A large and growing variety of mobile devices and a number of new forms of communication have been developed to accommodate expanding needs of people. Thus, for example, based on (i2SMS, 2008) almost every second person uses a mobile phone in 2008. But two years later as per (mobiThinking, 2011) there are already 77% mobile subscribers of the world population in 2010. However that has its drawback by making it difficult to develop services and applications accommodating a vast array of mobile devices and their platforms. Accordant innovative services are lacking a momentum of development. Frequently they are still mainly based on rather old technologies such as text messaging despite this wide acceptance of mobile phones. Thus there is a necessity for new developments and technologies in the area of mobile device service and application creation. Per (Koch & Rahwan, 2004) agent technology promises to be as such within this domain. In particular Java agent development environment (JADE) besides other possibilities proposes a way to develop mobile device based cross-platform applications.

By taking into account mobile and agent technologies possibilities we focus also on knowledge and especially on personal knowledge. As knowledge is increasingly valuated and used in business and in regular life situations then it points to a necessity for well educated people. Thus there is an implication for need of an effective personal knowledge management system (PKMS). Such system should lay foundation blocks for a new knowledge-based society, economy, and should allow ambient participation in a social and economic life. Per Jefferson currently available PKMS are just a bit more than just productivity tools (Jefferson, 2006). He suggests that there is a necessity for systems with ability to adjust to individual.

This chapter reports on several stages of broader research targeted at perspectives of developing a PKMS. The proposed solution is encompassing three personal knowledge management (PKM) aspects of well-rounded PKMS (Apshvalka, 2004; Apshvalka & Grundspenkis, 2005): social, psychological and technological. Technological aspect is based on agent and mobile technologies (Osis & Grundspenkis, 2009b; Osis & Grundspenkis, 2010; Osis & Grundspenkis, 2011a) utilizing mobile-cross platform solution based on JADE environment. In addition within this paper the technological aspect is elaborated in a detailed way and encompassing the whole PKMS perspective. Social and partially psychological aspect of PKM is based on proposed personal trinity model approach (Osis & Grundspenkis, 2011b) for developing a well-rounded PKMS. Within this aspect of PKMS is included the personal knowledge cone-spiral (PKCS) which makes it possible to avoid knowledge worker "burn-out" by detecting PKCS pattern in knowledge acquisition process. As well this aspect of PKMS includes five knowledge acquisition principles based on knowledge substance and its elements characteristics to support PKM.

The goal of this chapter is the following: using summary of existing PKM tools and systems and overview of approaches of their development taken over from the our previous research (Osis & Grundspenkis, 2011a) to propose a conceptually new approach for developing more well-rounded PKMS, which takes into account also a social and psychological aspect of PKM. As one area of usage of such PKMS is a learning environment support (Osis & Grundspenkis, 2010), which is briefly described in this chapter as well to provide a demonstrative example for potential utilization of proposed system. The main contribution of this chapter is an attempt to incorporate social and psychological aspects of PKM with its technological aspect into the PKMS, and to stimulate the debate in this regard.

Chapter is organized as follows. This brief introduction is followed by an overview of personal knowledge management from knowledge worker's perspective. Within this perspective a short summary of previous findings about existing PKM tools and systems is given. The third section describes personal knowledge management system's conception. This section includes description of social and partially psychological aspect of PKMS. In addition it contains a brief look into technological aspect of PKMS detailing several types of modules the proposed PKMS consists of. These modules include PKMS core or basic module, several supplemental modules, which are further divided into two types: frequently used modules and specific area modules. Description of specific area module "m-learning" focusing on learning environment support is given to illustrate a particular example of this type of module in more details. The fourth section is geared towards the development of proposed PKMS. This section includes a brief description of environment of mobile devices– types, platforms and ways of communication. Next it looks into strength and weaknesses of mobile devices in perspective of PKMS. That is followed by introduction of main elements of mobile Java environment. Then agent technology and mobile devices in perspective of PKMS and particularly also JADE and JADE LEAP environment, which focuses on mobile devices is described. All these pieces are put together and a detailed description of proposed PKMS architecture is given covering all types of modules involved. Specific attention is given to the core or the basic module, which encompasses also individual's knowledge profile, user profile and a special configuration area for adding supplemental modules to PKMS on a need basis. A conceptual specific area module "m-learning" is also described, which involves a case study at Vidzeme University of Applied Sciences to enhance a course grading system at the Faculty of Engineering as a learning environment supportive effort. The chapter ends with conclusions including summary of key results and the future work perspective. References section is included as well.

2. Personal knowledge management from knowledge worker's perspective

Personal knowledge management (PKM) is one of knowledge management (KM) sub-areas. KM research area exists already for a while, though PKM as a sub-area is not well enough researched one (Pauleen, 2009). Thus PKM has been chosen as one of basic research objects of this work.

By conducting research in this area it is determined that PKM includes series of processes an individual has to accomplish. In addition, analysis of this area has led to identification of several sets of such processes, which are summarized and systematized in Table 1. As in different sets several of these processes are very kindred or their essential is the same just each of them having a different name, then within this summary a number of processes (i.e. names of processes) are combined and should be considered as one. Accordant order of processes within each set (i.e. based on accordant researcher provided definition) is given by using numbers. At the same time these numbers indicate that particular PKM process is included within accordant researcher's given PKM definition.

Authors of this work provide a new view within PKM process context by taking into account summarized PKM processes in Table 1 and Barth's description of information processing skills and tools (Barth, 2005). Authors distinguish nine PKM processes, which include in PKM context comprehensive set of actions or functions to do. The nine PKM processes are: creation, access, processing, organizing, analysing, retrieving, collaboration, usage and sharing, and security.

PKM processes	(Apshvalka, 2004)	(Tsui, 2002)	(Jarche, 2009)	(Moghe, 2010)	(Frand & Hixon, 1999)	(Frei, 2006)
1. Composition or new ideas recital / creation					1	5
2. Searching / discovery	1	1				
3. Acquisition / aggregation		2		1	2	1
4. Processing / sorting			1	2		
5. Classification / organizing / categorizing		3	2	3	6	3
6. Reviewing / evaluation / analysis				4	3; 4	2; 4
7. Storing / codification	2	4	3		5	
8. Retrieving	4	5	4		7	
9. Connecting or socializing / dialogue creating			5			8
10. Contributing / usage	3		6			
11. Sharing / publicizing / presentation	5		7			6; 7

Table 1. Personal knowledge management sets of processes

Based on nine PKM processes, authors have developed a PKM process model which is shown in Figure 1. This model pictures processes to be used for knowledge element development and usage in PKM context. In process designating squares is an area in blue. It is a process sub-level, which if needed can omit particular process actions and to pass control to the next process. Dotted lines in context with security process means that accordant security action can or can not be applied during particular PKM process action(s). One can observe that security process is parallel to all other PKM processes.

With Barth words PKM essentially is responsible about what you know, who you know, and what they know (Barth, 2005). PKM cultural and collaboration edge is included in essential of this laconic definition. That points that PKM is not just focusing on individual as such. Rather it also focuses on cultural, collaborative and social aspects among knowledge workers.

PKM fosters creation of communities of practice (CoP) (Cakula & Osis, 2010; Martin 2006), which serves as a fertile ground for knowledge acquisition, sharing and usage, and as follows also for knowledge creation.

It is necessary to follow trends of own work areas and to continuously supplement own knowledge. In order for an individual to successfully manage these challenges authors see PKM as a solution and as a support provider for a knowledge worker and for an individual towards his / her growth and improvement. Thus it is also important that for a knowledge worker personal knowledge management system's (PKMS) support is available for simple information management tasks as well as for more intellectual activities.

By conducting analysis of PKMS it was determined that research in this area started relatively recently. So far PKM and PKMS is less researched KM area (Pauleen, 2009). As PKMS definition within this paper is considered one by Apshvalka and Grundspenkis (Apshvalka & Grundspenkis, 2005), which states that PKMS is a complex system and it contains social, psychological and technological aspects. Its operation is closely tied with a knowledge worker's perception, emotions, believes, surrounding society, environment, wishes and goals. Technology in PKMS context has an important role as well. A PKMS goal is to support as much as possible its owner in decision making and performing actions.

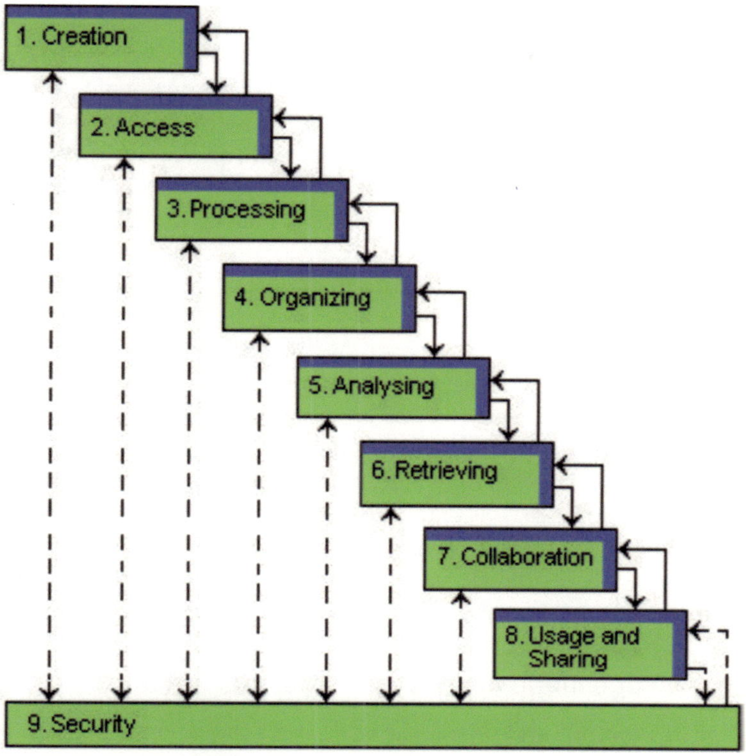

Fig. 1. Personal knowledge management process model

It is determined, that PKMS supports knowledge objects finding, acquisition, creation and sharing. PKMS also supports decision making and environment creation so that individual could share his / her knowledge with other knowledge workers or with CoP acquaintances. Miller considers that PKMS from practical point of view contains that how individual can find personal information sources in a computer or in a mobile device, and how this information can be adopted to particular situation to create intellectual and knowledge values to foster success at work or in personal life (Miller, 2005). In addition PKMS focuses not just to an individual personal information sources, but also to sources outside the set of latter mentioned sources.

So far observed PKM research areas can be divided in two directions. One direction mainly focuses on PKMS as a part of company's KMS (Völkel & Abecker, 2008) and it's interaction with KMS. Another direction focuses on usage of PKMS or PKM tools in individual's context thus paying less attention to company's KMS factor (Jarche, 2006; Li & Li, 2009).

Personal knowledge management tools and systems development approaches. By conducting PKMS analysis it is determined that there are several types of PKMS based on their structure. So far more known and developed PKMS are based on desktop approach (Doong & Wang, 2009), for example, Google Desktop, Windows Search, Apple Spotlight and Copernic Desktop Search. Other PKMS are based on Web technologies such as wiki, for example, WikiPad (WikiPad, 2010), or Web blogging (Li & Li, 2009). There have been attempts to combine latter mentioned approaches (Kim et al., 2007), thus trying to come up with such system, which would allow its user to avoid information doubling by using both desktop and wiki environment.

By conducting PKMS analysis it is also determined that there are several PKMS development approaches, for example, Maier's pier-to-pier KMS (Maier, 2004) with focus on individual level, Apshvalka's developed one based on brain functionality PKMS conceptual model (Apshvalka, 2004), Smedley's conceptual PKMS (Smedley, 2009) based on theoretical models in KM (Nonaka & Konno, 1999) and in learning (Kolb, 1984), Wright conceptual PKMS (Wright, 2005, 2008) based on four mutually connected scopes (analytical, information, social, learning). In the case of Smedley conceptual PKMS very important is that a knowledge sharing process is the trust factor (Smedley, 2009), but in Wright's approach very important is tight collaboration and networking (Wright, 2005, 2008).

So far created PKMS development approaches based on desktop and on Web social applications are applicable in PKM. However these approaches only partially support PKM requirements and conditions, and they do not combine all three PKMS aspects: social, psychological and technological. These PKMS are not scalable and / or are not adjustable to the particular knowledge worker and to his / her knowledge work and area of interest. Current PKMS can be considered as only a bit more than PKM productivity tools. Based on (Jefferson, 2006) there are needed systems with ability to adjust to individual style and working methods. By evaluating available information, we have to conclude, that so far are not known wholesome PKMS development approaches, which would focus directly on systems development and would combine previously mentioned three PKM aspects.

3. Personal knowledge management system's conception

An appearance of innovations and new ideas in the knowledge worker (KW) level happens in all environments and in all moments over individual's time frame. For the KW it is important to have a PKMS support. A PKMS only from technological aspect will not make a successful system's integration and usage for backing the KW's task supporting process. It is important that individual himself / herself is willing to use a PKMS and is willing to stick with PKM guidelines. Here stand out the social and psychological aspects of PKMS. It is important to realize individual's everyday needs, motivation and task accomplishing satisfaction.

A well-known hierarchy of needs was published more than fifty years ago (Maslow, 1954). Maslow proposed that individual's needs are hierarchically ordered in five levels: biological and physiological, safety, belongingness and love, esteem, and self-actualization. This hierarchy usually is depicted in the form of pyramid where at its basic level are positioned biological and physiological needs (Chapman, 1995). In 1970-s hierarchy of needs was extended with levels of cognitive and aesthetic needs, but in 1990-s there was added level of transcendence needs (Maslow, 1954; Chapman, 1995).

The theory of hierarchy of needs has been also criticized being subjective and the order of needs levels being not appropriate (Boeree, 2006). However from a PKMS perspective the Maslow hierarchy order is not important. More essential is to realize that such individual needs exist and they clearly have an impact on the KW. Thus these needs have to be taken into account when developing a PKMS.

Maslow realized the existence of attitude problems regarding workers such that they have certain human basic needs and that they have the rights for self-actualization (Chapman, 1995). There are also some other problems KW-s have to deal with (Etzel & Thomas, 1996). KW-s have to identify problems within themselves and should be willing to tackle them. Thus they can improve PKMS performance from all of its three aspects.

Important traits of KW about the done task are also motivation and satisfaction. In regard of satisfaction a considerable research is done by Herzberg developing theory of two factors (Herzberg et. al., 1959) which can be directly referred also to KW-s. Regarding motivation a valuable research effort is done by McClelland who developed a theory of motivation and researched individuals' needs for achievements (McClelland, 1967). It is considered that individual's needs are developing during his / her life. Haslam states that individual's motivation is dependent on his / her self-categorization (Haslam, 2004).

3.1 Personal trinity model – Social and psychological aspect

Authors have proposed a PKMS development approach taking into account several influencing factors of individuals (Osis & Grundspenkis, 2011b). This approach is named the personal trinity model (PTM) approach. It has three views:

- whole-human imitation point of view;
- individual needs point of view;
- PKMS development point of view.

Whole-human simulation point of view of PTM is described first. A personal knowledge is not a set of notifications, settings, expressions or actions that are stored for later use. "As organic beings we are embedded in situations and culturally formed, and we developmentally acquire and extend the learned activities that come to constitute our being in the world" (Day, 2007). As follows individuals act on behalf of their experience according to their surrounding customs and habits. An individual is developing as an oak tree which grows out of acorn with its encoding (i.e. having roots, trunk, branches and leaves). While growing it is affected by surrounding environment - sun and amount of warmth, precipitation and seasons. Similarly it is with individuals with their own initial "encoding" and further development influenced by surrounding environment. Thus the PTM can be considered as a symbolic simulation of human entirety in direct and indirect meaning. There are three basic parts: head, hart and body. The head part relates to a human cognitive and exploring aspect. The hart part relates to a human social, emotional and cultural aspect, while the body part relates to a human physiologic aspect.

From the whole-human simulation point of view authors will look more closely at the head part. Johnson talks about innovation and new ideas. He states that at the beginning there is a hunch (Johnson, 2010) in the mind of an individual. There it incubates. A new idea has not born yet. After a while another hunch appears in the mind of this individual. In the process of exchanging thoughts two or more hunches create a base for creation of new idea or directly foster it (Johnson, 2010). A thoughts exchange can take place within an individual herself / himself or among several individuals in the process of knowledge sharing. A hunch can be located in the mind of one individual or the same hunch can come up in the minds of several individuals.

Authors have defined the knowledge substance concept (Osis & Grundspenkis, 2011b). Based on the square of known-unknown (Frappaolo, 2004) the knowledge substance concept encompasses a breadth of all knowledge all around individuals and around the environment they live in as a community by communicating and interacting with each other. The knowledge substance is integrity of all knowledge, and it is not further dividable in knowledge sub-substances but only in knowledge elements (KE). In addition knowledge an individual is striving to acquire in the context of knowledge substance can not be seen only as a dichotomous item (or items) as it is in the case of knowledge domain stated in the knowledge space theory (DeRose, 2005; Cognitive Science Section, 2007). Meaning that there exist such KE-s which can not be fully cognizable or can not be identifiable at all. However they are also part of knowledge substance. Based on this concept authors have proposed five knowledge acquisition principles (Osis & Grundspenkis, 2011b) to support a PKM and knowledge elements acquisition.

The first principle: a KW has to posses an intuition to come to verity about those KE-s, which in a foreseeable time manner can not be find out or known, for example, NP complete problems (Fortnow, 2009), or which can not be known at all thus leaving them in a semi-find-out state (i.e. even they are found out in a hunch level though they stay as tacit knowledge, which further can not be explicated).

The second principle: an individual does not need to strive to find out and to pierce each and every surrounding KE till the last detail. They are too many. Instead one has to strive to common understanding about particular knowledge area to a certain level and to get additional knowledge how to acquire more detailed knowledge about this area in case it is needed later.

Nowadays regarding KE acquisition a KW is facing an increasing intensity tempo of acquiring new knowledge in particular time frame. Earlier individual obtained knowledge and all the main skills for his / her life during childhood or young adulthood. Once becoming an adult individual usually also possessed a craftsmanship to be relied upon for entire life. However nowadays there are much more dynamics in economics. Similarly as before much of knowledge is acquired in childhood or young adulthood. However it may turn out to be not good enough in our current world. Thus individual might have to be forced or stimulated to change occupation or to retrain pressed by economics, society or by other means. That means to learn substantially new knowledge and skills (i.e. vertical growth) as depicted in Figure 2 based on the proposed personal knowledge cone-spiral (PKCS).

For nowadays individual such additional knowledge and skills acquisition stages or spiral twines are more comparing with people centuries before. In order to be competitive in job

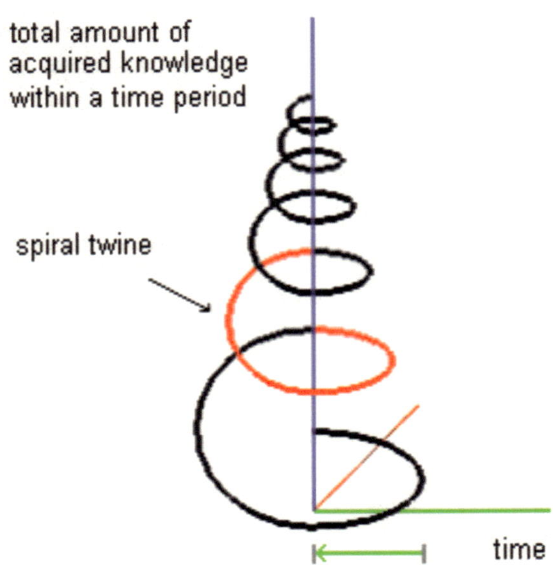

Fig. 2. Personal knowledge cone-spiral (Osis & Grundspenkis, 2011b)

market a KW has to acquire a qualitatively new knowledge even in shorter periods of time if to compare that with previous knowledge acquisition cycles or PKCS twines. That is similar to the coherence described by Moor's law regarding computer development (Intel, 2011). This pattern of even shorter spiral twines bears a potential side effect. Such pattern can indicate the potential of KW burn-out. Thus the PKCS not only describes nowadays the common pattern of even shorter periods of knowledge acquisition, but also may serve as warning signal built in the PKMS for a KW to adjust his / her learning intensity in order to avoid potential burn-out symptoms. This serves as an example that by using a PTM in development process and in execution of PKMS a KW has a support to voluntary leverage his / her life areas.

Regarding the PTM heads part there are proposed three more principles (Osis & Grundspenkis, 2011b) related with knowledge sharing and acquisition:

The third principle: in order to successfully acquire new KE-s an individual has to work out a desire to acquire them and to strive for this knowledge.

The fourth principle: there is a better chance to acquire new knowledge elements by collaborating (e.g. within communities of practice) rather than to try it alone. It is easier to maintain ones knowledge level by being within a group and by collaborating while by being alone knowledge gradually fades unless much more effort is applied to prevent that.

The fifth principle: sharing tacit knowledge is best accomplished by using analogies and similarities. In this way it is possible to transfer not only the direct meaning of knowledge but also the spirit of knowledge.

The PTM - individual needs point of view. The PTM is projected on the eight-level Maslow needs hierarchy described above. Accordingly individual needs are grouped into three parts, which correspond to the PTM three views (i.e. head – cognitive needs; heart – transcendence, self-actualization, esteem needs, aesthetic needs, belongingness and love needs; body – safety needs, physiological needs).

Usually it is important for a KW to reach needs stated in self-actualization level within hierarchy of needs. In this regard Maslow states that it is important to strive for specific set of fifteen values in order to be happy and to reach self-actualization (Maslow, 1954). However Boeree does not agree with this proposition. Rather he argues that individual being in such critical situations as war or economic crisis his / her desire to strive for this set of primary values will not exist due to more primary needs as food, warmth and home (Boeree, 2006). By taking into account these arguments authors propose that a knowledge workers should strive for other super-set of individual improving values (Osis & Grundspenkis, 2011b; Concordia, 1986) encompassing love for others and for themselves (LFO-FT):

- meekness and not being hot-headed;
- politeness and not being rude;
- wishing well and not being envious;
- simplicity and not being flatulent;
- low-keyed and not being indecent;
- unselfish and not being selfish;
- not being easily angered;
- forgiveness and not to remember/remind mischief;
- joy about truth and not delight about evil.

By taking into account human weaknesses, lust, etc. it is clear that this super-set is a running target which will never be reached. However the important point for an individual is to start to strive for this super-set of values constantly trying to achieve them. Then that will be the real gain for a KW from the individual perspective and even more valuable from collaboration with others perspective. Especially that applies to the 5th principle stated above.

The PTM - PKMS development point of view is described next. PKMS general development approaches based on robust framework and the PTM are dividable into two directions. First one focuses development principles and PKMS aspects including following PTM approach guidelines. This direction is dividable into two more parts - the PKMS social aspect and psychological aspect, and the technological aspect.

The PKMS social aspect and psychological aspect based on PTM focuses directly on a KW himself / herself. Partially they are connected with the technological aspect (note: this partial connection is true in opposite direction as well) by using previously defined 9 PKMS processes as a transition link. As a solution basis for these two aspects is previously described LFO-FT set of characteristics and 5 KE-s acquisition supporting principles. The PKMS technological aspect has a modular approach. Agent and mobile technologies are a solution basis for the technological aspect. In more details it is described in the fourth section of this chapter. PKMS general development approaches are depicted in Figure 3.

Another development direction focuses on a KW and his / her availability to further develop / customize PKMS by using 1st and 2nd level adjusting options. Thus a KW can develop his / her individual PKMS and also trying to include all three aspects of PKM - technical, social and psychological. These development approaches should be perceived as robust road maps for PKMS development.

3.2 Modular personal knowledge management system – The technological aspect

Modular PKMS architecture consists of basic module and several additional modules. The basic module contains basic functionality, which supports PKMS basic processing. This module contains knowledge worker's, so called, knowledge card or knowledge profile, user's card or user's profile, information and knowledge element searching, tacit knowledge elements externalization support tool, personal knowledge cone-spiral functionality, as well as time scheduling tool. The PKMS basic module from the architecture point of view is described in more details in fourth section.

3.2.1 Frequently used modules

PKMS additional modules are divided into two groups: frequently used modules and specific area modules. Frequently used modules contain modules suggested for minimal / small size PKMS while in the same time still maintaining scalability. Specific area modules contain such PKMS modules, which are considered for one or another group of KW-s with particular specifics of activities. For example, for ice cream development support (i.e. for developing a new ice recipe, solving with quality assurance tasks, external knowledge acquisition regarding competitors production development, and following development of European Union laws regarding diary area) in a milk processing company.

While keeping a PKMS size possibly small as frequently used modules are set the following ones: "goals and tasks management module" and "collaboration management module". Goals and tasks management module from a goal perspective allows a KW to set up personal goals in a simplified way, by using specific goals setting templates depending from chosen goal's type and specifics. From a tasks perspective this additional module supports a

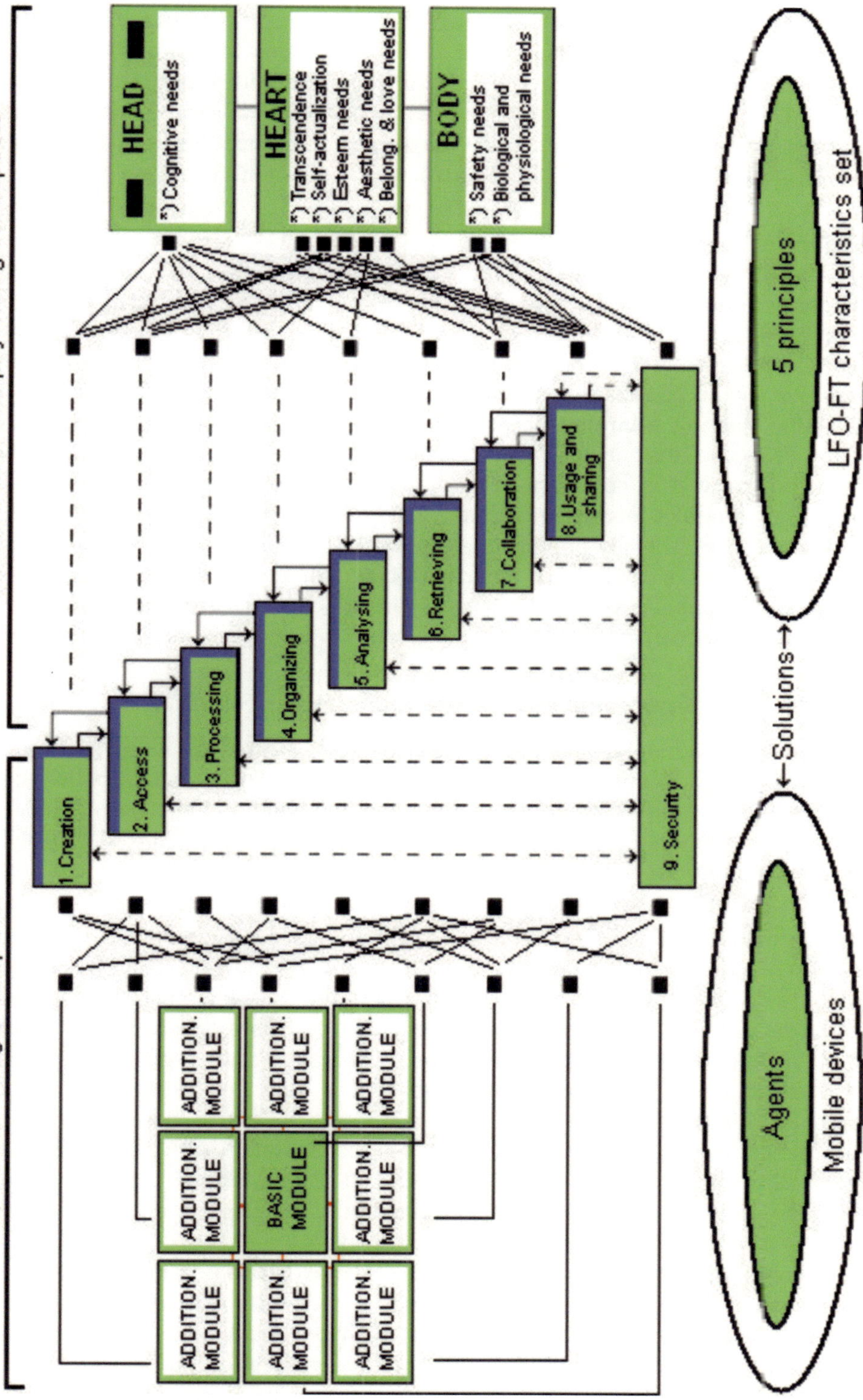

Fig. 3. PKMS aspects general development approaches

KW to set up to do tasks for himself / herself as well as for a PKMS. The collaboration management module provides support of several communication types (see user card – social aspect part) for knowledge worker's collaboration with other individual or for a PKMS collaboration agent with particular individual's PKMS representing agent. More detailed description about agent usage and frequently used modules from architecture and the technical solution perspective is given in fourth section of this chapter.

3.2.2 Specific area module "m-learning"

Each specific area module is intended for concrete group of KW-s with specific or partially specific tasks to do. As everyday work of one of the authors is connected with academic environment as a lecturer for professional bachelor study program in Vidzeme University of applied sciences, then m-learning module is chosen as a specific area module. As additional modules size should be kept as compact as possible, then this additional module is focused on providing learning environment support functionality by using mobile devices as the basis for a PKMS. So it is not considered as a universal m-learning module. However if for a particular company it is necessary to carry out additional m-learning support then by supplementing modules repository with new modules it is possible to add other m-learning modules to a PKMS. Thereby previous m-learning PKMS functionality is supplemented by additional one. In more details the particular specific area module is described also in fourth section of this chapter. As part of a work on particular specific area module authors have conducted research on mobile learning in PKM context (Osis & Grundspenkis, 2009a).

4. Development of personal knowledge management system

This section contains more detailed description of PKMS technological aspects in context of PKMS development. Within this section are stated mobile device characteristics, strengths and weaknesses, as well as smart phone and agent integration in context of PKM. Also is provided description of PKMS basic module, frequently used modules and specific area module "m-learning" architecture.

4.1 Mobile technology

By analysis of available information sources online and available literature it is determined that so far there have not done research exactly about PKMS development approaches based on mobile devices platform. Agnihotri and Troutt are even more categorical. They point out, that research about role of technologies in the PKM is only at its beginnings (Agnihotri & Troutt, 2009). For this reason within this work mobile device overview and evaluation in context of PKM is conducted.

One of the most important KW-s task is developing collaboration with other individuals, for example, as it is in case of Wright conceptual PKMS (Wright, 2005). Developing collaboration contains: ability to communicate, to share explicit and tacit knowledge elements, to do collaboration in any time and in any place.

It is important for KW to adjust mobile device from all PKMS aspects to his / her needs and requirements in order to conveniently and handy carried out everyday functions. It is also important so that this device (i.e. device physical shape) and available work environment within it is acceptable aesthetically (see PTM and individual needs). Device's shape based on it usage convenience (i.e. does it comfortably fit in palm, is there available convenient information input functionality) is one more mobile device characteristic. Based on PKM security process and on safety needs level (see PTM whole-human imitation point of view - body part) as another important characteristic can be named mobile device security functionality from unauthorized access to device point of view. An additional important point of view to look at is a PKMS ability to function on different mobile devices, i.e. reducing PKMS dependence from one particular mobile device model or even platform.

Within this work have been conducted mobile device summary and analysis, and have been determined that currently there are available many different mobile devices That included many different mobile device platforms. Each of them represents one mobile device operating system. As most used operating systems can be named Android, Symbian, iPhone OS, RIM and Microsoft developed mobile device operating systems (Gartner, 2011). Mobile device platforms and application development environments are also analysed. Within this aspect there is large diversity. Often development environments are specifically suited for particular platform. However in addition to mobile device basic platform no matter what operating system it runs on frequently there is provided support for Java environment. This is one of the reasons, which fosters to choose Java application developing environment for the PKMS development based on mobile devices. Later on we describe main Java mobile environment elements.

One of actual features of mobile devices is their ability to provide wireless communication and data transfer. Nowadays mobile devices usually are used for communication and data transfer with other mobile devices, for Web access or data synchronization with personal computer or notebook. Within our work we have determined and systematized mobile device communication and data transfer types in different parts of the World. In Table 2 these communication and data transfer types are depicted by focussing on European region.

Type, generation	Communication and data transfer types	Data transfer speed - download	Specifics and constraints
Basic-types	Wi-Fi (802.11n)	600 Mb/s	Operation range in indoors is till 46m, outdoors till 92m. Mobile device requires wireless network adapter.
	Bluetooth 2.0	2.1 Mb/s	Operation range till 10m.
	IrDA	115.2 Kb/s	Short range operation; required direct visibility.
2G	GSM	9.5 Kb/s	Operation range till 35km. Limited data transfer options.
	GPRS	53.6 Kb/s	GPRS is GSM extension (not available without GSM).
	EDGE/EGPRS	384 Kb/s	Mainly used as transition standard from GSM to UMTS.
3G	UMTS	1920 Kb/s	Data transfer rate 384 Kb/s for mobile phones.
	HSDPA	8-10 Mb/s	Only for download; upload not supported.
	CDMA2000	3.1 Mb/s	Limited amount of parallel connections - i.e. if a tight num. of clients, then some will be left without a service.
	WiMAX	75 Mb/s	Currently a comparably expensive service.
4G	3GPP LTE	100 Mb/s	Not widely available yet.
	UMB	275 Mb/s	Unclear future perspective can be discarded.

Table 2. Wireless communication and data transfer types in European region context

Usually knowledge worker conducts its work in company premises or in open air territory of company. Assuming company is located in populated area or within its vicinity and evaluating communication and data transfer ranges, then majority of 2G and 3G connections provide communication to mobile devices for conducting knowledge work. Data transfer basic types such as Bluetooth and IrDA operate in very limited range (till 10 meters). In addition IrDA requires direct visibility connection. There is also service coverage that can considerably differ from country to country. It is determined that Wi-Fi operation range allows its usage both in company premises and in open air territory of company.

An important aspect in KW's work is data transfer rate. From this point of view currently available best download rate is on 802.11n standard based Wi-Fi, which is 600 Mb/s.

Though latter mentioned data transfer rate is dependent on company used 802.11 standard versions. In many places there still is used one based on 802.11g which supports data transfer rate till 54 Mb/s. Also 3G technologies support a good data transfer rate, for example, WiMAX standard supports data transfer up to 75 Mb/s.

Additional aspect is based on costs of particular communication and data transfer rate. Bluetooth and IrDA are free of charge types of data transfer. However due to their limited operation range their usage to support the PKMS is not suitable. WiMAX data transfer type is suitable based on its operation range (till 50 km) and data transfer rate (up to 75 Mb/s). It is determined that it is rather expensive service and, for example, in Latvia it is not available yet even though for a testing time it was available in Lattelecom network. Also it is determined that there is not a wide range of mobile devices supporting WiMAX. Even there are a number of commercial Wi-Fi hot spots though there are available quite a few places (including company indoor and outdoor territories) with free of charge Wi-Fi hot spots as well. By evaluating latter mentioned aspects it is concluded that for KW and the PKMS support the most appropriate is Wi-Fi communication and data transfer type.

4.1.1 Strength and weaknesses of mobile devices in perspective of PKMS

By conducting mobile device strength and weaknesses analysis within this work it is determined that there are number of strength and weaknesses, which are related with mobile devices and which should be considered when involved in knowledge work. As weaknesses can be mentioned the following (Osis & Grundspenkis, 2009a): small and different size screens, small keyboards, small icons on touch screen displays, difficulties to access information and explicit knowledge elements (where add-ons are required), general navigation difficulties, diversity of mobile devices brands and each brand products diversity, mobile devices operating systems diversity (which creates difficulties for development of multi-platform PKMS applications), limited memory and processing power, limited buttery processing time, text messages and e-mail size limitations, difficulties to access Web content (originally designed for desktop computers screens sizes). At the same time several mobile devices strengths have been determined in the context of KW and the PKM which are actual both for m-learning and for mobile device based PKMS. They are (Mellow, 2005; Squire et al., 2006): portability, individuality, linking, context sensitivity; flexibility in a sense of time, place and new knowledge acquisition speed control; usage of technology, which is attractive to KW (i.e. from PKMS social and psychological aspects) and convenient.

By evaluating mobile devices strengths and weaknesses it is concluded that modern ones have several considerable strengths, which makes them especially attractive for use as a development basis for the PKMS. They are ubiquity, personalization, localisation functionality and interaction characteristic. In addition it is worth to point out that mobile devices supplemented with specific hardware obtain universal technical applicability characteristic. For example, accordingly supplemented mobile devices serves as a camera, pocket torch light, bicycle speedometer or mini-projector for providing slide shows (AT&T, 2009) to support such PKMS process as usage and sharing, and to satisfy individual's safety needs (see PTM individual needs point of view - body part).

The PKM means to know what knowledge do we posses, how can we organize it, mobilize, continue to create new knowledge and to apply it for reaching own goals (Martin, 2006). By reviewing latter mentioned mobile devices platforms, wireless communication and data transfer types, mobile devices weaknesses and strength, mobile devices characteristics, their ever increasing processing power and number of users (Hill, 2010) is acquired a base for confidence about mobile platform validity and conformity for the PKMS development.

4.1.2 Main elements of mobile Java environment

As a uniting element and cross platform unification solution for many mobile devices can serve Java programming language despite that these devices might operate on different operating systems (OS). Within mobile Java execution environment there are several differences based on mobile device technical specifications as well. That is why a short overview of main elements of Java execution environment is included.

This environment includes such elements as configurations and profiles. Configurations define the minimal requirements for the hardware of the device and what kind of Java virtual machine is included in the system. In turn profiles define the programming infrastructure available for applications intended to be run on top of particular configuration (Mikkonen, 2007). Two important configurations are distinguished: Connected Limited Device Configuration (CLDC) and Connected Device Configuration (CDC). Each of them sets requirements for underlying virtual machines which in turn are hosted on each particular mobile device operating system. CLDC is the simplest mobile Java configuration and it is available on low-end and middle-class mobile phones and smart phones. This configuration is based on simplified Java virtual machine. CDC configuration lays on standard-featured Java virtual machine even though it does not require all the libraries as in the case of desktop environment (Mikkonen, 2007). Therefore such configuration usually is available on most powerful mobile devices like tablet PC-s, communicators and PDA-s. Each of these configurations has profiles. They can be seen as a connecting element between Java environment creators and mobile application developers. CLDC has two closely related profiles: Mobile Information Device Profile (MIDP) and Information Module Profile (IMP). The first one is meant for mobile devices with small screens, as a minimum limited connectivity and a simple keyboard. Thus the MIDP profile actually is the most widespread one available. The IMP profile is geared for similar devices but lacking screen features like operate-able sensors. The CDC configuration has three profiles: Foundation Profile (FP) being a simplest profile among the three, Personal Basis Profile (PBP) extends the FP and Personal Profile (PP) basically mimicking standard Java running on desktop environment.

Currently in market the dominating configuration is the CLDC both among mobile phones and also among smart phones. Only few smart phones with the CDC configuration were in the market at the beginning of this century such as Nokia 9500 (Forum.Nokia, 2010). These devices were upper level smart phones with a very expensive price tag. As a result it turned out that there is no real business for the CDC configuration environment within a smart phone market. Also PDA-s (which are dominantly based on the CDC configuration) tend to disappear from market as smart phones are taking over their niche and offering even a wider variety of functionality. However the future of CDC is not necessarily dim. Thus, for example, Amazon Kindle e-Reader is taking over the run for the CDC configuration support. The Kindle software development kit (SDK) (Amazon, 2010) has been made available since spring 2010. Though for time being it is available for Amazon chosen or approved developers only.

4.2 Mobile devices and agent technology in perspective of PKMS

Research was conducted regarding software agent application areas in context of PKMS. It was determined that software agent can be used in a rather wide range of different areas such as searching for explicit knowledge elements localy within the PKMS, fostering collaboration among KWs and their representing PKMS, information searching in Web resources, supporting actions of KW in communities of practice and the PKMS hardware operation monitoring and supporting.

Regarding software agents, their characteristics and communication it is determined that first of all agent is a computer system existing in its environment, which can carry out autonomous operations within this environment in order to reach set goals (Jennings & Wooldridge, 1998). Agents ability to perform autonomous actions is one of the most important ones also due to that majority of researchers agree that agents should possess it (Wooldridge, 1999). Agents' autonomy is compared as equivalent characteristic to humans' free will (Vidal et al., 2011).

Agents possess abilities or characteristics (Jennings & Wooldridge, 1998). They are (Wooldridge & Jennings, 1995; Tveit, 2001; Padgham et al., 2008): autonomy, social abilities, ability to react, pro-activity, mobility, truth, benevolence, rationality. Based on Bradshaw (Bradshaw, 1997) some other agent characteristics include: temporal continuity, personality and adjustment.

An important area in agents' collaboration context is their ability to communicate. In case of humans in order to communicate they choose communication language which is understood by all involved parties. Similarly is used Agent Communication Language (ACL), which is based on (Bradshaw, 1997): vocabularies, Knowledge Interchange Format (KIF), and on Knowledge Query Manipulation Language (KQML). It is determined that a common vocabulary should be defined so that agents could mutually communicate. In addition communication is supported by using common ontology, which defines particular domain concepts and relations among them. Common ontology is used to design communication protocols. Also a common ontology is a support for vocabulary usage in agent communication. Agents should not be forced to use only one communication protocol in such a wide many sided environment as the Internet. Instead their collaboration must be regulated by using number of ontology protocols (Zack, 1999).

There are distinguished several types of agents. For example, there are collaboration agents, interface agents, information agents, reactive agents, hybrid agents, mobile agents and intelligent agents (Nwana, 1996). Within context of this work more attention is geared towards mobile and intelligent agents as the set of their characteristics is suitable for development of mobile device based PKMS.

Mobile agent is an execution unit which can autonomously migrate to another execution place by transporting along with it its code and execution status. Then it dynamically installs it code and seamlessly continue its execution in the new environment (Nwana, 1996; Lander, 1997; Lange & Oshima, 1999; Kelash et al., 2005; Kotz et al., 2002). Mobile agents use three types of messages (Kelash et al., 2005): proposal, knowledge based, and mobility message. There are several reasons to use mobile agents (Lange & Oshima, 1999): they decrease network load (by travelling themselves to data), they overcome network latency, they encapsulate protocols, they execute asynchronously and autonomously, they dynamically adjust, they are naturally heterogeneous (by naturally adapting legacy system), they are robust and fault tolerant.

Intelligent agents perceive their environment, make deliberate decisions based on their perception and react accordingly. Intelligent agents perceive their environment in different ways depending on environment characteristics. Agents obtain information about their environment by using sensors. Intelligent agent is a software component, which can operate autonomously by perceiving/understanding environment, by evaluating options, and making action decisions by not having communication with a user (i.e. agent owner) (de Carvalho & Tavares Ferreira, 2006).

Lightweight agent platform for mobile device based PKMS. Mobile devices get more popular and individuals become more demanding regarding available mobile device based services. For KWs even more important becomes to find the right information in the right time. More, in some cases it is desirable that software in mobile devices can act on behalf of their users. It is especially important in frequently changing and unpredictable environments. Koch and Rahwan (Koch & Rahwan, 2004) point out that this is the area where usage of agent technology is a promising solution to develop modern software based on mobile devices.

As a basis for agent and mobile technology integration serves created standards in this area. Such are Foundation for Intelligent Physical Agents (FIPA) developed agent based systems standards. FIPA specifications comprise a set of standards to facilitate collaboration of heterogeneous agents and their services (FIPA, 2009). Thus FIPA focuses not only on communication, but also on general meaning services such as standard approach to agent life cycle management (Bergenti et al., 2001).

Several world level companies such as Motorola, Siemens, British Telecom, Telecom Italia, etc. have realized the importance of this area and by joining effort they have started the Lightweight Extensive Agent Platform (LEAP) project. That is the first attempt of a kind to develop a FIPA agent platform that can run both on mobiles and on regular devices such as personal computers using wireless and land line networks. Main goal of the LEAP project is to develop a FIPA compliant agent platform, which is enough lightweight to run on mobile devices with limited resources, and is enough open and scalable to become a solution for devices with no particular resource limitations such as corporate servers (Bergenti et al., 2001).

There are several development platforms for software agent development on mobile devices. One example of such platform is MicroFIPA-OS (Tarkoma & Laukkanen, 2002), while the most popular one is Java Agent DEvelopment Framework (JADE) (JADE, 2009; Wang et al., 2003; Weng & Tran, 2007). It is a software platform fully realized in Java. It facilitates multi-agent systems development by using middle-ware, which is compliant with FIPA and combines several graphical tools for debugging and implementation phases. An agent platform can be distributed over several computers which not necessarily need to have the same operating system; configuration can be controlled using remote GUI. Configuration can be changed during run-time by moving agents from one computer to another whenever it is necessary. Agent communication is based on passing messages by using FIPA ACL as a communication language (JADE, 2009). There is developed the platform based on JADE agents for mobile devices called JADE-LEAP. It is based on FIPA standards and on latter mentioned LEAP project. This is also the frequently used agent platform, which is well documented and has active developers' community. It is determined that the JADE-LEAP is suitable as a development platform for mobile device based PKMS with built-in software agent support.

4.3 Architecture of personal knowledge management system

Based on PKMS general architecture, it is scalable and consists from modules combining the basic module and several supplemental modules. The basic module contains KW's knowledge profile and a user profile. The *knowledge profile* contains information about system's user: his / her knowledge level, knowledge specifics, information about desirable knowledge and also knowledge sharing frequency. In addition it contains a knowledge development plan and a knowledge element repository list. The *user profile* contains particular KW personal information, social aspect information, and psychological aspect information. Both these cards are used by the PKMS when there is collaboration with other KWs and accordingly with their PKMS. The *supplemental modules* contain two frequently used modules (i.e. the goal and task management module, and the collaboration module) and specific area modules. Within this work as a *specific area module* is chosen m-learning module, which provides functionality of learning environment support.

When there are developed new PKMS supplemental modules for inclusion in repository of supplemental modules, then there is updated also special supplemental module list. This list is transferred to the PKMS basic module along with installation of a new upgrade package. Based on this list the PKMS recognizes additional supplemental modules. In order to add frequently used module or specific area module to the PKMS there has to be used special PKMS settings and module configuration area called PUMKA. A KW uses PUMKA area only for PKMS configuration purposes and this area is not used during his / her everyday task processing. PUMKA combines the following functionality: adding frequently used modules or specific area modules to the PKMS, and PKMS (i.e. basic module) default settings configuration.

There is needed an intellectual support for a KW everyday to-do tasks in context of PKMS. Solution for this is an intelligent agents' community (see middle part of Figure 4) which creates a base for KW's environment. First of all agents can serve as hard work performers - as a driving force in so called "engine room". In basics it is hardware, software and technology integrated area to support knowledge acquisition, processing, storing and representation as it is mentioned in Grundspenkis approach (Grundspenkis, 2003) in companies' context. In this work it is used in context of PKMS. Secondly, there are agents supporting communication. And finally there are personal agents, which are tightly connected with KW.

"Engine room" agents idea is that nowadays a number of to-do tasks are connected with technical solutions, which should be done by KWs in order to streamline their everyday actions. These agents can appropriately react on changes in "engine room" environment. Such "engine room" environment consists, for example, from local network, wireless network, Internet and from KW used hardware. It is especially difficult and time consuming for majority of individuals to work with such environment. Other intelligent agents group is communication agents. They are responsible for communication support. Communication is an important aspect for an individual in multi-agent environment in order to perform knowledge creation, acquisition, sharing and distribution. Personal agents, which are directly influenced by a KW, support interaction with particular hardware device as well as provide support in knowledge work.

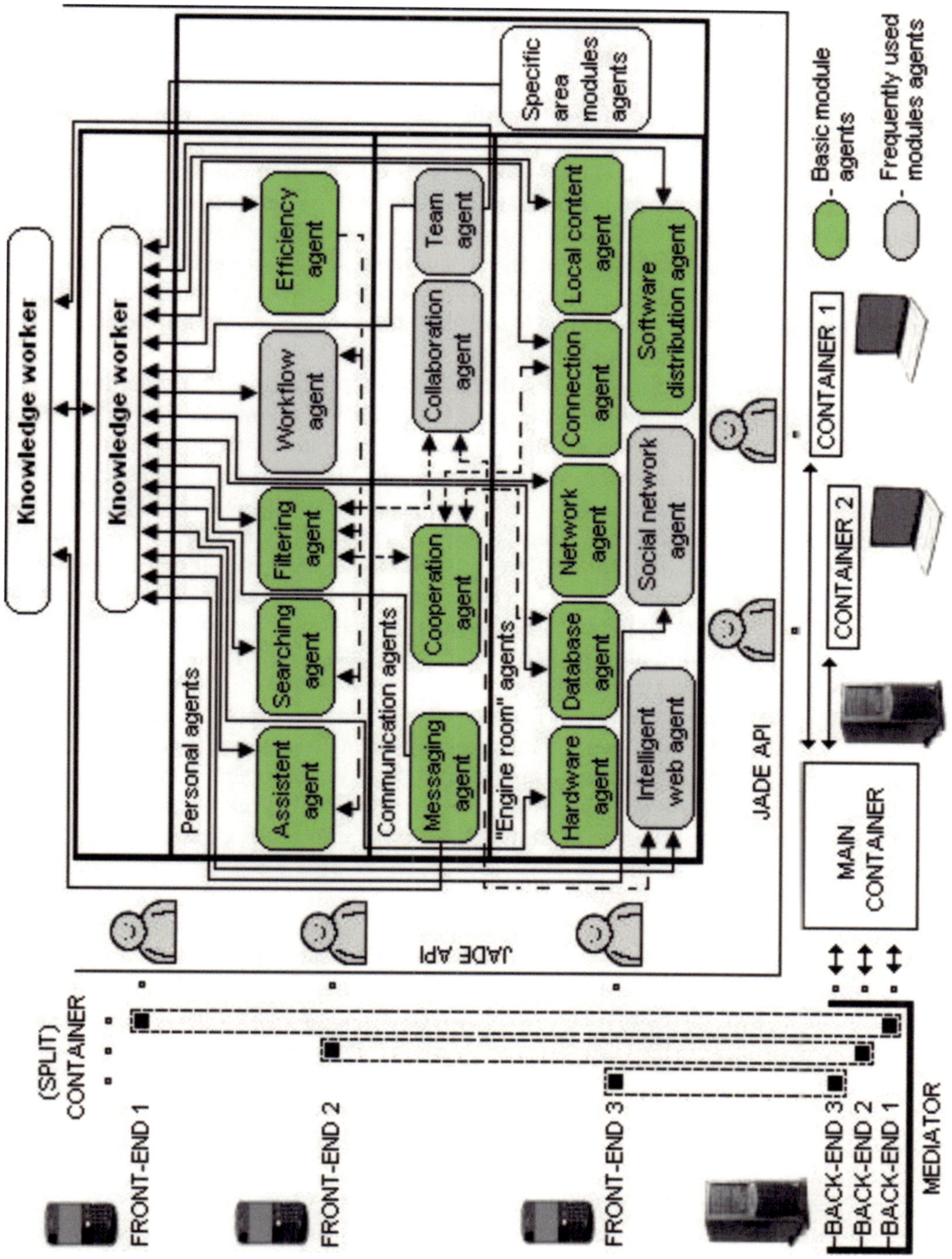

Fig. 4. PKMS three group agent environment in context of mobile devices and agent development environment JADE-LEAP

A KW and the PKMS three group agents environment in context of PKMS modules is depicted in middle part of Figure 4. In green are agents connected with PKMS basic module.

In grey are agents connected with PKMS frequently used modules. Meaning that workflow agent intelligent Web agent is connected with PKMS goal and task management module, but remaining grey-coloured agents are connected with collaboration module. Specific area modules agents should not be showed in details before accordant specific area module is not created and added to modules repository.

Solid lines in the middle part of Figure 4 (i.e. three group agents environment in context of PKMS modules) denote data, information and knowledge flow, but interrupted lines denote possible collaboration between accordant agents. PKMS three group agents' environment in context of mobile devices is depicted in Figure 4 entirely. It depicts the PKMS architecture by combining agent technology view, mobile device technology view, agent development environment JADE-LEAP view and five KWs using notebook computers and smart phones accordingly as a basis for PKMS.

Specific area module "m-learning" architecture. PKMS specific area module m-learning architecture from agent technology perspective is depicted in the middle part of Figure 5. Solid lines denote communication within specific area module m-learning, but interrupted lines denote communication with the PKMS. This module has four main agents types (Osis & Grundspenkis, 2010): instructor agent, operator agent, student agent and audit agent. The JADE-LEAP agent environment is used. There are included some more FIPA standard management agents. Architecture of PKMS specific area module m-learning in context of mobile devices and agent development environment JADE-LEAP is depicted in Figure 5. In particular solution m-learning module has the Main-Container (located on a server or can be located on a notebook computer) and five other containers: Container 1, Container 2 and three split Containers. The Main-Container contains audit agent and operator agent. It also has FIPA standard management agent Directory Facilitator (DF) and FIPA agent platform's mandatory component called Agent Management System (AMS). Containers 1 and 2 are located on notebook computers having regular Java environment. Other three split containers are located on smart phones (i.e. their front-ends). All back-ends of these split containers are located on a server (or can be located on a notebook computer). Automatic management of back-ends of all three front-ends is performed by the JADE-LEAP architectural unit called a mediator as depicted in Figure 5.

Specific area module m-learning has several scenarios. They are as follows: setting a mark, appealing, extending a deadline and scheduling an appointment. (1) *Setting a mark scenario* begins when instructor has corrected, for example, a home work and assigns points. The instructor agent provides option to create a batch collection of the student ID, a single item of points, and the exercise ID. Next it sends this batch collection to the operator agent. Then the operator agent saves that information. It uses help of DF agent (i.e. it is a JADE framework internal agent) and broadcasts this information to each student agent accordingly. In addition if student agents specifically request then they can receive a total summary status of assigned points at a given time. Meanwhile audit agent keeps track of done and not-yet-done exercises. It informs the student agent accordingly based on deadline proximity property value. This value can be set by the student agent. (2) *Appealing scenario* is started by the student. Then it is taken over by the student agent. It sends an appeal directly to the instructor agent. If it is too late and the appeal deadline is passed then the instructor agent on its own rejects this appeal. If that is not the case, then the instructor is informed. (3) *Extending deadline scenario* begins when the instructor decides to extend a deadline for a given exercise.

Then that information is transferred to the operator agent. There it is saved and communicated further with the audit agent and then student agents are informed. (4) *Scheduling an appointment scenario* provides possibility for the student agent to send a request directly to an instructor agent to schedule an appointment. If such request is received by the instructor agent then it consults with its PKMS time management module agent (i.e. if it is available). The latter one on its own decides if to accept or reject particular appointment request.

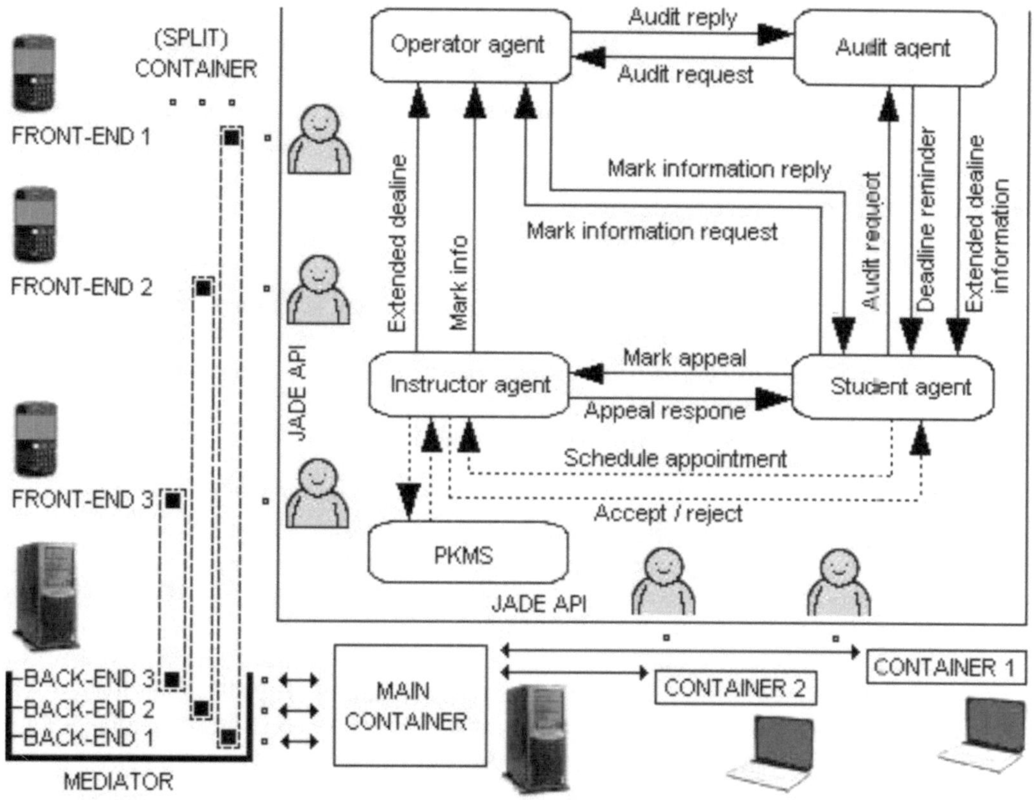

Fig. 5. PKMS specific area module m-learning architecture in context of mobile devices and agent development environment JADE-LEAP

5. Conclusion

The goal of broader research and to create within this work the personal knowledge management system conceptual development approach of combining technological aspect, social aspect and psychological aspect and such system's architecture solution based on mobile and agent technologies has been reached. Within this work is gained the following scientific novelty: (*) defined PKM nine processes and created PKM process model; (*) developed conception for united PKMS development based on suggested personal trinity model which combines technological, social and psychological aspects; (*) developed adaptable PKMS's architecture based on application of mobile and agent technology, and which contains all three latter mentioned PKMS aspects.

Possible directions of future work are: (*) based on created PKMS development conception to research company knowledge management system potential influence on conceptual PKMS and on KW using this system; (*) to conduct in-depth research how KWs can be motivated to use the PKMS from this system's social aspect and psychological aspect, as well as from its technological aspect.

6. References

Agnihotri, R. & Troutt, M., D. (2009) The effective use of technology in personal knowledge management - a framework of skills, tools and user context, *Online Information Review* (Emerald), Vol. 33 No. 2, pp.329-342, ISSN 1468-4527

Amazon (2010) Kindle development kit for active content, *Amazon.com*, 05.19.2010, Available from https://kdk.amazon.com/gp/vendor/sign-in?ie=UTF8&originatingURI=/gp/vendor /members/kindlepubs/kdk/home

Apshvalka, D. (2004) Personal knowledge management, *Proceedings of the 11th ECITE European Conference on Information Technology Evaluation*, pp. 17-22, Amsterdam, Netherlands, November 11-12, 2004

Apshvalka, D. & Grundspenkis, J. (2005) Personal and organizational knowledge management as a driving force for business process effectiveness, *Proceedings of the International Conference on Information Technologies for Business*, pp. 9–14, Vilnius University, Kaunas, May 27, 2005

AT&T (December 2009) AT&T unveils 1GHz Snapdragon-powered LG GW820 eXpo, GSM Arena, 04.19.2010, Available from http://www.gsmarena.com/at_t_unveils_1ghz_snapdragonpowered_lg_gw820_expo-news-1292.php

Barth, S. (2005) Self-organization: taking a personal approach to KM, In: *Knowledge management tools and techniques practitioners and experts evaluate KM solutions*, Rao, M., pp. 347-361, Elsevier, ISBN 8181478843, India

Bergenti, F. & Poggi, A. & Burg, B. & Caire, G. (2001) Deploying FIPA Compliant Systems on Handheld Devices, *IEEE Internet Computing*, IEEE, July, pp. 20-25, ISSN 1089-7801

Boeree, C. G. (2006) Personality theories - Abraham Maslow, 05.19.2010, Available from http://webspace.ship.edu/cgboer/maslow.html

Bradshaw J. (1997) An Introduction to Software Agents, The MIT Press, pp. 1-46, 04.19.2010, Available from http://www.cs.umbc.edu/agents/introduction/01-Bradshaw.pdf

Cakula, S. & Osis, K. (2010) Knowledge Management in Course Content Development and Teaching, *Proceedings of the International Conference on Education and New Learning Technologies (EduLEARN'10)*, pp. 87-96, ISBN 978-84-613-9386-2, Barcelona, Spain

Chapman, A. (1995) Maslow's hierarchy of needs, In: *Bussinessballs.com*, 04.19.2010, Available from http://www.businessballs.com/maslow.htm

Cognitive Science Section (2007) Knowledge Space Theory - Knowledge Domain, In: *University of Graz*, 04.19.2010, Available from, http://css.uni-graz.at/projects/CbKSTCourse/release/

Concordia (1986) Concordia Self-Study Bible - New International Version, Hoerber R., G., 1Co-13:4-6, ISBN 0-570-00505-1, Concordia Publishing House, Grand Rapids, MI

Day, R., E. (2007) Knowing and Indexical Psychology, In: *Rethinking Knowledge Management – From knowledge objects to knowledge processes*, McInerney, C., R. & Day, R., E., pp. 331-348, Springer-Verlag, ISBN 9783540710103, New York de Carvalho, R., B. & Tavares Ferreira, M., A. (2006) Knowledge management software, In: *Encyclopedia of knowledge management*, Schwartz, D., G., pp. 410-418, Idea Group Inc., ISBN 159140573-4, Hershey, PA, USA

DeRose, K. (2005) What Is Epistemology? A Brief Introduction to the Topic, In: *Yale University, Department of Philosophy*, 04.19.2010, Available from, http://pantheon.yale.edu/~kd47/What-Is-Epistemology.htm

Doong, H. & Wang, H. (2009) Predictors of diverse usage behaviour towards personal knowledge management systems, *Online Information Review* (Emerald), Vol. 33 No. 2, pp. 316-328, ISSN 1468-4527

Etzel, B. & Thomas, P. (1996) *Personal Information Management - Tools and Techniques for Achieving Professional Effectiveness*, New York University Press, ISBN 9780814721995, Washington Square, NY

FIPA (2009) Foundation for Intelligent Physical Agents, *FIPA*, 09.19.2009, Available from www.fipa.org

Fortnow, L. (2009) The Status of the P versus NP Problem, *Communications of the ACM*, Vol. 52, No. 9, pp. 78-86

Forum.Nokia (2010) Device details - Nokia 9500, *Forum Nokia*, 06.11.2010, Available from www.forum.nokia.com/Devices/Device_specifications/9500/

Frand, J. & Hixon, C. (1999) Personal Knowledge Management: Who, What, Why, When, Where, How, In: *UCLA Anderson School of Management*, 19.04.2010, Available from www.anderson.ucla.edu/faculty/jason.frand/researcher/speeches/PKM.htm

Frappaolo, C. (2004) What is Your Knowledge IQ, In: *Intelligent Portals*, 10.21.2008, Available from www.intelligentkm.com/feature/08/feat1.jhtml

Frei, U. (2006) The Spiral of PKM 2.0 (new graph), 19.04.2010, Available from http://ursfrei.wordpress.com/2006/11/05/the-spiral-of-pkm-20-new-graph

Gartner (May 2011) Gartner Says 428 Million Mobile Communication Devices Sold Worldwide in First Quarter 2011, a 19 Percent Increase Year-on-Year. Gartner, 05.21.2011, Available from: www.gartner.com/it/page.jsp?id=1689814

Grundspenkis, J. (2003) Development of hybrid intelligent systems: integration of structural modeling, intelligent agents and knowledge management techniques, *Scientific Proceedings of the Riga Technical University, 5th series computer science, applied computer systems*, Vol. 17, pp. 7–30, ISSN 1407-7493

Haslam, S., A. (2004) *Psychology in Organizations - The Social Identity Approach*, 2nd Ed., Sage Publications, ISBN 9780761942313, London

Herzberg, F. & Mausner, B. & Snyderman, B. (1959) *The motivation to work*, John Wiley & Sons, New York

Hill, A. (2010) The State of Mobile: EU5 Mobile Media Landscape and Trends, *comScore*, 05.19.2010, Available from http://www.comscore.com/Press_Events/Presentations_Whitepapers/2010/The_State_of_Mobile_EU5_Mobile_Media_Landscape_and_Trends

i2SMS (July 9, 2008) An Introduction to Mobile Technology: Information and Marketing in 2008, 10.21.2008, Available from http://www.tagonline.org/articles.php?id= 269

Intel (2011) Moore's Law, In: *Intel*, 02.21.2011, Available from, http://www.intel.com/technology/mooreslaw

JADE (2009) Java Agent DEvelopment Framework, 09.19.2009, Available from jade.cselt.it

Jarche, H. (2006) My PKM System, In: *Jarche.com*, 04.19.2010, Available from http://www.jarche.com/2006/08/my-pkm-system/

Jarche, H. (2009) Creating your PKM processes, In: *Jarche.com*, 04.19.2010, Available from http://www.jarche.com/2009/07/creating-your-pkm-processes

Jefferson, T., L. (2006) Taking it personally: personal knowledge management. *The journal of information and knowledge management systems*, Vol. 36, No. 1, pp. 35-37, ISSN 0305-5728

Jennings, N. & Wooldridge, M. (1998) Applications of Intelligent Agents, In: *Agent Technology: Foundations, Applications, and Markets*, pp. 3-27, Springer, 04.19.2010, Available from http://www.cs.umbc.edu/agents/introduction/jennings98.pdf

Johnson, S. (2010) *Where Good Ideas Come From: The Natural History of Innovation*, Riverhead, ISBN 9781594487712, New York

Kelash, H., M. & Amoon, M. & Ali, G., M. & Faheem, H., M. (2005) A Social Agent Interface for Resource Management in Distributed Systems, *Proceedings of the 2005 International Conference on Computational Intelligence for Modelling, Control and Automation, and International Conference on Intelligent Agents, Web Technologies and Internet Commerce* (CIMCA-IAWTIC'05), Vol.2, pp. 390-395

Kim, H., L. & Choi, J., H. & Kim, H., G. & Hwang, S., H. (2007) WANT: A Personal Knowledge Management System on Social Software Agent Technologies, In *Agent and Multi-Agent Systems: Technologies and Applications*, Carbonell, J., G. & Siekmann, J., pp. 785-794, Springer, ISBN 978-3-540-72829-0, Berlin, Heidelberg

Koch, F. & Rahwan, I. (2004) Classification of Agents-based Mobile Assistants, *Proceedings of the AAMAS Workshop on Agents for Ubiquitous Computing (UbiAgents)*, New York, USA, July, 2004

Kolb, D., A. (1984) *Experiential Learning: Experience as the Source of Learning and Development*, Prentice-Hall, ISBN 978-0132952613, New Jersey

Kotz, D. & Gray, R. & Rus, D. (2002) Future Directions for Mobile Agent Research, IEEE Distributed Systems Online, Vol.3, No.8, pp. 1-6, ISSN 1541-4922, 04.19.2010, Available from http://computingnow.computer.org

Lander, S., E. (1997) Issues in multiagent design systems, *IEEE Expert*, Vol.12 Issue 2, p.18-26

Lange, D. & Oshima, M. (1999) Seven good reasons for mobile agents, Communications of the ACM, Volume 42 , Issue 3, p. 88-89, ISSN 0001-0782

Li, G. & Li, Y. (2009) A Study on Blog Based Personal Knowledge Management, *Proceedings of the 2nd International Workshop on Knowledge Discovery and Data Mining*, pp. 248-251, Moscow, Russia

Maier, R. (2004) *Knowledge Management Systems, Information and Communication Technologies for Knowledge Management*, Springer, ISBN 978-3-540-20547-0, Berlin, New York

Martin, J. (2006) Personal knowledge management - the basis of corporate and institutional knowledge management, In: *Managing Knowledge: Case Studies in Innovation*, Martin, J. & Wright, K., Spotted Cow Press, Edmonton

Maslow, A., H. (1954) *Motivation and Personality*, Harper & Bros, New York

McClelland, D., C. (1967) The Achieving society, Free Press, New York

Mellow, P. (2005) The media generation: Maximise learning by getting mobile, *Proceedings of the ASCILITE 2005: balance, fidelity, mobility: maintaining the momentum*, Ascilite, pp. 469–476, Brisbane, Australia

Mikkonen, T. (2007) Programming Mobile Devices – An Introduction for Practitioners, John Wiley & Sons, Ltd, Chichester, West Sussex, England

Miller, R. (November 2005) The evolution of knowledge management this time it's personal, In: *EContent*, 04.19.2010, Available from www.econtentmag.com/Issues/222-November-2005.htm

mobiThinking (2011) Global mobile statistics 2011: all quality mobile marketing research, mobile Web stats, subscribers, ad revenue, usage, trends, 04.02.2011, Available from http://mobithinking.com/stats-corner/global-mobile-statistics-2011-all-quality-mobile-marketing-research-mobile-web-stats-su

Moghe, S. (January 2010) Here's how I'm approaching Personal Knowledge Management, In: *The learning generalist*, 06.11.2010, Available from www.learninggeneralist.com/2010/01/heres-how-im-approaching-personal.html

Nonaka, I. & Konno, N. (1999) The Concept of 'Ba': Building a foundation for knowledge creation, In: *The Knowledge Management Yearbook 1999-2000*, Cortada, J., W. & Woods, J., A., pp. 37–51, Butterworth-Heinemann, ISBN 9780750671224

Nwana, H. (1996) Software Agents: An Overview, *The Knowledge Engineering Review*, Vol. 11, No 3, Cambridge University Press, pp. 1-40, ISSN 0269-8889, 04.19.2010, Available from http://agents.umbc.edu/introduction/ao/

Osis, K. & Grundspenkis, J. (2009a) Perspectives of Integration of M-learning and Personal Knowledge Management, *Proceedings of the International Conference of Education, Research and Innovation*, pp. 6723-6733, ISBN 978-84-613-2955-7, Madrid, Spain

Osis, K. & Grundspenkis, J. (2009b) Perspectives on Usage of Agents in Personal Knowledge Management, *Proceedings of the International Conference on Knowledge Management (KMIS)*, pp. 332-337, ISBN 978-989-674–013-9, Madeira, Portugal

Osis, K. & Grundspenkis, J. (2010) Agent and Mobile Technologies and Their Usage in Development of Learning Environment Supportive System, *Proceedings of the 3rd WSEAS International Conference on Visualization, Imaging and Simulation (VIS)*, pp. 58-63, ISBN 978-960-474-246-2, University of Algarve, Faro, Portugal

Osis, K. & Grundspenkis, J. (2011a) Modular Personal Knowledge Management System and Mobile Technology Cross-Platform Solution Towards Learning Environment Support, *Proceedings of the Annual International Conference on "Virtual and Augmented Reality in Education" (VARE)*, pp. 114-124, ISBN 978-9984-633-13-3, Vidzeme University of Applied Sciences, Valmiera, Latvia

Osis, K. & Grundspenkis, J. (2011b) A different view to knowledge and personal knowledge management system, *Proceedings of the 12th European Conference on Knowledge Management (ECKM)*, (accepted for publication), University of Passau, Germany

Padgham, L. & Winikoff, M. & DeLoach, S. & Cossentino, M. (2008) A Unified Graphical Notation for AOSE, *Proceedings of the 9th International Workshop on Agen-Oriented Software Engineering at The 7th International Joint Conference on Autonomous Agents and Multi-Agent Systems (AAMAS 2008)*, pp. 1-12, Estoril, Portugal, 02.11.2008, Available from www.pa.icar.cnr.it/~cossentino/ paper/aose08-padgham.pdf

Pauleen, D. (2009) Personal knowledge management - Putting the "person" back into the knowledge equation, *Online Information Review* (Emerald), Vol. 33, No. 2, pp. 221-224, ISSN 1468-4527

Polanyi, M. (1966) *The Tacit Dimension*, Doubleday, London

Smedley, J. (October 2009) Modelling personal knowledge management, *OR Insight*, Palgrave Macmillan, Vol. 22, 4, pp. 221–233, ISSN 0953-5543

Squire, K. & Johnson, K. & Holland, W. & Nataf, Z. & Klopfer, E. (August 2006) MIT Games-To-Teach, Design Document for: A Platform For Augmented Reality Gaming, Environmental Detectives, In: *Literature Review into Mobile Learning in the University Context*, Cobcroft, R., S., Queensland University of Technology, 06.11.2010, Available from http://eprints.qut.edu.au/4805/1/4805.pdf

Tarkoma, S. & Laukkanen, M. (2002) Facilitating Agent Messaging on PDAs, *Proceedings of the Fourth International Workshop on Mobile Agents for Telecommunication Applications* (MATA-2002), pp. 259-268, ISBN 3-540-00021-6, Barcelona, Spain

Tiwana, A. (2002) *The knowledge management toolkit: orchestrating IT, strategy, and knowledge platforms*. Prentice hall, ISBN 0-13-009224-X, Upper Saddle River, New Jersey

Tsui, E. (2002) Technologies for personal and peer-to-peer (P2P) knowledge management, In: *CSC leading edge forum, technical report*, Australia

Tveit, A. (May 2001) A survey of Agent-Oriented Software Engineering, *Proceedings of the First NTNU Computer Science Graduate Student Conference*, Norwegian University of Science and Technology, 04.19.2010, Available from http://amundtveit.info/publications/2001/aose.pdf

Vidal, J. & Buhler, P. & Huhns, M. (2011) Inside an Agent, *IEEE Internet Computing*, IEEE, February, pp. 82-86, ISSN 1089-7801

Völkel, M. & Abecker, A. (2008) Cost-benefit analysis for the design of personal knowledge management systems, *Proceedings of the 10th International Conference on Enterprise Information Systems*, pp. 95-105, Barcelona, Spain, 04.19.2010, Available from http://www.slideshare.net/xamde/costbenefit-analysis-for-the-design-of-personal-knowledge-management-systems

Wang, A., I. & Sørensen, C. & Indal, E. (2003) A Mobile Agent Architecture for Heterogeneous Devices, *Proceedings of the 3rd IASTED International Conference on Wireless and Optical Communications*, pp. 14-16, 0-88986-374-1, Banff, Canada

Weng, Z. & Tran, T. (2007) An Intelligent Agent-Based Framework for Mobile Business, *Proceedings of the 6th International Conference on the Management of Mobile Business* (ICMB 2007), pp. 30-37, ISBN 0-7695-2803-1, Toronto, Canada

Wiig, K. M. (1997) Knowledge Management: Where Did It Come From and Where Will It Go? *Journal of Expert Systems with Applications*, Pergamon Press/Elsevier, Vol. 13, No.1., pp. 1-14

Wiig, K. M. (2004) *People-Focused Knowledge Management: how Effective Decision Making Leads to Corporate Success*, Butterworth-Heinemann, ISBN 0-7506-7777-5, Oxford

WikiPad (2010) WikiPad, *Jera Design*, 04.19.2010, Available from www.jera.com/wikipad

Wooldridge, M. (April 1999) Intelligent Agents, In: *Multiagent Systems*, Weiss, G., The MIT Press, pp. 1-51, 04.19.2010, Available from www.csc.liv.ac.uk/~mjw/pubs/mas99.pdf

Wooldridge, M. & Jennings, N. (1995) Intelligent Agents: Theory and Practice, *The Knowledge Engineering Review*, Cambridge University Press, Vol. 10(2), pp. 115-152, ISSN 0269-8889

Wright, K. (August 2005) Personal knowledge management: supporting individual knowledge worker performance, *Knowledge Management Research & Practice*, Palgrave Macmillan, Vol. 3, pp. 156–165, ISSN 1477-8238

Wright, K. (2008) Rethinking Knowledge Work, In: *Knowledge resources*, 04.19.2010, Available from www.knowledgeresources.ca/Knowledge_Resources/PKM_Model .html

Zack, M., H. (1999) Developing a Knowledge Strategy, *California Management Review*, Vol. 41, No. 3, 1999, p. 125-145, ISSN 0008-1256

10

A Challenge on Development of an Advanced Knowledge Management System (KMS) for Radioactive Waste Disposal: Moving from Theory to Practice

Hitoshi Makino, Kazumasa Hioki, Hideki Osawa,
Takeshi Semba and Hiroyuki Umeki
Japan Atomic Energy Agency
Japan

1. Introduction

In recent years there has been much discussion on the topic of knowledge management in many areas of nuclear science, particularly associated with the nuclear renaissance and the evident shortage of skilled manpower (e.g. Yanev, 2008). More generally, however, the exponentially expanding capacity of computer systems parallels an explosion in the documentation and databases supporting nuclear projects. This is nowhere more evident than in the field of radioactive waste management, characterised, as it is, by the extremely wide range of disciplines involved and very long project timescales (e.g. Kawata et al., 2006; Umeki et al., 2008; Umeki et al., 2009).

Although this may not yet be universally accepted, there is increasing evidence that the rapid rate of growth of material supporting complex technical projects – which we will term 'knowledge' – is rapidly reaching, if not passing, the point where conventional management systems show signs of collapse. Although tried and tested over millennia, the type of Knowledge Management System (KMS) developed to handle written documents is proving inherently incapable of being simply modified to cope with the present flood of electronic material. Although Moore's Law of expansion of data transfer speeds and storage capacity means that some of the simpler tasks involving document collation and archiving can be handled, there has been little progress in addressing the more difficult problems of how the huge volumes of documentation being produced can be critically reviewed/quality assured, synthesised, integrated and communicated to all the interested stakeholders in a form that they can understand.

A common blockage to progress is that, while many of the component problems (symptoms) may be acknowledged, it is not easy for organisations to perceive the magnitude of the approaching catastrophic system collapse and hence to implement the paradigm shift needed to introduce effective solutions. Indeed, it is a classic Catch-22 situation: the breakdown of conventional approaches means that those involved lack the overview required to see that their KMS is becoming increasingly dysfunctional.

The exponential growth in the knowledge base for radioactive waste management is a cause for concern in many national programmes. In the Japanese radioactive waste disposal field, the problems of information overload were recognised during a comprehensive assessment of High-Level Waste (HLW) disposal feasibility at the turn of the century (JNC, 2000). This problem is exacerbated by a Japanese volunteering approach to siting of a deep geological repository, which requires particular flexibility in the tailoring of site characterization plans, repository concepts and associated Performance Assessments (PAs). Recognition of this situation led, in 2005, to initiation by Japan Atomic Energy Agency (JAEA) of an ambitious project to develop an advanced KMS aimed to facilitate its role as the supplier of background R&D support to both regulators and implementers of geological disposal.

The chapter introduces the background to this initiative and the basic approach selected, and then review progress to date in this work, with emphasis on tailoring of existing Knowledge Engineering tools and methods to radioactive waste management requirements, and outline future developments and challenges (Umeki et al., 2009; Osawa et al., 2009b; Semba et al., 2009; Makino et al., 2009a; Makino et al., 2011).

2. Approach and features of the JAEA KMS

Recognition of the importance of knowledge management by JAEA led to establishment of a new Knowledge Office with the remit to develop and implement an advanced KMS tailored to the requirements of the Japanese geological disposal programme. This programme is coordinated with initiatives led by the responsible Government department 'ANRE' (Agency of Natural Resources and Energy) of METI (Ministry of Economy, Trade and Industry) and will, eventually, be formally linked to other relevant organisations in Japan that may be either producers or users of knowledge. Within JAEA, the Knowledge Office not only develops the new tools and organisational structures required to implement the KMS, but also provides executive support for synthetic analysis and evaluation of knowledge (including meta-analysis and top-level quality management).

It is important to emphasise here the particular boundary conditions for this KMS. At the most fundamental level, JAEA is charged with providing scientific and technical support to both implementing and regulatory organisations and also interested stakeholders – including the general public. This requires that all parties recognise JAEA to be a competent and unbiased organisation and that the KMS incorporates a rigorous Quality Management System (QMS) that is accepted by all.

For geological disposal in Japan, the implementer 'NUMO' (Nuclear Waste Management Organisation of Japan) has selected a volunteering approach for initiation of the siting process, which introduces technical challenges in terms of assuring flexibility of site characterisation planning, repository concept development and associated PA (e.g. Kitayama et al., 2005). Additionally, attracting volunteers and developing dialogue with local communities involve challenges in public communication.

On the regulatory side, development of guidelines and licensing procedures for deep geological repositories is ongoing, but one clear aim is to maximise consistency with already established regulations for near surface disposal facilities for lower level radioactive waste (NSC, 2004). This is complicated in Japan due to its location on an Island Arc, with its associated high tectonic activity and geological complexity (e.g. Apted et al., 2004).

Although current emphasis is on existing inventories of radioactive waste, the Japanese long-term commitment to nuclear power and a reference development programme over the next 100 years has to be considered in order to develop a consistent and compatible long-term waste management programme (Makino et al., 2009b). In addition, various types of waste caused by Fukushima Dai-ichi accident occurred in 2011 will become significant subject to the Japanese waste management programme.

Taken together, these constraints on the KMS lead to a requirement for a holistic approach that will form the core of a programme to be implemented over a period extending beyond the 21st century. Clearly, major developments in technology are to be expected over this period, although these are inherently unpredictable in detail. Emphasis is thus placed on development of a fundamental KMS concept that will evolve in line with advancing technology, supported by tools and approaches that are, to the maximum extent possible, scale and platform independent.

The overall structure and key components of the KMS are illustrated in Figure 1. It should be noted that the remit of the Knowledge Office is very wide and the KMS thus includes all aspects of tacit knowledge management (e.g. focused training and experience transfer schemes - often denoted as human resource management), focused quality management (discussed in more detail below) and anticipation of technology developments and future requirements (e.g. using a think tank approach - elsewhere often part of strategic planning or requirements management). Therefore, the combination of the challenging boundary conditions and wide remit led to the decision to establish a support team (Knowledge Office) composed of staff with wide experience of radioactive waste management, and knowledge engineering, who can tailor established methodology and tools effectively and efficiently to the various requirements needed for development of the KMS. In retrospect, this strategic decision probably contributed significantly to the successes achieved to date.

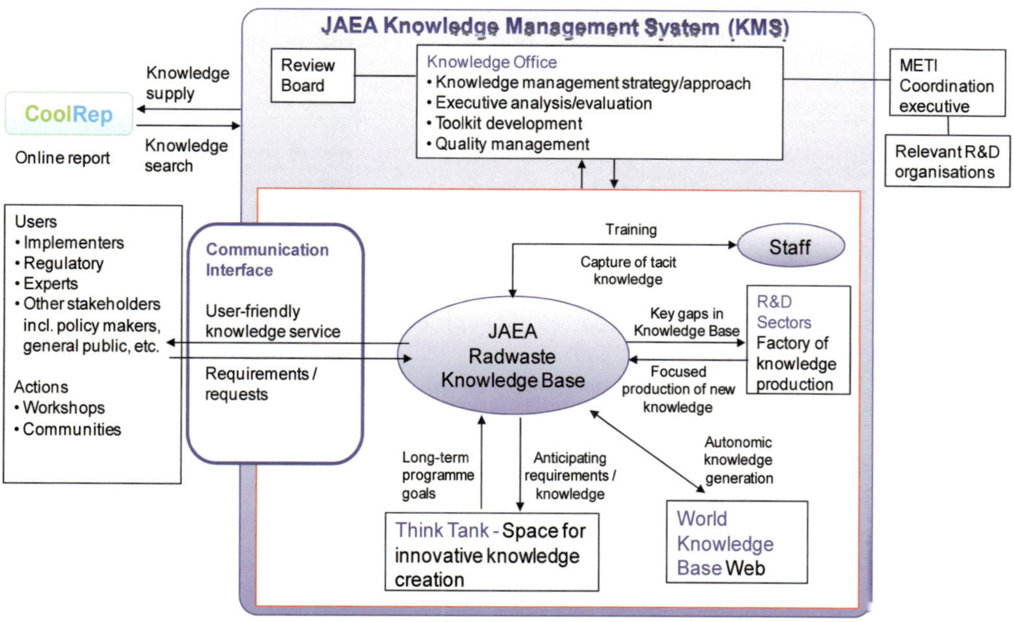

Fig. 1. Outline KMS concept: Structure and key elements

The various different types of knowledge involved and the management functions required are summarised in Table 1. This table also notes which functions have the potential to be, at least partially, automated or facilitated using advanced knowledge engineering tools. Automation and/or computer support of knowledge management functions is a key to implementation of this novel approach – providing the potential to respond to the exponentially increasing rate of information production, but also giving the greatest challenge to the Knowledge Office team. The essence of what is aimed for has been summarised as an 'intelligent assistant' – an electronic toolkit that allows project leaders and coordinators to manage the huge fluxes of data that they have to control and to efficiently use their time by carrying out only the weighting and top-level synthesis and decision making that cannot be automated.

Form of knowledge	*Management functions*	*Content*	*Planned/ongoing developments**
Data	Data management	- raw data (internal) - solicited data (external) - processed data	**- robust archive** **- internal and external data mining** **- autonomic data processing** **- autonomic QA** **- formal approaches for QA**
Documents	Document management	- internal documents - key external documents	**- robust archive** **- autonomic QA/cataloguing/ cross-referencing**
Software	Software management	- archive of all relevant codes/databases - archive of manuals and handbooks - archive of relevant input/output	**- robust archive** **- autonomic change management** **- formal approaches for QA**
Experience and methodology	Resource management	- procedure manuals and guidebooks - expert systems - training materials	**- use of expert systems to capture and transfer tacit knowledge** **- advanced training and experience transfer**
Synthesis	Knowledge integration	- experienced synthesis team - expert systems	**- formal description of key integration processes** **- formal approach for QA**
Guidance	Knowledge coordination	- experienced coordination team	**- prediction of requirements (Think Tank)** **- process for filling key gaps in knowledge**
Presentation	User/producer dialogue	- user friendly interfaces (interactive – allowing dialogue)	**- high-end graphical methods for presenting complex information**

Note: *Of the required developments, those highlighted in bold text may be supported by advanced IT/KE technology

Table 1. Typical contents and structure of a KMS based on initial studies carried out by JAEA

A key component of the KMS is the JAEA Radwaste Knowledge Base (KB). This is a dynamic entity, which will be constantly supplemented by new input – through focused production by Japanese (or international partner) R&D programmes or autonomically generated by directed searches of the internet. Unlike traditional databases, there is no imposed structure on the KB: it is simply an electronic library of all relevant information and documentation that is applicable to specific radioactive waste applications. It will be used to generate application-specific sub-databases, which are frozen and archived as required to ensure transparent documentation of the background to all major project milestones or decisions that utilise this KB. Utilisation of the KB will be facilitated by a user-friendly interface that allows the mode of access and the form and technical level of output to be tailored to the needs of different knowledge users.

The information explosion noted in the introduction is the key problem when considering how the KB will be utilised by the main user organisations such as implementer and regulator. Although huge volumes of material are already available and very much more will be generated in coming decades, much of this is (or will become) irrelevant for actual implementation or regulation of a repository project. A strict filtering process to develop application-specific subsets of the KB is thus essential for practical use – and also to develop a unified approach to quality management.

The process of developing a project-specific KB from the requirements specified by end users is illustrated in Figure 2 (Umeki et al., 2009; Umeki et al., 2010). Ideally, this would be facilitated with a direct interface to a formal Requirements Management System (RMS),

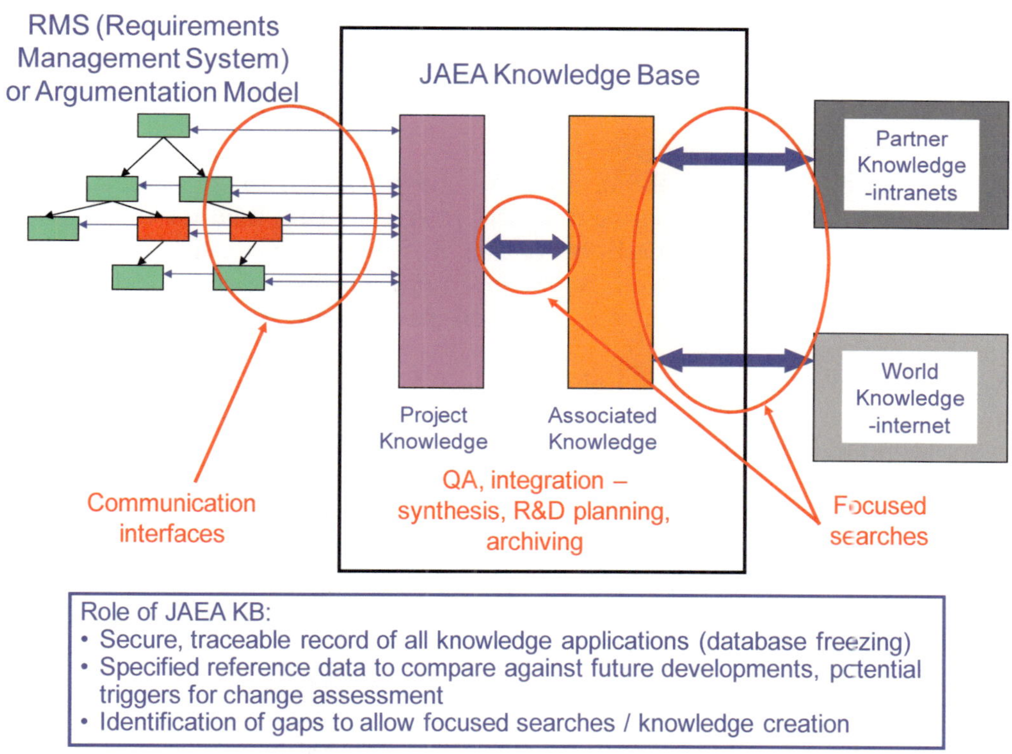

Fig. 2. The knowledge base and its interfaces to users and knowledge resources

which provides a hierarchy of project needs, identifies potential conflicts and establishes priorities or weightings (possibly as a function of programme progress). Although requirements management is recognised to be essential by NUMO and a formal system is under development (NUMO, 2007), it is not yet operational. To initiate work in the absence of clearly defined requirements, therefore, a prototype project-specific KB is being developed using a basic structure of a geological repository safety case, which will certainly be a key requirement for the implementer and a focus of programme review by the regulators (JNC, 2005; Umeki et al., 2008). In this context, the safety case can be clearly a common frame for R&D activities carried out in all relevant organisations. The safety case is also of great interest for all stakeholders.

A safety case is an extremely complex synthesis of a vast array of different information. Although this is supported by much of the technical work carried out by JAEA and other R&D organisations, development of the safety case is actually carried out by NUMO and reviewed by the regulators. To make the benefits of this advanced KMS by JAEA apparent to all relevant parties, it is important that it eases the work of specialists by highlighting the relevance of their research to the safety case and simplifying the processes of accessing relevant literature, synthesising data, producing and reviewing documentation and communicating their results to interested parties (see Section 3). Here argumentation modelling mentioned in Section 3.1 have played an additional key role of overviewing the essence of the safety case in an easily understandable manner.

3. Tools developed in the JAEA KMS project

This section will discuss about development and application of tools comprising the JAEA KMS with practical examples.

3.1 Argumentation modelling

The safety case can be seen as the top-level goal of all works carried out within a geological disposal project. Knowledge can be classified in terms of its role in the safety case and prioritised in terms of its impact on overall safety case argumentation (Figure 3). The resultant argumentation model can be developed in a top-down manner, highlighting the constraints on decisions set by upper level requirements and the consequences of decisions on all interlinked topics.

Argumentation modelling is a well-established tool in Knowledge Engineering (e.g. Kirschner et al., 2003) and can be implemented in a number of different ways. In all cases, an initial claim is analysed to determine possible counter-arguments which are, in turn, analysed to identify supporting arguments that counter these. The process iterates until unambiguous hard evidence is provided or an open question is identified. Although such processes are well established in areas such as philosophy and law, they are less often used in technical fields. Nevertheless, experiences to date within the JAEA KMS project have shown that this approach is well suited to breaking down complex multidisciplinary problems in radioactive waste management.

Use of an argumentation model to represent key components of a safety case has certain advantages:

- The starting point of the argumentation model is a clear claim in natural language; this could be, at the top level, "The safety case justifies proceeding with the repository project at a particular programme milestone" or, at a lower level, "a particular system component contributes to the safety case". This puts any lower level input clearly into context.

- The initial claim must be supported by arguments, which can be usefully classified into different types. At present, different classes of arguments are used: these range from consideration of "hard" laws of science or defined exclusion criteria to "softer" assessments of common understanding and requirements for public acceptance.
- Some, or all, of the arguments may give rise to counter arguments. The advantage of classifying the arguments is that particular classes of supporting argument lead naturally to counters. For example, in the case of "Argumentation based on analogy", some of the critical questions that might be considered would be the possible extent of any sampling bias or the potential existence of analogue counterexamples.
- These counter arguments then lead to further supporting arguments, generally going into further technical detail, with links wherever appropriate to the supporting knowledge base. This is continued until the case is considered to be sufficient – which inevitably involves expert judgment. In practice, especially early in a programme, it may not be possible to develop a complete argument – some aspects must be covered by assumptions or result in open questions. These can be highlighted and used to focus and set priorities for associated R&D.

The formalised method involves classification of arguments, which allows the relative strength of associated evidence to be assessed (e.g. arguments based on scientific laws vs. those based on empirical data) and also allows associated typical 'critical questions' to be reviewed to check if the argumentation model is complete (Figure 4). Inevitably, argumentation models become increasingly complex as they go into finer technical detail and rapidly lead to cross-linking between different sub-systems. To manage the network, software tools are essential and after a number of existing packages were examined, a tailored argumentation model editor called Scarab (**S**upporting tool for **Co**nstructing **AR**gumentation models with **A**ssociated knowledge-**B**ase) has been developed (Osawa et al., 2009b). Figure 5 shows an example of screenshots of the argumentation model editor.

Additional functions of Scarab include:

a. Storing existing argumentation models in a case-base, allowing users to key-word search cases similar to the one at hand;
b. Storing base information of arguments which is called knowledge note (Figure 6);
c. Recording all the revisions made to each argumentation model, with comments explaining the reason for changes;
d. Supporting discovery of new counter-arguments by using "deep" knowledge of the safety case structure;
e. Link with group-ware that provides a collaborative internet working environment;

Finally, it should be mentioned that an even simpler form of argumentation modelling has proven useful in developing new communication methods, particularly aimed at non-technical (or, at least, non-expert) audiences. Here the argumentation model is developed not as a network as shown in Figure 4, but in the form of a dialogue between cartoon characters. Such presentation is very familiar in Japan and this option will be implemented in both static (*manga*) and animated (*anime*) forms. In addition, presentation form like common FAQ might be necessary for understanding of citizens.

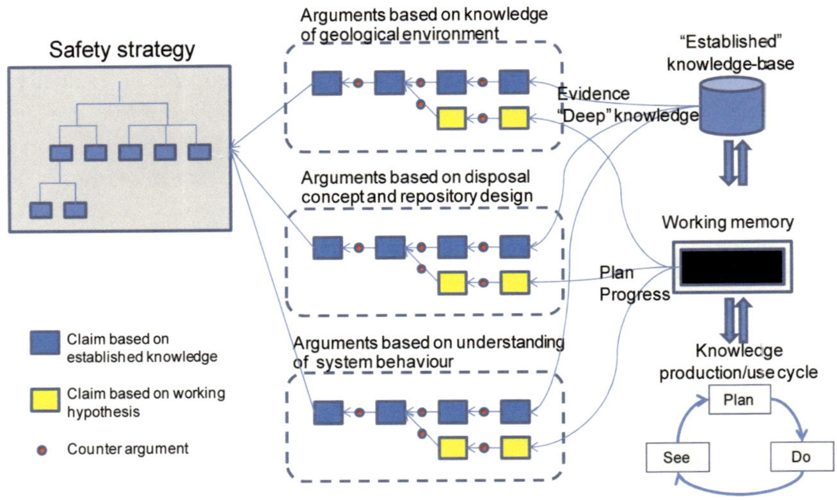

Fig. 3. Role of argumentation models in developing the safety case knowledge base

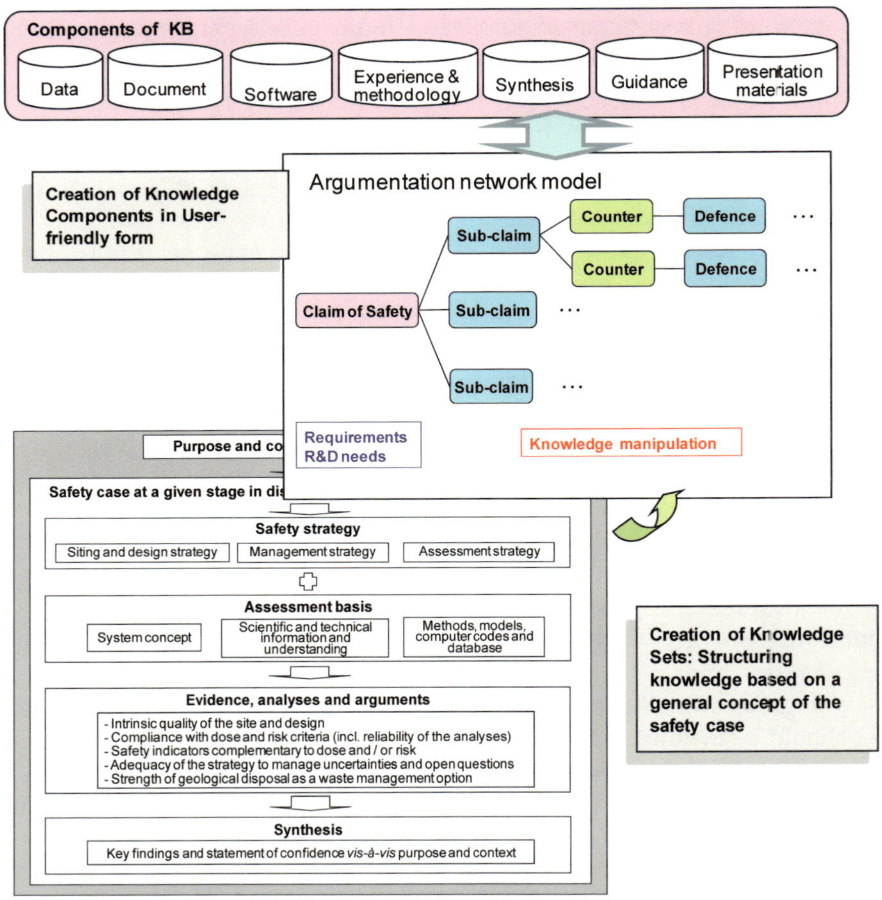

Fig. 4. Representing the safety case as an argumentation model in order to structure the KB

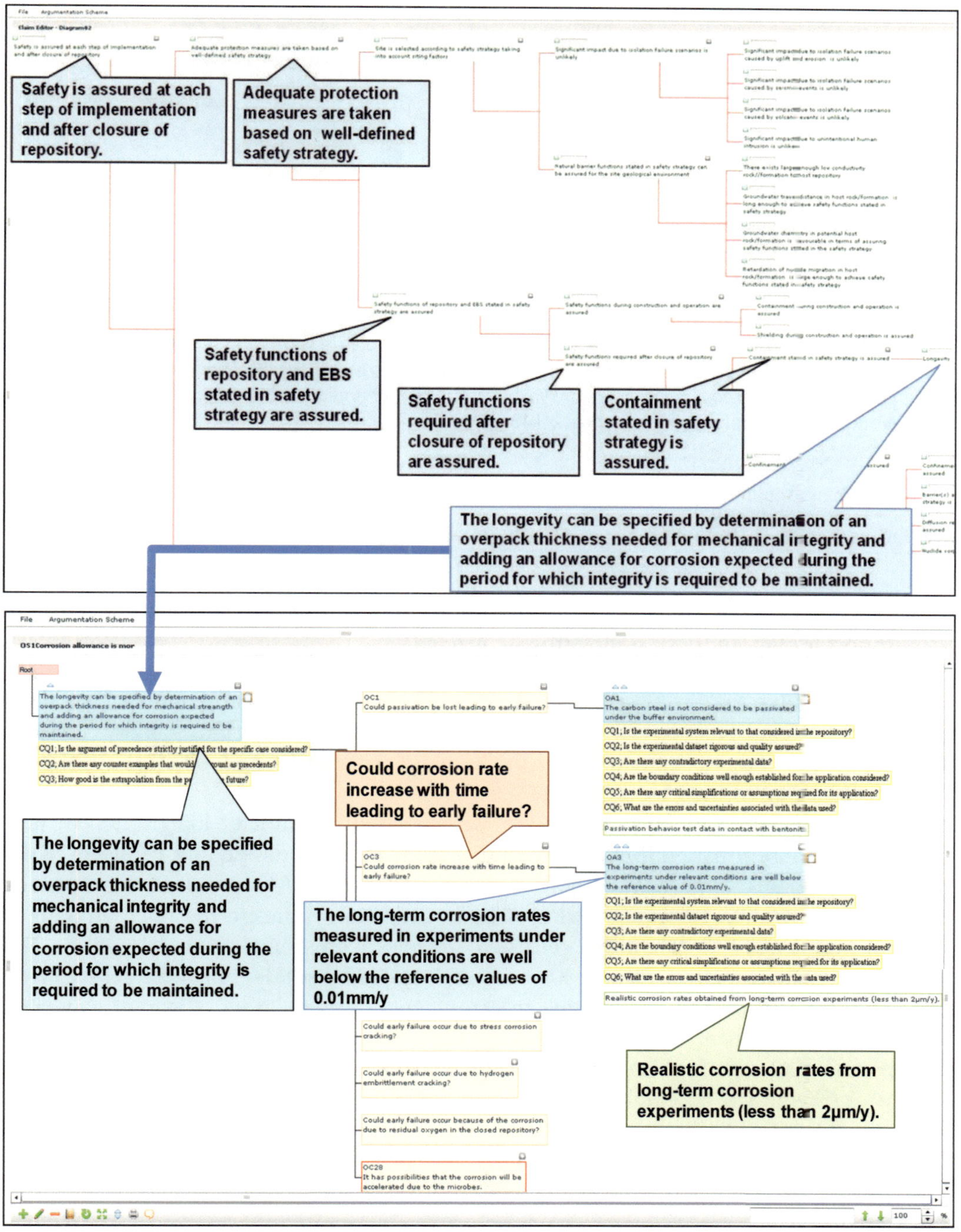

Fig. 5. Screenshots of the argumentation model editor (Scarab)

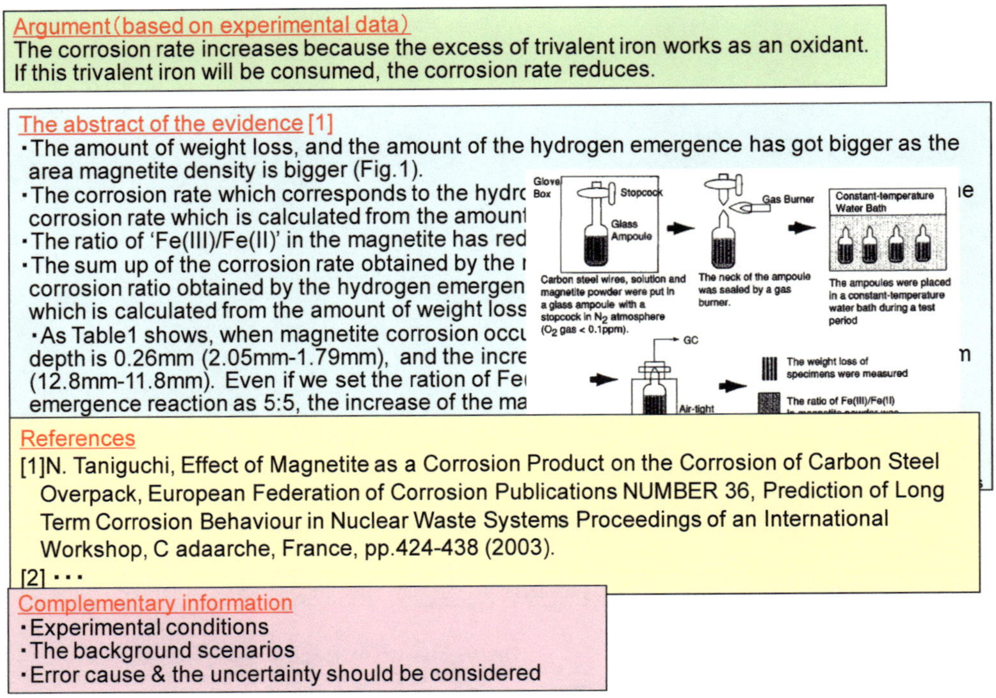

Fig. 6. Illustration of a knowledge note

3.2 Support tool/method for geosynthesis process

The characterisation of potential repository sites is one of the most resource-intensive and politically-sensitive tasks facing the Japanese geological disposal programme. This work will process huge volumes of information that must be corrected, quality assured, integrated, analysed, documented and archived in a rigorous and efficient manner, a process often referred to as "geosynthesis".

A geosynthesis methodology has been developed to facilitate integration of site characterisation information flow, incorporating feedback from design and PA users. Trial application of this approach is now ongoing within JAEA studies at two generic underground research laboratory (URL) sites in order to synthesise the huge amount of practical experience and data into a consistent geological environment model (GEM) . The methodology of site characterisation has evolved from initial studies of simple geosynthesis data flow diagrams, which traced how measurements during site investigation generated data sets for end-users in a transparent and quality-assured manner.

A particular feature of JAEA's activities involves R&D in two URL projects: one at Mizunami (Saegusa & Matsuoka, 2010), central Japan, in crystalline rock and the other at Horonobe (Ota et al., 2010), north of Japan, in sediments. These URLs are generic research facilities and thus distinct from site-specific underground facilities that will be constructed by NUMO at volunteer sites, during the detailed investigation stage of site characterisation (NUMO, 2004).

If the experience and know-how obtained in the URL projects is to be used at other sites (for example by NUMO), it is necessary to have flexibility to respond to considerable differences in boundary conditions. While some of the site characterisation tasks involve rather routine data handling that may be easily automated, much of it requires input of "tacit knowledge" (Nonaka & Takeuchi, 1995; IAEA, 2005), which involves the experience of expert staff. In particular, planning and managing the characterisation programme results in challenges, due to the inherent uncertainty in site understanding and the inevitable surprises that will occur.

To provide support for NUMO, which may need to run several field programmes in parallel - and also the regulator, which is expected to follow these and provide input for key decisions - JAEA is attempting to capture both Japanese and international geosynthesis experience within a KMS component, termed the Information Synthesis and Interpretation System (ISIS) (Osawa et al., 2009a; Semba et al., 2009).

ISIS is being developed by applying advanced electronic information technology and knowledge engineering approaches; it will include an extensive knowledge base, expert systems utilising an inference engine and an archive for rule-based and/or case-based reasoning as major constituent elements (Figure 7).

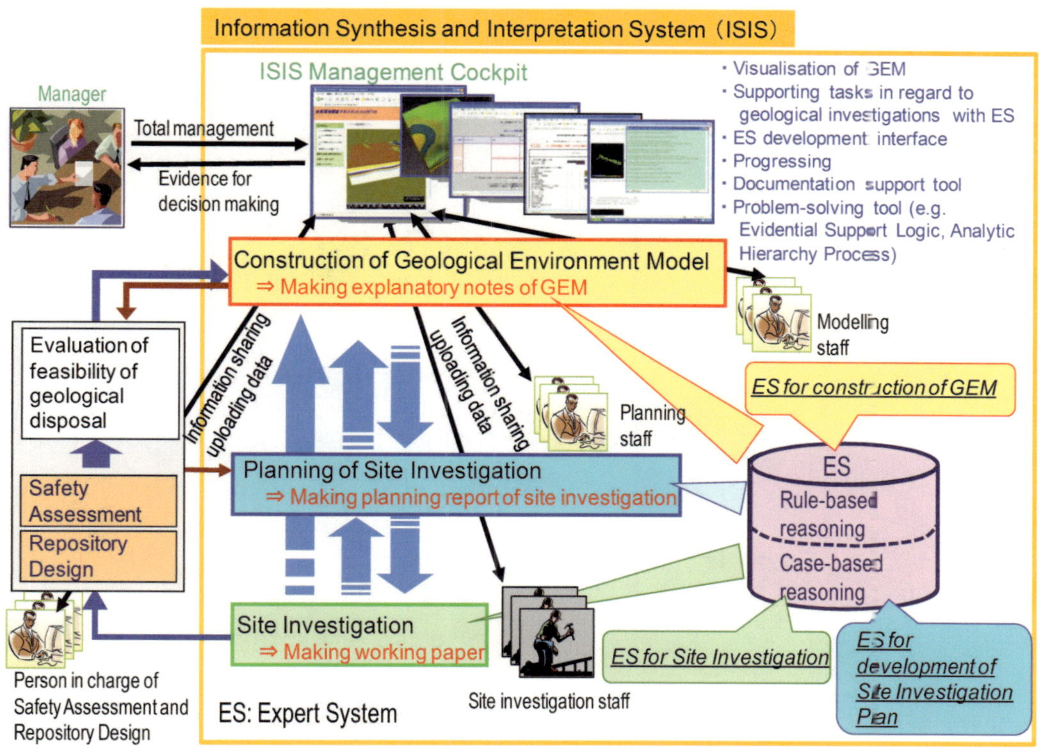

Fig. 7. Basic concept of ISIS

Although the Japanese knowledge base will need to be complemented by input from international partner programmes with wider practical experience, all indications to date suggest that development of such an intelligent system is feasible with existing technology.

Based on the requirements and goals specified above, ISIS has investigated implementation of the following tools:

1. Expert system (ES) development tools: particularly focused on capturing tacit knowledge using rule-based or case-based approaches.

2. Management cockpit: integration of ISIS tools and communication tool.
3. Problem-solving methodology: formal approach for identifying and resolving conflicting requirements.

The first stage of ES development involves a formal process of knowledge acquisition. This can be illustrated as a detailed task flow diagram resulting from expert elicitation. An example is shown in Figure 8, which shows the sequence of tasks for establishing on-land seismic reflection surveys resulting from interviews with experts.

The next stage involves knowledge modelling; carrying out syntax analysis of the component rules and cases (Figure 9a). This allows representation of knowledge in a form that is accessible to methods from the field of knowledge engineering.

The final stage is creation of the operational ES; this involves establishing a user interface based on established templates (Figure 9b) and formulating knowledge elements as a menu, based on the results of the syntax analysis. The interface is used to create the rule-based and case-based procedures, by selecting appropriate knowledge elements and syntax. A knowledge engineering tool then produces the ES automatically, based on this formalised input.

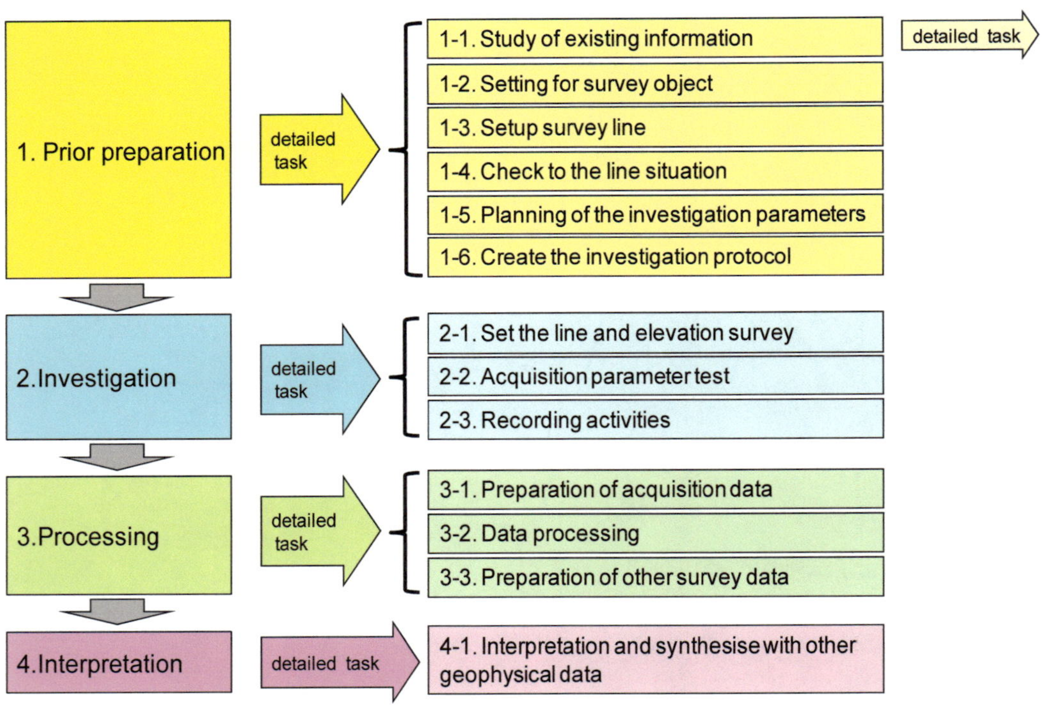

Fig. 8. An example of flow of elicitation of task knowledge

3.3 Support tool/method for performance assessment

Regarding total system performance assessment, it was recognised that routine tasks in PA, e.g. development of input datasets, groundwater flow and transport modelling, interpretation of model output, integration within a total system PA, etc., are repeated many times. This may occur whenever there are changes in assessment scenarios, geological environment models, repository design, relevant databases, etc. Introduction of advanced

Rule-base	Decision-making rules within tasks of site investigation, represented using IF...THEN format	e.g. Selection of drilling methods If full core recovery needed YES: Then a wireline drilling method should be selected NO: then a non-core drilling method should be selected (tricon bit etc.)
Case-base	Cases how a problem in site investigation was solved in the past, to suggest ways to handle similar problems in the future	e.g. Troubleshooting of drilling fluid loss

a. Identification of relevant knowledge elements

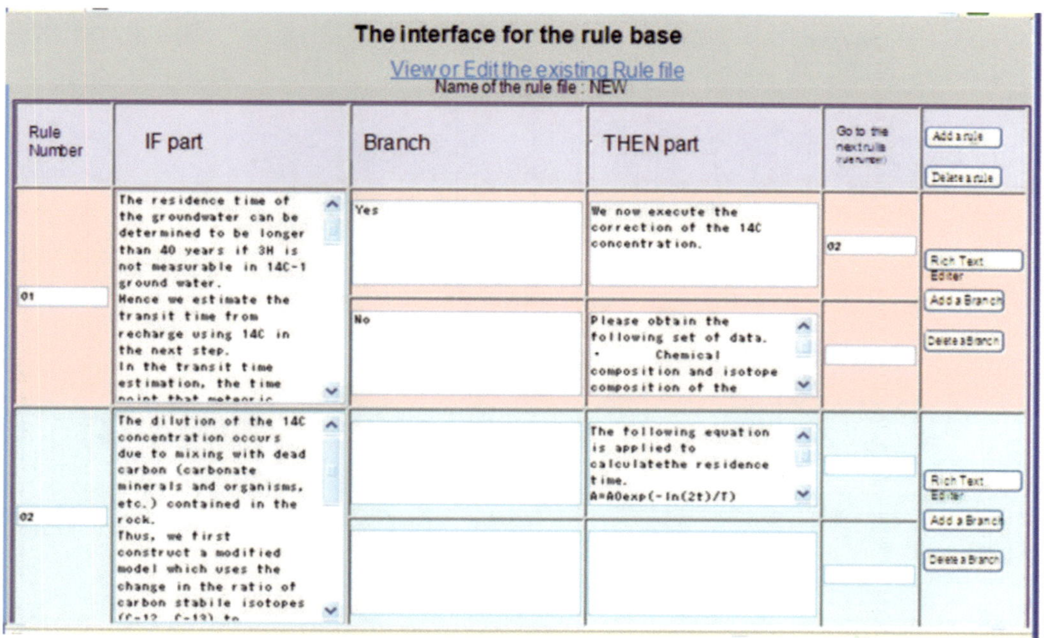

b. ES development interface for the rule-base

Fig. 9. Knowledge modelling and ES development

knowledge management technologies and tools should increase efficiency, traceability, transparency and repeatability of such PA tasks (Makino et al, 2009a). They will also ease the process of auditing contents of PA and support QA of the input, analytical methodology and resulting output.

The overall toolkit under development is termed PAIRS (Performance Assessment Integrated Report System) (Figure 10). A significant feature of the PAIRS is that this comprises a linked set of not only text, tables and figures corresponding to conventional PA report but also applications that have been used through PA tasks. The key components of this system are as follows:

- Electronic Performance Assessment Report (e-PAR): the electronic report developed with support of PAIRS, which contains a core of quality-assured text, tables and figures linked to calculation by encapsulated tasks for a specific dataset (e-PAR case-base means a library of developed e-PARs)
- Operator: an encapsulated application library that includes numerical tools and assessment softwares used for certain tasks in a user friendly form
- User interface: an intelligent user interface facilitates reconfiguring the input dataset and encapsulated tasks, management of calculations and then editing the resultant output to create/modify contents of e-PAR; this will be supported by change management tool to provide a top-level overview of all changes implemented, their justification and their consequences in terms of overall performance
- Application knowledge base: a central library of all PA data (both raw and derived) together with all relevant information supporting their selection and application, together with an associated historical record of all changes and modifications.

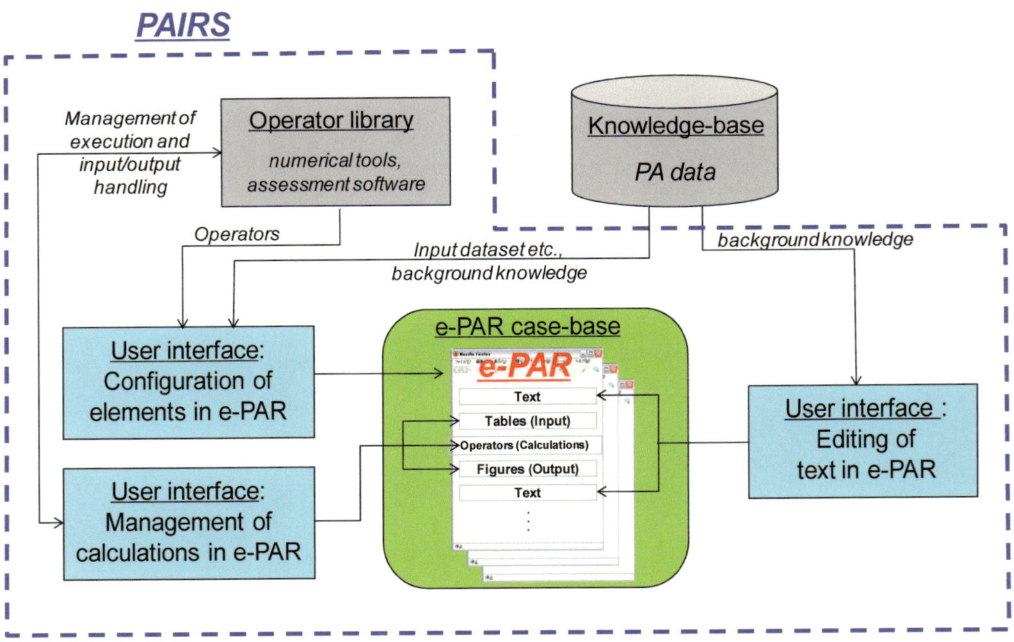

Fig. 10. Schematic overview of PAIRS and component tools

Figure 11 shows an example of e-PAR and outline of operation on e-PAR (browse, edit and reanalysis). Functions of operator library and calculation management on e-PAR are currently being tested with an existing post-closure PA code (for example, a code based on GoldSim (Golder Associates, 2001)), but will be flexible enough to incorporate other existing codes and next generation models/databases when they arise.

Main features and advantages of e-PAR in practical viewpoints are:

- Easy access and operation with browser
- Easy execution of PA tasks in an easy and understandable operation, which allow application of PA tools by non-PA experts and expedite communication among different disciplines
- Storing context and procedure of PA tasks with all relevant data, information and knowledge (both domain knowledge and task knowledge) in an easily accessible format
- Recording all the changes in a systematic manner for future reference
- Dynamic, interactive and user-friendly, while a conventional paper/electronic report is static, one-way and, to some extent, user-unfriendly.

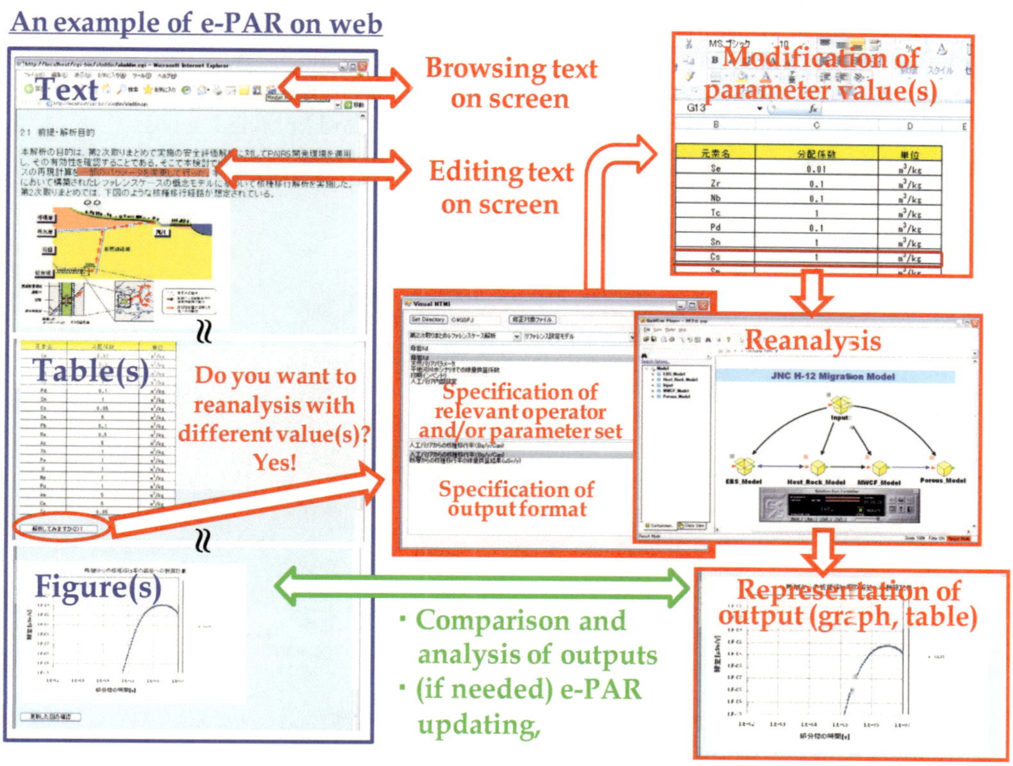

Fig. 11. Flow of functions and operations on e-PAR (browsing, editing and reanalysis)

3.4 CoolRep

As indicated in Figure 12, at a top hierarchical level the key tools utilised are, in addition to Scarab for argumentation model development, CoolRep and a smart search engine.

'CoolRep' is an advanced, internet-based approach to management of documentation and providing an interface with users – both technical and non-technical. It allows the vast volumes of relevant information to be presented in a user-friendly manner, with different access options for different stakeholder groups. Since March 2010, the CoolRep 2010 version in Japanese language is available (http://kms1.jaea.go.jp/CoolRep/) and demonstrates the capability of JAEA (in the future, together with other Japanese R&D organisations) to support production and review of safety cases for deep geological disposal (Figure 12). An

English version is under development. Here, the name 'CoolRep' was chosen for this environment friendly option that minimises the use of hard copy, which was developed on the basis of lateral thinking by analogy to the CoolBiz campaign in Japan (http://en.wikipedia.org/wiki/Cool_Biz_campaign).

The CoolRep is produced entirely in electronic form and is provided on the internet in the form of a short, easily readable overview (2010 Japanese version is equivalent to around 75 pages) with extensive hyperlinks to:

- support text providing more detailed technical input of major technical components (termed KERNELs - Knowledge Elements incorporating Requirements, Novelty, Experience and Limitations)
- both the generic, overall safety case structure and the component KERNELs in the form of argumentation models
- further nested hyperlinks in both text and argumentation models that provide more technical detail, including ultimately full text of key references
- provide access to other knowledge management tools and knowledge base
- visual support material, including graphics, videos and animations
- all review and QA records
- provide access to relevant external websites.

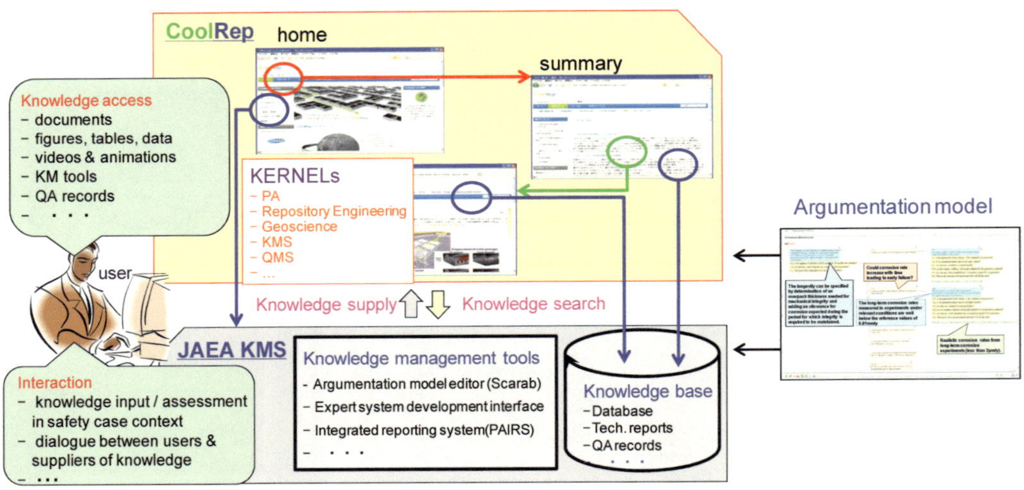

Fig. 12. Links between CoolRep, the JAEA KMS and argumentation models

The advantages of this approach include:

- The overview can focus on logical presentation of the safety case; technical support information is accessed directly when desired, rather than either clogging development of argumentation model with superficial detail or being isolated in abstruse specialist reports
- Technical depth can be increased to the level desired by the user via the nested hyperlinks
- Wherever relevant, contained material is reviewed via a rigorous internal quality management system: comprehensive quality records (review comments, author responses, issue resolution forms) can be viewed by direct links

- During production, a single read-only master exists containing the accepted version; amendments of components may be produced in parallel, but contain digital signatures of the authors and are opened officially only after acceptance and digital signature of the report coordinator (assures implementation of the QMS and prevents different versions of information and data being used by different groups).

So far, not all functions are fully implemented - but sufficient test cases are available to assure fundamental applicability of this tool.

As noted previously, transparent quality management is particularly important for the JAEA knowledge base. Even though guidelines are not yet agreed by all stakeholders, a demonstration of QA review for some text in CoolRep 2010 version and supporting kernels has been implemented. A further contribution to technical QA is the capability to solicit feedback from users. Such feedback can, in addition, be used to improve the structuring of information and the presentation software and play an important role in establishing dialogue with users, which includes the implementer, regulators, involved researchers, academics and the general public. CoolRep provides a portal that not only gives technical users access to KM tools and the KB, but also includes demonstration cases and user manuals (both conventional and video format).

In terms of the tools shown in Figure 12, progress has been slowest on smart search engine development. This is because an early decision to develop new software can be seen in retrospect to have been made without realisation of the extremely rapid rate of progress in this field. The effort is now focused on tailoring existing tools to the particular requirements of the JAEA KMS. In order to use smart search engines, it is critical to establish a clear vocabulary or taxonomy for the complex and multidisciplinary waste disposal field, in order to allow structured contextual searches that go beyond simple keywords. Much of the ongoing development in this area involves some form of semantic analysis, which has been claimed to be the key to 'next generation' knowledge management (e.g. Kawata et al., 2006; Umeki, 2007; Umeki et al., 2008). In order to form the basis to test such approaches, efforts have first concentrated on definition of clear ontology and examination of approaches to 'ontology cleaning' that have been used in other areas (e.g. Borrego-Díaz and Chávez-González, 2006).

4. Discussion and conclusion

The structured approach to initiating the development of a new KMS seems to paying off - tools and methodology have been seen to be applicable to a wide range of JAEA activities for deep geological disposal of radioactive waste and provide a better overview of context that was previously available. The need for a major change in approach of the JAEA activities to introduce KMS concept, processes and technologies/tools is now widely accepted by senior managers and younger staff, in particular, has provided positive feedback to the initiatives investigated. Nevertheless, in some critical areas - especially associated with the development of smart search engines - progress has been limited to defining project specifications and a key challenge will be assembling the support team to carry out the required software tailoring work. Probably most promising is the observation that, even at an early stage, the tools used provide hints of how increasing numbers of knowledge management functions can be automated, which will be a key to any next generation system.

So far, progress on the knowledge communication side has been focused on CoolRep and the range of concepts and proposals implemented within this platform, utilising the concept of cultivating communities of practice (e.g. Wenger et al., 2002).

Further development here will, however, be one of the main focuses of work in the coming years as the Japanese geological disposal programme moves closer to site-specific work. It is also applicable to implement disposal of many types of radioactive waste generated by the accident of the Fukushima Dai-ichi nuclear power station. There is no doubt that the envisaged system is at (or even beyond) the limits of what is feasible with existing technology. Nevertheless, this is an extremely dynamic and fast-moving field and there seem to be good chances that all defined goals can be met.

The works will be very challenging but, as the fundamental requirement for a 21st century approach to the management of knowledge becomes more widely accepted, the opportunities to share the load in collaborative projects will expand. Certainly, JAEA will work closely with other relevant organisations in Japan that are producers and/or users of knowledge, but extended cooperation with international partners is also a high priority goal for the near future.

5. Acknowledgment

The authors gratefully acknowledge the support in developing and applying this KMS from many individuals within both JAEA and supporting organisations. Special thanks go to Dr. Ian G. McKinley (McKinley consulting) and Dr. Hiroyasu Takase (Quintessa Limited K.K.). The authors also thank the ASME (American Society of Mechanical Engineers) for granting permission to use excerpts from the Proceedings of the ICEM'09: 12th International Conference on Environmental and Radioactive Waste Management (Osawa et al., 2009b; Semba et al., 2009). This study includes the output of research carried out under a contract with METI (Ministry of Economy, Trade and Industry) as part of its R&D support programme for developing geological disposal technology.

6. References

Apted, M.; Berryman, K.; Chapman, N.; Cloos, M.; Connor, C.; Kitayama, K.; Sparkes, S. & Tsuchi, H. (2004). Locating a radioactive waste repository in the ring of fire, *EOS, Transactions, American Geophysical Union*, Vol. 85, No. 45, 465–471

Borrego-Díaz, J. & Chávez-González, A.M. (2006). Visual Ontology Cleaning: Cognitive Principles and Applicability, *Lecture Notes in Computing Science*, Vol. 4011/2006, 317-331, Springer-verlag, Berlin, Heidelberg

Golder Associates (2001). *GoldSim Contaminant Transport Module, Users Guide*, Golder Associates Inc

IAEA (2005). Nuclear Knowledge Management Glossary of Terms,

Available from: http://www.iaea.org/km/documents/NKM-Glossary.pdf

JNC (2000). *H12: Project to Establish the Scientific and Technical Basis for HLW Disposal in Japan, Project Overview Report*, JNC TN1400 2000-001

JNC (2005). *H17: Development and Management of the Technical Knowledge Base for the Geological Disposal of HLW, Knowledge Management Report*, JNC TN1400 2005-022

Kawata, T.; Umeki, H. & McKinley, I.G. (2006). Knowledge management: Emperor's new clothes?, *International High-Level Radioactive Waste Management Conference (IHLRWM) 2006*, 1236–1243, Las Vegas, NV, USA, 30 April – 4 May 2006

Kirschner, P.A.; Buckingham-Shum, S.J. & Carr, C.S. (Eds.) (2003). *Visualizing Argumentation: Software Tools for Collaborative and Educational Sense-Making*, ISBN 1-85233-6641-1, Springer-Verlag, London

Kitayama, K.; Ueda, H.; Sakabe, Y.; Umeki, H.; McKinley, I.G. & Kaku, K. (2005). A structured approach for stepwise design of HLW repositories tailored to volunteer sites, *Proceedings of the IAEA Conference on Safety of Radioactive Waste Disposal*, Tokyo, Japan, 3–7 October 2005

Makino, H.; Hioki, K.; Umeki, H.; Yang, H.; Takase, H. & McKinley, I.G. (2009a). Practical application of the KMS, 1; Total system performance assessment, *Proceedings of the ICEM'09: 12th International Conference on Environmental and Radioactive Waste Management*, ICEM2009-16348, Liverpool, UK, 11–15 October 2009 (CD-ROM)

Makino, H.; Umeki, H.; Hioki, K. & McKinley, I.G. (2009b). The challenge of development of a holistic waste management approach to support the Nuclear Renaissance, *Proceedings of the International Waste Management Symposium 2009 (WM '09)*, Phoenix, AZ, USA, 1–5 March 2009 (CD-ROM)

Makino, H.; Hioki, K.; Umeki, H.; Yang, H.; Takase, H. & McKinley, I.G. (2011). Knowledge Management for radioactive waste disposal: moving from theory to practice. *International Journal of Nuclear Knowledge Management*, Vol. 5, No. 1, 93–110

Nonaka, I. & Takeuchi, H. (1995). *The Knowledge-Creating Company*, ISBN 0-19-509269-4, Oxford University Press, New York Oxford

NSC (2004). *Commonly important issues for the safety regulations of radioactive waste disposal*, 10 June 2004, Nuclear Safety Commission of Japan, Unofficial Translation v2 (050727), Available from: http://www.nsc.go.jp/haiki/page3/050728.pdf

NUMO (2004). *Development of Repository Concepts for Volunteer Siting Environment*, NUMO-TR- 04-03

NUMO (2007). *The NUMO Structured Approach to HLW Disposal in Japan*, NUMO-TR-07-02

Osawa, H.; Umeki, H.; Ota, K.; Hama, K.; Sawada, A.; Takeuchi, S.; Semba, T.; Takase H. & McKinley, I.G. (2009a). A structured approach for stepwise development of next-generation technology for integrated site characterization of deep geological repositories, *Proceedings of the International Waste Management Symposium 2009 (WM '09)*, Phoenix, AZ, USA, 1–5 March 2009 (CD-ROM)

Osawa, H.; Hioki, K.; Umeki, H. & Takase, H. (2009b). Use of the safety case to focus KMS applications, *Proceedings of the ICEM'09: 12th International Conference on Environmental and Radioactive Waste Management*, ICEM2009-16348, Liverpool, UK, 11–15 October 2009 (CD-ROM)

Ota, K.; Abe, H. & Kunimaru, T. (Eds.) (2010). *Horonobe Underground Research Laboratory Project: Synthesis of Phase I Investigations 2001-2005, Volume "Geoscientific Research"*, JAEA-Research 2010-068

Saegusa, H. & Matsuoka, T. (Eds.) (2010). *Final Report on the Surface-based Investigation Phase (Phase I) at the Mizunami Underground Research Laboratory Project*, JAEA-Research 2010-067

Semba, T.; Osawa, H.; Hioki, K.; Tachibana, S. & Takase, H. (2009). Practical application of the KMS: 2) site characterisation, *Proceedings of the ICEM'09: 12th International*

Conference on Environmental and Radioactive Waste Management, ICEM2009-16355, Liverpool, UK, 11–15 October 2009 (CD-ROM)

Umeki, H. (2007). A Challenge for computing in the 21st century: radwaste knowledge management, *Joint International Topical Meeting on Mathematics & Computation and Supercomputing in Nuclear Applications (M&C + SNA 2007)*, Monterey, CA, USA, 15–19 April 2007, American Nuclear Society, LaGrange Park, IL (CD-ROM)

Umeki, H.; Osawa, H.; Naito, M.; Nakano, K.; Makino, H. & McKinley, I.G. (2008). Knowledge management: the cornerstone of a 21st century safety case, *OECD-NEA/EC/IAEA International Symposium on Safety Cases for the Deep Disposal of Radioactive Waste: Where Do We Stand?*, Paris La Défense, France, 23–25 January 2007

Umeki, H.; Hioki, K.; Takase, H. & McKinley, I.G. (2009). Overview of the JAEA knowledge management system supporting implication and regulation of geological disposal in Japan, *Proceedings of the ICEM'09: 12th International Conference on Environmental and Radioactive Waste Management*, ICEM2009-16354, Liverpool, UK, 11–15 October 2009 (CD-ROM)

Umeki, H. & Takase, H. (2010). Knowledge-based management systems for geological disposal, In: *Geological Repositories for Safe Disposal of Spent Nuclear Fuels and Radioactive Materials*, Ahn, J. and Apted, M.J. (Eds.) Crc Pr I Llc, ISBN-978-1-43983-109-2

Wenger, E.; McDermott, R. & Snyder, W. M. (2002). *Cultivating Communities of Practice*, ISBN-978-1-57851-330-7, Harvard Business Press, Boston, Massachusetts

Yanev, Y. (Ed.) (2008). Special issue on nuclear knowledge management: IAEA perspective. *International Journal of Nuclear Knowledge Management*, Vol. 3, No. 2, 115–209

11

Knowledge Crystallisation Supported by the KnowCat System

Ruth Cobos
Universidad Autónoma de Madrid
Spain

1. Introduction

Nowadays, it is commonly accepted that the World-Wide Web is the most popular tool for sharing knowledge and information (Berners-Lee, 1996). However, there is a huge and growing amount of information and it is getting more and more difficult to make sense out of it. The research work presented in this paper is an effort to address this Overload Information problem (Gross, 1964).

The main proposal of this work consists in managing the knowledge of a user community by means of a mechanism for knowledge construction in a distributed and incremental way. More specifically, knowledge evolves towards a structured and refined state by means of user interactions.

The aim of this mechanism is to achieve the crystallisation of user community knowledge as a result of user interactions, and without the need of an editor or manager of this task. The crystallised knowledge is the most accepted one by the community and, on the other hand, the knowledge that has not obtained enough acceptation will be likely to be removed.

It is important to highlight that knowledge is constantly evolving. Even crystallised knowledge may receive interactions from the community for further improvement. The key point is the evolution and improvement of knowledge by means of user evaluation.

The user community knowledge is subject to a maturation process involving two main phases. At first, due to the lack of critical mass of knowledge and interaction, a steering committee needs to be in charge of knowledge evaluation. Once enough mass is reached, knowledge crystallisation turns to be based on the evaluation performed by virtual communities of experts.

Those users who have added knowledge that has been crystallised are considered as experts, that is, their work have been recognised by the rest of the community. Virtual communities of experts are constructed in terms of sub areas of knowledge community, and they are in charge of the collaborative evaluation of the knowledge of their sub areas. This is similar to the peer review mechanism.

A collaborative Knowledge Management system called KnowCat has been designed and implemented ("Knowledge Catalyser"). KnowCat is based on the concept of Knowledge Crystallisation, supported by virtual communities of experts. KnowCat allows a user community to share, evaluate and structure collective knowledge. The system allows building Web sites where relevant and structured knowledge about some area or topic can be found (Cobos, 2003).

The KnowCat system is presented in the Section 2. Its Knowledge Crystallisation mechanism is detailed in Section 3. The system has evolved for the last twelve years, during this period it has been used with several user communities and a great amount of research data and results have been obtained, which are presented in Section 4. Finally, this paper concludes with some conclusions and future works in Section 5.

2. The KnowCat system

KnowCat (acronym for "Knowledge Catalyser") is a fully consolidated and thoroughly tested and validated Knowledge Management system which has been developed at Universidad Autónoma de Madrid (Spain) an in active use since 1999 (Alamán and Cobos, 1999; Cobos, 2003).

2.1 The characteristics of the KnowCat community knowledge

KnowCat enables us to build up community knowledge sites or knowledge areas. Each knowledge site is divided into three workspaces:

- Community knowledge workspace, which shows the knowledge elements contributed by the users.
- Communication community space, which supports the communication among the users through e-mail lists.
- Personal user workspace, a workspace in which each user can see their own contributions to the knowledge site and can receive information about the interactions of other users related to their contributions.

More specifically, the community knowledge is organised around several knowledge elements. These knowledge elements and the relationships among them are shown in figure 1.

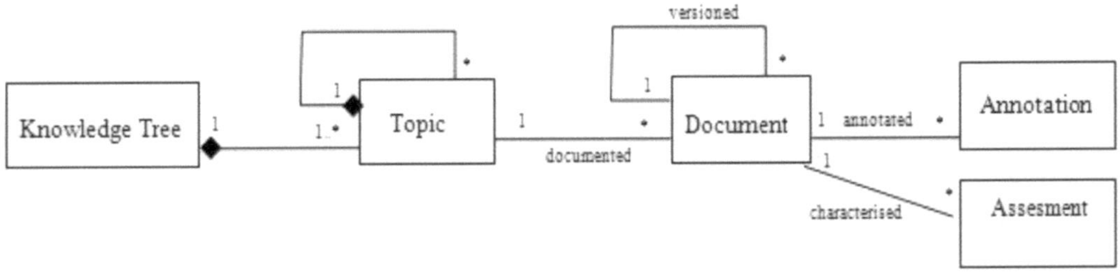

Fig. 1. KnowCat knowledge elements

Firstly, the knowledge tree, which is a hierarchical structure of topics, displays the organisation of the knowledge site in several topics.

Secondly, each topic contains a set of mutually alternative documents that describe the topic. At any given time, all documents contained in the same topic compete with each other to be considered as the "best" description of the topic. This competitive environment is achieved by the Knowledge Crystallisation mechanism of the system, which is supported by virtual communities of users. Furthermore, each document has a "crystallisation degree", which determinates the social acceptation of this one for the user community (more details in Section 3). At any time, the author of a document can contribute with a new version of his/her document.

Thirdly, each document can receive annotations -or note, for short-. A note is a review about the information presented in a document. Each note has a type that determinates its purpose. We have the following note types:

a. "Clarification" note: this is useful to clarify some parts of the document. E.g. "The following link, that it appears in my document, it doesn't work now, but it worked a week ago ...".
b. "Support" note: this is useful to express agreement with the document. E.g. "This document is very useful in my opinion and it is easy to read it".
c. "Review" note: this is useful to make suggestions about adding, removing, or changing some parts of the document, or for making comments regarding it. More specifically, we have the following note types:

i. "Addition" note: to suggest additions to the document. E.g. "In my opinion, it is necessary to add in this document an index with its most important sections".
ii. "Delete" note: to suggest deletions from the document. E.g. "In the summary there are some examples which, may be, are not necessary".
iii. "Correction" note: to suggest changes to the document. E.g. "I think that there is an error in the first paragraph of the conclusion section, it appears 'motor' instead of 'motivation'".
iv. "Criticism" note: to criticise the document. E.g. "...Moreover the arguments are not properly in our opinion in order to justify author position".
v. "Question" note: to make open questions about the document. E.g. "I think that the document author didn't express clearly his opinion about the document topic, please, can you give us your opinion in the next document version?".

Finally, each document can receive assessments. An assessment represents a "weight assertion" which can be used by the users in order to determinate how good (with a value from 1, minimum value, to 10, maximum value) a specific aspect (i.e. correctness, innovation, etc.) of a specific part of a document (i.e. introduction, references, etc.) is. E.g. References.Completeness=9 *(Part.Aspect=value)* means that a specific document, in the opinion of the user, has the 90% of appropriated references (i.e. some few number of references are missing in this document).

2.2 The collaborative work supported by KnowCat at the community knowledge workspace

The KnowCat users can collaborate in a knowledge site trough the following potential interactions: modifying the knowledge tree, adding a document to a selected topic, voting a document, annotating and contributing with assessments about a document, adding a document version, accessing to documents and document versions, accessing to notes and assessments.

In figure 2, we can see an example screenshot of the community knowledge workspace of "Technical Office" KnowCat site.

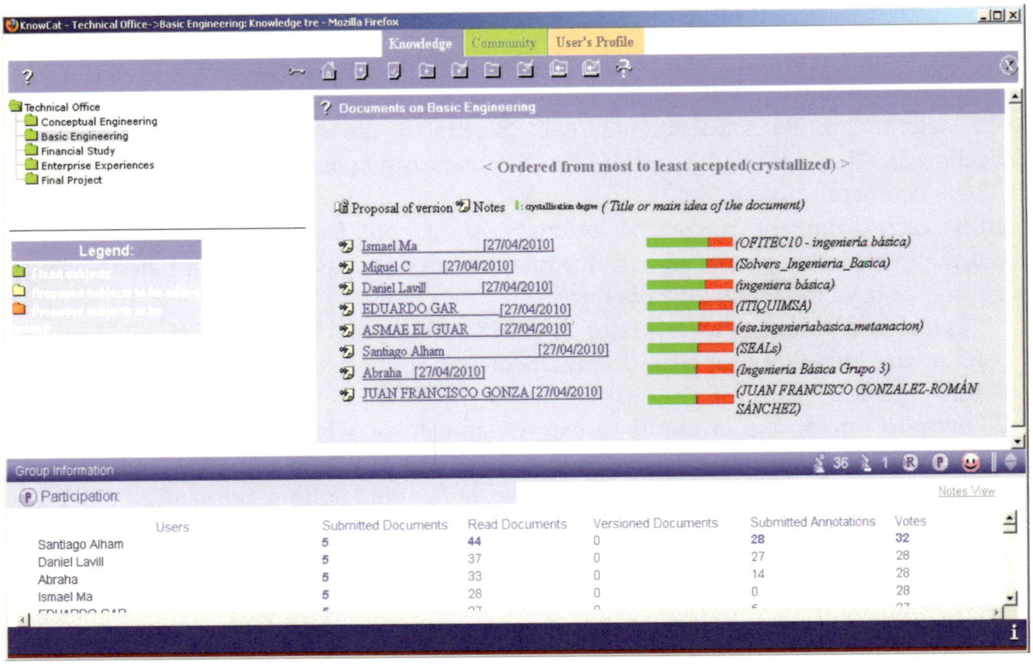

Fig. 2. KnowCat example screen of a knowledge site about "Technical Office".

The details of the user operations provided by KnowCat are:

a. Modifying the knowledge tree, which is displayed on the left side of the screen in Figure 2. The user can participate in the collaborative construction of the knowledge tree. They can suggest adding, deleting or modifying topics of the knowledge tree.
b. Adding a new document to a selected topic. A user contributes with a document (normally a Web page located in a Web server) related to a specific topic of the knowledge tree. From this moment on, the document can receive votes from other users, notes and assessments (normally from other users) and a revised version from the original author. As seen on right side of the screen in Figure 2, the documents are identified by the author's name, arrival date and title. They are ordered by their crystallisation degree, which is shown to the right of the identification heading of each document (with the green-red bar). On the left side of the identification heading of each document are the icons indicating whether a document has received notes and assessments and whether a new version of the document is available. For example, the document identified by "Ismael Ma [27/04/2010] (OFITEC10 - ingeniería básica)" shows the highest crystallisation degree in the topic called "Basic Engineering".
c. Displaying the content of a document (accessing to a document). When a topic is selected from the knowledge tree (it is displayed on the left of the screen) the identification of its documents are shown on the right of the screen. A user can display the content of a document by clicking its identification. The document is then displayed on the right side of the screen.
d. Voting a document. A user can express with a vote the degree to which s/he is in agreement with a document. There are two types of voting mechanisms available in KnowCat: i) a value from a range (1-5, where 1 is the minimum value and 5 the maximum one) and ii) with the single value "1" to denote agreement with the

document. The latter is by far the most popular voting mechanism in the system and has been validated as the most useful way of expressing agreement with a document.

e. Adding an annotation to a document. A user contributes a note to a document in order to make suggestions and/or give comments or opinions. It is possible to annotate a specific document when displayed on the screen. In order to use this operation, a user has to contribute with the following: i) a text, which expresses the assistance that the user wants to provide to the author of the annotated document and ii) a note type (see previous section).

f. Adding assessments to a document: A user contributes with assessments to a document at the same time that s/he is annotating it. In order to use this operation, a user has to contribute with the following: i) select an element of the document (i e. introduction, references, etc.), ii) select an aspect to evaluate (i.e. correctness, innovation, etc.) of the selected element (i.e. introduction, references, etc.) and iii) a value from 1 to 10 (1 minimum value, 10 maximum value).

g. Displaying the content of a note and the content of assessments. When the content of a document is displayed, it is possible to access the list of its received notes and assessments on the left side of the screen.

h. Adding a new version of a document. The author of a document can contribute with a new version of her/his document at any time. This operation is available as a sub-case of the "Adding document" operation.

i. Displaying the content of a new document version. When the content of a document, which is versioned, is displayed, it is possible to select to display its proposed new version.

2.3 Virtual communities and knowledge evolution

A virtual community (Schlichter et.al., 1998) is a group of users that are considered experts in one or more related topics. In this work the opinions from experts are important because they should have more impact than opinions from novices or occasional users.

Virtual communities of experts are constructed in terms of the knowledge tree. For each topic, the community of experts in this topic is composed of the authors of the crystallised documents on the topic, on the parent of the topic, on any of the children of the topic or on any of the sisters of the topic. There is a virtual community for each topic of the knowledge tree, and any successful author usually belongs to several related communities.

When it is started a knowledge area there is only a root node with the main topic. Probably, there will not be enough people and interactions to make the knowledge crystallisation mechanism credible. In relation with this bootstrapping problem, virtual communities have also proven to be handful. Virtual communities behave in a different way when they are just beginning. So, it is proposed a maturation process that involves several phases. Figure 3 shows this evolution.

At the beginning stages the user community work in a "supervised" mode. During this supervised phase there will be a steering committee in charge of proposing knowledge structures (initial refinements of the root node) and voting for them. The members of the steering committee are defined in the moment of creation of the knowledge area; new members can be added by consensus of the current members.

In this phase, descriptions (documents about some topic) may be added to the system both by the members of the steering committee and by other users that are considered as collaborators. However, only the members of the steering committee have the complete capability of voting on the documents, and thus in deciding which documents crystallise. Collaborators may have limited capability of voting, if the steering committee decides so.

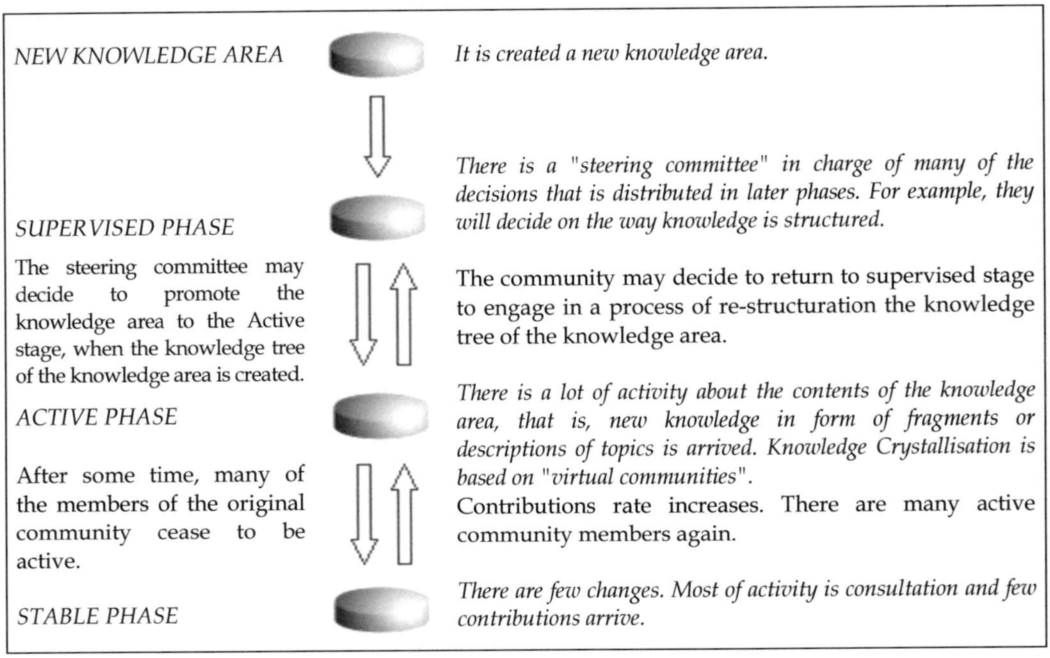

Fig. 3. Knowledge evolution of a knowledge area

Eventually, the steering committee may decide to advance the area of knowledge to the "active" mode, possibly when a critical mass of participants and interactions is achieved. In this moment there should be a single tree structure for the area, decided by consensus. Then the steering committee is dissolved and the subsequent crystallisation of the knowledge is based on virtual communities.

During the "active" phase, when one user contribution crystallises, s/he receives a certain amount of "votes" that s/he may apply for the crystallisation of other documents (of other authors) in the virtual community where her/his crystallised document is located. As in the previous phase the descriptions may be added both by experts and collaborators; in fact all users start using the system as collaborators and when a document of a user crystallises s/he becomes an expert in related communities of the topic where the document is located.

The other aspect of knowledge crystallisation is the evolution of the structure of the knowledge tree. If a member of a virtual community proposes to add a new subject to a topic, remove a subject from a topic or move a subject from one topic to another topic, then a minimum quorum of positive votes from other members of the community will be necessary for the change to be made.

Finally, an active community may reach the "Stable" phase. Many of the community members are not active any longer, so different rules should be applied to ensure some continuity of the crystallisation. Changes are rare, and most of the activity is consultation. Few new contributions arrive, and they will have much more difficulties to crystallise comparing to the previous phase. However, if activity raises to a minimum again, the node may switch to "Active" status, and engage in a new crystallisation phase.

3. Knowledge crystallisation

A central concept in this work is the "Knowledge Crystallisation" mechanism. With this mechanism it could be possible to have, in each moment, the best knowledge elements in a knowledge area, in opinion of the user community.
The mentioned KnowCat knowledge elements -documents, notes, version documents, topics- are produced by the users and their lifetime depends on the patterns of their usage. Any of these elements will stay longer in the knowledge area if it is frequently used and receive favourable opinions from other users. In that case, its crystallisation degree will rise, and thus its probability to stay in the knowledge area. However, if one knowledge element is not used or it doesn't receive favourable opinions by the users, then it will eventually disappear from the knowledge area as a consequence of its crystallisation degree going down. This mechanism is called Knowledge Crystallisation.
Firstly, it is shown in the next section the crystallisation of documents. Secondly, it is shown the crystallisation of annotations, and version documents. Finally, it is shown the crystallisation of the structure.

3.1 Documents' crystallisation process

The Knowledge Crystallisation mechanism takes into account the users' opinions about the documents and the evolution of its received opinions in order to determinate which documents have enough acceptation during a determinate period of time. They will then crystallise.
Each document has a value called "crystallisation degree" or "social acceptation degree"-or acceptation degree, for short-, which is a value between 0-1. A document "crystallise" when his acceptation degree stay for a period of time called "time for crystallising", e.g. 2 weeks, over a determinate "crystallisation point" , e.g. 0.65.
The acceptation degree of a document takes into account:

- The explicit received opinions concerning the document are computed in the *ExplicitAcceptationDegree* value. These explicit opinions are: the received votes (ratings) and how theses votes have been received; and the received assessments, notes and their types.
- The implicit received opinions concerning the document are computed in the *ImplicitAcceptationDegree* value. These implicit opinions are the accesses to the document.

The acceptation degree, which is called as *AcceptationDegree,* of each document, doc_i, in a concrete moment ,t_j, is calculated from the mentioned elements in the following way:
It is considered that the explicit opinions are more useful in order to determinate the acceptation of a document, because they are more elaborated opinions that implicit opinions, so the $coef_E$ is higher than $coef_I$ (e.g. $coef_E = 0.9$; $coef_I = 0.1$).

$$AcceptationDegree(doc_i,t_j)=\begin{bmatrix} ExplicitAcceptationDegree(doc_i,t_j)\times coef_E + \\ ImplicitAcceptationDegree(doc_i,t_j)\times coef_I \end{bmatrix}\times History(doc_i,versionDoc_i,t_j) \quad (1)$$

The knowledge crystallisation mechanism deals with knowledge in evolution. The documents evolves through a sequence of document versions, how is this evolution is calculated in the "history degree" value, i.e. $History(doc_i, versionDoc_i, t_j)$. This value is used in the calculation of the acceptation degree of a document in order to correct its social acceptation taking into account its evolution through several document versions. See Section 3.2.

The first idea in order to calculate the *ImplicitAcceptationDegree* of a selected document doc_d is to compare the number of the received access by doc_d with the received access by all the documents that are in the same topic that doc_d.

$$percentageAccess(doc_d,t_i)=\frac{numberAccess(doc_d,[t_0,t_i])}{\sum_j numberAccess(doc_j,[t_0,t_i])} \quad (2)$$

where,

t_0 the moment when the knowledge area was created.

t_i the actual moment.

$numberAccess(doc_d,[t_0,t_i])$ is the number of received access by doc_d from t_0 to t_i.

doc_j is a document which is in the same topic than doc_d.

This measurement needs to be normalised because it is depends of the context where the document is located, so it is proposed the Formula 3 in order to obtain the implicit social acceptation degree of a document doc_d.

$$ImplicitAcceptationDegree(doc_d,t_i)=\frac{percentageAccess(doc_d,t_i)}{\max\left(percentageAccess\left(doc_j,t_i\right)\right)} \quad (3)$$

where:

$max(percentageAccess(doc_j,t_i))$ is the highest percentage of the received access from the document which are in the same topic than doc_d.

The explicit social acceptation degree of doc_d is calculated taking into account the following values: the value concerning the received votes, *ExplicitAcceptationDegree_Votes*, the value concerning the received notes, *ExplicitAcceptationDegree_Notes*, and the value concerning the received assessments, *ExplicitAcceptationDegree_Assessments*.

$$ExplicitAcceptationDegree(doc_d,t_i)=\begin{bmatrix} ExplicitAcceptationDegree\_Votes(doc_d,t_i)\times coef_{EV} + \\ ExplicitAcceptationDegree\_Notes(doc_d,t_i)\times coef_{EN} + \\ ExplicitAcceptationDegree\_Assessments(doc_d,t_i)\times coef_{EA} \end{bmatrix} \quad (4)$$

It is proposed that $coef_{EV}$ is higher than $coef_{EN}$ and $coef_{EA}$, because the votes are realised by expert users while every community user can realise notes and assessments (e.g. $coef_{EV} = 0.8$; $coef_{EN} = 0.1$; $coef_{EA} = 0.1$).

The *ExplicitAcceptationDegree_Votes* of doc_d is calculated taking into account the normalised percentage of the received votes by doc_d, *normalPercentageVotes*, and a value concerning how theses votes have been received in time by it, i.e., the evolution of the number of received votes in time, *evolutionVotes*.

$$ExplicitAcceptationDegree\_Votes(doc_d,t_i) = normalPercentageVotes(doc_d,t_i) \times evolutionVotes(doc_d,t_i) \quad (5)$$

where,

$$normalPercentageVotes(doc_d,t_i) = \frac{percentageVotes(doc_d,t_i)}{\max\left(percentageVotes(doc_j,t_i)\right)} \quad (6)$$

$$percentageVotes(doc_d,t_i) = \frac{numberVotes(doc_d,[t_0,t_i])}{\sum_j numberVotes(doc_j,[t_0,t_i])} \quad (7)$$

evolutionVotes is a value in the rank 0.95-1.10 when doc_d has a good evolution of the number of the received votes in time, e.g. doc_d receives constantly votes. However, *evolutionVotes* is a value in the rank 0.80-0.95 when doc_d has a bad evolution, e.g. doc_d received at the beginning a lot of votes but close to t_i it doesn't receive new votes.

ExplicitAcceptationDegree_Notes of doc_d is calculated taking into account on the one hand the received "support" annotations and on the other hand the received "review" annotations.

$$ExplicitAcceptationDegree\_Notes(doc_d,t_i) = \begin{bmatrix} normalPercertageSupportNotes(doc_d,t_i) \times coef_{SA} + \\ normalPercertageReviewNotes(doc_d,t_i) \times coef_{RA} \end{bmatrix} \quad (8)$$

where,

normalPercentageSupportNotes(doc_d,t_i) is the normalised percentage of the received "support" notes by doc_d until the moment t_i.

normalPercentageReviewNotes(doc_d,t_i) is the normalised percentage of the received "review" notes by doc_d until the moment t_i.

It is proposed that $coef_{SA}$=1 and the following function is used in order to calculate the coefficient $coef_{RA}$.. With this function the following two cases are distinguished: if a document receives few "review" notes means that this document has social interest and $coef_{RA}$ is close to value 1; if it receives a lot of "review" notes means that the document needs to be improved and $coef_{RA}$ has a value close to 0.

$$coef_{RA}(x) = \begin{cases} 0.5\,x + 0.5 & \text{when } x = numberReviewNotes(doc_d,t_i)/average(numberReviewNotes(doc_j,t_i)) \\ & x > 0 \text{ y } x \le 1 \\ -1/(k-1)\,x + k/(k-1) & \text{when } k = 3\,\sigma / average(numberReviewNotes(doc_j,t_i)) \\ & x = numberReviewNotes(doc_d,t_i)/average(numberReviewNotes(doc_j,t_i))\ ;\ x > 1 \end{cases} \quad (9)$$

ExplicitAcceptationDegree_Assessments of doc_d is calculated taking into account the normalised average value of the received assessments.

$$ExplicitAcceptationDegree\_Assessments(doc_d,t_i) = \frac{averageValueAssessments(doc_d,t_i)}{\max\left(averageValueAssessments(doc_j,t_i)\right)} \quad (10)$$

where,

$$averageValueAssessments(doc_d,t_i) = \frac{\sum_j valueAssessments_j(doc_d,[t_0,t_i])}{numberAssessments(doc_d,[t_0,t_i])} \quad (11)$$

$valueAssessments_j(doc_d,[t_0,t_i])$ is the value of the assessments identified as j for the doc_d.

3.2 Notes and document versions' crystallisation process

As it is shown in the previous section, a social accepted document can "crystallise", however a social accepted annotation can "stay" in the knowledge area and a social accepted proposal of a document version can "consolidate".
The annotations receive votes, too. These votes can be "in favour" or "against" the annotation. The knowledge crystallisation mechanism calculates per annotation the number of the received votes of each type in this way:

$$AgainstDegree(note_a,t_i) = numberVotesAgainst(note_a,t_i) - numberVotesInFavour(note_a,t_i) \quad (12)$$

If *AgainstDegree* of a selected annotation $note_a$ is higher than the average of received votes by the annotations which are in the same location as $note_a$ then this annotation is delete from the knowledge area, in another case the annotation "stay" in the knowledge area.
The documents' assessments don't receive votes, therefore, they don't have a crystallisation mechanism associated.
In each moment, it is possible to have a proposal of a new document version, $versionDoc_i$, of a document, doc_i. The knowledge crystallisation mechanism determinates when a new document version replaces the previous one, i.e., the new document version "consolidate". For this matter, the members of the virtual community of the topic of a document with a new proposal of version have to give their opinions about the following characteristics of the new document version:

- Continuity: that is, if the new document version deals the content of the previous one in a similar way.
- Improvement: that is, if the new document is an improvement of the previous one.

With the received opinions concerning the first characteristic is obtained the "continuity degree", *ContinuityDegree,* of the new document version (a value between 0-10, 10 the maximum value), with the received opinions concerning the second characteristic is obtained the "improvement degree", *ImprovementDegree,* of the new document version (a value between 0-10). If the continuity degree is higher than a determined value called "continuity point" (for example, 5) then the new document version replace the previous one. The history degree, which is used in Formula 1, is calculated as a function of the improvement degree as follows:

$$History(doc_i, versionDoc_i, t_j) = funHistoryDoc(ImprovementDegree(versionDoc_i,t_j)) \quad (13)$$

$$funHistoryDoc(x) = \begin{cases} 0.02 * x + 0.88 \text{ when } x = ImprovementDegree(versionDoc_i,t_j),\ x \geq 0 \text{ and } x < 6 \\ 0.05 * x + 0.7 \text{ when } x = ImprovementDegree(versionDoc_i,t_j), x \geq 6 \text{ and } x \leq 10 \end{cases} \quad (14)$$

3.3 Structure's crystallisation process

The last aspect of knowledge crystallisation is the evolution of the structure of the knowledge tree. If a member of a virtual community proposes to add a new subject to a topic, remove a subject from a topic or move a subject from one topic to another topic, then a

minimum quorum of positive votes from other members of the community will be necessary for consolidating the change.
This minimum quorum, *MinimumQuorum,* of positive votes for a selected proposed change in the structure $propChangeStruct_p$ is calculated as follows:

$$MinimumQuorum\left(propChangeStruct_p,t_i\right)=\left\lceil \begin{array}{l} percentageExperts\times \\ numberActiveExperts\left(propChangeStruct_p,t_i\right)\end{array}\right\rceil \quad (15)$$

where,
percentageExperts is a configurable value, e.g. 0.8
numberActiveExperts is the number of active member of the virtual community where $propChangeStruct_p$ is proposed.

4. Research studies supported by KnowCat

KnowCat has been tested for more than ten years in several research studies with student communities at Universidad Autónoma de Madrid (UAM, Spain), Universitat de Lleida (UdL, Spain) and Universidad Pontificia Bolivariana (UPB, Colombia), among others. Table 1 shows a summary of the participants'communites of these research studies
Most of these research studies have corroborated these design hypotheses of KnowCat (Alamán & Cobos, 1999; Cobos & Alamán, 2002; Cobos, 2003; Cobos & Pifarré, 2008; Diez & Cobos, 2007; Gómez, Gutiérrez, Cobos & Alaman, 2001):

- When a set of people having a certain level of knowledge engage in a reasonable interaction with the system, the result converges to some consensus. This consensus is closely related to an objective measurement of "quality" of the contributions.
- The knowledge classification through a tree structure has been exposed as a suitable approach for managing and organising the knowledge.
- The use of document annotations is useful for motivating document authors in generating new document versions. If a document author takes into account the received notes in the creation of a new document version of his/her annotated document, the new document version will improve.
- The knowledge area resulted by the user community interactions and the Knowledge Crystallisation mechanism represents the social interests of its community.

These research studies took the form of longitudinal case studies conducted in authentic university environments. In order to illustrate the research methodology of these studies, an example about how the system could be used for any community is exposed:

1. Both students and instructors supported the creation of a common frame of reference before using the KnowCat system. They shared the study's common values and pedagogical goals, and the collaborative tasks were coordinated in advance - i.e., the tasks and the timetable were agreed on previously between instructors and students. Moreover, the students, who needed it, received formation about how to use KnowCat features.
2. The main procedure of the students' work with the KnowCat system was as follows:
   a. The students were distributed into the topics that were established by the instructor in the knowledge tree. Normally, there were between five to ten students

working in the same topic. Individually, students read some information about a specific topic course.

b. The students wrote an individual report (document) about the topic and entered it into KnowCat. These reports contained a personal reflection on the content of the read information, or suggested a personal solution to a specific problem.

c. The students read some peers' report and annotated them –i.e. by giving assistance– in order to help the fellow classmates improve on it. For each individual topic, the students were asked to annotate a minimum number of classmate's report (e.g. to write at least three notes and to write at least five assessments, these notes and assessments could be done on one or more documents). During the study, the students were strongly encouraged to annotate the reports of different classmates. In most of the research studies, the students' documents received a different number of interactions, for instance, none of the students' documents received less than three notes. In some studies, the students voted for the best document on a topic. In this way, the knowledge crystallisation mechanisms could be started to generate an initial classification.

d. The document's author read the notes concerning her/his report, taking into account her/his classmates scaffolds, re-wrote the report and entered it back into the system again, as a new document version.

e. Finally the students voted for the best document on a topic. Moreover, they gave their opinions about the "continuity" and "improvement" characteristics of the new document versions (see Section 3.2) in order to facilitate the system the decisions over which documents had to be replaced with their new document version.

3. Students answered to a questionnaire about the work realised with KnowCat. In some cases, they were interviewed. To enable coding and analysing, the interviews were transcribed word by word.
4. The data analysis was generated by the instructors. Both a qualitative content analysis and a quantitative analysis were made about the students' contributions in the system. These analyses were useful in order to corroborate both the common mentioned system design hypotheses as specific ones formulated in the context of each specific research study (see some examples below).

Some specific research studies carried out with communities at UdL have contributed the following corroborated hypotheses (Pifarré & Cobos, 2009; Pifarré & Cobos, 2010):

- The pedagogical application of the KnowCat system may favour and improve the development of the students' metacognitive learning processes. The content analysis of the students' interviews revealed the existence of metacognitive knowledge regarding the learning processes that students develop while interacting with KnowCat knowledge elements. Students showed high levels of consciousness about learning new strategies and about the conditional use of these strategies to solve specific tasks efficiently.
- The instructional application of the KnowCat system may favour and improve the development of students' self-regulated skills. Small group interaction patterns appear while their members are working together throughout the instructional process supported by KnowCat. These interaction patters were related with an increasing number of self-regulated processes, specially planning, asking for clarification and monitoring skills.

COURSE	ACADEMIC YEARS	#PARTICIPANTS PER YEAR	DEPARTMENT, UNIVERSITY
Operating Systems	1998/1999 - 2006/2007 (nine years)	250	Computer Engineeting, UAM
Uncertain Reasoning	1999/2000 - 2002/2003 (four years)	15	Computer Engineeting, UAM
Mathematics for Children's Training	2000/2001 – 2004/2005 (five years)	40	Theory of Education, UAM
Learning Strategies	2002/2003	31	Pedagogy and Psychology, UdL
Psychopedagogy Intervention	2002/2003	18	Pedagogy and Psychology, UdL
Artificial Intelligence	2004/2005 - 2007/2008 (four years)	250	Computer Engineeting, UAM
Automata Theory and Formal Languages	2004/2005 - 2006/2007 (three years)	90	Computer Engineeting, UAM
Biology for Development	2004/2005 - 2006/2007 (three years)	40	Biochemistry, UAM
Computers Systems II	2005/2006 – 2006/2007 (two years)	200	Computer Engineeting, UAM
Psychopedagogy Intervention in children development disorders	2006/2007	26	Pedagogy and Psychology, UdL
Technical Office	2007/2008 – 2009/2010 (three years)	35	Chemical Engineering , UAM
Collaborative Systems	2008/2009 - 2010/2011 (two years)	10	Computer Engineeting, UAM
Technology Management	2009/2010 – 2010/2011 (two years)	15	Computer Engineeting, UPB
Informatics I	2009/2010	20	Law, UPB

Table 1. Courses and participants in the realised research experiences.

On the one hand, KnowCat system has been involved since the first system version in 1999 until nowadays, due to the results obtained and the users' opinions from all the research studies. Moreover, the system was extended with new services.

Firstly, a console with awareness services was added to KnowCat (Cobos, Claros & Moreno-Llorena, 2009). These services are: brief information about registered users (what have these users done?), brief information about connected users, a radar view (where and what are the connected users doing?), participation-meter (How many times have the registered users done each task?), a fish eye view (when, where and what has each registered user done?) and a map of interaction among users in the annotating task (who has annotated the document of whom?).

These new services provide users useful information about how KnowCat users are interacting with the system. This console is shown in the bottom part ("Group Information") of the KnowCat screen. In Figure 2, we can see the participation-meter service.

Secondly, in this mentioned console a motivation booster service was added, which provide users feedback information about its work progress in KnowCat (Echeverria & Cobos, 2010). These extensions to the system have corroborated these hypothesis related to user community feelings:

- The users are aware of their participation in a collaborative work, in other words, they feel that are working in a collaborative way.
- When users receive feedback information about their activities progress, then they increase their interactions with the system performing their activities in a better manner, and they become more motivated to interact with the system.

On the other hand, a prototype called Semantic KnowCat (SKC) was developed on KnowCat to investigate solutions to information overload in ICT-based systems, using knowledge management systems as a model (Moreno-Llorena & Alamán, 2006; Moreno-Llorena 2008). SKC uses for this purpose some hidden aspects of such systems, as the residual energy of their activity, and properties of both the elements and the activities involved (see the chapter about this prototype in the book).

5. Conclusion and future work

In this paper, the KnowCat (acronym for "Knowledge Catalyser") system is presented. KnowCat deals with knowledge in evolution and its main contribution is a Knowledge Crystallisation mechanism, which is supported by virtual communities of experts. This mechanism maintains in the KnowCat knowledge areas the collective accepted knowledge by its user community.

There is a crystallisation process for each knowledge element that can receive user interactions in the community knowledge areas: documents, annotations, version documents and topics. In the case of documents, each document has a social acceptation degree (a value between 0-1, 1 is the maximum value), which takes into account: i) explicit received opinions (i.e. the received votes and how theses votes have been received; and the received assessments, notes and their types); ii) implicit received opinions (i.e. accesses to the document) and iii) its evolution through several document versions. A document, which have enough social acceptation during a determinate period of time, may "crystallise". Therefore, its author wil become and expert in the topic where the document is located.

The annotations receive votes, which can be "in favour" or "against" the annotation. The knowledge crystallisation mechanism calculates per annotation the number of the received votes of each type and determinates its social acceptation. A social accepted annotation can "stay" in the knowledge area.

Documents' versions receive votes about the content continuity (i.e. if the new document version deals the content of the previous one in a similar way) and the content improvement (if the new document is an improvement of the previous one). When a document version has social acceptation about the content continuity then it replaces the previous one, i.e., the new document version "consolidate". The social acceptation about the content improvement is used to calculate an specific part of the social acceptation degree of the corresponding document: the part related with its evolution through several document versions.

KnowCat has been tested for twelve years in several research studies with student communities at several universities. These research studies have corroborated the KnowCat design hypotheses and the details of these studies and their results are a great contribution of this research work (Alamán & Cobos, 1999; Cobos & Alamán, 2002; Cobos, 2003; Cobos & Pifarré, 2008; Diez & Cobos, 2007; Gómez, Gutiérrez, Cobos & Alaman, 2001; Pifarré & Cobos, 2009; Pifarré & Cobos, 2010).

The system was extended with: i) awareness services, which provide users useful information about how they are interacting with the system and supports users to be aware of their collaborative interactions with the system (Cobos, Claros & Moreno-Llorena, 2009) and ii) a motivation booster service, which provide users feedback information about its work progress in KnowCat and supports to maintain user motivation to interact with the system (Echeverria & Cobos, 2010).

An interesting open research issue is the integration of KnowCat with other Web platforms or Knowledge Management systems. A first effort in this directions is an initial version of the integration of KnowCat and another Knowledge Management system called Sofia (Cobos, et.al., 2010). Sofia system provides the ability to externalize tacit knowledge, through the group storytelling approach and it has been developed at Federal University of Rio de Janeiro (Luz, et.al., 2008). This integration proposal supports both tacit and explicit knowledge management thanks to the characteristics and functionalities of both systems.

Finally, the KnowCat system is in evolution, furthermore more research studies are planned, both with new user communities and with some of the communities that have used it in previous academic years.

6. Acknowledgment

This research was partly funded by the Spanish National Plan of R+D, project numbers: TIN2008-2081/TIN and TIN2011-24139; by the CAM (Autonomous Community of Madrid), project number: S2009/TIC-1650.

7. References

Alamán, X., Cobos, R. (1999). KnowCat: a Web Application for Knowledge Organization. In: *LNCS 1727*, Chen, P.P., et al. (Eds.), pp. 348-359, Springer, ISSN 0302-9743.

Berners-Lee, T. (1996). *The World Wide Web: Past, Present and Future*. September, 2011. Available from: <http://www.w3.org/People/Berners-Lee/1996/ppf.html>.

Cobos, R. Alamán, X. (2002). Creating e-books in a distributed and collaborative way. *Journal of Electronic Library on Electronic book for Education*, Vol. 20, No. 4, (May 2002), pp. 288-295, ISSN 0264-0473.

Cobos, R. (2003). *Mechanisms for the Crystallisation of Knowledge, a proposal using a collaborative system*. Doctoral dissertation. Universidad Autónoma de Madrid.

Cobos, R., Pifarré, M. (2008). Collaborative knowledge construction in the web supported by the KnowCat system. *Computers & Education*, Vol.50, No. 3, (April 2009), pp. 962-978, ISSN 0360-1315.

Cobos, R., Claros, I., Moreno, J. (2009). A proposal of Awareness Services for the Construction of Quality Community Knowledge supported by the Knowledge Management system KnowCat. *Proceedings of International Conference Human-Computer Interaction*, pp. 365-374, ISBN 978-3-642-02555-6, San Diego, USA, July 19-24, 2009.

Cobos, R., Cajías, R., Barros, L., Borges, M.R.S. (2010). Towards the Construction of a Knowledge Building Environment. *LNCS 6240*, Luo, Y. (Ed.), pp. 27-30. Springer, ISSN 0302-9743.

Díez, F, Cobos, R. (2007). A Case Study of a Cooperative Learning Experience in Artificial Intelligence. *Journal Computer Applications in Engineering Education*. Vol. 15, No. 4, (december 2007), pp. 308-316, ISSN 1061-3773.

Echeverria, l., Cobos, R. (2010). A Motivation Booster proposal based on the monitoring of users' progress in CSCL environments. *Proceedings of the 2010 14th International Conference on Computer Supported Cooperative Work in Design (CSCWD 2010)*, pp. 671-676, ISBN 978-1-4244-6763-1, Shanghai, China, April 14-16, 2010.

Gómez, M., Gutiérrez, A., Cobos, R., Alamán, X. (2001). Collaborative Learning with computer-based support in the design of material for the development of abstract thought in Preschool Education. An Experiment in the teaching of mathematics. *Proceedings of the International Symposium of Computers in Education 2001*, pp. 241-254.

Gross, B. M. (1964). *The Managing of Organizations: The Administrative Struggle (Vol. 1)*, New York: Free Press of Glencoe.

Luz, C.M., Borges, M.R.S., Campos, M.L.M. (2008) Sofia – A framework for the Development of Group Storytelling Tools, *Proceedings of the ACM Workshop on Story Representation, Mechanism and Context (SRMC 2008)*, pp. 41–47, ISBN 978-1-60558-315-0, ACM Press, Vancouver, Canada, October 31, 2008.

Moreno-Llorena, J., Alamán, X. (2006). A Proposal of Design for a Collaborative Knowledge Management System by means of Semantic Information. In: *HCI related papers of Interacción 2004, Navarro*-Prieto, R. et al. (Eds.), Springer, pp. 307-319, 2005. ISBN 978-1-4020-4204-1, Dordrecht, The Netherlands.

Moreno-Llorena, J. (2008). *Collaborative Knowledge Management By Means Semantic Information*. Doctoral dissertation. Universidad Autónoma de Madrid.

Pifarré, M., Cobos, R. 2009 Evaluation of the Development of Metacognitive Knowledge Supported by the KnowCat system. *Educational Technology Research and Development Journal (ETR&D)*, Vol. 57, No. 6 (March 2009), pp. 787-799. ISSN 1042-1629.

Pifarré, M., Cobos, R. 2010. Promoting Metacognitive Skills through peer scaffolding in a Collaborative Learning Computer-based environment. *International Journal of Computer-Supported Collaborative Learning*, Vol. 5, No. 2, (March 2010), pp. 237-253. ISSN 1556-1607.

Schlichter, J., Koch, K. & Chengmao, X. (1998). Awareness The Common Link Between Groupware and Communityware. In : *Community Computing and Support Systems*, T. Ishida (Ed), pp. 77–93, Springer Verlag, ISBN 3-540-65475-5, London, UK.

12

Enhancing Knowledge Management for Engineers Using Mind Mapping in Construction

Chun-Sung Chen[1] and Yu-Cheng Lin[2]

[1]*Ching Yun University, Department of Applied Geomatics*

[2]*National Taipei University of Technology, Department of Civil Engineering*

Taiwan

1. Introduction

Knowledge management (KM) is the collection of processes governing the creation, storage, reuse, maintenance, dissemination and reuse of knowledge. KM refers to the collection of processes controlling the creation, storage and usage of experience in a particular situation or problem solving context. To transfer knowledge between experienced engineers, construction professionals have traditionally used techniques ranging from formal annual meetings to face-to-face interviews. Construction KM focuses on the acquisition and management of important issues and experience from participating engineers.

To enhance the quality of KM gained by engineers involved in construction projects, this study proposes a knowledge flow approach integrated with mind mapping to achieving KM solutions in the construction industry. Combined with web-based technology and mind mapping, this study proposes a Construction Web Topic-based Knowledge Management (CWTKM) system enabling engineers to reuse domain knowledge and experience by dynamically exchanging and managing knowledge during the construction phase of a project. In the proposed CWTKM system, the topic-based experience exchange environment in the mind map enables engineers to illustrate and share their experience with other engineers effectively. Engineers are, thus, invited to exchange and share their knowledge based on their previous experience.

By integrating web-based technology and mind mapping, engineers can obtain problem solutions and experience directly from senior engineers, decreasing the time and reducing the cost of on-the-job training. By exchanging and sharing previous experiences among engineers, similar and related experiences used to execute similar projects can clarify domain knowledge and enable the exchange of knowledge through web KM. The CWTKM system provides a web-based platform for users who can request assistance from selected or all engineers in the enterprise who have relevant experience. The user can also submit knowledge description using mind mapping in CWTKM system. Moreover, senior and junior engineers can effectively and easily exchange knowledge and experience regarding a specific aspect of their current construction project. In this study of a Taiwan construction building project, the survey (questionnaire) results indicated that the CWTKM system, integrated with mind mapping approach is effective for construction knowledge exchange and management.

2. Problem statement

When completing projects, these engineers and experts typically accumulate domain knowledge and valued knowledge, but share little or no knowledge with others. In view of KM, these significant issues and experiences of construction engineers and experts are particularly valuable due to associated factors such as manpower, significant cost and time. The complicated nature of the construction industry makes it an important field for KM, particularly regarding knowledge gained from experienced engineers. Sharing knowledge between engineers can improve construction management during the construction phases of projects, thus helping avoid mistakes that past projects have already encountered. Transferring construction knowledge between projects can significantly contribute to achieving project objectives such as cost, schedule, quality and safety (Reuss and Tatum, 1993). Learning from experience, also, avoids problem-solving from scratch, i.e., problems that have already been solved need not be solved repeatedly. However, no effective platforms are available to assist engineers or experts in exchanging and sharing their know-how and experiences when contractors execute construction projects. The inability to share the knowledge of engineers and experts represents a major loss for contractors in the construction industry.

The primary problems derived from the questionnaire survey of twenty junior and senior engineers from five participating construction building projects, in the sharing and exchanging of knowledge, specifically during the construction phase of projects, are as follows: (1) difficulty in determining which engineers and experts have helpful and relevant knowledge; (2) limited efficiency and quality when using only document-based media for knowledge management; (3) difficulty in finding engineers with relevant knowledge in similar projects; and (4) unease with illustrating knowledge in current commercial information management systems. Documenting and applying knowledge may avoid problem-solving from the outset, i.e., problems already solved need not be solved repeatedly. However, few suitable design platforms have been developed to assist engineers in illustrating and sharing their knowledge when needed. Although enterprises in the A/E/C industry have begun to collect and store explicit information in KM databases, they have not always been successful at retrieving and sharing tacit knowledge (Woo et al., 2004). Sharing and using previous tacit knowledge in construction projects is, therefore, the primary and significant challenge of this study.

3. Research objectives

This study proposes a novel and practical methodology for capturing and representing the knowledge and project knowledge of engineers by utilizing mind mapping and topic-based maps (TBM) approach. Furthermore, this study develops a construction topic-based Maps Knowledge Management (CWTKM) system for engineers. The CWTKM provides a knowledge exchange and management service in the construction phase of a project for the reuse of domain knowledge and experience (see Fig. 1). Contractors often execute similar projects; accordingly, the problems encountered in like projects can provide a reference for comparable projects in the future. To be competitive, a contractor needs to make innovative use of knowledge, accumulate knowledge through previous projects and apply it in relevant projects. Senior engineers that participate in projects act as knowledge workers; they facilitate the collection and management of knowledge from previous projects.

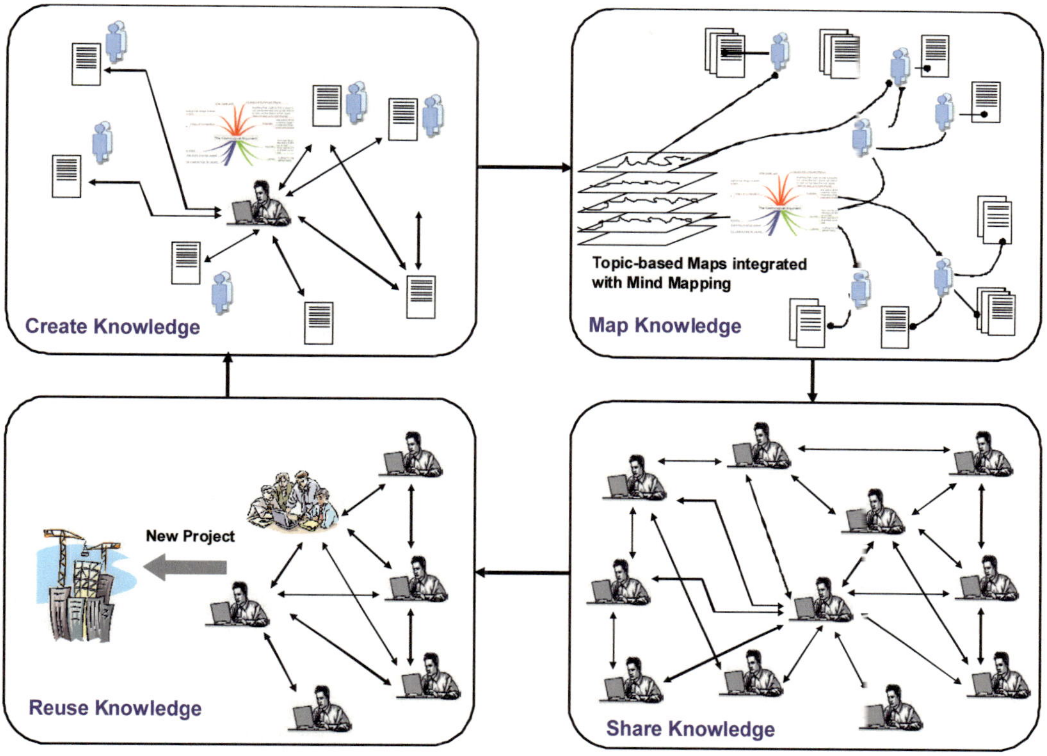

Fig. 1. The application of CWTKM in construction projects.

This study concentrates on new approaches for managing and reusing past specific knowledge for a construction project framework. With the newly proposed TBM approach and integration of mind mapping techniques, service engineers and practitioners can exchange original ideas, experience, knowledge and commands. By integrating TBM and mind mapping techniques, engineers can obtain problem solutions and experience directly from senior engineers, decreasing the time and reducing the cost of on-the-job training. By exchanging and sharing previous knowledge among engineers, similar and related knowledge used to execute similar projects can clarify domain knowledge and enable the exchange of knowledge through web-based KM platform.

To apply KM to new or other construction projects, the process and content of project knowledge must be collected, recorded and stored effectively in the CWTKM system. To assist the participating engineers in illustrating and managing their own project experience, Topic-based mapping is presented to help them explore their acquired experience. . The main objectives of this study are as follows: (1) enhance the illustration capabilities using the TBM approach and mind mapping techniques of captured experience of engineers and experts related to construction projects; (2) optimize the communication of tacit experience among participating engineers in the exchanging environment; and (3) design an efficient topic-based mapping for users to effectively locate parallel experience from relative engineers. The CWTKM system is then applied in selected case studies of a Taiwan construction building project to verify the proposed approach and demonstrate the value of sharing experience in the construction phase.

4. Background research

4.1 Previous research in knowledge management in the construction industry

In the construction industry, KM is a discipline that promotes an integrated approach to the creation, capture, sharing and reuse of the domain knowledge of a profession obtained from projects that have been previously undertaken. Most project-related problems, solutions, experience and know-how are in the minds of individual engineers and experts during the construction phase of a project. Implicit knowledge is generally undocumented or stored in a system database. To preserve implicit knowledge as corporate property, capturing the implicit knowledge and making it in the form of explicit experience is a vital aspect of KM. Two broad categories of knowledge are tacit knowledge and explicit knowledge. Tacit knowledge is personal, context-specific experience that is difficult to formalize, record or articulate; it is stored in the minds of people (Malhotra, 2000). Tacit knowledge is personal knowledge acquired through individual experience, which is shared and exchanged through direct, face-to-face contact (Malhotra, 2001; Malhotra, 2000; Tiwana, 2000).

Numerous research efforts have focused on applications of knowledge management in construction. A Hong Kong study examined the main barriers to effective knowledge sharing, as well as critical factors and benefits in the construction companies in Hong Kong and the United Kingdom (Fong and Chu, 2006). Intelligent representation structures store and access construction domain knowledge and couple it with advanced planning tools to facilitate rapid formulation and assessment of initial construction project plans (Udaipurwala and Russell, 2002). Fong et al. (2007) pointed out that the knowledge-creating capability of value management teams not only enhances the reputation of value management, but also, helps to dispel the perception of value management as an outdated problem-solving tool.

4.2 Previous research on knowledge maps in construction

A knowledge map includes the sources, flows, and points of knowledge within an organization (Liebowitz, 2005). All captured knowledge can be summarized and abstracted through the knowledge map. The knowledge map, also, provides a blueprint for implementing a knowledge management system. Well-developed knowledge maps help users identify intellectual capital, socialize new members and enhance organizational learning (Wexler, 2001). A knowledge map is a consciously designed medium for communication between makers and users of knowledge by a graphical presentation of text, model numbers or symbols (Wexler, 2001). Knowledge mapping helps users understand the relationship between stored knowledge and dynamics. Knowledge maps have been applied in various applications, including development of knowledge maps for knowledge management software tools (Noll et al., 2002). Numerous research efforts have focused on the use of knowledge maps to support various knowledge management tasks (McAleese, 1998). Davenport and Prusak (1998) observed that developing a knowledge map involves locating significant knowledge in an organization and publishing a list or image that indicates a roadmap to locate it. Mind maps (Buzan and Buzan, 1993) illustrate the structure of ideas in an associative manner which attempts to represent how ideas are stored in the brain. A concept map provides a structure for conceptualization by groups developing a concept framework that can be evaluated by others (Trochim, 1989). Dynamic knowledge mapping can assist in the reuse of experts' tacit knowledge (Woo et al., 2004).

5. Methodology

Although maps of knowledge representation have been developed for knowledge-based applications, no knowledge map has been developed for knowledge management (KM) in construction. To assist engineers in extracting the knowledge gained from their own experience in projects with which they have been involved, this study proposes a novel topic-based maps (TBM) approach for the application of KM in construction. The TBM help to efficiently illustrate the experiences in the minds of engineers to generate and organize experience within a core topic. The TBM are based on associations flowing outward from a central image in a free-flowing, yet organized, and coherent way. The above content also functions as the experience acquisition tool in the CWTKM system. Furthermore, engineers may access and edit many resources, as attachments, in the system. Hence, the CWTKM system can provide engineers with an experience exchanging environment, as well as a web-based platform for acquiring experience from more experienced engineers.

5.1 Concept of topic-based maps

The proposed TBM are specific approaches to KM in the construction field. Although knowledge and concept maps are easily recognized in knowledge management, the proposed TBM approach is a novel concept and is specific to construction KM. TBM can be defined as a diagrammatic and graphic representation of experience linking relationships between knowledge and attributes of MAP. The TBM mainly provide assistance for easily and effectively obtaining the necessary experience of users. The primary advantages of TBM are as follows: (1) TBM are simply, clearly and dynamically represented in the CWTKM system; (2) users can easily navigate the CWTKM in order to: a) understand and determine which engineers and experts own special experience related to a problem as it arises, and b) edit their experience based on what the situation may require; (3) TBM enable users' ability to expand flexible knowledge illustration and linkage; and (4) TBM enhance the available visual knowledge illustration in the maps.

TBM are designed to be easily integrated with mind mapping and their construction experience. The key reason for using TBM is the ease with which the combined experience can be understood and reapplied. Figure 2 illustrates an overview and conceptual framework of TBM utilized in construction KM. Like construction project management, KM is based on the concept of undertaking project planning and control activities. Knowledge and experience gained from activities in previous projects can be collected, managed and applied in future projects. Acquired experience from participating engineers can be accessed and saved as map units in categories for efficient collection, management and finally, retrieval for use in the current projects.

5.2 Framework of topic-based maps

Topic-based Maps (TBM) are defined in multiple levels, and constructed from variables which can be broken down by decomposing the knowledge units into smaller map units into which the acquired knowledge is stored. TBM may be comprised of several layers. The project unit is modelled in the first layer. The second-level layers model Map units (drawing illustration). The lower-level layers model knowledge units. Similarly, any map unit in this lower layer can be broken down further to incorporate other components in lower layers. The map contents can be viewed as either a single point or as ranges. The structure of TBM enables users to access stored knowledge through layers based on the

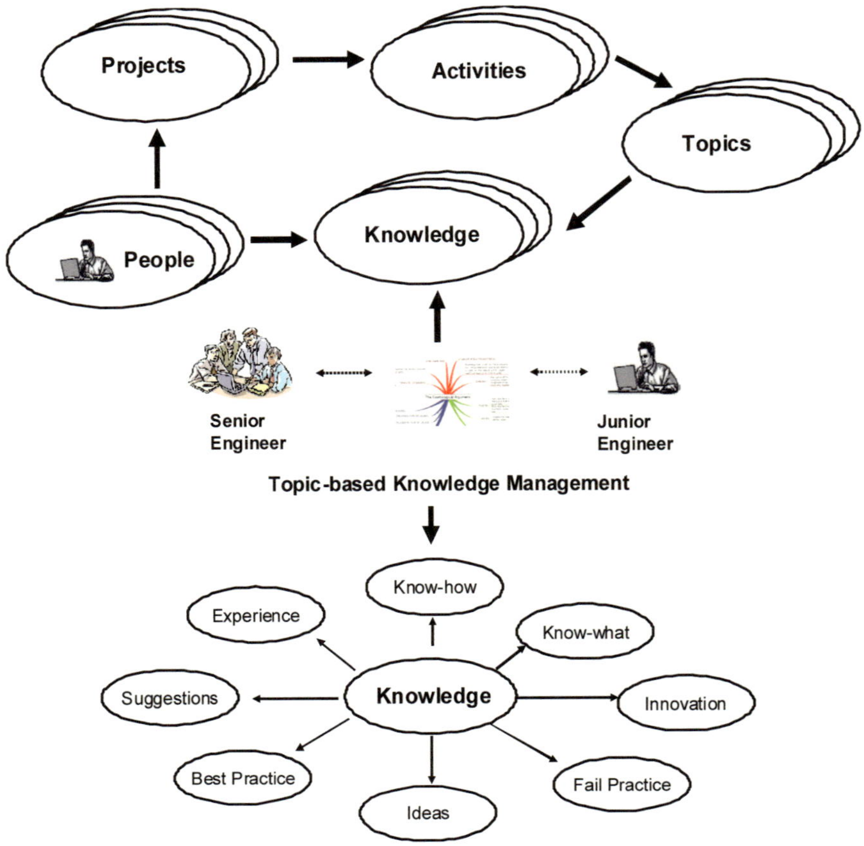

Fig. 2. The application of TBM integrated with mind mapping in knowledge management

attributes and types of acquired knowledge. Knowledge stored in map units of a project map includes both tacit and explicit knowledge. Explicit knowledge may be comprised of an knowledge topic, knowledge description and knowledge attachments (documents, reports, drawing and other explicit sources). Tacit knowledge may include problems-faced descriptions, problems-solved explanations, solution suggestions, and know-how explanations. Additionally, TBM give users an overview of available and unavailable knowledge in core project areas, enabling effective management of tacit and explicit knowledge. Identifying the relationship between main topic and subtopic map units is significant for users to link related knowledge together. The system is naturally designed to automatically or manually link activities which are highly similar. For example, the knowledge of a current project can be utilized, and the same or similar map units contributed by past projects can be accessed while the knowledge of current users is being recorded.

Fig. 3 shows the flowchart of TBM in knowledge management. TBM have components and procedures based on construction project management and, thus, differ from existing knowledge maps. The proposed TBM consist of seven components. These seven components are number of knowledge, knowledge topics, knowledge relationships, knowledge owners, knowledge diagrams, knowledge packages, and knowledge attributes. Procedures are presented for constructing TBM based on a knowledge management framework. The procedure consists of the following five primary phases: knowledge determination; knowledge extraction; knowledge attribute; knowledge validation; and, knowledge sharing.

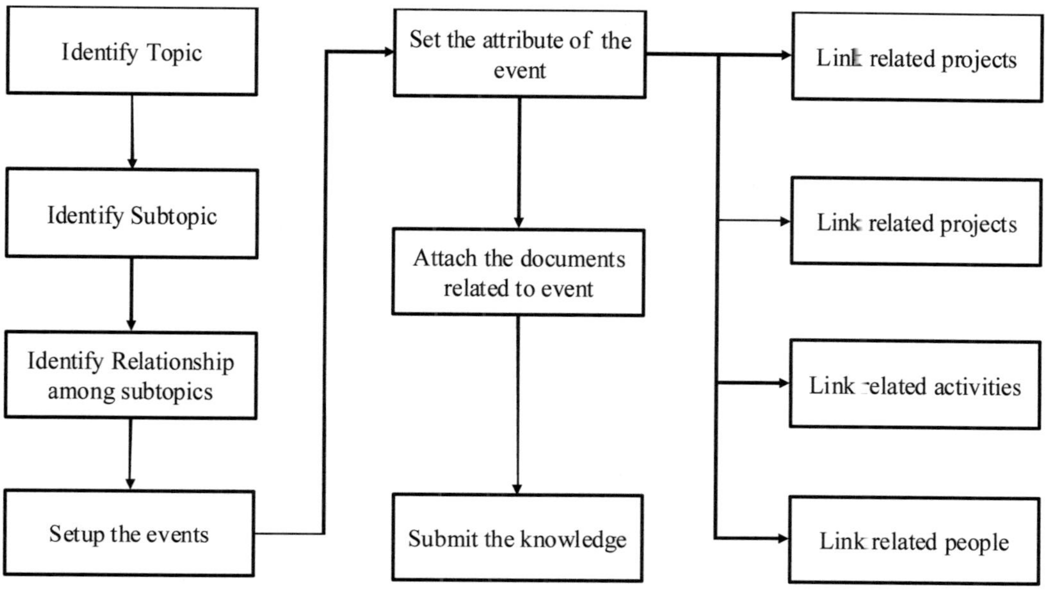

Fig. 3. The Flowchart of TBM in knowledge management

6. System implementation

This section describes the details of the Construction Web Topic-based Maps Knowledge Management (CWTKM) system. The CWTKM system is based on the Microsoft Windows 2003 operating system with Internet Information Server (IIS) as the web server. The prototype is developed using Java Server Pages (JSP), which are easily incorporated with HTML and JavaScript technologies to transform an Internet browser into a user-friendly interface. Software MindManager is used as mind mapping in the study.

Three search functions are supported in the system. The server of the CWTKM system supports four distinct layers: interface, access, application and database layers; each has its own responsibilities. The interface layer defines administrative and end-user interfaces. Users can access information through web browsers such as Microsoft Internet Explorer or FireFox. Administrators can control and manage information via the web browser or by using a separate server interface. The access layer provides system security and restricted access, firewall services and system administration functions. The application layer defines various applications for collecting and managing information. These applications offer indexing, knowledge map edition, digital photo/video management functions, full text search, collaborative work and document management functions. The database layer consists of a primary SQL Server 2003 database and a backup database (also based on SQL Server 2003).

All knowledge information in the CWTKM system is centralized in a system database. Project participants may access some or all of these documents through the Internet according to their levels of access authorization. Any information/experience about the project can be obtained from and deposited into the system database only through a secure interface. The web and database servers are distributed on different computers, between which a firewall and virus scans can be built to protect the system database against intrusion.

The CWTKM system provides project category search, keyword search and expert category search. The project category and keyword search functions enable users to find the knowledge they need directly from the activities of selected projects. The system, also, provides another function in the expert category for users to find related knowledge according to domain experts. The information held by each domain expert is provided to the users seeking the domain knowledge-related experts. One of the main features of the CWTKM system is enabling users to request assistance in knowledge support and exchange from specific selected engineers or all engineers in the enterprise through the TBM.

7. Case study

The following case study involves a contractor with seven years of specific experience in Taiwan high-tech construction projects. The contractor hoped to take full advantage of knowledge management (KM) to obtain the valued experience from participating engineers and effectively manage it for exchange and reuse in other comparable projects. The contractor, therefore, announced that all engineers would be encouraged to use the CWTKM system to apply KM to effectively manage acquired knowledge from participating engineers. The CWTKM system was utilized in the Taiwan construction building project to verify the proposed methodology and demonstrate the effectiveness of sharing previous knowledge in the construction phase. The case study was undertaken in a 11-month construction project with a schedule including approximately 1,450 activities. Moreover, all engineers were encouraged to explore and edit their own experience in the CWTKM system.

In the knowledge acquisition phase, senior engineers and knowledge workers undertook most work knowledge acquisition, since tacit knowledge must be acquired directly from the minds of engineers. Further, the tacit knowledge may be transferred into explicit knowledge by senior engineers and knowledge workers themselves. Most tacit knowledge extracted for reuse and storage may be available from the memories of experts and engineers. In a broader view, knowledge extraction may also include capturing knowledge from other sources such as from problem-solution descriptions, suggestions, innovation and collaboration.

In the case study, the senior engineer attempted to edit domain knowledge and experience in the "Contract management among subcontractors" learning lesson. The learning lesson experience in contract problem-facing description among subcontractors, detailed situation description and problem-solution explanations. The knowledge workers and senior engineer initially sketched the main knowledge map based on the original project network-based schedule plan. After the main map was identified, the five experienced senior engineers were invited to edit their experience in the TBM regarding contract problem-facing. Related information/documentation was then collected and converted into a digital format. The attached files included digital documents, video and photo files. After the related attached files were digitized, the senior engineer packaged them as an experience set for submission. The knowledge workers, also, assisted the senior engineers in completing the above digitization work and conferred with them weekly to accelerate the problem solving process. The project activities continued for ten months. All engineers were required to provide their own knowledge regarding the tasks for which they were responsible. Each engineer created a knowledge map and summarized his experience and domain knowledge in the map to enable the reuse of the solution process for future projects. The knowledge map included: the knowledge topic, knowledge descriptions, knowledge diagram, knowledge attribute, knowledge packages and linkage, the solution to the problem, including related documents, photographs and videos of processes, and expert suggestions, including notes, discussions and meeting records. Knowledge was extracted based on every process defined as it related to the map units of a project. Domain knowledge and knowledge were organized according to the attributes of the map units concerned. When the submitted knowledge set was approved, the system illustrated the process automatically, and an assistant in the KM team attributed the knowledge and classified the knowledge by placing it in an appropriate position (map units in the TBM) in the system. Restated, users can locate and directly access related knowledge simply by clicking on these map units located on the multilevel knowledge maps. In the knowledge storage phase, all knowledge was centralized and stored in the central database to avoid duplicating data. All knowledge can be stored in the system by ensuring that data are all electronic and in a standard format for each file type such as a specific document or drawing format. All knowledge maps must be validated to perform well before the knowledge maps are published. All validation is performed in enterprise KM terms by domain experts, knowledge workers and knowledge map makers. Finally, the knowledge set is automatically backed up from the knowledge database to another database. The system automatically sends a message confirming the update to the appropriate users after approving and storing the experience.

A new project is started after completion of the construction project ten months earlier. A senior engineer encounters two different problems in a new project whose information is unavailable in the CWTKM System. After referring suggestions and assistance from senior engineers, the senior engineer solves the problem and shares the new solution with senior engineers. Finally, the senior engineer creates a new map unit and knowledge package, and submits the obtained suggestion and experience to the map unit of the knowledge map, linked with the related knowledge topics. Moreover, the knowledge is later updated when further feedback and another solution to the same problem are added. The updated knowledge set is republished in the map units of the knowledge map after completing the approval process, and a notice is transmitted to the authorized members.

8. Field tests and results

During the field trials, verification and validation tests were performed to evaluate the system. The verification process was proposed to determine whether the system operated as intended while validation was performed to evaluate the system's usefulness. The verification test was conducted by checking whether the CWTKM system could perform tasks specified in the system analysis and design. The validation test involved asking selected case participants to use the system, who then provided feedback via questionnaire. The seventeen respondents included two project managers with 5 years of experience; five senior engineers with 20 years of experience; four engineers with 10 years of experience; four junior engineers with 1 year of test experience; two knowledge workers with 5 years of experience; and one Chief Knowledge Officer (CKO) with 3 years of experience. The CWTKM System was demonstrated to the respondents, who were then requested to express their opinions of the system via the questionnaire. To evaluate system function and satisfaction with system capabilities, questionnaires were distributed, and the system users were asked to separately rate the conditions of system, system function and system capability, in comparison with the previous system using a five-point Likert scale. A 1, 3 and 5 on the Likert scale corresponded with "not useful", "moderately useful" and "very useful," respectively. Table 1 shows system evaluation result. Some comments for future improvements in the CWTKM system were also obtained from the project participants.

The functionality of system	**Mean Score**
Ease of knowledge sharing	4.6
Reliability	4.2
Applicable to Construction Industry	4.1

The use of system	**Mean Score**
Ease of Use	4.5
User Interface	3.9
Over System Usefulness	4.5

The capability of system	**Mean Score**
Reduce Rework Problems	4.3
Reduce Unnecessary Costs	4.2
Reduce Happening Mistake Percentage	4.1
Ease of finding previous experience	4.2
Improve Problems Solutions	4.1
Enhance the relationship of knowledge and people	3.9
Improve Experience Sharing Problems	4.5

Note: the mean score is calculated from respondents' feedback on fivescale questionnaire: 1(Strongly Disagree), 2, 3, 4 and 5 (Strongly Agree)

Table 1. System Evaluation Result

The integration of mind mapping and TBM technique to share and illustrate available experience significantly enhanced the efficiency of KM processes. Based on the user satisfaction survey, most users agreed that the CWTKM system enables engineers to exchange and share previous experience and knowledge using TBM to express their ideas and thoughts. Furthermore, the TBM provided clear and dynamic representations of experience and effectively identified Map units with experience and knowledge related to the project. The survey revealed a user satisfaction rate of 87 %, indicating that the CWTKM system is useful for assisting engineers in editing their previous knowledge through the mind mapping and TBM approach to enhance knowledge acquisition and management. The experimental results showed that the CWTKM system significantly enhanced progress in the construction knowledge exchange progress and management. Overall, the use of CWTKM system minimized ineffective experience communication and exchange among engineers.

The significant findings of the case study are summarized as follows: (1) the total number of knowledge units in the system was 317 with 97 knowledge packages during execution of the project; (2) most senior engineers and experts considered recording and editing their experience to be too time consuming; (3) assisting more senior engineers in transferring tacit knowledge can be problematic, because most senior engineers cannot type their knowledge by themselves, and (4) most engineers agreed that the TBM approach and mind mapping are helpful to enabling knowledge sharing and management in construction projects.

9. Conclusions

This study proposed a novel and practical methodology for capturing and representing the experience and project knowledge of engineers by utilizing mind mapping and TBM approach. Furthermore, this study developed a Construction Topic-based Map Knowledge Management (CWTKM) system for engineers that provides a concept experience exchange and management service for the reuse of domain knowledge and experience. TBM divide knowledge into map units, thus forming an effective knowledge management tool in construction projects. Effective integration of web technology in CWTKM system has been demonstrated in the case study in the Taiwan construction building project. The CWTKM system enables engineers to exchange and share previous knowledge using TBM to express their ideas and knowledge. Furthermore, the CWTKM system enables users to request knowledge support and to exchange knowledge with selected engineers or all enterprise engineers by submitting problem descriptions through TBM. Novice engineers directly accessing the system can effectively share and exchange knowledge. The integration of the TBM and mind mapping appears to be a promising means of enhancing construction KM during the construction phase of a project. In summary, the CWTKM system can assist engineers in illustrating their ideas clearly and sharing their knowledge. Furthermore, CWTKM system and TBM approach enable users to survey and access effectively the tacit and explicit knowledge of previous engineers and experts in similar projects.

Although further effort is needed to update the explicit/tacit knowledge related to various projects, the proposed system benefits construction knowledge management by (1) providing an effective and efficient web-based environment for exchanging knowledge specifically regarding construction projects; and (2) providing users options by requesting assistance from selected engineers or all engineers in the enterprise who have relevant knowledge by submitting a problem description.

The use of the TBM approach integrated with mind mapping in the study mainly provides assistance to help engineers illustrate their own knowledge easily and effectively. The questionnaire results indicate that the primary advantages of TBM in the system are as follows: (1) the TBM provide clear and dynamic representations, thus identifying the experience and knowledge of engineers relevant to the project, (2) the TBM clearly identify the available engineers or experience to request for experience exchange regarding the special knowledge in the current project and (3) users can locate needed knowledge easily and effectively based on TBM illustration.

During field tests phase, most engineers need to handle the knowledge management progress directly in the jobsite. Therefore, the CWTKM system will be developed for smart phones or Tablet PCs use to enable jobsite engineers edit knowledge and experience directly in the jobsite in the future.

10. References

Buzan T. & Buzan B., (1993), The mind map book: How to use radiant thinking to maximize your brain's untapped potential, New York; Plume.

Davenport, T.H. and Prusak, L. (1998), Working Knowledge, Harvard Business School Press

Fong, P. S. W. and Chu, L. (2006), Exploratory study of knowledge sharing in contracting companies: a sociotechnical perspective. Journal of Construction Engineering and Management, 132(9), 928-939.

Fong, P. S. W., Hayles, C. S., and Hills, M. J. (2007), Dynamic knowledge creation through value management teams. Journal of Management in Engineering, 23(1), 40-49.

Liebowitz, J. (2005), Linking social network analysis with the analytic hierarchy process for knowledge mapping in organizations, Journal of Knowledge Management, Vol. 9 No.1, 76-86.

Malhotra, Y. (2000), Knowledge management and virtual organizations. Idea Group Publishing, Hershey, PA.

Malhotra, Y. (2001), Knowledge management and business model innovation. Idea Group Publishing, Hershey, PA.

McAleese, R. (1998), The knowledge arena as an extension the concept map: reflection in action, Interactive Learning Environments, Vol. 6 No. 1, 1-22.

Noll, M., Frohlich, D. and Schiebel, E. (2002), Knowledge maps of knowledge management tools: information visualization with BibTechMon, in Karagiannis, D. and Reimer, U. (Eds), Practical Applications of Knowledge Management 2002 Conference Proceedings, Springer-Verlag, New York, NY.

Reuss, Mark C. and Tatum, C. B. (1993). "Requirements and Tools for Transferring Construction Experience between Projects." Technical Report # 78, Center for Integrated Facility Engineering, Stanford University, CA, Feb 1993.

Tiwana, A. (2000), The knowledge Management Toolkit – practical techniques for building a knowledge management system. Prentice-Hall, New Jersey.

Trochim, W.M. (1989), An Introduction concept mapping for planning and evaluation, Evaluation and Program Planning, 12(1), 1-16.

Udaipurwala, A. and Russell, A.D. (2002), Computer-assisted construction methods knowledge management and selection. Canadian Journal of Civil Engineering, 29(3), 499-516.

Wexler, M. (2001), The who, what, and why of knowledge mapping. Journal of knowledge management, 5(3), 249-263.

Woo, Jeong-Han, Clayton, Mark J, Johnson, Robert E., Flores, Benito E., and Ellis, Christopher (2004), Dynamic Knowledge Map: reusing experts' tacit knowledge in the AEC industry. Journal of Automation in Construction, 13(2), 203-207.

13

Knowledge Integration to Support Networking for Laboratory Preparedness and Response to Emerging Pathogens

Shamir N. Mukhi[1], Lai King Ng[1], Theodore I. Kuschak[1] and May Chu[2]
[1]*Public Health Agency of Canada*
[2]*Centers for Disease Control and Prevention*
[1]*Canada*
[2]*United States of America*

1. Introduction

Laboratories play a critical role in facilitating timely recognition of and response to public health threats. However, capabilities and capacities vary widely among laboratories around the world. The scientific community recognizes that: 1) no single laboratory or network can effectively cover all health hazard threats and 2) connecting laboratories through networks enables scientific communities to harness and contribute their expertise in response to public health threats, while adding value and enhancing opportunities to enrich their own work. However, a consolidated and accessible inventory of laboratories that would enable this to happen does not exist.

Public health laboratories serve the essential function of identifying etiologic agents of disease in an accurate and timely manner. However, the practicality and potential of these laboratories in the detection, monitoring, and reporting of threats over a wider geographic range is limited by unclear case definitions, inadequate laboratory capacity, and often, limited political will of local authorities to comply with International Health Regulations (IHR) 2005 (Baker and Fidler, 2006) to be prepared to respond to public health emergencies of international concern (PHEIC). Furthermore, some countries are not member states of World Health Organization (WHO) and therefore have no obligation to comply with IHR.

Global, regional, and national laboratory networks serve to alleviate these issues by streamlining the detection, monitoring, and reporting procedures for communicable diseases in order to effectively and significantly reduce the global or regional burden of disease. Laboratory networks are useful in establishing and maintaining standards such as molecular disease confirmation by providing member laboratories with standardized testing and reporting procedures, reagents, equipment, training, reference materials, quality control indicators, and technical support. Such collaboration between and among laboratories facilitated by networks allows for rapid and accurate provision of information regarding the magnitude of disease and the strains that are circulating in particular regions, leading to faster response and more effective control of the threat. Some example networks include the Global Polio Network (Hull et al, 1997) and the Global Measles and Rubella Network (Featherstone et al, 2003).

Although significant scientific knowledge has been developed, tested and translated into successful public health interventions and leading to reduced infectious disease burden, the public remains vulnerable to epidemics and pandemics. Emerging infections such as HIV, SARS, avian influenza and the recent H1N1 pandemic are further exemplified by the emergence and global spread of multi-drug resistant pathogens, which threatens our ability to treat viral and bacterial infections in hospitals and in the community. Taken together these acts of nature have put enormous pressure on governments to act quickly to protect the public's health. The public have in turn, incurred high costs in terms of lives and implementation of countermeasures. These public health problems have resulted in society disturbance, economic loss and political expectations.

2. Global laboratory directory

The WHO revised the IHR in 2005. This revision updated the practice of reporting and monitoring emerging threats of international concern and calls for strengthening of core capacities, including the laboratories of its 194 member countries (WHO, 2008).

The implementation of IHR capacity plan is often an iterative process. The global scientific community recognizes that no single laboratory or country has the resources to control all health hazards at all times. In this chapter, we focus on infectious diseases, but these principles also apply to chemical and radio-nuclear threats.

Infectious diseases do not recognize geographic borders. Cross-border collaborations and information sharing are necessary for early mitigation of a PHEIC caused by infectious agents. Therefore, it is important that laboratories also tap into existing external resources while strengthening their own capacity at the same time. One such resource is the vibrant community of laboratory networks. In this age of rapid communication and creation of virtual communities of practice, connectivity and information accessibility becomes easier, yet loses the assurance of scientific scrutiny. Networks of laboratories that come together as a community of practice can provide reliable information and expertise. In Canada, we have established many different types of networks to serve different purposes. These include disease specific networks, public health networks, hospital networks and networks of networks. There are also many successful international and global networks that serve as invaluable resources to public health. However, locating specific laboratories or networks can be laborious using publically available search engines, especially since many are not visible on the web.

Over the last decade, we have witnessed significant change in the way scientific communities share experiences, exchange methods and ideas, expertise and resources through use of emerging Internet and satellite technologies. The ease of travel, access to e-journals, rapid Internet searches, daily outbreak updates and virtual meetings further create opportunities to meet and connect in ways never possible in the past. These electronic gateways are becoming more accessible to even those laboratories that have been the most remote and isolated. Scientists, laboratories, and networks have embraced these developments, but the remaining challenge is to capture and share this ever-expanding, vibrant, and science-based knowledge in a simple and intuitive manner. Some of the recent attempts to developing web based search engines are not truly designed for laboratories and, as such do not have an efficient means of filtering information relevant to laboratories. Even some of the popular websites have proven difficult to navigate. The connectivity to experts and access to information is important for global laboratory capacity building. It is important to sustain laboratory networks that could serve as irreplaceable repositories of experience and knowledge.

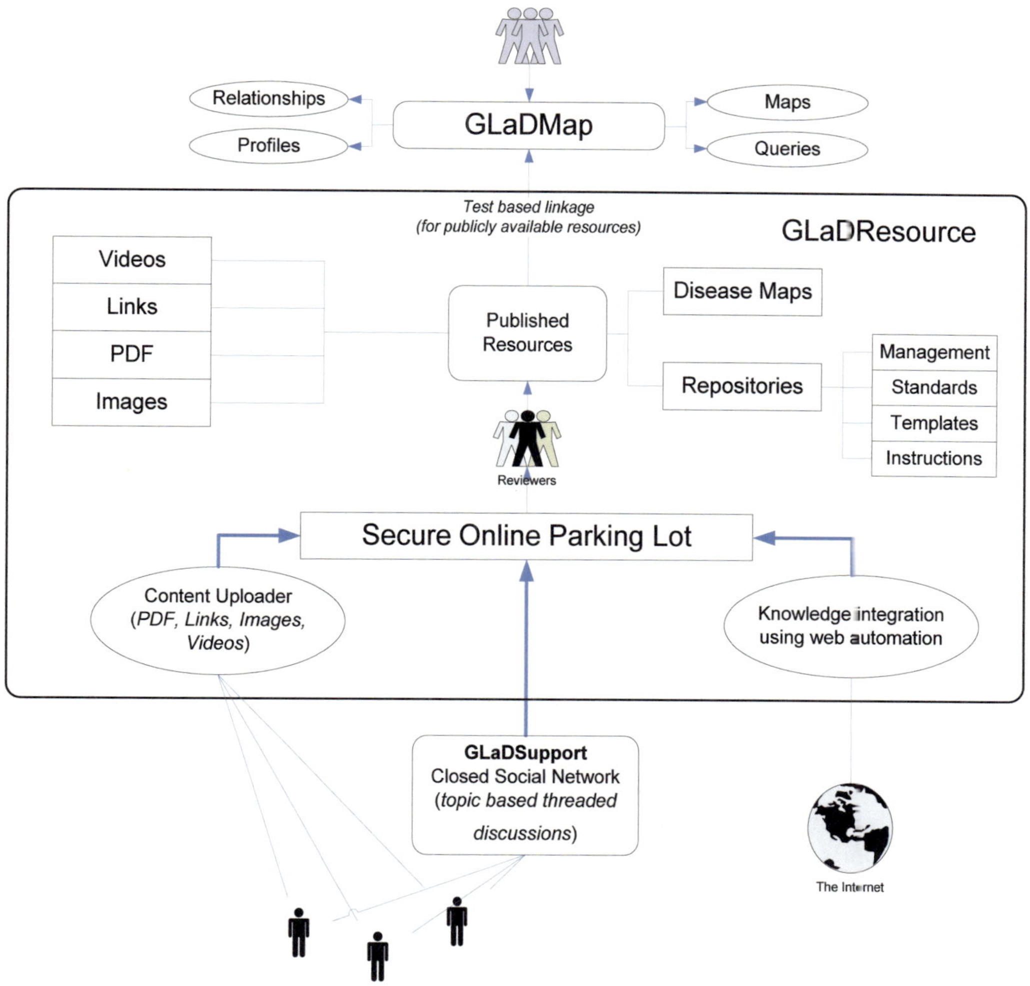

Fig. 1. Global Laboratory Directory Vision

The WHO, the National Microbiology Laboratory, Public Health Agency of Canada and Centers for Disease Control and Prevention, USA collaborated on developing the Global Laboratory Directory (GLaD) to map, connect, and support the laboratory networks and their members. GLaD is conceived as a support system to encourage laboratory networks to be part of a global community of peers. It is to connect laboratories among and between networks to leverage their capabilities and capacities in support of effective preparedness and in compliance with the IHR. GLaD, as depicted in Fig. 1, comprises of three main components: GLaD*Map*, GLaD*Resource* and GLaD*Support*.

It is easy to undervalue laboratories as assets for health protection and to question the need for investment into them and their existence. Moreover, the power of networking as a means of achieving public health goals is not always explored or harnessed. GLaD aims to support laboratory networks and advocate for their support and sustainability for the following reasons:

- Networks embody collaborative spirit and enthusiasm as players in the health sector
- Their collective work enriches scientific knowledge and range of expertise
- They contribute critical resources, capacity, and capability in the form of organization, technical experts, materials, information and innovation
- Scientific knowledge must be built through multi-disciplinary partnerships, and participation of many members and organizations is more comprehensive and timely than those derived from individual efforts
- Supporting networks is a practical and efficient way to capture and retrieve the technical and corporate knowledge, experience and resources for the public good

GLaD priorities and activities are aligned and complimentary to the United Nations Millenium Development Goals, with existing global health regulations and codes in animal, plant, and human sectors, and with global laboratory initiatives. The GLaD project adheres to the following core principles:

- Ensure equity for all participants
- Respect community rights and national sovereignty
- Listen and respond to the needs of the stakeholders
- Respect autonomy of existing networks - Add value to their core functions and activities
- Consult with wide-ranging experts and users to obtain a balanced view
- Recognize laboratory expertise wherever it resides
- Acknowledge participant contributions
- Operate with transparency and adhere to highest ethical practices

GLaD platform is developed using the established Canadian Network for Public Health Intelligence (CNPHI) technology framework (Mukhi et al, 2007), which is a comprehensive framework of applications and resources designed to fill critical gaps in Canada's national public health infrastructure. CNPHI's innovative Program/Information Technology approach supports data sharing and collaboration by integrating disparate data sources and facilitating intelligence generation and dissemination to enhance public health coordination and response activities for the direct benefit of local, regional, provincial/territorial and national stakeholders.

2.1 GLaD*Map*

2.1.1 Overview

The GLaD*Map* component provides an intuitive multi-faceted search engine with visual depiction of the interactive relationships of the networks and their member laboratories using a visualization tool that displays information provided by the network and by member laboratories themselves. GLaD*Map* enables users to: (1) find laboratories or networks that are dedicated to a specific objective or function, (2) connect with those located in geographical locations of interest, and (3) search for specific type(s) of services and, expertise/experts.

GLaD*Map* comprises of three fundamental hierarchical information units: 1) Laboratory, 2) Institution and 3) Network. A laboratory is defined as a place (room, building or facility) set apart for a group of scientists to conduct practical investigations in science (e.g. bacteriology, virology, toxicology, parasitology) or production of reagents for such investigations (animal facility, media preparation) and analysis and interpretation of results (e.g. bioinformatics, biostatics, mathematical modeling) from undertaking the investigations. A laboratory can be complex, multi-faceted or very simple, set up for basic sample collection as its sole function. A laboratory is the most basic information unit within the GLaD*Map* system. The following rules apply for including a laboratory on GLaD:

- Every laboratory named in a network is included in GLaDMap
- All national reference centres, including those not currently in laboratory networks, but which have the mandate from their respective state/national authority to provide a laboratory service to the public in a country
- Regional reference centres that have been nominated by peers or by official authorities to provide public health laboratory services to a specific region
- WHO Collaborating Centers that provide specific laboratory services

The following types of laboratories are to be excluded from GLaD:

- Laboratories in profit-driven institutions
- Laboratories that conduct research that generates intellectual properties that reduces global equity in access to laboratory services or diagnostic tests
- Laboratories or those institutions that market products of public health risks.

It is understood that the management structure and organization of institutes may differ so as to optimize the delivery of laboratory services to their external stakeholders, clients, or communities. Laboratories established within an institution may be set up based on specific syndromes (e.g. respiratory, diarrhoeal), methodology platforms (serology, DNA based or genotypic methods (e.g. PCR, DNA sequencing, culture or phenotypic methods), specific functions (research and development, technology transfer, surveillance, reference services, emergency preparedness and response), or a combination of approaches. GLaD*Map* does not place restrictions for participation on size, types, or management system of laboratories, but it is important to be able to easily locate the appropriate person responsible for further communications.

The second information unit within GLaD*Map* is an institution, which is defined as an organization established to provide public services. It has one or more laboratory units, which are the official workspaces of scientists and principal investigator(s) where they carry out their scientific work. An institution is a legal entity that has an official designation that gives them the mandate or authority to house the laboratory units. Any number of laboratory units may be co-located within the same institution. The following rules apply for including an institution on GLaD:

- Institutions that host laboratories that are member of networks included in GLaD*Map*
- Those that have national reference laboratories
- Institutions that have mandate from the state to provide reference services to the public
- Institutions that host WHO Collaborating Centres having a laboratory function Institutions hosting laboratories that provide data for national or global laboratory surveillance
- Institutions hosting laboratories that conduct research to answer specific public health questions, health hazard characterization, hazard identification, and hazard detection without profit.

All profit driven institutions that are not members of networks within GLaD should be excluded.

The third information unit with GLaD*Map* system is a network, which is defined as an interconnected entity (usually championed by a "leader" or "manager") and linked by common interest (a community of practice). Members develop a working relationship for professional benefit and visibility. Often these networks are established to achieve common goals that are accomplished more easily together than by one or two entities on their own. These networks may have formal or informal organizational and administrative structures. The following rules apply for including a network on GLaD:

- Societies, consortiums, and committees that provide laboratory service to public without monetary profit.
- Laboratory network members that are representatives of their laboratories or institutions that are part of the public health system.
- Laboratory networks that do not endorse a specific commercial organization or institution
- Public health institutions or states that could benefit from the promotion of laboratory networks found in GLaD*Map*
- Laboratory networks of importance for improving preparedness in prevention, response, and control of public health emergencies of global concern.
- Laboratory networks that provide data required for public health functions and decision-making e.g. surveillance, patient diagnosis, reference services, research and development, transfer of laboratory technologies and human resource development.

The following types of networks must be excluded from GLaD:

- Professional societies based on contributions of individual members to advance the knowledge in science. Their members represent their own achievements and positions, and rarely those of their institution, organizations, laboratories or employers.
- Societies, consortiums or advisory committees (groups, bodies) that play an active role in a policy advisory capacity. These societies could be linked to GLaD, but not part of GLaD*Map*
- Societies or networks who could be players in public health, but represent the interests of private or commercial organizations
- Networks that play an active role in advocacy of specific subject matter that may be in conflict with government or government funded laboratory policies.

2.1.2 Functionality

The GLaD*Map* system includes three information units as mentioned earlier, including Laboratory, Institution and Network. Each of these units is represented on the system by a collection of data elements referred to as a profile. The laboratory profile form consists of the following sections that may be completed by the participating sites as available:

- Identity: Laboratory name, website information, and contact information including geographical information so that the laboratory can be mapped.
- Disciplines: Classification information, such as, bacteriology, chemistry, immunology, toxicology, et cetera.
- Functions: Main role and responsibilities of the laboratory. Some examples include, clinical diagnostics, surveillance, outbreak investigation, vaccine production, specimen banking, training, reference services, quality assurance and veterinary.
- Specimen: Environmental (such as, food, water, soil, air), Clinical, Toxicology, Animal, and information on number of containments units at each level for handling specimens.

- Tests: Bacteriology, Immunology, Mycology, Parasitology, Toxicology, Virology, including information on estimates of number of specimens handled yearly and quality management system.

The institution profile form consists of the following sections that may be completed by the participating sites as available:

- Identity: Institution name, website information, and contact information including geographical information so that the institution can be mapped.
- Laboratories: List of member laboratories associated with the institution or network.
- Networks: List of networks that the institution is affiliated with.

The network profile form consists of the following sections that may be completed by the participating sites as available:

- Identity: Network name, website information, and contact information including geographical information so that the network can be mapped.
- History: Captures the purpose of network's establishment and any associated history including governance body, funding sources, terms of reference and founders.
- Activities: Descriptions that best describe the network activities including workshops and annual meetings.
- Disciplines: Classification information for member laboratories, such as, bacteriology, chemistry, immunology, toxicology, etc.
- Functions: Main role and responsibilities of the member laboratories. Some examples include, clinical diagnostics, surveillance, outbreak investigation, vaccine production, specimen banking, training, reference services, quality assurance and veterinary.
- Type: Local, national, international, global or regional.
- Laboratories: List of member laboratories associated with the institution

The GLaD*Map* tool has been developed as an online web-based system to enable quick access to posted profiles and to provide the ability to seamlessly create or update new profiles while keeping the ownership of data in mind. In order to begin the data entry, GLaD has defined the persons expected to enter the information as follows (as illustrated in Fig. 2):

- The leader or manager (or a designate) of a network is the person to enter information for the network profile in GLaD*Map*
- The director of the institution is the official representative (or a designate) to enter the data for the institutional profile.
- The leader of the laboratory unit is the responsible person (or a designate) to enter data for the laboratory profile.

A laboratory must be affiliated with a network for it to exist within the GLaD*Map* system. This relationship defines the basis of the integrated search engine to define relationships between networks and their members. Optionally, a laboratory might be associated to an institution as intermediary organization between a network and laboratory. This hierarchical structure enables multi-dimensional relationships to co-exist between networks, institutions and laboratories. For example, one laboratory can be a member of multiple networks; an institution can have multiple laboratory members and be affiliated with multiple networks.

Fig. 3 is a functionality chart illustrating the data flow of the application including the searching functionality as well as the update/submit new profile functionality. Note that a laboratory may belong to a network directly without belonging to an institution.

In summary, a user needs to follow the following steps upon visiting the home page:

- Select the profile: Network, Institution or Laboratory
- Enter the relevant information in each of the sections
- Submit the profile with associated email address for confirmation and follow-up if required

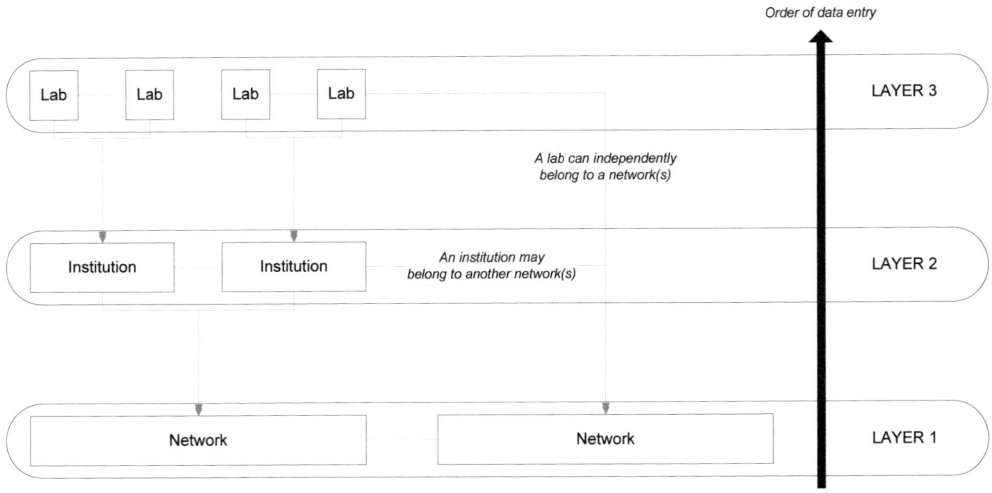

Fig. 2. GLaD*Map*: Illustration of three hierarchical data entry layers

Once the profiles have been entered, the information is automatically submitted into a restricted pending box within the online GLaD*Map* system. The profiles are then reviewed and approved by the GLaD*Map* Reviewer (who may consult with the data provider before approving the profile). Once approved, the profile immediately becomes publicly available for searching and the submitter is notified *via* automatically generated email.

The GLad*Map* system includes a mechanism to update existing profiles by the responsible individuals using a built-in email based one-time use access links. This mechanism alleviates the need for user account management. This is achieved by sending an automatically generated single use link in an email to the profile lead requesting an update. Fig. 4 illustrates steps required to submit/update each of the profiles using the GLaD*Map* system.

The search functionality provides an interactive mechanism for users to find laboratories using one of the four available search methods: Laboratory Name, Network, Geographical Location, and Tests performed. These methods may be combined to further filter the results. The system provides the results in one of three ways: Simple line list (which displays the results in a list highlighting some of the key data elements including name, primary contact, country and link to the detailed profile); color coded geographical point maps using integrated Google Maps; and proprietary interactive visualization tool called interactive relationship diagram (IRD), as illustrated in Fig. 5.

The IRD is a used to visualize multi-dimensional relationships between and among laboratories, institutions, networks, countries, and WHO regions. The tool allows user to visually interact with the relationships and analyze various patterns that can emanate from such interaction.

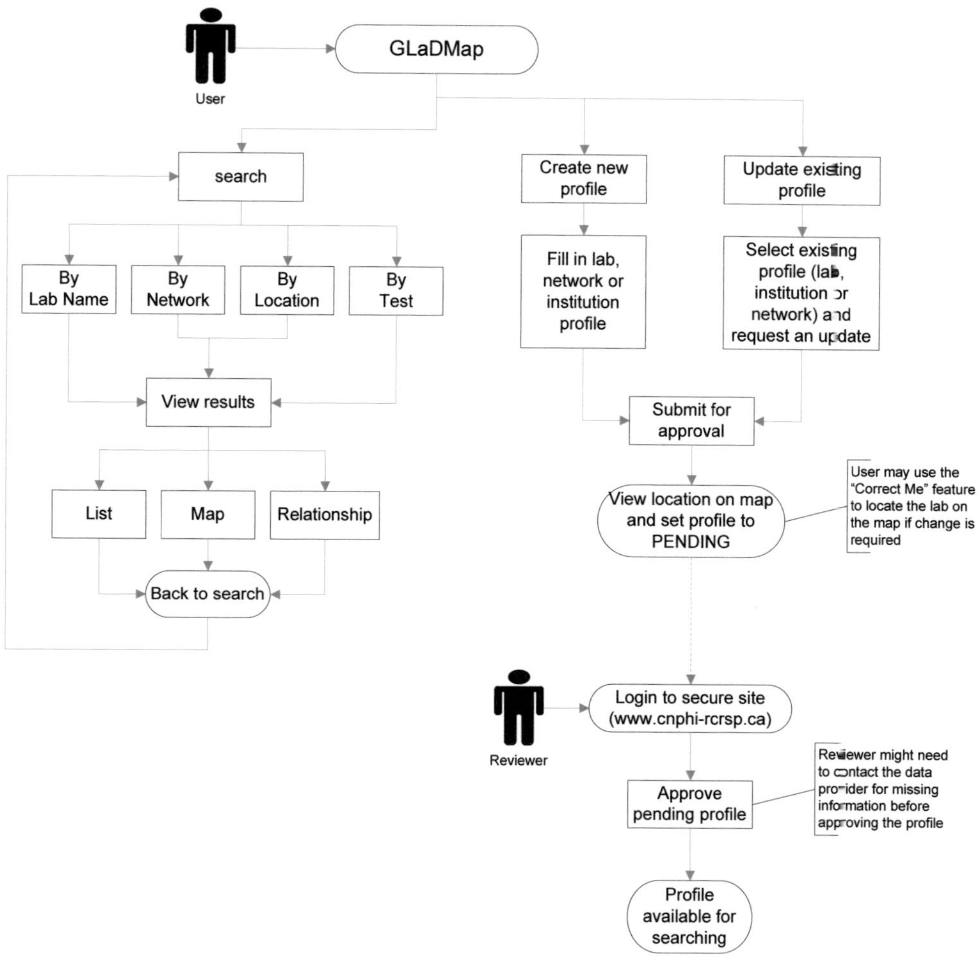

Fig. 3. GLaD*Map*: Application data flow for searching, creating and updating profiles

2.1.3 Preliminary analysis

GLaD*Map* currently contains 33 laboratory networks and over 1,000 laboratories. Analysis of network and laboratory profile completion has shown that gaps still exist in the completeness of the networks, and only 10% of laboratories have complete profiles at this time. Some preliminary analysis of search usage data has shown that the most commonly used search fields were network and test performed. This underscores the importance of network and profile completion, as it increases the likelihood of the search term appearing in the search results.

The next step is to perform in-depth analysis of the data that has been collected using the GLaD*Map* tool to identify missing data, most commonly completed fields, fully completed networks, and search usage. Such analysis will aid in understanding the use of the system and assist in planning the next steps.

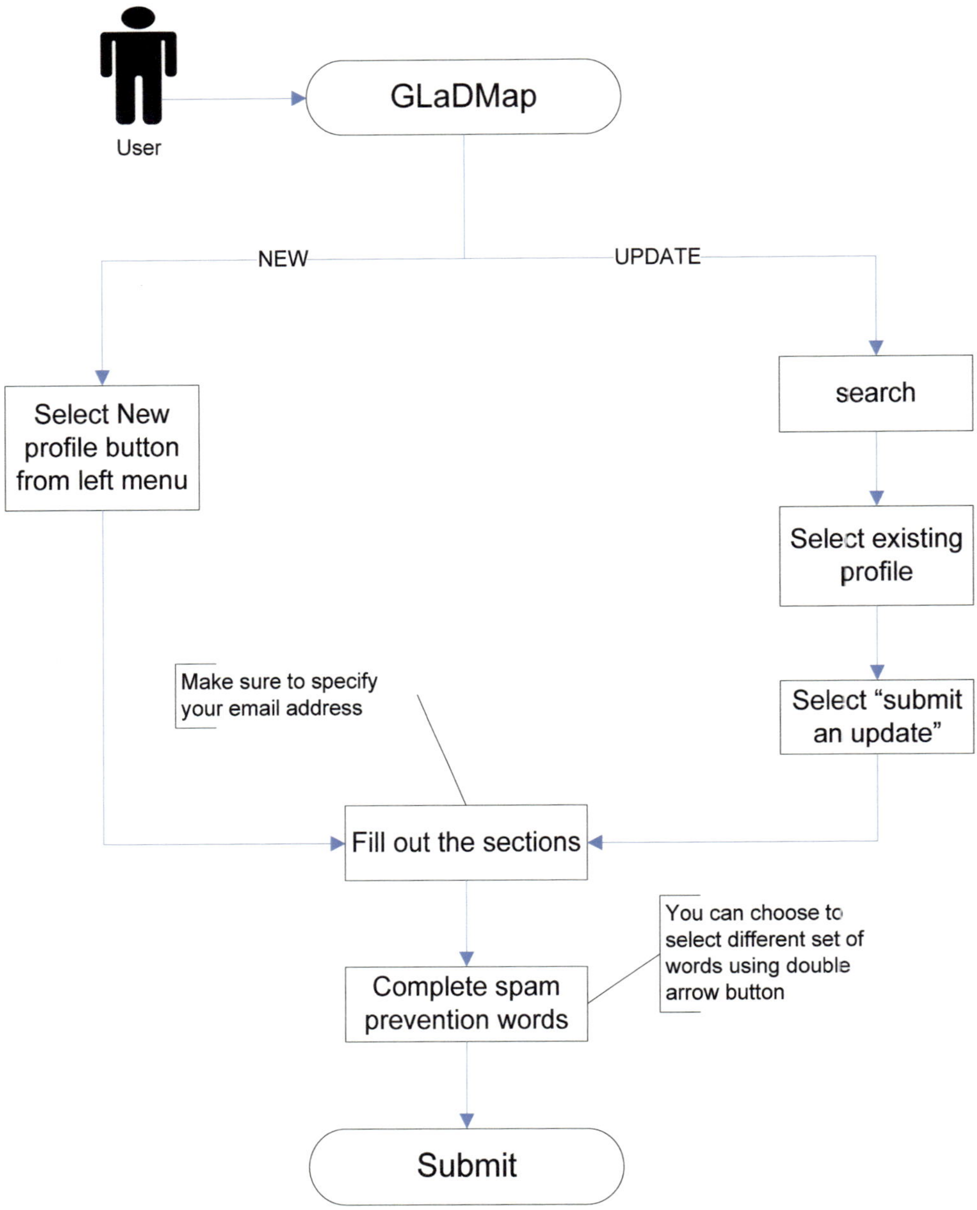

Fig. 4. GLaD*Map*: Process for submitting new profile and updates

2.2 GLaD*Resource*

GLaD*Resource* component of the GLaD platform is intended to be a dynamic, shared repository for archiving templates, tools/"best use" advice, and self-learning materials. It is intended to provide access to: 1) templates (agreements, contracts, multi-center study formats, etc.), 2) network tools (*i.e.* lexicon, managing membership, quality standard monitoring, etc.), protocols (for evaluations, reference panels, wet-laboratory exercises etc.)

and successful solutions and techniques (advocacy techniques, shipping specimens, etc.), and 3) a self-learning e-platform offering topics for professionals so they can learn about scientific advancements, management practices and organizational skills.

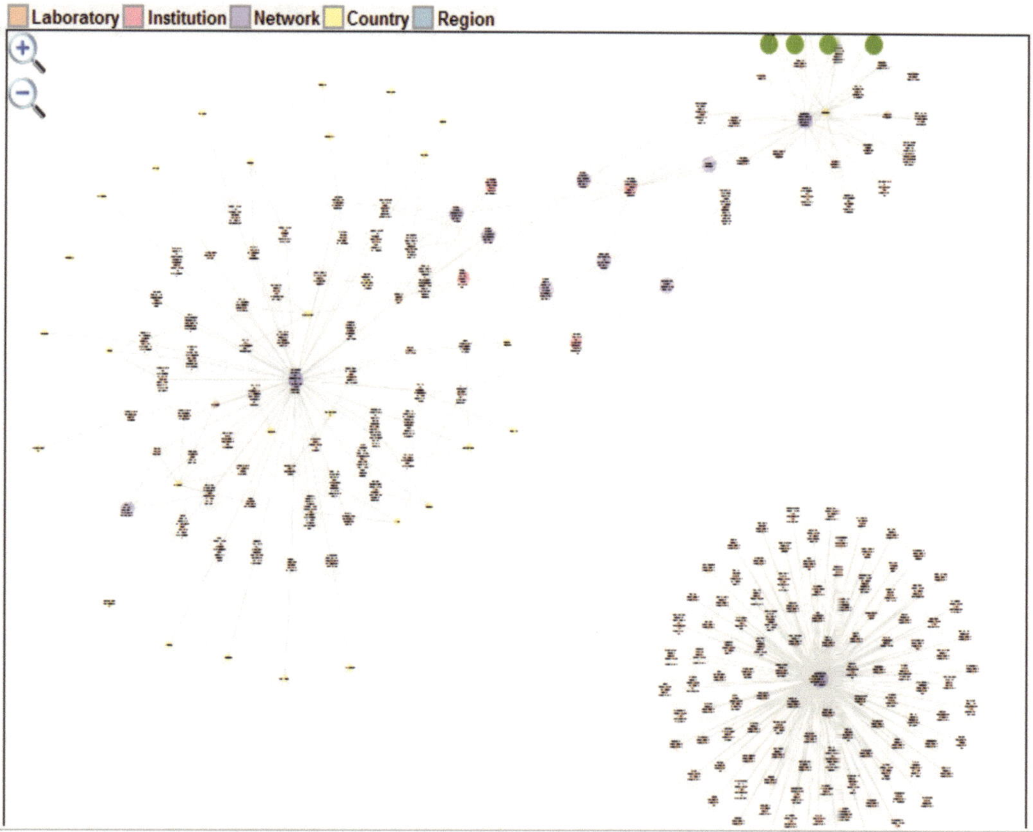

Fig. 5. Interactive Relationship Diagram: Illustration of multidimensional relationships

GLaD*Resource* will be a secure site available to laboratory professionals. Resource sharing will be based on two concepts. First, participants would be able to upload video tutorials, PDF files, images or web links to a secure parking lot. The parking lot will enable users to ask questions and leave comments on the various resources within the lot, thus fostering rapid collaboration and assessment of resources on a global scale. Second, a system will be developed to automatically identify resources on the web using automated search engines to provide faceted searching, full-text searching, dynamic clustering and geospatial searching. Such a system will enable rapid identification of resources available on the Internet (such as, YouTube, e-journals,) and create an instant pool of such resources for the users.
Some of the examples of resources that will be considered for inclusion within the GLaD*Resource* components include:

- Self-learning material to see how tests are done in various countries
- Quality standards for tests that are set by accreditation bodies (ISO, CAP, CLIA)

    - How various laboratories work within these systems, and how they differ based on tests, laboratory, network, country
- Use of proficiency panels and biosafety around the globe
- Protocols from highly regarded laboratories such as WHO reference centers

The following key concepts will be considered during the development of the GLaD*Resource* component, keeping in mind that it needs to be user-driven system that empowers and encourages users to input resources and maintain them:

- Resources should be targeted to scientists, technicians laboratory directors, and network managers
- Format of files to make sure they are sharable, printable, et cetera
- Language of resources to make sure they can be translated with ease
- Quality of resources:
    - Where do the protocols originate?
    - What is the "status" of the author?
- Legal considerations

It is well understood that the willingness of users to collaborate and share documents will require the generation of immediate value-added to the community.

2.3 GLaD*Support*

GLaD*Support* is planned to be an activities platform linking networks and their members to interact within their network and with others using "closed" social networking platform. GLaD*Support* will: 1) keep a message board for networks to post announcements, open invitations to meetings and training opportunities, 2) give strategic guidance and assistance to existing and new networks, 3) create opportunities to connect laboratory network managers and, 4) organize meetings and forums for sharing practical information, and proven best practices that keep networks functional and active.

A Social Network is a set of Processes, Methods and Information, Communication Technology (ICT) to bring communities and likeminded people together to interact for common purposes or serving common goals through provision of a platform for participants to socially interact with each other. Twitter, Facebook and LinkedIn are young (less than 10 year old) companies which have already proven the benefits of virtual social networking - reports of high profile events first appear on Twitter and Facebook, before the media network catches on. The individuals engaged in these social networks have a sense of belonging to the virtual society, and are interested in notifying their "social circle" about breaking events.

According to a recent article in the Wall Street Journal (Vascellero, 2007), social networking opportunities for professionals have been burgeoning with the recent advent of websites such as Sermo.com for physicians, AdGabber.com for advertising, and InMobile.org for the wireless industry. These websites are intended as a place for individuals in the same industry to connect, network, and share ideas. These websites differ from message boards in that they include features such as personal blogs, profiles with professional credentials, links to friends, instant messaging, and event invitations.

Online communities of practice can allow users to interact with others in their field without geographic or temporal barriers. This anywhere/anytime communication increases access to information from others in their field, and facilitates professional growth and knowledge transfer. According to (Sherer *et. al.*, 2003), asynchronous Internet communication can supplement a community of practise by providing the following services:

- Question and answer: Such as a message board
- White pages: A directory of members
- Subject matter experts: A topical directory of experts
- Professional Development activities: informal, self- directed learning or a listing of face to face or online professional development programs
- Library: Resources to support the community focus
- Best practices: What has been done and what works well, including templates and examples
- Lessons learned: History and documentation of the community's progress
- Community management tools: following participants, traffic, most popular documents and discussions
- Community workspace: Collaborative tools for discussion (chat, discussion board, white board, videoconferencing) and ability of members to create their own special interest groups
- Site search engine: For ease of access to documents
- Other related communities: Links to other communities and websites

Because these communities may include a large amount of information pertaining to different topics, (Sherer *et. al.*, 2003) also recommend allowing users to customize their experience so that they only see the information most relevant to themselves.

In designing an interactive community for professionals, it is necessary to understand how the community will be used and what type of knowledge will be shared. A study conducted in 2007 (Hara & Hew, 2007) investigated why and how nurses used an online community of practise. The study found that nurses' use of the online community arose from a need to ask questions and interact with other nurses that are doing the same job that they do. Because it is necessary for nurses to be knowledgeable about current best practise methods and literature, they found the information available in the community useful. Many well-known nurses were members of the community, and this gave the community a level of expertise and professionalism that attracted more members. In terms of content of the community, researchers found that 51% of the messages regarded knowledge sharing, 33% solicitation of help, and the remainder pertained to appreciation, job posting, empathy, greetings, administration, clarification, compliments, and encouragement. Furthermore, of the 51% of messages involving knowledge sharing, only 8.7% contained book knowledge being shared, while the rest contained practical knowledge. This shows that by far, participants were sharing practical knowledge acquired through practice in order to reduce gaps advance their skills as practitioners. The authors conclude that in order to sustain knowledge sharing in an online community, you need six factors:

1. Self- selected members: To ensure knowledge sharing is informal, voluntary, and natural
2. Validation of practise: To establish identity and reinforce role of practitioners
3. A need for knowledge: A need to be knowledgeable about current best practises, technology, and advancements in the field

4. A non-competitive environment: Sharing knowledge with peers from different organization reduces competition and increases willingness to share, as there is no individual recognition involved
5. Asynchronous communication: Convenient, anytime- anywhere access
6. A moderator: To ensure ease of use by members and to keep the discussion focused and professional

Finally, in a global community, it is important to understand any cultural barriers to access. In a 2006 study done by the engineering firm Caterpillar (Ardichvilli *et. al.*, 2006) in it's international offices, located in Brazil, China, and Russia, researchers investigated what factors might prevent employees from participating in an online community of practise with their international affiliates. They found that the most commonly cited barriers were:

- Modesty; fear of looking boastful or immodest
- Language barriers; concern that their English was not good enough to communicate with international colleagues
- Competitiveness and job security; the notion that knowledge is the key to employability, and by sharing that knowledge they lose their competitive edge
- Hierarchy; higher level employees may not find the time or may not see value in participation
- Preference for face-to-face communication over online communication
- Reluctance to share knowledge with members of "other" groups

The GLaD*Support* component will utilize some of the above-mentioned principles and lessons learned in developing a novel closed social network for laboratory professionals to facilitate global collaboration and consultation.

2.4 Scenarios

The GLaD platform can provide significant benefits to the laboratory community. The following lists some example scenarios on how GLaD contributes to global collaboration and consultation while providing efficient means of finding relevant information:

- Toxicology Testing for Melamine: Traditionally, responsible organization would spend significant amount of time looking for information on laboratories that could perform melamine testing, typically through word of mouth. GLaD's search engine, if populated with such laboratory profiles ahead of time, can interactively and rapidly locate all toxicology laboratories and their locations, and provide the means to further narrow the search for melamine testing.
- Influenza Diagnostic Capability and Capacity: A laboratory network spends great effort and resources assessing Influenza capacity within its member laboratories, information, which becomes quickly out of date. GLaD provides a mechanism for laboratory profiles to be available online and kept up to date. Diagnostic gaps can be quickly addressed and equipment supplied without costly surveys.

Typical current practice is to search the Internet for information, which can be extremely time consuming and oftentimes misleading, or to use traditional approach of using phone calls to search for expertise. GLaD platform can provide a one-stop-shop for laboratory related information, which is fast, continually evolving, and universally accessible with a multi-faceted approach to searching and sharing.

3. Conclusion

Global health security is everyone's responsibility. Uniting scientists and their expertise into networks is one way to strengthen response, build capacity and share with others at local, regional and global levels. Successful models of cooperative networks-- Global Outbreak and Response Network, the UN agencies (WHO, Food and Agriculture Organization)-supported networks, the World Animal Health Organization (OIE) reference networks, PulseNet International and its sub-regional networks-- are examples of functional networks and a testament that networks do provide the connection and are irreplaceable repositories of experience and knowledge. Paradoxically, even as the scientific community recognizes that it is easy to form a network, it also recognizes that sustaining the work of the networks can often be challenging. The development of knowledge management tools for this project is intended to assist the GLaD laboratory community to meet their challenges.

4. Acknowledgment

The authors would like to convey sincere thanks to Ms. Kashmeera Meghnath who performed literature review and usage analysis and assisted with editing of this chapter. The authors are grateful to the World Health Organization for supporting developing the GLaD conceptual ideas under the International Health Regulations Coordination Office, Geneva, Switzerland and to the laboratory technical advisers of their experience in managing global laboratory networks.

5. References

Ardichvilli, A, Maurer, M, Li, W, and Wentling, T. (2006). *Cultural influences on knowledge sharing through online communities of practise.* Journal of Knowledge Management. *10,* 94-107.

Baker, M.G. & Fidler, D.P. (2006). *Global public health surveillance under new international health regulations.* Emerging Infectious Diseases. 12:1058-65.

Featherstone, D., Brown, D., & Sanders, R. (2003). *Development of the global measles laboratory network.* J Infect Dis. 187(Suppl 1):S264–9

Hara, N and Hew, KF. (2007). *Knowledge sharing in an online community of health professionals.* Information Technology & People. *20,* 235- 261.

Hull, B.P. & Dowdle, W.R. (1997). *Poliovirus surveillance: building the poliovirus laboratory network.* J Infect Dis. 175(Suppl):S113-6

Mukhi, S. N., Aramini J. and Kabani A. (2007). *Contributing to communicable disease intelligence management in Canada,* Can J Infect Dis Med Microbiol. November; 18(6): 353–356.

Sherer, PD, Shea, TP, and Kristensen, E. (2003). *Online Communities of Practice: A Catalyst for Faculty Development.* Innovative Higher Education. *27,* 183- 294.

Vascellero, J.E. (2007). *Social Networking Goes Professional*. Wall Street Journal. Retrieved from http://online.wsj.com/article/SB118825239984310205.html

World Health Organization (2008). *International Health Regulations, 2005*. ISBN 9789241580410. Accessed on September 03, 2011. Available from: http://www.who.int/ihr/9789241596664/en/index.html